# TEACHING KNOWLEDGE AND INTELLIGENT TUTORING

EDITED BY

PETER GOODYEAR

ABLEX PUBLISHING CORPORATION
NORWOOD, NEW JERSEY

Printed in the United States of America

**Library of Congress Cataloging-in-Publication Data**

Teaching knowledge and intelligent tutoring / edited by Peter
  Goodyear.
     p.    cm.
   Includes bibliographical references (p.  ) and indexes.
   ISBN 0-89391-628-5. — ISBN 0-89391-629-3 (pbk.)
   1. Intelligent tutoring systems—Great Britain.   2. Teaching.
 I. Goodyear, Peter, 1952-
 LB1028.5.T383   1990
 371.1'02—dc20                                            90-44662
                                                            CIP


Ablex Publishing Corporation
355 Chestnut Street
Norwood, New Jersey 07648

# CONTENTS

# ACKNOWLEDGMENTS

I am pleased to be able to thank the following for their contributions to the evolution of this book:

The American Psychological Association, for permission to reprint a modified version of Gaea Leinhardt and James Greeno's article "The Cognitive Skill of Teaching," which first appeared in the *Journal of Educational Psychology,* Volume 78, 1986.

Lawrence Erlbaum Associates, for permission to reprint a modified version of Allan Collins and Albert Steven's chapter "A Cognitive Theory of Inquiry Teaching," which first appeared in *Instructional Design: Theories and Methods,* C. Reigeluth, (Ed.), 1983.

The Leuven University Press, for permission to reprint a modified version of the chapter by Erik de Corte and his colleagues, which originally appeared in *Teacher Thinking and Professional Action,* J. Lowyck, C. Clark, and R. Halkes (Eds.), 1989.

Methuen & Co. for permission to reproduce the extract from R. Hull (1985), *The Language Gap,* in the chapter by Rimmershaw and Beveridge.

The American Association for Artificial Intelligence and the University of Lancaster for financial support for the 3rd CeRCLe Workshop (Ullswater,

1988). The British Council for financial support for the link between the University of Lancaster and the Learning Research and Development Center, University of Pittsburgh.

All the colleagues who participated in the CeRCLe workshop and contributed to its success.

Pierre Dillenbourg (le roi du Mac), for stimulating discussions and assistance with graphics.

Alison Walker, for invaluable assistance in workshop organization and subsequent help with preparation of the manuscript.

All the authors but one, for their observance of deadlines and subsequent patience.

Lastly, to Valerie, for knowing why 10 minutes means an hour and an hour means a week.

Peter Goodyear
*Farleton, Lancashire, May Day 1989, 3:40 a.m.*

# SECTION I

## TEACHING KNOWLEDGE FOR INTELLIGENT TUTORING

# 1

RESEARCH ON TEACHING AND THE
DESIGN OF INTELLIGENT
TUTORING SYSTEMS

PETER GOODYEAR

## 1. INTRODUCTION

### 1.0. Teaching

A stereotypical image of teaching is of someone giving us an extended solution for a problem we don't have. The method may involve a lengthy exposition, or a series of bogus questions eliciting rhetorical answers. The prototypical objection to this approach to teaching rests on the lack of engagement between the teacher's aims and preoccupations and those of the students. The teacher's aims and actions derive from some notions of a valuable curriculum, which connects only tangentially with the students' conscious interests. We can imagine many reasons why the teaching may be ineffective. The students fail to see a point of application for what they are hearing; it does not help with the problems that currently worry them, and so on.

A stereotypical image of learner-centered education is of someone working on a problem which has emerged from events in his or her own life, or from personal interests. (I'll call this their *project*.)[1] They work with enthusiasm

---

[1] I use the term *project* with two connotations. One is its everyday usage in education. The second subsumes the first, is more abstract, and derives from hermeneutic sociology. It

and concentration on the project until they hit some seemingly insurmountable obstacle. At this point, they turn to someone (who may be drawing a salary as a teacher) for help. The help they get is focussed, local in its application, and they return to their project. The prototypical objection to this approach to education has two roots. One is a worry about the patchy, superficial, narrow quality of students' projects. The other is a concern about the lost opportunities for suggesting generalizable solutions to specific problems, for making connections between the local and the global, or between the current and previous problems, and for stimulating reflection.

Each of these stereotypes can provide a script for the teacher. I would argue that the challenges which give character to teaching are those which arise from the difficulty of producing a performance which acknowledges both, and adheres to neither.

The need to understand the distinctive character of teaching is deepening as we move forward in the so-called "information age." The tools of information technology are increasing our access to discrete fragments of information. In consequence, the role and value of "information-in-the-head" and of the teacher as disseminator of information are in question. (Such questions are old ones within the field of teaching. My emphasis here is on their diffusion through the population more generally.) The accessibility of information renders obsolete the rote acquisition of disconnected, decontextualized facts and demands a reexamination of what it means to be educated and what education is for. One response is to shift the focus towards higher level skills—to "knowing how to find out," to generalized problem-solving strategies, to collaborative work and communicative skills. It becomes harder for teachers to know how their interventions can be helpful, what precise purposes they serve. It is far from the case, however, that teaching becomes redundant. Higher-level skills need fertile, problem-rich contexts in which to emerge. They need content on which to work. They grow best if encouraged with yet higher order activities, such as reflection.

People who want to teach need rich knowledge of several kinds. First and above all else, they must have knowledge about those they try to teach. They must understand the projects in which those cast as their learners are engaged. They must know what their learners know, in so far as this can be used to guide their interventions.

Secondly, they must have knowledge about the world. They must be able to distinguish those areas of knowledge which their culture sees as essential for its own reproduction. They must have methods for valuing knowledge, not only in terms of its cultural importance but also in its relation to learning: they must know good projects and how to generate them. They must know

---

emphasizes the personal relevance, purposive nature, and coherence of activities in which someone may be engaged.

some of the problems such projects will turn up. They must know where the opportunities are for stimulating reflection, or generalization, or synthesis.

Thirdly, they must know how to intervene (and when not to intervene). They must know how to act in order to evoke the response (cognitive, behavioral) they want from the learner. This demands a very subtle knowledge of how the learner interprets their teaching action—an interpretation which can be influenced by many contextual factors as well as by the learners' perception of the relations between themself, their project, and the teacher.[2] Knowing how to intervene also requires the teachers to be clear about their own eventual purposes, to know how to manage the interaction between their goals and their constraints on the methods for reaching such goals.

Teaching thus described, is a complex, demanding activity. It is pervasive. It is certainly not restricted to those who are trained, licensed, and paid as teachers. The knowledge required to teach is complex, of many forms, and is acquired in diverse ways. Some is specialized from the knowledge we all acquire and use in order to engage in social interaction. Some is formally described, taught as part of the teacher education curriculum, embodied in the educational research literature, argued about. Some is invisible, ineffable, embodied only in action, used unconsciously, acquired like a chameleon acquires its color.

The principal reason for the existence of this book is the proposition that teaching can be done by machines.[3] Exploring such a proposition causes us to look at teaching, the activites comprising teaching, and the knowledge which enables teaching to take place, at a more abstract level than we usually do. It also requires us to be more precise about teaching. When artificial intelligence (AI) comes into contact with a new area of human activity, we often find ourselves forced to clarify many previously implicit or ill-formulated beliefs. Even if AI cannot create a computerized teacher, its presence may illuminate our own educational practices.

## 1.1. Scope of this Book

In one way or another, all the contributors to this book are involved in the study of teaching. Some are primarily interested in understanding the work of professional teachers—usually for the purposes of improving teacher educa-

---

[2]"Teaching is seen as an activity involving teachers and students working jointly. The work involves the exercise of both thinking and acting on the parts of all participants. Moreover teachers learn and learners teach. Both these functions of each actor can be considered an essential part of the inquiry" (Shulman, 1986, p 7).

[3]The reader is free to interpret this as either (a) people *are* machines, teaching can be done by machines (human or otherwise); or (b) machines (such as computers) can be programmed to teach.

tion, sometimes for enhancing our understanding of complex, cognitively demanding activities in general. Other contributors are primarily interested in the construction of sophisticated computer-based educational devices, using methods from the field of artificial intelligence. Some of these developers are motivated by what they believe to be entrenched failings of established educational systems that depend on inadequate human teaching. They may be reluctant to look at teaching by people as a source of ideas for the design of computer-based devices. They may even be reluctant to use terms like teacher or tutor to refer to their artificial learning aids. On a second dimension, some of these developers are directly involved in solving near-horizon computational problems: They are concerned with implementation and the pragmatics of engineering and are impatient with what appears to be computationally intractable. Others see the challenge of building intelligent computer-tutors as a long-range project, demanding extensive rethinking of fundamental issues. For them, intelligent tutoring systems research involves basic research into the nature of teaching.

This book has some of its roots in an exploration I began 3 years ago—an attempt to examine the proposal that studies of human teaching might be used to inform the design of intelligent computer-tutors. Implicit in this is a reciprocal proposal that our understanding of teachers' knowledge and actions might be able to benefit from the models and methods of AI and cognitive science. The exploration led to a link with the work of people such as James Calderhead (at Lancaster) and Gaea Leinhardt and Stellan Ohlsson (at LRDC, Pittsburgh). Out of this grew the 3rd Research Workshop of CeRCLe—the Centre for Research on Computers and Learning—(Ullswater, April 1988) on "Teaching Knowledge and Intelligent Tutoring." The workshop brought together a number of researchers from different countries who were directly involved in building intelligent tutoring systems (ITSs), or were carrying out empirical studies of teaching to help think about the design of ITSs, or had been taking a cognitivist stance in studying teaching, or had been using AI-based systems to help in teacher education. Others were involved in fundamental research into attributes of human interaction and human–computer interaction (such as dialogue or explanation) that are of relevance to understanding teaching by machines and by people.

Out of that workshop comes this book.[4] Its final composition probably reflects the trajectory of my own path in the last 3 years: that I have been thinking more about what a better understanding of the nature of teaching can do for the design of knowledgeable teaching artifacts than I have about the value of cognitivist perspectives on teaching and teacher education. Of course, the two are not separable. Accounts of teaching that are to be of value

---

[4]The book has grown from a core of talks presented at the workshop, supplemented by some specially invited chapters and reprints of two "landmark" papers.

to the design of knowledgeable artifacts need to be of a kind which can *eventually* be rendered in computational terms. The literature of educational research abounds with accounts which are cognitively implausible. We are still struggling to understand how to use the imperative of (eventual) computational expressibility as a useful constraint on accounts of teaching.

So this book contains a mixture of pieces. Some concern the pedagogical knowledge of ITSs which have been built, or at least are on somebody's drawing board. Others report empirical studies of teaching by those concerned with ITS design. A few look at the cognitive demands of teaching and review perspectives on the nature of teachers' professional knowledge. Rather more describe systems that have roots in AI and are being used to support teacher education and teaching tasks more generally. The painstaking analysis which accompanies the creation of such systems casts a cool light on aspects of teaching and teaching knowledge.

Since it is our hope that this book will encourage more of our colleagues from the ITS and research-on-teaching fields to engage in a dialogue about teaching, the next two sections attempt to give a brief overview of the salient concerns in each field.

## 1.2. Intelligent Tutoring Systems

Computers have been used for educational purposes for more than 30 years. During the 1960s, significant resources were invested in the development of computer-based teaching systems following principles derived from programmed learning. Since then, the range of philosophical, pedagogical, and technical approaches to the educational use of the computer has broadened very substantially. Educational applications in which the computer actually takes on a recognizable *teaching* role are currently in the minority. Cutting across the styles of application, we find different technological orientations. As far as AI is concerned, we see its methods and tools being applied to straightforwardly expository systems as well as to "learning environments" designed with the intention of promoting learning by discovery (see, e.g., Lawler & Yazdani, 1987).

Interest in the application of AI to systems which (in some sense) try to *teach* emerged from the impossibility of designing adaptive systems using conventional programming methods. A key element in the rhetoric of computer-assisted learning is the goal of individualization. There are two main ways of enabling a system is to adapt its teaching to the individual needs of different learners. Using conventional programming techniques, the system builders must prespecify all available routes through the space of teaching possibilities. Every test, every decision, every branch to some remedial material and every exposition must be written in advance. For teaching with any significant complexity, the combinatorial problem is enough to render the design, comprehensibility, and subsequent maintenance of the system highly problematic. This suggests a second approach, which is to enable the system to make decisions, to reason during the teaching interaction. AI provides an expanding set of tools for simulating reasoning—for carrying out inference—in computer systems. A prerequisite for such reasoning is that the system must have available to it an explicit representation of the knowledge it needs (in its domain of expertise). By *explicit*, we mean available in a form on which the algorithms of inference can work.

Much of the labor involved in constructing artificially intelligent systems revolves around this problem of formalizing relevant knowledge. In the case of artificially intelligent teaching systems, it conventionally revolves around the formalization of three (or four) sets of knowledge.

1. Most systems teach *about* some subject, about the content of some domain. In so far as they need to be able to solve problems in that domain, they need explicit representations of *domain knowledge*.

2. Most systems adapt their teaching to the needs of the particular learner with whom they are interacting, by building and dynamically updating some explicit representation of attributes of the learner (especially his or her presumed knowledge or misconceptions in the domain). Such a representation is called a *student model* or a *learner model*, and the process involved in its construction and maintenance is sometimes referred to as cognitive diagnosis.

3. Most systems have *teaching knowledge*, often explicitly represented as rules comprising one or more teaching strategies. The simplest of such rules may be of a form:

> If the state of the student model is x, and the teaching goal is y, take teaching action z.

4. Many systems have some explicit representation of rules for dialogue, for conducting some form of conversation across the computer–learner interface. In earlier systems, this knowledge may often have been intimately bound up with the teaching knowledge. More recently, attempts are made to separate higher-level pedagogical reasoning from reasoning about the details of how to display a particular piece of information, for example.

The current state of the art (1989) in building intelligent teaching systems is hard to determine. It is clearly more advanced in those domains which seem to lend themselves more readily to formalization (some areas of physics, elementary mathematics, computer programming, equipment control and maintenance, for example). It is also more advanced where system builders have adopted pedagogical models which could be described as instructional, goal-directed, system-led or content-driven rather than models which favor learner-directed exploration, negotiation of purposes, or the acquisition of higher-level cognitive skills. More learner-centered models *are* being explored, and their advocates tend to distance themselves from the main stream research, for example by rejecting the most widely used descriptive term for an AI-based teaching system—intelligent *tutoring* system.

What does now seem clear about the state of the art is that progress is to be made through at least two styles of working. Firstly, the three or four sets of knowledge identified above are each sufficiently rich and elusive to warrant independent study. Many researchers believe that the field is still too young to justify tackling the construction of a complete ITS. Rather we will learn more (for the moment) by studying BITS (Bits of an ITS). Others see the central problems as being to do with integration or interdependence—that knowing about the BITS will not tell us how to put them together, or that the nature of each of the BITS is strongly determined by its relation to the whole.

Currently, there are a number of strategic sites for research. These include problems of learner modeling (especially, methods for enriching or extending the content and utility of learner models), the implementation of less didactic teaching styles (e.g., through collaborative learning or guided exploration), inproved methods for the acquistion and representation of pedagogical and domain knowledge, and the exploitation of better methods for learner–computer communication (e.g, through graphic interfaces and more sophisticated dialogue modeling). Many of the more inspiring projects at the moment do not involve attempts to build fully functioning ITSs, but are investigations of important interdependencies in systems design.

In this book, we are generally interested in the knowledge that enables a person or a computer system to teach. Our focus could be said to be on the third of the knowledge sets listed above. However, it soon becomes clear that this focus cannot be a exclusive one; thinking about teaching soon causes us to question many basic premises about the organization of knowledge. Not least, we soon realize that there are no simple answers about the modularity of knowledge, pedagogic or otherwise.[5]

## 1.3. Research on Teaching

Studies of teaching have long been a major preoccupation of educational research. During the postwar years, both the foci and the pace of research

---

[5]Further reading: The interested reader new to this area now has a good choice of books which will provide an introduction to the field. The following are recommended: Wenger (1987), Mandl and Lesgold (1988),Self (1988), and Psotka, Massey, and Mutter (1988).

have varied considerably. At different times, reviewers of the field have found cause to celebrate and to lament the rate of progess (e.g., Wittrock, 1986; Travers, 1973). The model of Dunkin and Biddle (1974) has been influential in shaping our perceptions of method and substantive concerns in research on teaching. They identified four sets of variables implicated in teaching: presage, context, process, and product.

> *Presage variables*—are characteristics of teachers (e.g., training experiences, teaching skills, subject knowledge, gender)
> *Context variables*—are properties of the learners, the school, the community and culture, and of the classroom (e.g., prior learning experiences, school size, ethnic mix of the catchment area, the availability of textbooks)
> *Process variables*—represent observable actions and interactions of teacher and learners in the classroom
> *Product variables*—include short- and long-term learning outcomes (cognitive, affective, etc.)

Partly by providing a working vocabulary for the field, Dunkin and Biddle's model lent further strength to the main current of research on teaching: the process–product studies which have dominated research in the last 25 years. Such studies have commonly adopted a behaviorist stance, restricting their attention to observable teaching behaviors and to learning outcomes as revealed in attainment tests. The reaction to behaviorism came relatively late (Shavelson, 1973; Shulman & Elstein, 1975) and has been manifested in two polarized programs—one interpretive, borrowing from ethnography, the other cognitive, borrowing from cognitive science. Despite their many differences, these two programs have a common purpose in seeking to understand the ways in which teachers construct representations of the world and act in accordance with those representations (cf. Shulman, 1986).

There has been a growing allegiance to a cognitive mediational model of teaching, which gives a central place to teachers' thinking (Winne & Marx, 1977). The focus on knowledge and reasoning turns many researchers towards cognitive psychology for models and methods and a number of the key studies in this subfield will be recognizable to workers from ITS as instances of expert–novice research (e.g., Leinhardt, 1983). What reduces the interest of ITS people in this body of work is its breadth, since most of it is concerned with the classroom teacher and the tasks of the classroom teacher are many and varied. While ITS researchers are looking for the knowledge underpinning demonstrably effective teaching strategies (often in specific domains), the research on teachers' thinking ranges across all the areas of classroom management.

The general and specific utility of research on teaching for designers of ITSs remain to be explored. One dimension of this question in constituted by the scale of the ambition of ITS research. To the extent that ITS research is concerned with the fundamental nature of teaching, research on human teaching will be of relevance. Where ITS research is seen in terms of incremental improvements on the adaptivity of existing teaching systems, the potential of research on human teaching will be strictly limited. That said, many of the questions now on the agenda of research on teaching resonate with basic work in the field of AI and ITS.

Current preoccupations in cognitively oriented research on teaching include the following. What might constitute an adequate pedagogical knowledge base for beginning teachers (e.g., Reynolds, 1988)? What features of knowledge (content and structure) distinguish between novice, experienced and expert teachers (e.g., Berliner, 1986; Leinhardt & Greeno, this volume)? What are the relations between pedagogic knowledge and subject matter (domain) knowledge? How is subject matter knowledge encoded in a teachable form—as "pedagogic content knowledge" (Wilson, Shulman, & Richert, 1988)? How does the teacher's orginal acquisition of subject matter knowledge influence its later transformation into pedagogical content knowledge (e.g., Leinhardt, 1988)? What knowledge is entailed in noninteractive teaching, such as lesson planning and evaluation (e.g., Clark & Yinger, 1987)? How do teachers cope with cognitive overload in interactive teaching; what is the nature of "teaching routines" and self-monitoring (e.g., Olson, 1984)? How do teachers acquire, structure, and use knowledge about learners—both generally and in individual cases (e.g., Anning, 1988)?[6]

## 2. USING RESEARCH ON TEACHING TO GUIDE ITS DESIGN: PROBLEMS AND POSSIBILITIES

### 2.1. Misconceptions about the Claim

In a moment, I want to provide two brief illustrations of work which involves the investigation of some selected aspects of teaching. One of the purposes of this work is to contribute to the knowledge base available for ITS design. Before offering the examples, I need to attend to four common misconceptions about the nature of the claim that empirical studies of human teaching *can* be used to inform thinking about ITS design.

---

[6]Further reading: Wittrock (1986) is the most comprehensive contemporary review of research on teaching. Calderhead (1984) gives a concise introduction to research on teachers' decision making. His two more recent collections (1987, 1988) give a good overview of current concerns in this field. Influential positions with regard to teaching, pedagogical science, and the artistry of practice can be found in Gage (1978) and Schon (1983).

### 2.1.1. Human Teachers are Poor Models.   The most common objection
runs as follows. ITSs represent an opportunity to escape from the inadequacies of human teachers. Computers have powers that are different from those of human beings (e.g., they have very reliable memories, they can produce vivid illustrations very quickly, they can monitor very closely the performance of the learner, they are not biased by irrelevant beliefs about the learner). To model ITSs on human teaching would be to replicate all the failings of teachers and to ignore the special advantages of the computer.

There are three related responses to this objection. They are at their weakest when addressed to ITS developers who are concerned with the pragmatics of implementing complete systems *now*. They are given more serious consideration by those who believe that we are a long way from knowing how to construct a system which has any claim to being able to teach intelligently—those who regard ITS research as a long-term investigation into the fundamental nature of teaching.

The first response is to acknowledge that computers and human beings have different capabilities but that they also share many attributes, at least at some useful level of abstraction. An intelligent teacher should be able to reason about its own pedagogic limitations, capabilities, and resources, for example.

A second response is to say that a number of the claimed strengths of computers rely on the simplistic level of computation which they are capable of performing. (It is easy to have a reliable memory if that memory has no significant structural complexity. It is easy to have reliable powers of inference if one is limited to deductive reasoning.) We can argue that the knowledge structures and methods of reasoning necessary to support activites as demanding as teaching will have to be orders of magnitude more complex than they currently are, will be unreliable, and may best be understood (at least at first) by modeling human beings.

The third response relates to the comprehensibility of complex artifacts. We know from human–computer interaction research that the user's mental model of a computer system is an important element in determining the use they make of it. As computer tutors become more complex, so the problem of forming a mental model of their methods, purposes, and limitations will grow. This problem will be shared by users of all artificially intelligent artifacts. We do not yet know how best to help users acquire appropriate mental models, though analogy to the familiar is a common strategy. Using human analogies (anthropomorphizing the system) has a number of clear dangers (Weizenbaum, 1974; Turkle, 1986), but it is difficult to imagine other sources of analogy.

### 2.1.2. Individualized Teaching.   Another objection to empirical research
on teachers says that ITSs are meant for individualized teaching, for

one-to-one interaction, whereas human teachers teach whole classes. Their skills are irrelevant. This is easily disposed of. Teaching is not restricted to classroom teachers. Many people engage in teaching without being called teachers, and much of this teaching is one-to-one. Studied examples include private tutors, sports and musical coaches, therapists, university dons, and computer center advisory staff. Moreover, many school teachers *do* actually engage in a great deal of one-to-one interaction. The teacher who spends all his or her time talking to the whole class is a caricature found only in myth or university lecture halls. Finally, we should note that one-to-one teaching is a special case of teaching chosen as safe ground by ITS developers. There are no sound theoretical reasons why ITSs should be restricted to one-to-one interactions. The argument that theoretical work on learner modeling should be inhibited by the current perceptual limitations of an AI workstation does not deserve to be taken seriously.

*2.1.3. Lack of Formal Accounts of Education.* Those who, on first reading, accept that research on teaching may be of relevance to ITS design are sometimes subject to another class of misconception—that the educational research literature is replete with computational accounts of teaching. The serious point here is that our methods of mining this literature are still primitive. We have not evolved good techniques for extracting what may be valuable, so it may often seem that the only solution (for the ITS designer) is to do the work of educational researchers again, but this time to do it thoroughly. This seems an extreme response and one which underlines our lack of certainty about the proper forms for theoretical analysis in the ITS field.

*2.1.4. Lack of Expert Models.* Finally we must deal with the claim that there are no expert teachers on whom expert ITS could be modeled. It is certainly true that it is very difficult to get universal agreement on the quality of a teaching performance, even harder to get agreement on the validity of the knowledge on which that performance may be based. This both misstates the problem and begs some questions about expert performance. We could argue that the pressing need in the ITS field is not for knowledge about optimal ways of teaching, but for knowledge about how to do any kind of teaching. Given the state of the art, it seems perfectly valid to ask questions like "how do tutors manage to use learner models in interactive tutoring" rather than "what is the best way of using a learner model." Driven by the exigencies of the computationally tractable and sporadic introspection, the development of a "theory of teaching" in many ITS projects is rudimentary indeed. There is a strong argument for work on such a theory, even in descriptive rather than prescriptive form.

The two case studies which follow are an attempt to illustrate how we

might strenghten our descriptions of teaching by conducting selected empirical studies, or by attempting to reinterpret some of the theoretical literature
on teaching. In each case, the goal has been to illuminate issues of relevance
to the design of artificial teachers.

## 2.2. First Case Study—Coaching PC-Paint

The first illustrative example concerns an attempt to investigate some
attributes of teaching in a context where few of the unacknowledged supports
common it ITS research are available. A first support is reliance on domain
knowledge to direct teaching action. It can be argued that many ITSs do not
contain domain-independent teaching knowledge at all, and that the teaching
actions taken by the system emerge quite directly from the structure of the
domain representation. A second support is reliance on a simple goal
structure. Many systems are incapable of supporting teaching other than as
movement through a single goal hierarchy in which the primary learning
objective provides the top-level goal and the subgoals are all learning
prerequisites.

Neither of these supports were available to the teacher in the teaching
activity we chose to investigate. The teaching context was a course for adult
learners studying art. The part of the course in progress at the time of our
investigation was concerned with nonrepresentational art. Students were
making close studies of the paintings of a number of celebrated artists, and
this included attempting to produce works in the style of certain chosen
artists, in order to get closer to those artists' thought, manner, and
technique. As well as using traditional media for producing their works, the
students also had access to a "paintbox" program on a personal computer.
This was their first experience using the paintbox software.

The teacher had at least two purpose in mind—that the student should
acquire some skills (by no means a well-defined set) in using the paintbox
program, and that they should acquire these skills in the context of producing
and talking about a picture in the style of a selected artist. These purposes are
simultaneously conflicting and complementary. They conflict in that they
compete for the student's time and attention. They are complementary
insofar as work on the picture creates an authentic context for the acquisition
of skills.

The teaching context does not lend itself to any straightforward domain
analysis. The students' learning task could not be equated with the acquisition of a set of concepts or skills. One of the teacher's stated aims was that the
students should be given an opportunity to improve their ability to *discuss*
issues involved in the creation and criticism of abstract art. He admitted no
firmer idea about intended learning outcomes.

We had several goals in conducting this investigation. We were learning about methodology—about appropriate techniques for eliciting teaching knowledge. We had a goal of testing a multi-level elicitation methodology which we hoped might enable us to link the details of the teacher's action to his more global statements about his educational aims and values. Secondly, we were interested in trying to unearth some of the congnitive resources drawn on by the teacher in carrying on a complex and cognitively demanding task in which he could not get much leverage from well-specified targets or detailed plans. We predicted that his activity would be akin to coaching, and we know very little about how to conduct this kind of teaching (Breuker, 1988). Thirdly, we were aware of a growing consensus in the ITS research literature that "teachers don't use student models." It was clear to us that, if this were true, current ITS conceptions of a student model were grossly impoverished.

The elicitation method derives from Adelman's use of "accounts"(see, for example, Adelman, 1981).[7] This prefers methods which involve *in situ* study and which perturb the teaching activity as little as possible.The elicitation of accounts proceeded as follows. We spent some time, before the part of the course in which we were directly interested, discussing with the teacher his purposes for the course. After this discussion, the teacher produced a writtten account of his plans, which included detailed observations about character- istics of his students and about the logistics of his proposed activity, as well as high-level discourse on his personal values as an artist and art educator.

The teacher then organized several sessions with his students in which they would be creating abstract pictures in chosen styles using the paintbox program. He videotaped each students's work in one or more sessions. The tape also recorded his comments to the student concerned. (The teaching activities recorded are between 30 minutes and an hour; each is continuous and is of the work of one student; the teacher is in shot, watching over the student's shoulder and making occasional comments for almost all of the time.)

After the teaching sessions, the teacher wrote a second account in which he looked back on and evaluated the activity. Finally, we replayed the tapes to the teacher and elicited a retrospective protocol from him —a third account stimulated by the tape (cf. Calderhead, 1981; Anning, 1988).

Several observations emerge from the study. Firstly, it very soon became clear that analysis of the teacher's action could not take place without recourse to his own accounts. That is, our interpretations as researchers of the nature of the task(s) on which he was working were insufficient to provide a framework onto which his decision making could be mapped (cf. Breuker,

---

[7]The approach can also be seen as a rapprochement between the ethnographic and cognitivist traditions in the study of teachers' thinking.

1988, p. 327). In contrast to most studies of problem solving undertaken within the information-processing paradigm, we did not have privileged access to a representation of the problem space. The explanatory value of the teacher's accounts made careful interpretation of their status all the more important. Therein lies the second observation: that an actor's account of his actions is an account produced for a purpose and not a pure description. This does not render the account worthless. It does demand a theory of accounts which will support a principled interpretation of them. Triangulating accounts with each other and with a representation of the action (such as the videotape) gave us some leverage in unraveling the teacher's action and decision making. We have no reason to believe that the teaching we observed was unique in this regard: that the fragments of real teaching action cannot be understood without access to the structure of beliefs, intentions, and values within which they are set.

A third observation relates to the use of student models. The teacher's preliminary statements about his proposed teaching were suffused with references to the characteristics of the individual students with whom he would be working. These characteristics included student's knowledge about computer operations, artistic ability, dexterity, articulacy, confidence, and attitude to or tolerance of the teacher's guidance or interference. In many cases, these statements were linked to descriptions of appropriate teaching actions ("Fred will not take kindly to me telling him how to use the mouse"). In planning, the teacher was clearly working with some elaborate mental representation of the students. However, in action, he could not be said to be maintaining a student model at the fine grain-size we associate with student modeling in ITSs. When he did, it was for limited periods of time, was very localized in scope, and was tightly bound to one of his active teaching goals. When sufficient progress was made towards that goal, the modelling behavior appeared to be abandoned and the content of the model lost from working memory.

A final observation concerns the teacher's interweaving of goals and the impact of this on the frequency and type of his interventions. He had described two main purposes for the students' activity. During the teaching sessions he attempted to stimulate reflection and discussion about the work of the artist whose style was being emulated by asking (at widely and irregularly spaced intervals) questions such as "Do you feel it's working yet?" or "Are you happy with the way the textures relate just here?" The openness and high ambiguity of these prompts were clearly effective in provoking the desired response. (A more extensive study might elicit a set of heuristics for quite generally applicable prompts of this kind.) His second purpose, supporting the acquisition of PC-Painting skills, led to a different pattern of interventions. These too were unevenly distributed through time but, once begun, would continue, with the teacher taking over the direction of the work, for some significant period of time—usually until some discernable objective was reached. The precipitating circumstances for these interventions were varied but often included some evidence of floundering (at an operational level) on the student's part. Three or four repeated unsuccessful attempts at the same action would usually be sufficient. It was evident that both student and teacher accepted the unspoken contract that the student's learning would in some way be better if the teacher did not intervene at the first sign of floundering. The student was aware and accepting of the teacher's task of balancing immediate aid against the opportunity for enduring learning.

The next steps with this kind of study, I would suggest, are not to engage in a detailed analysis of the teaching protocols in order to move towards a specific computational model. This is not an attempt to elicit expertise in coaching PC-Paint or abstract painting. Rather, the implications include the following.

1. We are in urgent need of better high-level conceptualizations of teaching. In the field of ITS, the dominant image of teaching is of a chess game, in which the teacher as grandmaster has a single objective and the learner has at best a rudimentary knowledge of the pieces, moves, and purposes of the game. In actuality, many instances of teaching necessitate a great deal of effort (by all parties) in negotiating and clarifying the nature and purposes of the activity *while it is in progress*

2. We do not yet take seriously the *interactive* nature of teaching. In characterizing teaching as a simple, goal-driven, top-down, plan-execute process, we not only ignore the constraints that interactivity imposes, we also ignore the problem-solving *resources* that interaction makes available. We have only rudimentary accounts of the opportunistic, situated character of teaching.

## 2.3. Second Case Study—Self-Improving Systems

The second brief example is concerned with work on self-improving ITSs. Self-improving systems use algorithms which simulate learning in order to improve aspects of their performance. Learning may be aimed at improving one or more of the knowledge bases used by the system (in the case of ITSs —domain knowledge, pedagogical knowledge, learner model, dialogue model), though the few self-improving systems which have been built concentrate on improving the efficacy of their teaching (Dillenbourg, 1988). In effect, this means refining the teaching rules used by the system—usually through some process of experimentation in which the system acquires data on learner performance and makes judgments about more and less effective teaching actions. There are a number of hard problems obstructing the development of better self-improving systems, and the area is very underexplored. Among the problems are the following:

In order to learn (to self-improve), systems need experience of teaching real students. Sessions with ITSs tend to be quite lengthy. Accumulating sufficient contact hours to make significant experimetation can be a problem. There is an associated moral difficulty concerned with the use of real learners as experimental teaching subjects.

Secondly, self-improving systems usually have to learn on the basis of little knowledge. Their improvement is driven by regularities in learner performance data rather than by any kind of deep knowledge about why certain teaching actions might prove better than others. The learning is data driven rather than theory guided.

Thirdly, there is a problem of credit assignment. It is difficult for a system (and for a human teacher of course) to determine what combination of actions and events caused a particular change in learner behavior. Establishing a firm link between a cognitive state change in the learner and a particular teaching action or sequence of teaching actions is a nontrivial task.

Fourthly (by no means finally), the system's current possibilities for acquiring data about the learner are very limited. Communication across the interface is sparse and stilted. The bandwidth of information transfer from learner to system is extremely narrow compared with human communication. Noise in the data is also a problem.

In collaboration with Pierre Dillenbourg I have been trying to establish whether research on teachers' professional development [8] (self-improvement in human teachers) can give any insight into the problem of self-improving ITSs (Dillenbourg & Goodyear, 1988,1989). As I have argued above, such thinking needs to proceed at a relatively high level of abstraction—one at which the differences between human and artificial teachers become less salient. We believe we have identified a number of similarities that may provide guidance for the design of self-improving ITSs.

We believe that reflective thinking is central to the process of self-evaluation and self-improvement (cf. Schon, 1983,1987). Reflective thinking is thinking about oneself and one's personal experience. In the domain of teaching, it is thinking about oneself as a teacher, about the knowledge and actions implicated in oneself as a teacher. I have observed already that a teacher's access to their knowledge about teaching may be problematic. Not all knowledge is available to introspection, and very little is represented in the form of declarative pedagogical theory. However, one *can* reason about the knowledge embedded in action, about tacit pedagogical knowledge, just as

---

[8]*Professional*—although we do not see teaching as an activity reserved for professionals, most of the research literature on which we draw implicitly does.

one can manipulate mental representations of one's performance of any task.[9]

There is a resonance with teaching knowledge in ITSs here. An idealized view of an ITS's teaching knowledge is that it should be represented in some declarative form, that it should be a complete and coherent theory of teaching with which the system can reason in order to make teaching decisions in real time. At the moment, we seem a long way from such a theory. What we have implemented, very often, are teaching rules or procedures for teaching which may *conform* to the designer's espoused (often fragmentary and informal) theories about teaching but which are in no way *directly derivable* from them. So the system's proceduralized teaching knowledge is rather like the human teacher's *knowledge-in-action*: What this suggests is that a self-improving ITS, like a reflective practitioner, needs a good self-representation. Recent work on computational reflection (e.g.,Maes & Nardi,1988) suggests that progress may be made on the *structuring* of reflection in AI systems. The empirical task facing us now is one of examining the *content* of teachers' self-representations in order to discern what kinds of knowledge an ITS might use to annotate and theorize about its teaching procedures (for a more complete account, see Dillenbourg & Goodyear, 1989).

## 3 AN OVERVIEW OF THE BOOK

The chapters in this book have been divided between four sections, though many of them have close affinities with contributions in other sections and some themes emerge and re-emerge throughout the book.

The first section attempts to introduce some issues concerning teaching knowledge that arise in the context of thinking about ITSs. They are by workers who have been intimately involved in ITS design and construction. Stellan Ohlsson's chapter presents three theories of teaching: teaching viewed as the communication of subject matter, as the remediation of incomplete or incorrect mental representations, and as the facilitation of knowledge construction. He illuminates the distinctions between these three views by reference to his recent work on an intelligent tutor for fractions. This is followed by a piece from Mark Elsom-Cook, based around work on his IMPART and DOMINIE systems. The emphasis here is on styles of teaching interaction and on links between models of interaction and models of dialogue. The section concludes with a chapter by Geoff Cumming and John Self which arises from their reflections on the difficulties of learner modelling and the potential of defining the interaction between system and student as a collaborative learning experience.

---

[9]This is not to say that the representation is necessarily a good one (which is a problematic issue in itself).

In the second section we move to some empirical studies of teaching (defined to include the teaching of so-called *parateachers* and to include some classes of action underpinning teaching). The contributions are by people who have a strong interest in the design of intelligent tutoring systems and use empirical methods to improve our understanding of teaching processes. David Littman's work is part of a larger project concerned with the design of an intelligent tutor for introductory computer programming. He reports on some studies of teaching knowledge (tutorial planning schemas) used when tutors prepare to help students who have written programs containing multiple errors. The next contribution is by Sarah Douglas, who reasserts the importance of the interactive character of teaching. She reminds us that communication failures are common in human interactions and focuses on the failure detection and repair strategies that make communication between tutors and learners robust. Barbara Fox shares in the insistence on tutorial interaction as a collaborative production and takes another detailed look at the cognitive/interactional processes that make tutoring possible. Following this, Derek Sleeman and colleagues describe several strands of work carried out over the period 1984-87 in connection with their PIXIE system. This includes field studies of teachers' practices in diagnosing and remediating errors in introductory algebra, experiments investigating the efficacy of remediation based on student modelling, and an account of the use of TPIXIE ( a BUGGY-like derivative of PIXIE) in improving teachers' diagnostic skills. Paul Kamsteeg and Dick Bierman discuss the use of multiple source protocol elicitation and analysis methods in pedagogical knowledge acquisition. Their work is particularly unusual and interesting in the way it takes an incremental, iterative approach to modelling tutoring knowledge. The section closes with a reprint of a classic paper by two originators of the field—Allan Collins and Albert Stevens. The chapter provides a cogent summary of their extensive work in observing and building formal representations of the activities of a number of highly skilled teachers.

In Section III we move from researchers whose primary allegiance is to ITS building to those whose main focus is on teachers' thinking and teacher education. The section begins with another classic paper—by Gaea Leinhardt and Jim Greeno. In this chapter, the authors provide an articulate exposition and illustration of the analysis of teaching as a skilled, knowledge-based activity. The next chapter is from James Calderhead, who broadens the frame by offering an account of the complex task of classroom teaching and of the knowledge which supports it. In discussing the representation of teaching knowledge, he also begins to elaborate on some of the attributes of a genuinely intelligent tutor which I outlined above. Finally, Rachel Rimmershaw and Mike Beveridge look at the fundamental activity of explanation, as perceived in teaching and in tutoring/expert systems research. Like other contributors to this volume, they emphasize the collaboration necessary to achieve a fruitful teaching interaction, in this case through the negotiation of explanations.

In the fourth and final section are gathered together a number of reports on the development and use of computer systems for supporting teaching tasks and teacher education. Most of these systems are knowledge-based or derive their inspiration from work in AI. The imperatives of formalization, as always, prove a rigorous test of our understanding. In addition to the direct or eventual utility of the systems described, the intellectual by-products of their creation are also impressive. The first chapter in this section is by Sharon Wood and describes the "Trainee Teacher Support System" developed at the University of Sussex. Construction of an intelligent system for advising trainee teachers has as a prerequisite the formalization of teachers' knowledge about classroom processes. Sharon Wood's work represents a significant achievement in modelling such a complex domain. Philip Winne also describes a system (DOCENT) which is intended to advise student teachers in instructional planning. To be an expert instructional planner means that DOCENT must have explicit formal representations of research-based and practitioner-derived knowledge about educational processes. Winne and colleagues have developed representational tools (ELI, BLEEP) tuned to such a purpose. The third system reported in this section, described by Anne Shelly and Ernest Sibert, was created in the Syracuse STDM project (Simulation on Teacher Decision Making). The system allows student teachers to practice making teaching decisions in a simulation environment and provides tools for each student teacher to record the path of his or her thinking. This record provides a valuable resource for reflection and discussion. Erik de Corte and colleagues are also interested in computer simulation. Their chapter gives an account of the use of a BUGGY-like program for studying student teachers' thinking while they are engaged in diagnosis of arithmetic errors. This work picks up once more the theme of teachers' use of student models—discussed above and by Sleeman et al. and Kamsteeg and Bierman. The final chapter is by Marlene Jones and Kevin Wipond. It moves us on to a consideration of pedagogy, which once again transcends the boundaries between human- and computer-based teaching. Irrespective of the eventual details of teaching action (such as whether a lesson is to be offered by a human teacher or a computer-based system), planning and reasoning about teaching requires explicit representation of higher-level knowledge about such things as course and curriculum design.

## 4. SUMMARY

Teaching is a complex form of human action. Developments in artificial intelligence now make it possible to think of machines that can teach. To progress towards such a goal, we are in need of much more explicit and detailed accounts of teaching—we have to engage in a fundamental study of what teaching is and of what knowledge supports it. This book is a contribution to the first phase of such a study.

## REFERENCES

Adelman, C. (1981). On first hearing. In C. Adelman (Ed.), *Uttering muttering: Collecting using and reporting talk for social and educational research*. London: Grant McIntyre.

Anning, A. (1988). Teachers' theories about children's learning. In J. Calderhead (Ed.), *Teachers' professional learning* (pp. 128-145). London: Falmer.

Berliner, D. (1986). In pursuit of the expert pedagogue, *Educational researcher, 15*, 5-13.

Breuker, J. (1988) Coaching in help systems. In J. Self (Ed.), *Artificial intelligence and human learning* (pp. 310-337). London: Chapman & Hall.

Calderhead, J. (1981). Stimulated recall: A method for research on teaching. *British Journal of Educational Psychology, 51*, 180-190.

Calderhead, J. (1984). *Teachers' classroom decision making*. London: Holt Rinehart & Winston.

Calderhead, J. (Ed.). (1987). *Exploring teachers' thinking*. London: Holt, Rinehart and Winston.

Calderhead, J. (Ed.). (1988). *Teachers' professional learning*. Lewes, England: Falmer Press.

Clark, C., & Yinger, R. (1987) Teacher planning. In J. Calderhead (Ed.), *Exploring teachers' thinking* (pp. 84-103). London: Cassell.

Dillenbourg, P. (1988). Self-improving tutoring systems. *International Journal of Educational Research, 12* (8), 851-862

Dillenbourg, P., & Goodyear, P. (1988). *Reasoning about tutoring in self-improving systems* (CeRCLe Tech. Report). Lancaster, England: University of Lancaster.

Dillenbourg, P., & Goodyear, P. (1989, May). *Towards reflective tutoring systems: self-representation and self-improvement*. Paper presented at the 4th International Conference on AI and Education, Amsterdam.

Dunkin, M., & Biddle, B. (1974). *The study of teaching*. New York: Holt Rinehart & Winston.

Gage, N. (1978). *The scientific basis of the art of teaching*. New York: Teachers College Press.

Lawler, R., & Yazdani, M. (Eds.). (1987). *Artificial intelligence and education: Learning environments and tutoring systems* (Vol. 1). Norwood, NJ: Ablex Publishing Corp.

Leinhardt, G. (1983). Novice and expert knowledge of individual students' achievement. *Educational Psychologist, 18*(3), 165-179.

Leinhardt, G. (1988). Situated knowledge and expertise in teaching. In J. Calderhead (Ed.), *Teachers' professional learning* (pp. 146-168). London: Falmer.

Maes, P., & Nardi, D. (Eds.). (1988). *Meta-level architectures and reflection*. Amsterdam: North Holland.

Mandl, H., & Lesgold, A. (Eds.). (1988). *Learning issues for intelligent tutoring systems*. New York: Springer Verlag.

Olson, J. (1984). What makes teachers tick? Considering the routines of teaching. In R. Halkes & J. Olson (Eds.), *Teacher thinking*. Lisse, Netherlands: Swets & Zeitlinger.

Psotka, J., Massey, L.D., & Mutter, S. (Eds.). (1988). *Intelligent tutoring systems: Lessons learned*. Hillsdale, NJ: Erlbaum.

Reynolds, M. (Ed.). (1988). *Knowledge base for the beginning teacher*. New York: Pergamon.

Schon, D. (1983). *The reflective practitioner*. New York: Basic.

Schon, D. (1987). *Educating the reflective practitioner*. San Francisco CA: Jossey Bass.

Self, J. (Ed.). (1988). *Artificial intelligence and human learning*. London: Chapman & Hall.

Shavelson, R. (1973). What is *the* basic teaching skill? *Journal of Teacher Education, 24*, 144-151.

Shulman, L. (1986). Paradigms and research programmes in the study of teaching: contemporary perspectives. In M. Wittrock (Ed.), *Third handbook of research on teaching* (pp. 3-36). New York: Macmillan.

Shulman, L., & Elstein, A. (1975) Studies of problem-solving, judgement and decision making: implications for educational research. *Review of Research in Education, 3,* 5-42

Travers, R. (Ed.). (1973). *Second handbook of research on teaching.* Chicago, IL: Rand McNally.

Turkle, S. (1986). *Computers and the human spirit.* London: Granada.

Weizenbaum, J. (1974). *Computer power and human reason.* San Francisco, CA: Freeman.

Wenger, E. (1987). *Artificial intelligence and tutoring systems.* Los Altos, CA: Morgan Kaufman.

Wilson, S., Shulman, L., & Richert, A. (1987). "150 ways of knowing": Representations of knowledge in teaching. In J. Calderhead (Ed.), *Exploring teachers' thinking* (pp. 104-124). London: Cassell.

Winne, P., & Marx, R. (1977) Reconceptualising research on teaching. *Journal of Educational Psychology, 69,* 668-678.

Wittrock, M. (Ed.). (1986). *Third handbook of research on teaching.* New York: Macmillan.

# 2

## KNOWLEDGE REQUIREMENTS FOR TEACHING: THE CASE OF FRACTIONS*

### STELLAN OHLSSON

## 1. THREE THEORIES OF TEACHING

The characteristic feature of artificial intelligence (AI) systems is that they operate with an explicit representation of the knowledge that is required for successful performance. Intelligent tutoring systems are no different from other types of AI systems in this respect. The construction of an artificial teacher is possible only if we explicitly describe the knowledge requirements of successful teaching.

Different conceptions of teaching imply different knowledge requirements. The first goal of this chapter to outline three theories of teaching that are relevant for intelligent tutoring system research, and to describe the knowledge requirements implied by each theory. The three theories imply different knowledge requirements, because they view the teacher as carrying out different types of decisions. The first-order theory views teaching as *the communication of subject matter*. I shall call this the *traditional* view, without necessarily implying that any particular researcher has proposed this view. The second order theory views teaching as *the remediation of incomplete or incorrect mental representations*. This is the *current* view. The intelligent tutoring systems

*Preparation of this chapter was supported by NSF grant MDR-8470339. The opinions expressed do not necessarily reflect the position of the sponsoring agency, and no endorsement should be inferred.

25

that have been implemented to date are typically based on this view. The third-order theory views teaching as *the facilitation of knowledge construction*. This is a *future* view. Research has not yet progressed to the point where we can build systems that are based on this view. The three theories form a sequence, in the sense that each theory is a response to an inherent problem in the preceding theory.

Intelligent tutoring systems are typically based on the second-order theory of teaching. I argue later in the chapter that there is no reason to expect such systems to provide instruction that is radically better than instruction based on intuition and common sense. Only the third view of teaching holds a promise for radical improvements in instruction. The research needed to construct systems based on the third order theory is not research in intelligent tutoring systems *per se*, but research in learning theory.

The second goal of this chapter is to analyze the knowledge requirements for teaching fractions. The domain of fractions is interesting, because it is a necessary bridge between arithmetic and algebra, and because the learners' difficulties in this domain are conceptual rather than procedural in nature. The analysis of fractions is part of an ongoing effort to design an intelligent tutoring system that can teach conceptual understanding of fractions (Ohlsson, 1986, in press; Ohlsson, Nickolas, & Bee, 1987). The specific analysis provides an example of the distinctions between the three theories and their knowledge requirements. Conversely, the three theories provide a framework for the specific analysis.

Before I proceed, I need to make three caveats. First, by a theory of teaching I do not mean a psychological theory of the behavior of teachers. The kind of theory I have in mind cannot be tested against videotapes of classroom events. Like other types of design, the design of instruction—and teaching is online design of instruction—has a *prescriptive* aspect: We prefer good designs over bad ones. But "good" and "bad" are not scientific terms. It is helpful to consider the analogous case of architecture. There are theories of architecture, but they cannot be either verified or falsified by observations of architects. A theory of architecture is not a psychological theory of house-designing behavior, but rather an effort to capture the essence of house design (Lloyd Wright, 1954). Similarly, a theory of teaching that is useful for the implementation of intelligent tutoring systems is a theory that tells us *what teaching is*, rather than one that tells us what teachers do.

The fact that a theory has a prescriptive aspect does not imply that it is exempt from rational critique and evaluation, or that empirical observations play no role in that evaluation. Architects cannot afford to ignore the regularities of material nature, but the way in which those regularities enter into the evaluation of an architectural design is very different from the way they enter into the evaluation of a theory of physics. Similarly, a theory of teaching must take the regularities of mental life into account, but it is not charged with the task of explaining or predicting those regularities.

My second caveat is that, by teaching, I mean, for purposes of this chapter, *targeted teaching* that is, teaching that aims to establish a particular predefined subject matter in the mind of the learner. I do not consider teaching as nondirective encouragement of cognitive growth. Self (1985) has proposed that intelligent tutoring systems can be designed to encourage cognitive growth rather than to teach a particular subject matter. There is much to be said for this idea, both pedagogically (in order to get maximal motivation, let the learner's current interest be the sole ground for the choice of topic), morally (do we have a mandate to decide what the next generation should be interested in?), and practically (there is now so much knowledge that any path through it is radically incomplete, so what reason is there to choose one path over another?). Nevertheless, it seems likely that targeted teaching will always have a role to play in the educational system, and that for the foreseeable future it will continue to play the lead role.

My third caveat is that, by teaching, I mean, for purposes of the present chapter, *one-on-one tutoring*. The pragmatics of one-on-one tutoring are different from the pragmatics of regular classroom teaching, which in turn differs from the pragmatics of reciprocal teaching—to list just three different teaching scenarios. What is true for one scenario may or may not be true for another. I am primarily interested in one-on-one tutoring, because this is the natural mode of operation for an intelligent tutoring system.

## 2. THE COMMUNICATION OF SUBJECT MATTER

The first-order theory of teaching says that to teach is to communicate the relevant subject matter to someone who does not yet know it. In this view teaching is seen as a kind of *conversation*. For instance, I can say to a friend that "I promise to meet you at the theater tomorrow," and thereby communicate to him or her the promise that I will meet him or her at the theater tomorrow. Similarly, I can, according to this view, say to my friend that "a physical body continues in uniform, rectilinear motion unless a force acts on it," and thereby communicate to him or her the fact that physical bodies tend to go their merry way unless interfered with. This theory of teaching is radically inadequate, but the issue being investigated here is not its adequacy but its knowledge requirements.

The first-order theory implies that a teacher has two types of decisions to make, namely what to say and how to say it. More precisely:

1. The teacher has to decide which subject matter unit, which *topic*, to teach. This type of decision recurs at many levels, because topics vary in scope

and are nested within each other. A topic of wide scope, such as *arithmetic,* contains within it topics of intermediate scope, such as *fractions,* which, in turn, are made up of topics of minimal scope, individual knowledge items, such as *the concept of equivalent fractions.*

2. Having chosen a topic, the teacher has to choose a way of presenting that topic to the learner. This involves sequencing the subtopics, selecting exercises, formulating explanations, etc., as well as designing the graphical details of visual illustrations, etc.

The two decision types of the first-order theory imply two knowledge requirements: The teacher needs to have a codification of the subject matter, and he or she needs to know effective methods for the presentation of each unit of the subject matter. The first-order theory thus generates two of the main issues of traditional educational research, namely subject matter analysis and the effectiveness of different modes of presentation.

Subject matter analysis has become subject to stringent criteria as a result of the birth of A I and its application to the modeling of human cognition (see Ohlsson, 1988a, for an overview). A subject matter analysis is now expected to take the form of a computer program that can solve problems within the relevant domain. The major discovery that this demanding standard has produced is that *we do not know what we know.* We are discovering that, for most knowledge domains, there exists, no standard codification of the relevant knowledge. Medical experts cannot tell us how they perform a diagnosis, and mineral prospectors are only dimly aware of the basis for their location of drillholes. The rules they are applying cannot be found in any handbooks. Interviewing experts about the basis for their decisions turns out be a difficult task. Surprisingly, the conclusion that we do not know what we know is not limited to complex or ill-structured knowledge domains. Even mathematical treatises turn out to be incomplete and sketchy when approached with cognitive science methodology (Bundy, 1983; Michener, 1978; Resnick, in press). Unsuspected levels of complexity are discovered in even the most elementary topics (Greeno, Riley, & Gelman, 1984; Smith, Greeno, & Vitolo, 1989). In short, the stringent criteria of clarity and completeness that computer implementation imposes on subject matter analysis have led to the conclusion that *teachers have always worked with inadequate codifications of the knowledge they were supposed to teach.* It is obvious that a clear and precise codification of the subject matter is an important requirement for effective teaching, whether the teaching is delivered by a human or a machine. Cognitive science research, while raising the standards for what counts as a subject matter analysis, implies that such analyses are even more urgent than we used to believe.

## 2.1. Example: The Subject Matter of Fractions

The domain of fractions poses an interesting pedagogical challenge. It is an apparently simple topic which is necessary for continued study of mathematics, but which children master only with great difficulty. What is a fraction? Since number theory is *the* most analyzed domain of mathematics—itself the paragon of clarity and precision—we expect this question to have a standard, well-defined answer. However, mathematical expositions of the number system do not recognize a separate category of entities called *fractions* (Thurston, 1956). It is tempting to identify fractions with rational numbers, but this is incorrect, as shown by the fact that, for instance, 1/2 and 2/4 are two different fractions, although they denote the same rational number. To a first approximation, fractions are mathematical objects—ordered pair of integers—that are used to *denote* rational numbers.

Although the view of fractions as symbols for rational numbers is mathematically correct, it does not capture the variety of ideas that are expressed by the fraction notation $x/y$:

1. To *partition* a quantity into parts. Fore instance, "6/3 = 2" means "six partitioned into three equal-sized parts yields parts which have size two."
2. To *extract* one quantity from another. For instance, "6/3 = 2" means "three can be extracted from six two times."
3. To *circumscribe* a part of a quantity. For instance, "3/7" means "three out of seven."
4. To *measure* a quantity in relation to another quantity. For instance, "$x = 3/7 \times y$" means "$x$ is equal to the result of partitioning $y$ into seven equal-sized parts, and then combining three of those parts."
5. To *compare* one quantity to another. For instance, "6/3 = 2" means "six is twice as big as three."
6. To *distribute* one quantity over another. For instance, "6/3 = 2" means "if six $x$:s are distributed over three $y$:s, there will be two $x$:s for each $y$."
7. To *change* a quantity. For instance, "$3/7 \times x$" means "shrink $x$ until it becomes three sevenths of its current size."

These ideas are commonly referred to as *partitive quotient, quotitive quotient, proportion,*[1] *fraction, multiplicative comparison, ratio,* and *operator respectively,* but

---

[1] The term *proportion* has two distinct meanings in English. In the *colloquial* meaning, a proportion is a part of a quantity. For instance, *the proportion of the Earth's surface that is ocean is 3/4.* In the *mathematical* meaning, a proportion is an equality between two ratios. Both meanings are listed in any comprehensive dictionary. I am here referring to its colloquial meaning.

the usage of these terms varies. In-depth analyses of these and other fraction concepts can be found in Ohlsson (1987a, 1988b)

The seven ideas listed above are semantically related, but not identical. It is not obvious how to describe their relations to each other. For instance, ideas 1,2,5, and 6 are naturally applied to the case in which the numerator is larger than the denominator, ideas 3 and 4 are naturally applied to the case in which the numerator is smaller than the denominator, while idea 7 is equally applicable in both cases. It is not obvious why this should be so, or why concepts that apply to mutually exclusive sets of cases have come to be expressed by the same notation. Furthermore, ideas 3,4,5, and 6 build on idea 1, while ideas 2 and 7 are independent of it. How should this dependence/independence be described? Similarly, ideas 1,2,3,5, and 6 assign a meaning to $x/y$ independently of other quantities, while ideas 4 and 7 only assign a meaning to $x/y$ in relation to an implicitly assumed multiplier (3/7 of $x$). Furthermore, the mathematical behavior of $x/y$ is not the same across all its interpretations. If 2/7 and 3/7 are fractions in the sense of idea 4 above, then their sum is 5/7, but if they are ratios (see idea 6 above), then their sum is better represented by 5/14. Mathematical expositions of the number system are oblivious of these and other conceptual puzzles with respect to fractions.[2] Extensive analyses by educational researchers have so far failed to provide a complete and satisfactory account of the entire set of fraction concepts (Hiebert & Behr, 1988).

The rest of this section focuses on fractions in the sense of idea 4 above. The analysis of this fraction concept has progressed further than the analyses of the other fraction concepts. The presentation here summarizes the intellectual purpose of fractions, the concepts and principles of fractions, and the fraction notation.

*The Intellectual Purpose of Fractions.* The intellectual problem that fractions solve can be stated as follows: *How do we assign a numerical description, a measure, to a quantity that cannot be assigned an integer value because it falls between two integers?* Suppose that we have assigned a continuous quantity U, to be called the *unit quantity,* the value 1. What numerical description can we then assign to some other quantity T, the *target quantity, if T* is a part of U, i.e., if T is smaller than U? If U equals 1, then T falls between 0 and 1, and so cannot be described by an integer.[3] How can we numerically describe the size of T?

---

[2]Unfortunately, the term *fraction* has to make double duty in this discussion. In the *wide* sense, the term fraction refers to any entity symbolized by x/y. In the *narrow* sense, fraction refers only to such an entity when it is interpreted as in idea 4 above. I shall rely on context to distinguish between these two senses of the term.

[3]We can imagine situations in which U has some other value than 1, and T falls between other values than 0 and 1. However, all such situations can be reduced to the situation being discussed here without loss of generality.

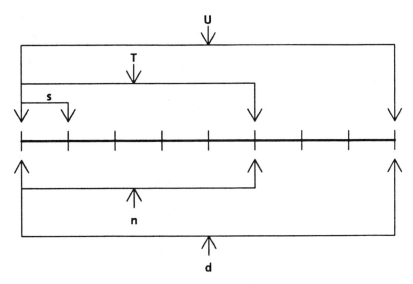

Figure 2.1. The construction of a fraction.

The solution to this problem consists of two steps. Figure 2.1 illustrate the two steps with respect to the quantity length: First, we seek a partitioning of $U$ into equal-sized parts, such that the boundary between two adjacent parts coincides with one endpoint of $T$ (assuming that the other endpoint of $T$ coincides with the endpoint of $U$). Suppose a partition of $U$ into 8 equal-sized parts fulfills this criterion. Second, we count the number of such parts required to create a quantity equal to $T$. Suppose that $T$ is equal to the combination of 5 parts. We then describe $T$ by saying that $T$ *is five eights of U*, or if $U$ can be left implicit, $T = 5/8$.

This method for measuring $T$ (in relation to $U$) has a number of interesting features. There is only space here to mention two of them. First, the fraction bridges the gap between the continuous and the discreet. The operation of partitioning the unit quantity into equal-sized parts enables us to quantify a continuous quantity by counting, because it replaces the continuous quantity with a set, namely the set of its parts. Pedagogically, this means that fractions should be introduced in the context of continuous, rather than discrete, quantities. Second, a fraction is a protomeasure.[4] The target quantity is expressed in relation to another quantity. Pedagogically, this means that

---

[4]True measurement requires a *standard* unit quantity and a *standard* partitioning. For instance, the metric system for measuring length uses the meter as the standard unit quantity and partitioning by ten as the standard partitioning. Fractions in the sense of idea 4 are similar to measures, except that they use an arbitrary unit quantity and an arbitrary partitioning. Hence the term *protomeasure*.

fractions should be introduced in the context of measuring. Unless the inadequacy of the integers for measuring continuously variable quantities is understood, the student has no intellectual need of fractions.

*The Concepts and Principles of Fractions.*   The central notion of fractions arithmetic is the concept of *equivalent fractions*. Equivalent fractions exist because the problem of expressing a target quantity $T$ in terms of a unit quantity $U$ does not have a unique solution. If partitioning $U$ into four parts and combining two of those parts does the job, then so does partitioning $U$ into 12 parts and combining six of them. Understanding his concept requires knowledge of at least the following four principles:

1. *Any given quantity can be constructed in different ways.*

   In terms of numbers, this principle says that any number is the sum of many different sets of addends, e. g., that the number 6 is the sum of both $(3+3)$ and of $(1+1+1+1+1+1)$. This principle has been identified by Lauren Resnick (see, e.g., Resnick & Omanson, 1987), who calls it the *principle of additive decomposition*. It is a central part of the rationale for the place-value algorithms of integer arithmetic.

2. *If a quantity is cut into parts, the combination of the parts is equal to the original quantity.*

   This principle is an idealization, because in the case of the partitioning of a physical quantity, as in cutting a crumbling cake, some amount is, in fact, lost. Similarly, sawing through a piece of wood turns a small amount of wood into sawdust. We do not know whether the idealization presupposed by this principle is a stumbling block for children.

3. *If a given quantity is cut into a larger number of equal-sized parts, the size of each part is smaller, and vice versa.*[5]

   This principle requires counterfactual reasoning, because it speaks (implicitly) about alternative partitionings of a given quantity. In many physical situations the alternative partitionings of a given quantity are mutually exclusive. Once a particular piece of wood has been sawed into parts, that piece of wood has ceased to exist and so cannot be sawed into parts again. Consequently, the comparison implied by this principle is necessarily an *imaginary* comparison ("if we *had* sawed it into twice as many parts, then"). We do not know to what extent children are capable of counterfactual reasoning.

---

[5]The formulation of the principle is admittedly awkward. Using technical terminology we can say that *the size of the part is inversely proportional to the number of parts.* But this language is not available to children.

4. *If a given quantity U is cut into d parts, and it takes n of those parts to construct a second quantity T, then, if U is cut into (m × d) parts instead, then it takes (m × n) of those parts to construct T.*

*This principle introduces the notion that the inverse relation between the number of parts and the size of a part can be described numerically, so that if there are m* times as many parts, then it takes exactly *m* times as many of those parts to construct a given amount.

There are other abstract principles about fractional quantities that children need to understand in order to calculate with fractions, but these principles suffice to illustrate that such principles constitute a central part of the subject matter of fractions, that such principles cannot be identified by opening a treatise on number theory, and that whether children at a given age understand such principles is an empirical question.

*Knowledge About Fraction Notation.* Fraction notation is, like place-value notation, a composite notation. Fractions are represented by symbols that consist of a combination of two integer symbols. But fraction notation has a peculiar feature that distinguishes it from place-value notation: There is no canonical representation for a particular number. For instance, the sum of 10/6 + 5/6 can written as either 15/6, 2 and 3/6, 2 and 1/2, or as 5/2. Whereas the integer notation has a one-to-one mapping of symbols onto numbers, the fraction notation has a many-to-one mapping.

*Discussion.* Mastery of a mathematical domain includes the ability to solve problems in that domain. The subject matter of fractions includes the procedural knowledge required to decide whether two fractions are equivalent or not, to find a common denominator for two given fractions, to find the sum, difference, product, and quotient of two fractions, to translate an improper fraction into a mixed fraction, and so on. The procedures for solving these problems are simple. They can be reduced to the following three rules: (a) multiplying both numerator and denominator of a fraction with the same number yields an equivalent fraction; (b) the sum of two fractions with equal denominators is found by adding their numerators and copying the denominator; and (c) a multiplyer to a fraction can be moved onto the fraction bar. It is unlikely that procedural complexity is the cause of children's difficulties with fraction. The core of the domain of fractions consists of conceptual, as opposed to procedural, knowledge, and the application of that knowledge in the construction of the rationale for the procedures. Learning fractions is not primarily a matter of acquiring certain cognitive skills, but rather a matter of learning to think with a new type of abstract entity.

The subject matter analysis suggests at least the following four specific sources of difficulty: (a) since the fraction notation is used to express at least half a dozen different ideas, learners are likely to confuse those ideas, unless the instructor carefully separates them; (b) learners are unlikely to understand the intellectual purpose of fractions unless fractions are introduced in the context of the inadequacy of an integer scale for measuring continuous quantities; (c) since the principles of fractions require abstraction and counterfactual reasoning, it is possible that young learners do not understand those principles; and (d) learners are likely to expect the fraction notation to have a one-to-one mapping between symbols and numbers, and thus be confused by the existence of equivalent fractions.

The example of fractions illustrates the necessity of subject matter analysis. No instructional program for fractions, computerized or not, can succeed in teaching conceptual understanding of fractions if it ignores the difficulties listed above. No domain-independent pedagogical design principle can specify how to overcome the problems caused by ambiguity of basic terms, lack of intellectual purpose, missing prerequisites, and incorrect presuppositions. These obstacles to learning must be counteracted with domain-specific instructional actions.

## 2.2. Problem: The Diagnosis of Previous Knowledge

The first-order theory of teaching implicitly assumes that the teacher knows the extent of the student's previous knowledge. This follows from the fact that every knowledge item has prerequisites. For instance, the concept of a fraction can be traced back to the principle of additive decomposition and to the procedure for counting the elements of a set. These knowledge items can, in turn, be traced back to their prerequisites, and so on. But if all knowledge builds on previous knowledge, then there is no absolute starting point for teaching. The selection of a particular topic as the target for teaching is therefore warranted only if the teacher knows that the student has previous knowledge of the prerequisites of that topic.

In classroom instruction the structure of the curriculum provides a gross estimate of the student's previous knowledge in the form of the sequence of courses he/she has passed through. This estimate errs in two ways. First, it does not take into account that the student might acquire relevant knowledge elsewhere. Second, the fact that the student has gone through a particular course does not imply that he or she has mastered the content of that course. These two factors introduce individual differences between students who are at the same place in the curriculum.

It follows that in order to have an accurate estimate of previous knowledge, the teacher must *diagnose* the knowledge state of the individual student. Cognitive diagnosis consists of inferring what the student does and does not know on the basis of his or her performance on some diagnostic task. *But expertise in how to diagnose knowledge of a particular subject matter does not belong to that subject matter, but to psychological theory.* Since the result of the diagnosis refers to what is in the student's head, rather than to the subject matter, diagnosis presupposes a theory of how knowledge is mentally represented in general, and how students mentally represent the subject matter in particular. The need to diagnose the previous knowledge of the individual student introduces a new type of decision on the part of the teacher—what does this student know?—and, consequently, a new knowledge requirement. The problem of cognitive diagnosis takes the theory of teaching out of the codification of subject matter and into the theory of mental representations.

## 3. THE REMEDIATION OF MENTAL REPRESENTATIONS

The second-order theory of teaching says that to teach is to correct the learner's mental representation of the subject matter. According to this view the learner is on the way to mastery of the subject matter. He or she has *some* representation of the subject matter, but, by definition, that representation is incomplete or incorrect—that is why he or she is still learning. The job of the teacher is to provide remediation for the discrepancies between the learner's representation and the complete and correct representation. I call this theory of teaching the *current* theory, since it is the basis for almost all intelligent tutoring systems that have been implemented to date.

According to the second-order theory a teacher makes four different types of decisions:

1. Which subject matter topic is to be taught?
2. How does an expert represent that topic?
3. Which deficiency does the mental representation of *this* student suffer from at *this* moment in time?
4. How can that deficiency be remediated?

The first decision is the same as decision 1 in the first-order theory. Consistent with the focus on targeted teaching, all three theories discussed here claim that teaching begins with a decision about which topic to teach. Hence, the knowledge requirements of the second-order theory includes those of the first-order theory.

Decision 4 in this theory corresponds to decision 2 in the first-order theory: How to teach? However, an act of teaching is in this theory conceived as a corrective action instead of as a communication of a knowledge item. A corrective action can take many different forms other than stating—or restating—the relevant knowledge item, for example, asking a question or providing a counterexample. The difference between the first and second-order theories is reflected in a somewhat curious shift in language:Whereas someone who works within the first-order theory is likely to talk about *teaching a concept,* i.e., communicating that concept to the learner, researchers who operate with the second-order theory often talk about *teaching an error,* i.e., helping the student to overcome that error.

The knowledge requirements introduced by the second-order theory are implied by questions 2 and 3: How is the subject matter encoded in the mind of someone who knows it, and how is it encoded in the learner (at some particular moment in time)? Both questions presuppose that we have a theory of how knowledge is encoded in general, i.e., of the syntax and semantics of the language of thought. Cognitive psychology has produced a handful of different hypotheses about the format of mental representations. Episodic and factual information is often assumed to be encoded in a *semantic network* and/or in a collection of *frames.* The network or the collection of frames constitute *long-term memory.* The perceptually available properties of the situation that a person find himself/herself in are most often represented as a set of logic-like *propositions* which are stored in *working memory.* The learner's intentions are often assumed to be encoded in a *goal-subgoal hierarch.* Procedural knowledge is typically assumed to be encoded in so-called *production rules,* condition-action pairs that specify the circumstances under which a particular action is executed. In short, cognitive psychology has proposed relatively precise hypotheses about the mental representation of previously learned factual information, the immediately available situation, intentions, and cognitive skills.

The codification of the relevant subject matter and the theory of mental representation are the basic ingredients of an expert model. A first-approximation model is constructed by encoding the subject matter into the relevant format. There are two complexities. First, a standard codification of the subject matter is typically not available, or else so vague and incomplete as to be useless. Second, the problem of encoding a given subject matter into a given format usually has more than one solution. For example, the heuristics used by medical doctors to diagnose diseases can be encoded as production rules in a variety of ways (Clancey, 1987). The question of how the expert encodes the subject matter must be answered empirically, by collecting and interpreting data from experts' performances.

The purpose of the expert model is to facilitate the description of errors. Once a model of the correct representation is available, the learner's mental representation of the subject matter can be described as a *deviation* (a gap or a misconception) from the correct one. If the correct representation is stated precisely, the set of psychologically plausible deviations can (sometimes) be stated precisely as well. The power of this approach was first explored in the well-known BUGGY model of subtraction errors (Brown & Burton, 1978;

Burton, 1982). Identification of the psychologically plausible deviations requires empirical observations of learners' errors.

The purpose of a precise description of errors is, in turn, to facilitate the tailoring of teaching actions to particular errors. In order to make use of this possibility, the teacher must know how to identify *which* perversion of the correct representation a particular student is suffering from at a particular moment in time. This is the problem of *cognitive diagnosis:* Given a performance by a particular learner at time *t*, infer (the relevant portion of) his/her knowledge state at time *t*. The standard solution is to make a list of the psychologically plausible perversions, to match those perversions one by one against the record of the student's performance, and to select the best match as the most plausible diagnosis. This solution has a number of weaknesses. To compile a reasonably complete error catalogue might require large amounts of empirical research. Also, to identify the best match at runtime may require huge amounts of computation. Furthermore, it is unclear how to describe performances that are inconsistent and performances that do not match against any of the plausible perversions. Other approaches to cognitive diagnosis have been tried (Langley, Wogulis, & Ohlsson, 1990; Ohlsson & Langley, 1988), but it is generally agreed that the problem is intractable in its general form. VanLehn (1988) provides a systematic discussion of problems and methods. Self (1988) has proposed ways to circumvent the intractability of the problem.

The study of cognitive errors takes the theory of teaching outside the boundaries of the subject matter in two respects. First, the theory of a particular subject matter does not include knowledge about perversions. For instance, physics does not encompass all possible wrong ideas about physical phenomena. But the *psychology* of physics does study all possible mental representations of physical phenomena, including the incorrect ones. Second, errors must often be described in terms of how a mental representation is used, rather than in terms of the representation itself, so the study of errors introduces the notion of *cognitive processes* into the theory of teaching.

In summary, the second-order theory of teaching poses the following knowledge requirements, over and above the requirement of having a codification of the subject matter: (a) knowledge of the format(s) of mental representations and the processes that operate upon them, (b) knowledge of the mental representation of somebody who knows the subject matter well, (c) knowledge of the different perversions of the subject matter that are likely to occur in human learners, and (d) knowledge of how to identify which of these perversions a particular learner is suffering from at a particular moment. These knowledge requirements take the theory of teaching out of the concern with subject matter and into the realm of psychological theory. There are still very few subject matter topics for which all of these knowledge requirements are satisfied.

### 3.1. Example: The Mental Representation of Fractions

Why do children have difficulties with fractions? Which characteristics of their mental representations of fractions make it so hard for them to operate correctly with fractions? Educational researchers have proposed that *children do not associate a value, a number, with the fraction symbol as a whole* (see, e.g., Behr & Post, 1988). The only numbers they associate with the fraction symbol, according to this hypothesis, are the integer values associated with the numerator and the denominator, respectively. Such a deviation from the correct representation would indeed be crucial. As Behr and Post (1988) point out, if learners do not associate numbers with fraction symbols, they will have problems with the idea of equivalent fractions, i.e., with the idea that several fraction symbols can be associated with the *same* number. They will also have problems with the procedures for calculating with fractions. The notion of, say, adding two fractions can hardly make sense unless fractions correspond to numbers. I shall refer to the failure to associate numbers with fraction symbols as the *No Value Error,* and to the hypothesis that this error is the root of children's difficulties with fractions as the *No Value Hypothesis.*

The No Value Hypothesis would be strengthened if we could explain *why* children fail to associate numbers with fraction symbols. If a child can associate a number with a symbol like "13", why can he or she not associate a number with a symbol like "1/3"? One possible explanation is that pedagogical practice does not encourage children to associate numbers with fractions. This explanation is consistent with the casual observation that fractions are sometimes introduced by partitioning a unit quantity and selecting some number of the resulting parts. This presentation avoids introducing the target quantity (see Figure 2.1) as a quantity of independent interest. The only quantities which are explicitly defined in this type of presentation are the unit quantity, the number of parts in the unit quantity, and the number of so-called selected parts. The fact that the sum of the so-called selected parts is the quantity of interest is not emphasized. As a result, learners may never realize that the fraction is a numerical expression for the size of the target quantity. This explanation is optimistic because it claims that the difficulty is shallow. If children were told directly and explicitly to associate fractions with numbers, this explanation claims, they would do so. However, the frequency and persistence of children's errors indicate that the difficulty of associating a number with a fraction symbol has a deeper cause than mere lack of opportunity. At the current time we have no satisfactory explanation for the No Value Error.

Is the rest of the fractions curriculum easy to learn, once the No Value Error has been overcome? Can children easily learn, say, the concept of equivalent fractions, once they understand that a fraction symbol as a whole denotes a number or a quantity? Unfortunately, this is not the case. Both developmental and educational research suggests that children can be expected to have difficulties with the concept of equivalent fractions, even if they are not victims of the No Value Error. As the subject matter analysis showed, understanding equivalence between fractions requires an understanding of the inverse relation between the number of parts in a unit quantity and the size of each part. To repeat the crucial principle, if $U$ is divided into, say, $d$ parts, and it takes $n$ of those parts to make up some quantity $T$, then, if we divide $U$ into $(m \times d)$ parts, we need $(m \times n)$ of those parts to make up the quantity $T$. The change in the number of parts is *compensated* by the change in the size of each part in such a way that the quantity $T$ remains unchanged.

This principle is an instance of a more general schema involving three quantities $x_1, x_2$, and $y$. The schema is defined by two characteristics. The first characteristic is that $y$ is a function of both $x_1$ and $x_2$. They are therefore called the *determinants* of the schema, while $y$ is called the *resultant*. If one of the determinants is held constant, a change in the other determinant will cause a change in the resultant. The second characteristic of the schema is that $x_1$ and $x_2$ are related to each other in such a way that they mutually compensate each other: If both determinants are free to vary, $y$ remains constant. A change in one determinant is counteracted by a corresponding change in the other determinant in such a way that the resultant is unchanged. I will call this schema *constancy under multiplicative compensation*.

Do children understand constancy under multiplicative compensation at the age at which we try to teach them fractions? Can they mentally represent the interactions between the three variables in this schema? The empirical evidence indicates that the answer is ''no.'' The first source of evidence is the research on children's conservation of physical quantities initiated by Jean Piaget and his co-workers. The classical finding is that children cannot infer the equivalence of a quantity before and after a change in an object, because they focus on a single determinant of that quantity. For instance, they believe that a volume of water increases (decreases) in volume when poured into a taller container, because they do not realize that the increase in height (decrease in width) is compensated by the corresponding decrease in width (increase in height) in such a way as to keep the volume, the resultant quantity, constant. This result has been replicated many times (Flavell, 1963). A second source of evidence is Siegler's studies of children's understanding of the balance beam (Siegler, 1978). Correct performance on the task of predicting when a balance beam will remain level requires understanding that the torque on one arm of the beam is a function of both the amount of weight on that arm and of the distance of the weight from the fulcrum. It also requires understanding that weight and distance are mutually compensatory, so that a change in one of the determinants of torque can be counteracted by a corresponding change in the other determinant in such a way that the torque remains constant. Siegler calls this conception of the balance beam *Rule IV*. His data show that children do not reach this understanding of the balance beam before the age of 17 years. In summary, developmental research is consistent with the hypothesis that children cannot operate with the schema of constancy under multiplicative compensation at the age at which we try to teach them fractions. I shall call this hypothesis the *No Compensation Hypothesis.*

If inability to understand constancy under multiplicative compensation is the root of children's difficulties with equivalent fractions, we would expect them to deal with problems involving equivalence in the same way that they deal with problems involving conservation of physical quantities:by focusing on a single aspect of the situation. Research on children's performance on tasks in which they have to compare fractions is consistent with this expectation. For instance, Behr, Wachsmuth, Post, and Lesh (1984) and Post, Wachsmuth, Lesh, and Behr (1985) observed what they call a *whole number strategy*. According to their observations, children judge the relative size of fractions by comparing a single pair of integers, either the numerators or the denominators. Smith (personal communication, November 1988) found that a majority of children's equivalence judgments are based on pairwise comparisons of numerator with numerator (the larger the numerator, the greater the fraction), and denominator with denominator (the large the denominator, the smaller the fraction), but without any interaction between the two comparisons. This strategy will yield *correct* judgements for several problem classes: (a) problems in which the numerators are equal, (b) problems in which the denominators are equal, and (c) problems in which the two pairwise comparisons have the same outcome (e.g., 1/5 compared to 2/3). This strategy fails only when the two judgments have contradictory outcomes, as in 3/5 vs. 1/4. The comparison of the numerators indicate that 3/5 is the larger number because it has more parts, while the comparison of the denominators indicates that 1/4 is the larger number because it has larger parts. Comparisons of this type cannot be carried out without considering the compensatory relation between the numerator and the denominator. Thus, according to Smith's observations, children acquire a strategy for judging the relative size of fractions that generate correct answers to many problems, but which does not require understanding of constancy under multiplicative compensation.

In summary, the concept of equivalent fractions is an instance of the general schema of constancy under multiplicative compensation. Both developmental and educational research support the hypothesis that children have not mastered this schema at the age at which we try to teach them fractions. Their difficulties with equivalent fractions should therefore be no surprise.

The two hypotheses advanced here—the No Value Hypothesis and the No

Compensation Hypothesis—would be strengthened if we could use them to explain children's procedural errors in calculating with fractions. The most persistent and frequent error with respect to fractions is the so-called *freshman error* (Silver, 1986), in which children add fractions with equal denominators correctly, but add fractions with unequal denominators by adding the numerators *and adding the denominators*. This error is common and resistant to remediation.

If children do not associate numbers with fraction symbols, then the request to add two fractions must generate an *impasse,* a cognitive state in which the mental procedure that is being executed cannot continue. The child's procedure for addition presumably expects two numbers as inputs; hence, if that procedure is given two entities which are not numbers as inputs, it can be expected to run into an impasse. Brown and VanLehn (1980, 1982) have proposed a hypothesis, called *repair theory,* which claims that a person deals with impasses by editing the control state of the procedure with domain-independent editing functions, called *repairs*. The repairs operate on the local control state and cannot foresee the consequences of the changes they introduce. As a result, although a repair may enable execution to continue, there is a high probability that continued execution will result in a wrong answer. Repair theory has been successfully applied to the description of procedural errors in the domain of subtraction. Unfortunately, repair theory does *not,* in fact, predict the freshman error. The repairs postulated in the description of subtraction errors do not edit the control state of the procedure for adding equal-denominator fractions (which children solve correctly) so as to generate the freshman error for fractions with unequal denominators. Either we have not yet discovered all psychologically relevant repairs, or else the impasse-repair type of explanation is not applicable to the freshman error. The point of reporting this negative result here is to illustrate that we do not yet have precise explanations for even the most basic errors in the domain of fractions, let alone for the bewildering array of more complex procedural errors in the addition and subtraction of mixed fractions that have been documented by Evertz (1982) and Tatsuoka (1984). Careful observation and analysis of cognitive errors is a crucial component of instructional design in the domain of fractions.

## 3.2. Problem: The Content of Remedial Messages

The basic pedagogical principle of the second-order theory is that instruction—tutorial messages—should be tailored to the knowledge state of the learner. Presentation of the subject matter is not enough, because the subject matter can be misunderstood in different ways, and the instructional message that corrects one misunderstanding is not the same message that corrects another misunderstanding. Hence, individualized design of instruction, based on an online diagnosis of the particular learner's knowledge state, is essential.

Given a particular deviation from the correct representation, *which* tutorial message would make the learner correct that deviation? For instance, suppose that the learner is adding multicolumn numbers incorrectly, and we diagnose the errors as forgetting to add the carry when processing a column. How can that deviation of the correct addition procedure be remedied? The straightforward approach is to say "you are supposed to add the carry." Will this message cause the learner to correct his or her procedure so that he or she adds the carry in the future? I do not know of any data to which to turn for an answer, but my intuition tells me that it will be effective only in a small number of cases. Be that as it may; the main point of the example is that the description "forgets to add the carried digit" does not reveal which intervention would make the learner remember to add the carried digit. It is even less clear which tutorial messages are needed to overcome the No Value Error, or to develop the ability to operate with the schema of constancy under multiplicative compensation. In general terms, *the description of a deviation between student's mental representation of the subject matter and the correct representation does not entail any conclusion about which tutorial message might cause the learner to correct that deviation*.

The problem is that both the expert model and the student model are theories of *performance*. But the contrast between the novice and the expert models does not tell us how, by what route, the novice turns into an expert. There are many different types of changes that could transform a novice into an expert. Only some of those changes correspond to how humans learn. If the purpose of a tutorial message is to cause such a change to happen, then the content of the message cannot be a function only of the particular deviation between the student model and the expert model, but must also be a function of the type of change that the message is supposed to trigger. Hence, the content of the tutorial messages cannot be derived without a theory of *learning*.

The claim that some intelligent tutoring systems are based on learning theory is thus only partially true. The expert model, the student model, and the diagnostic component of such systems are in some cases based on psychological theory. In the tutoring systems developed by John Anderson and co-workers (Anderson, Boyle, & Reiser, 1985; Anderson, Boyle, & Yost, 1985; Reiser, Anderson, & Farrell, 1985), the *timing* of the tutorial messages is also derived, in a general way, from the principles of the ACT* theory. However, there are no systems in which the *content* of the tutorial messages is derived from a learning theory. To the best of my knowledge all existing tutoring systems output tutorial messages that have been designed by the system programmer, and they are designed on the same basis as all other instruction: intuition, common sense, and guesses about what might work. The choice of which message to output and when to output it might be based on theory, but the content of the messages is not.

This observation has implications for the assessment of the current stage of development of intelligent tutoring systems. A tutorial system cannot be expected to be stronger than its weakest component. Hence, there is no reason to expect instruction based on the second-order theory to be radically better than instruction based on intuition and common sense. Such tutoring systems are like space shuttles in which every component has been designed in accordance with physical theory except, say, the wings, the design of which has been left to common sense. It is unlikely that such a bird would fly. Similarly, it is unlikely that a tutoring system in which all components except the tutorial messages have been designed in accordance with theory would have any radical effects. The advantages of theory-based instructional design cannot be cashed in, as it were, unless *all* components of the tutoring system are designed in accordance with theory. If intelligent tutoring systems are to realize their full potential, they must be based on cognitive theory in the strong sense that the content of the tutorial messages is derived from theory. This requirement takes the theory of teaching outside the concern with cognitive errors, and into the realm of cognitive change.

## 4. THE FACILITATION OF KNOWLEDGE CONSTRUCTION

The third-order theory of teaching says that to teach is to help the learner improve his or her current world view. The learner is continuously in the process of constructing his or her view of the world, including his or her view of the particular subject matter. To learn means to improve one's world view so that it becomes more comprehensive, connected, consistent, nuanced, and parsimonious. There are many different types of improvements: to replace a vague idea with a clearer one, to connect previously unconnected ideas, to distinguish two different but similar ideas, to weed out mistaken factual information, to add factual information, to generalize an idea, to work out the implications of an idea, to subsume a particular instance under a general idea, to identify conflicts between ideas, to resolve conflicts, and so on. Occurrences of these and similar processes will here be called *learning events*.[6] A sequence a learning events is a *learning sequence*. If the learning sequence leads to a better view of the subject matter, I will call it a *productive* learning sequence.

---

[6]This useful term has been introduced, I believe, by Alan Shoenfeld. He may or may not agree with the use I am making of the term here.

According to the third-order theory the job of a teacher is to act in such a way that productive learning sequences occur in the learner.

In order to cause productive learning sequences, the teacher has to make six types of decisions:

1. Which subject matter topic is to be taught?
2. How does an expert represent that topic?
3. Which deficiency does the mental representation of *this* student suffer from at *this* moment in time?
4. Which productive learning sequences are possible in the learner's current knowledge state?
5. Under which circumstances will those productive learning sequences occur?
6. How can those circumstances be brought about?

Decisions 1, 2, and 3 are the same as for the second-order theory. The third-order theory does not escape the need to identify the subject matter, to describe the expert's representation of the subject matter, and to diagnose the learner's current knowledge state. The question of how to teach has been transformed once again. To teach is, in this theory, neither to communicate the subject matter, nor to remedy cognitive errors, but to arrange situations in which productive learning sequences are likely to occur.

The knowledge requirement introduced by the third-order theory is that a teacher must know how learning happens. Modern learning theory assumes that the cognitive processes of the learner include a small set of fixed *learning mechanisms,* i.e., editing functions that take a symbol structure as input and revise it in some well-specified way. Each learning mechanism has *triggering conditions* that specify when, under what circumstances, the mechanism will be activated. For instance, a mechanism of rule composition may be activated when two problem-solving rules repeatedly apply in sequence, when a subgoal is satisfied, or under some other set of circumstances. A learning mechanism also has *information requirements* that must be satisfied for it to apply successfully. For instance, a generalization mechanism must have at least two instances to generalize over. Like all other cognitive processes, learning mechanisms must operate under *capacity limitations* of some sort. For instance, the amount of information that can be taken into account in a single learning step is probably small, the computation performed by a learning mechanism is likely to be simple, the number of learning steps that can occur in a particular time period is probably limited, and so on. This perspective implies that a cognitive structure is not infinitely malleable. The applicability conditions, information requirements, and capacity limitations constrain the possible improvements of the learner's current knowledge state.

For instruction to be effective, it must be consistent with the constraints on the possible changes. The *one disjunct at a time* constraint provides a good example. VanLehn (1986, 1987, 1990) argues that children learn the standard place-value algorithm for multicolumn subtraction with regrouping mainly by inducing the algorithm from solved examples. The type of learning mechanism that is required for this has been studied in artificial intelligence research under the name *grammar induction*. It is well known that one of the information requirements of grammar induction is that there are no multiple disjuncts, i.e., places in which a nonterminal node in the grammar can be rewritten in alternative ways. The implication is that, if the construction of the subtraction procedure happens through grammar induction, the teacher should arrange his or her practice problems so that the learner only encounters one (new) disjunct at a time. There is as yet no empirical confirmation that adherence to his pedagogical principle facilitates the construction of procedures. If such data are forthcoming, the one disjunct at a time principle has extensive and well-defined implications for the design of instruction in arithmetic and other highly procedural domains.

Anderson (1983, 1986) has proposed a set of learning mechanisms that collectively go under the name *knowledge compilation* and which operate in the context of the ACT$^*$ theory of the human cognitive architecture. The knowledge compilation hypothesis claims that the verbally presented infor-mation is *proceduralized* into problem solving rules. For instance, a theorem of plane geometry which says, schematically, that, *if P* is true, then *Q* is true, can give raise to several rules, including the subgoaling rule *if the goal is to prove that Q is true, then set the goal to prove that P is true.* The knowledge compilation hypothesis also claims that several simple problem-solving rules can be *composed* into a more complex rule that controls a larger segment of problem solving behavior. The ACT$^*$ theory has mainly been applied to learning situations that have *fixed* declarative inputs such as geometry theorems (Anderson, 1982) or descriptions of logic circuits (Anderson, in press). The theory can be used to derive what the resulting procedure will be after learning has been completed. However, it ought to be possible to apply the theory backwards, as it were. In such an application one would begin with the target procedure that one wants the learner to construct, and deduce which declarative inputs would lead to that procedure with a minimum of cognitive strain. To the best of my knowledge, the ACT$^*$ theory has not been applied in that fashion.

Many other hypotheses about learning have been proposed recently, but their instructional implications have not been explored. For instance, the hypothesis that learning occurs when subgoals are satisfied, common to both the UPL model of Ohlsson (1987c) and the Soar model of Laird, Rosen-bloom, and Newell (1986), imply that a teacher should supply the learner with easy-to-reach subgoals. The theory of discrimination learning proposed by Langley (1987) implies that the learner must encounter both correct and incorrect applications of a problem-solving operator in order to learn the correct use of that operator. This hypothesis has obvious implications for the design of problem-solving exercises. The learning theory proposed by Ohlsson and Rees (1988) claims that learners revise their procedures when they find themselves producing problem states that are inconsistent with what they know about the problem environment. This hypothesis implies that instructional messages should refer to the *the state of the problem,* rather than to the performance of the learner. For instance, a tutorial message might say *the denominators should be equal* rather than *you should find a common denominator before you add the numerators.* None of these instructional implications have been empirically validated.

As these examples show, modern learning theory has focussed on *procedural* knowledge. All the theories mentioned above refer to the construction of procedures for well-defined tasks. However, the core content of most subject matter topics consists of *conceptual* knowledge. The goal of instruction is usually to help the learner construct the concepts and principles that are central to the subject matter. The skill of performing a particular type of exercise is often unimportant in itself; the exercises are only tools for teaching the principled content of the domain. Unfortunately, there are no precise learning theories that explain the construction of conceptual knowledge. Instruction in concepts and principles, whether computerized or not, cannot be based on theory at this time, for lack of an appropriate theory. If intelligent tutoring systems are to be built on learning theory, and if they are to teach conceptual (as well as procedural) knowledge, then research must focus on the invention of learning mechanisms that construct conceptual knowledge.

### 4.1. Example: The Construction of Fractions

Consider once again the concept of equivalent fractions. What is required for a learner to construct this concept? What are the cognitive circumstances under which this construction will take place? How do the prerequisites for this concept come together into a grasp of this fundamental idea? What *happens* when the learner grasps this idea? The learning theories mentioned above are of no help in answering these questions. The notion of equivalent fractions is not a procedure or a skill, but an *idea,* and its acquisition cannot be explained by theories of skill acquisition.

Although we do not have a learning theory for conceptual knowledge, the previous discussion implies that instruction in the conceptual basis of fractions must focus on two relations: (a) the relation between fraction symbols and physical quantities, and (b) the inverse relation between the

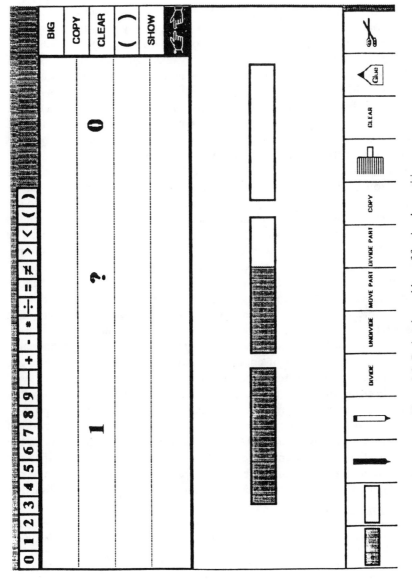

Figure 2.2. Posing the problem of fractional quantities.

number of parts a quantity is divided into, and the size of each part. The construction of fractions is likely to be facilitated by a learning environment in which those relations can be manipulated and studied. This conclusion is embodied in the design of the Fractions Tutor, an intelligent tutoring system that is intended to help learners construct, first, the concepts and principles of fractions, and, second, the procedures for operating with fractions.[7] The Fractions Tutor is implemented in the Loops environment and currently runs on a Xerox 1109 workstation. The screen organization of the Fractions Tutor is illustrated in Figure 2.2. There are two windows. The top window is called the *Notebook* and the bottom window is called the *illustration window*.

The Notebook functions like an ordinary notebook: it provides a surface on which one can write and erase number symbols. Unlike a paper-and-pencil notebook, the Notebook does not require skill in shaping symbols. A character is written in the Notebook with the help of the mouse. Digits and other characters that can be written in the Notebook correspond to the icons at the top of the Notebook window (see Figure 2.2). When the cursor is positioned over an icon and the mouse is buttoned, the cursor turns into the character in the icon. The character can then be moved to its intended location by moving the mouse, and put down, as it were, by buttoning. The learner need never use the keyboard to write and manipulate symbols in the Notebook. Also unlike a paper-and-pencil notebook, the computerized Notebook allows the student to pick up an already written symbol and move it to another place on the writing surface. It is possible to pick up and move entire expressions, e.g., a mixed fraction, as well as single characters. The characters can be written in either of two font sizes, called *big* and *small*, respectively. The larger font is used for integers, and the smaller for fractions. The switch BIG at the right edge of the Notebook controls the size of the next character to be written. The switch is toggled by mousing it.

The bottom window in Figure 2.2 is the illustration window, in which the learner can create and manipulate (graphic representations of) physical objects. Conceptually, the illustration window provides a view of a world of objects, a so-called *illustration world*. Three different illustration worlds for the Fractions Tutor have been implemented to date. They are named after the type of objects they contain: the *Strips World*, the *Rectangles World*, and the *Marbles World*. Switching from one illustration to another is accomplished in

---

[7]The Fractions Tutor is a team effort. Lauren Resnick is principal investigator; Stellan Ohlsson is project leader. Jeffrey Bonar and Pearla Nesher have acted as advisors to the project. Gaea Leinhardt has generously shared her data on instruction in fractions. The implementation of the tutor is the work of Stewart Nicholas, with contributions by Ernest Rees and Ruedi Nicholas Stuessi. Nancy Bee and Pat Zeller have carried out the field evaluations of the tutor. Barbara Grover, Jeremy Resnick, Janice Singer, and Susan Sterrett have at various times and in various capacities contributed important insights into the analysis behind the tutor. The analysis of the subject matter is continued by Kate Bielaczyc.

approximately 2 seconds in the current implementation. I will only describe the Strips World here. The other two illustrations have been described by Ohlsson (1987b) and by Ohlsson, Nickolas, and Bee (1987).

The *objects* in the Strips World are strips, rectangles of fixed length and width. The length of the strip is the unit quantity in the Strips World. A strip can be white, partially grey, or completely grey. The length of the grey part of a strip is continuously variable. It serves as the target quantity in the Strips World. The *actions* on the strips are summarized in Table 2.1. Strips can be created and thrown away, moved and copied. A strip can be painted wholly or partially grey, and the grey can be erased. Since a strip can also be divided, and since the parts can be filled in independently of each other, a strip is characterized by (a) the total length of the grey area, (b) the number of parts, (c) the size of each part, (d) the number of grey parts, and (d) the number of white parts.

The icons below the Strips window (see Figure 2.2) represent the actions. The action icons are activated by mousing them. For instance, to divide a strip, the student would mouse the icon containing the word DIVIDE. The cursor turns into a labeled arrow that says *Divide this strip*. The student moves the arrow until it points to the relevant strip and inputs the desired number of parts. The system carries out the partitioning. The user need not use the keyboard to execute the actions in any of the illustration worlds.

Number symbols can only appear in the Notebook window and strips can only occur in the illustration window. A major feature of the Fractions Tutor is the facility for *yoking* the two windows to each other. The icon labeled SHOW at the right edge of the Notebook turns the cursor into a labeled arrow when moused. The label in *Show this object*, and when the arrow is pointed at a strip and the mouse clicked, the number referring to the length of the grey area in

Table 2.1.  **Actions in the Strips World.**

| Action | Result |
|---|---|
| CREATE | Creates a new strip. |
| COPY | Creates a copy of an existing strip. |
| MOVE | Moves a strip from one place to another. |
| DELETE | Deletes an existing strip. |
| CLEAR | Deletes all existing strips. |
| DIVIDE | Divides a strip into $n$ equal-sized parts. |
| UNDIVIDE | Erases the divisions between parts in a strip. |
| FILLIN | Changes an *entire* strip or an *entire* part of a strip from white to grey. |
| ERASE | Changes an *entire* strip or an *entire* part of a strip from grey to white. |
| PAINT | Increases or decreases the length of the grey area in a strip, or in a part of a strip, in a *continuous* fashion. |
| MOVE PART | Moves the grey color from a single part to some other location. |
| SUBDIVIDE | Divides a part of a strip (which has the effect that all other parts of that strip are divided as well). |

that strip appears in the Notebook. Similarly, if the SHOW icon is moused and the arrow pointed at a number in the Notebook, the corresponding strip appears in the Strips window. If a fraction symbol is changed, the tutor carries out the corresponding change in the yoked strip, and vice versa. For example, if a grey part of a strip is erased, the number one is subtracted from the numerator of the corresponding fraction. If a number is picked up and moved, the corresponding strip moves accordingly. And so on.

In accordance with the analysis of the intellectual purpose of fractions, fractions are introduced to the learner by posing the problem of how to measure a quantity that falls between zero and one. This problem can be posed in the following way with the help of the tutor (see Figure 2.2):

1. The tutor creates a white strip and uses the yoking relation to show that it corresponds to zero. The tutor then creates a grey strip and shows that it corresponds to unity.
2. The tutor creates a white strip, places it between the two existing strips, and paints it *partially* grey. The tutor asks the child what number the partially grey strip corresponds to, pointing out that the amount of grey in that strip is somewhere between the amount of grey in the other two strips.

The idea of dividing a strip and counting the number of grey parts is then introduced as a solution to the problem of how to measure the length of the grey area in a partially grey strip, i.e., what number corresponds to such a strip.

The concept of equivalent fractions can be introduced to the learner through the following exercise (see Figure 2.3):

1. The tutor writes two fractions in the Notebook, and asks the student to judge which is greater.
2. Having made a judgment, the student requests the strips that correspond to the two fractions. He or she undivides the strips and verifies his or her judgement by visually comparing the amount of grey in the two strips.
3. After a few trials with unequal fractions, the tutor produces two equivalent fractions, and asks the student to make a judgment as to relative size. Upon checking his judgment in the above manner, the student discovers that the two fractions correspond to strips that have grey areas of equal lengths.

The basic Fractions Tutor does not have built-in, preprogrammed demonstrations or exercises. Instead, both the Notebook and the illustration worlds are programmed to be as consistent as possible with their conceptual

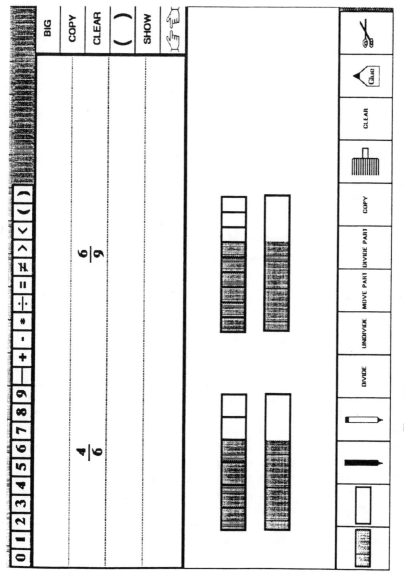

Figure 2.3. Introducing the concept of equivalent fractions.

1. I: *So now let's see, can you tell me what we got on the screen there now?*

2. S: We got, we got four-eights.

3. I: *Four-eighths, that's right. Now, let's see if we can find, we can find a, divide it, make a copy of it to begin.*

(The subject is reminded of how to copy a strip.)

4. I: *Now let's see. Can we find another division with more parts in it that will also work, to be four-eighths now?*

5. S: Maybe.

6. I: *What would you guess? If it's four-eighths now, what's another division that would work?*

7. S: I don't know. I know what I'm gonna try, though.

(There are some difficulties with the system due to a bug in the program.)

8. S: I'll try nine. See what nine does. And then I'll just keep on going up.

(The subject verifies that nine does not work.)

9. I: *Now try another division.*

10. S: I'll try, I was gonna try eleven.

(The subject verifies that eleven does not work. She looks for the next division to try.)

11. S: Up, up, up, and away! I hope ten works. It works!

12. I: *Okay.*

13. S: Five-tenths!

Figure 2.4. Protocol exerpt, Part1.

definitions. All actions can be executed in any context, and they almost always have the effects that one would expect them to have, given their conceptual definitions. Demonstrations and exercises are quite literally programmed on top of the illustration worlds. The internal representations of the actions in the illustration world (see Table 2.1) are used as a high-level programming language in which to specify demonstrations and exercises.

Since the specification of demonstrations and exercises is independent of the implementation of the illustration worlds, those worlds can be used to support different teaching styles. The exercise for equivalent fractions summarized above is an example of a guided exercise. The following is an example of a more open-ended, discovery exercise for equivalent fractions:

1. The tutor creates the strip corresponding to, say, 4/8, and asks the student to find other partitionings of the same strip that work, i.e., partitionings that divide the strip in such a way that a boundary

1. I: *Can you find another higher one that would work?*

2. S: Six-twelfths.

3. I: *Try it.*

   (The subject creates the required strip.)

4. S: Okay. Now I want to divide it again. And I want to divide it into, I said, twelve. It works! See?

5. I: *That works!*

6. S: Six-twelfths!

7. I: *That's right. Okay.*

8. S: Fourteenths!

9. I: *And how many colored, if you divide it into fourteen, how many colored pieces will there be?*

10. S: There's seven.

   (The subject tries a new method for creating a strip, and so needs some advice about the commands. Having created the strip, she resumes the exercise.)

11. S: I was gonna try fourteenths.

12. I: *Fourteenths. That's right.*

13. S: It works!

   (The subject explores how many divisions the computer system allows.)

Figure 2.5. Protocol exerpt, Part2.

between two parts coincides with the boundary between the grey and the white areas.

2. The student copies the given fraction, and experiments with alternative divisions. For each division that works, the strip and the corresponding number is saved on the screen.

3. Finally, the student is encouraged to discover some regularity in the set of divisions that works.

Can the Fractions Tutor help students construct the idea of equivalent fractions? The Notebook and the illustrations worlds have been tested in field studies in which a human tutor used the software as a tool for one-on-one tutoring. The protocol excerpt in Figures 2.4, 2.5, and 2.6 shows an interaction in which the student is working on the discovery exercise described above. She was given 4/8 as her initial fraction. At the beginning of the exercise she could not predict which alternative partitions would work (see Figure 2.4, fragment 7). When encouraged to find other partitions of

1. I: *Suppose that we tried to find, can we find divisions that are smaller, with fewer number of parts, that work for this one.*

2. S: Oh, with fewer?

3. I: *Yes, with fewer. What would you ... .*

4. S: Let's try six!

5. I: *Six. And ... ?*

6. S: And four and two.

7. I: *Okay. Go ahead; that's a good plan.*

8. S: Yes! It's not gonna work!

9. I: *It, it won't ... ?.*

10. S: I just found out the way!

11. I: *How?*

12. S: We just have half of any number!

13. I: *Okay.*

14. S: Any number except for the odd numbers!

15. I: *Okay. That sounds right to me.*

16. S: Like eleven! Yes, like eleven.

17. I: *Okay, what about eleven?*

18. S: It's an odd number. It won't work.

Figure 2.6. Protocol exerpt, Part3.

4/8, she tries division by seven, then by nine, and then by 10, expressing surprise that 10 works. She then predicts that 12 will work, expressing her prediction as "six-twelfths" (Figure 2.5, fragment 2). Seeing that 12 works, she exclaims "fourteenths!" (Figure 2.5, fragment 8).

When prompted, the subject predicts that there will be seven grey parts if the strip is divided into 14 parts (see Figure 2.5, fragment 10). When asked to find partitions into smaller number of parts than eight, she immediately generates six, four, and two as her alternatives (Figure 2.6, fragment 6). Shortly after that, she exclaims, "I just found the way" (Figure 2.6, fragment 10); she has discovered that "we just have half of any number." This discovery enables her to predict that 11 will not work. In a second phase of the exercise, not covered in the excerpts, she transferred her discovery to other fractions.

The protocol excerpt illustrates both the power and the shortcoming of the current version of the Fractions Tutor. There is little doubt that the subject constructed a conceptual insight during this learning event. Which features of the software facilitated the learning event? First, the implementation of the illustration worlds allowed the student to try anything that came to mind, when it came to mind. If a particular number seemed like a good bet, she could try it immediately. Second, the convenience of having the machine perform onerous duties like partitioning a strip into equal parts allowed the student to get rapid feedback on her actions. This student took maximum advantage of this. Her work was characterized by a high rate of interaction with the system. Third, the yoking feature enabled her to get *mathematical* feedback on her *physical* actions. Fourth, the copy command, in conjunction with the size of the Xerox 1109 screen, enabled her to compare the outcomes of several actions without working memory overload.

However, as the attentive reader has realized, *she achieved the wrong insight*. The principle that we would have wanted her to discover is that one fraction gives raise to an equivalent fraction if its numerator and its denominator are multiplied with the same number. Instead, she constructed the idea that equivalent fractions have a constant relation between numerator and denominator: "we just have the half of any number." She constructed the principle that $x$ divided by 2 over $x$ is equivalent to $1/2$, rather than the principle that $x/y$ is equivalent to $(x \times m)/(y \times m)$. The principle she discovered is true, but its application is only obvious in the case of fractions that are generated from a unit fraction.

The example illustrates the problem of basing the design of instruction on a learning theory. It would be useful to know what determined the outcome of the exercise. Why did the student construct one idea rather than another? Would it have been possible to predict before the event that this exercise would produce this particular insight? Is one of these ideas inherently simpler than the other, so that learners can generally be expected to reach one idea before the other? How can we design an exercise that has a higher probability of guiding the learner towards the more general principle? Even more urgent is the question whether the unintended discovery is a step on the way towards the intended discovery, or whether it is a blind alley. Can the student build on her idea about a constant relation between numerator and denominator in order to attain the more general idea? Or does this insight block attainment of the more general idea so that it has to be *un*learned before she can make further progress? Successful instruction requires a theory that can answer these and similar questions about the construction of conceptual knowledge.

### 4.2. Problem: The Social Nature of Learning

Application of the first-order theory leads to the necessity of diagnosing previous knowledge, a problem which cannot be solved within that theory.

Similarly, application of the second-order theory leads to the problem of designing the content of remedial messages, a problem that cannot be solved within that theory. Will application of the third-order theory lead us to a problem that cannot be solved within that theory, and thus point the way to a fourth-order theory?

The concept of teaching ultimately rests on the fact that people can learn from other people. This is fortunate, because if it were not so, each individual would have to discover everything on his or her own, and accumulation of knowledge across generations would not be possible. But if people learn mainly from other people, it is plausible that the relation between the learner and the teacher enters into the learning process in some fundamental way. Can the third-order theory deal with the social aspects of learning?

It is important to distinguish between a weak and a strong formulation of the notion that learning is a social phenomenon. Learning is obviously a social phenomenon in the weak sense that the learner has to understand the teacher's messages in order to learn from them. This makes teaching subject to the same difficulties and complexities as other forms of human communication. This fact has no particular implications for either learning theory or the theory of instruction, and poses no threat to the third-order theory.

The more radical possibility is that learning is a social phenomenon in the strong sense that *the learning mechanisms take the learner's view of the teacher among their inputs*. This implies that the learner's mental model of the teacher determines which revision of the current knowledge state occurs as a consequence of a particular instructional message. If this should turn out to be so, then the relevant description of the learner's knowledge state includes his or her mental representation of the teacher; hence, the teacher's model of the learner has to include the learner's representation of the teacher, which as we just noticed, includes the teacher's view of the learner, and so on. There is no recovery from this recursion within the third-order theory. Hence, increased attention to the social nature of learning might eventually force us to abandon that theory. However, history cannot and should not be anticipated; there is much work to be done before we have learned enough from the third-order theory to know in what direction the theory of teaching should go next.

## 5. CONCLUSIONS

Different conceptions of teaching imply different knowledge requirements. The traditional view of teaching as the communication of knowledge implies that the teacher needs to know the relevant subject matter. However, cognitive science research has shown that standard codifications of even well-structured and precise knowledge domains are sometimes nonexistent and often vague and incomplete. For instance, mathematical treatments of the number system do not deal with the conceptual ambiguity of the fraction notation, the intellectual purpose of fractions, the concept of equivalent fractions, the inverse relation between the number of parts and the size of a part, or any of the other aspects of fractions that are crucial for the design of instruction in this domain. Subject matter analysis remains a crucial step in the design of instruction, whether that instruction is to be delivered by a human or by a machine.

The current theory views teaching as the remediation of learners' errors. This conception implies that the teacher knows how knowledge is mentally represented, which mental processes make use of that knowledge, and which errors learners are likely to suffer from on the way to mastery of the subject matter. This theory also implies the need for a method for inferring which particular error the learner is suffering from at a particular moment in time. In the case of fractions we are still in the process of constructing a theory of how children represent fractions that can explain the frequency and persistence of their errors. It is unlikely that any instructional program for fractions can succeed without such theory. Error analysis remains an an essential component of instructional design in general, and of intelligent tutoring systems in particular, despite recent pessimism with respect to the possibility of diagnosing errors.

We are moving towards a view of teaching as the facilitation of knowledge construction. This conception requires that the teacher has a theory of the learning mechanisms in the student's head, and that he or she knows how to act in order to trigger those learning mechanisms. However, current learning theory focuses on the construction of procedural knowledge, rather than on conceptual knowledge. No current learning theory explains how concepts and principles are constructed, nor under which circumstances such a construction is likely to occur. But the core of a subject matter topic like fractions consists of concepts and principles, not of cognitive skills. Theory-based design of intelligent tutoring systems requires the development of a learning theory that focuses on conceptual rather than on procedural knowledge. Consequently, the research that is needed in order to construct better tutoring systems is not research into system building per se, but research into learning theory.

## REFERENCES

Anderson, J.R. (1982). Acquisition of cognitive skill. *Psychological Review, 89*(4), 369-406.

Anderson,J.R. (1983). *The architecture of cognition*. Cambridge, MA: Harvard University Press.

Anderson, J.R. (1986). Knowledge compilation: The general learning mechanism. In R. S. Michalski, J. G. Carbonell, & T. M. Mitchell (Eds.), *Machine learning:An artificial intelligence approach* (Vol. II, pp. 289-310). Los Altos, CA: Morgan Kaufmann.

Anderson, J.R. (in press). Practice, working memory, and the ACT* theory of skill acquisition: A comment on Carlson, Sullivan, & Schneider. *Journal of Experimental Psychology: Learning, Memory, and Cognition.*

Anderson, J.R. Boyle, C.F., & Reiser, B.J. (1985). Intelligent tutoring systems. *Science, 228,* 456-462.

Anderson, J.R., Boyle, C.F., & Yost, G. (1985). The geometry tutor. *Proceedings of the Ninth International Joint Conference on Artificial Intelligence* (pp. 1-7). Los Angeles, CA: Morgan Kaufmann.

Behr, M.J., & Post, T.R. (1988). Teaching rational number and decimal concepts. In T.R. Post (Ed.), *Teaching mathematics in grades K-8* (pp. 190-231). Boston, MA: Allyn and Bacon.

Behr, M. J., Wachsmuth, I., Post, T.R., & Lesh, R. (1984). Order and equivalence of rational numbers:A clinical teaching experiment. *Journal for Research in Mathematics Education, 15*(5), 323-341.

Brown, J.S., & Burton, R.R. (1978). Diagnostic models for procedural bugs in basic mathematical skills. *Cognitive Science, 2,* 155-192.

Brown, J.S., & VanLehn, K. (1980). Repair theory: A generative theory of bugs in procedural skills. *Cognitive Science, 4,* 379-426.

Brown, J.S., & VanLehn, K. (1982). Towards a generative theory of "bugs". In T.P. Carpenter, J.M. Moser, & T.A. Romberg (Eds.), *Addition and subtraction: A cognitive perspective* (pp. 117-135). Hillsdale, NJ:Erlbaum.

Bundy, A. (1983). *The computer modelling of mathematical reasoning.* London: Academic Press.

Burton, R. R. (1982). Diagnosing bugs in a simple procedural skill. In D. Sleeman & J.S. Brown (Eds.), *Intelligent tutoring systems* (pp. 157-183). London:Academic Press.

Clancey, W.J. (1987). *Knowledge-based tutoring. The GUIDON program.* Cambridge, MA: MIT Press

Evertz, R. (1982). *A production system account of children's errors in fraction subtraction* (Tech. Rep. No. 28). Milton Keynes, UK: The Open University, CAL Research Group.

Flavell, J.H. (1963). *The developmental psychology of Jean Piaget.* Princeton, NJ:Van Nostrand.

Greeno, J.G., Riley, M. S., & Gelman, R. (1984). Conceptual competence and children's counting. *Cognitive Psychology, 16,* 94-143.

Hiebert, J., & Behr, M. (Eds.). (1988). *Number concepts and operations in the middle grades* (Vol. 2). Reston, VA: The National Council of Teachers of Mathematics, Inc. & Hillsdale, NJ: Erlbaum.

Laird, J.E., Rosenbloom, P.S., & Newell, A. (1986). *Universal subgoaling and chunking: The automatic generation and learning of goal hierarchies.* Boston, MA: Kluwer Academic Publishers.

Langley, P. (1987). A general theory of discrimination learning. In D. Klahr, P. Langley, & R. Neches (Eds.), *Production system models of learning and development* (pp. 99-161). Cambridge, MA: MIT Press.

Langley, P., Wogulis, J., & Ohlsson, S. (1990). Rules and principles in cognitive diagnosis. In N. Frederiksen, R. Glaser, A. Lesgold, & M.G. Shafto (Eds.), *Diagnostic monitoring of skill and knowledge acquisition.* (pp. 217-250) Hillsdale, NJ: Erlbaum.

Lloyd Wright, F. (1954). *The natural house.* New York: Meridian.

Michener, E.R. (1978). Understanding understanding mathematics. *Cognitive Science, 2,* 361-383.

Ohlsson, S. (1986). Some principles of intelligent tutoring. *Instructional Science, 14,* 293-326.

Ohlsson, S. (1987a). *A semantics for fraction concepts* (Tech. Rep. No. KUL-87-01). Pittsburgh, PA: University of Pittsburgh, learning Research and Development Center.

Ohlsson,S. (1987b). Sense and reference in the design of interactive illustrations for rational numbers. (pp. 307-344) In R. W. Lawler & M. Yazdani (Eds.), *Artificial intelligence and education* (Vol. 1, pp. 203-237). Norwood, NJ: Ablex Publishing Corp.

Ohlsson, S. (1987c). Transfer of training in procedural learning:A matter of conjectures and refutations? In L. Bolc (Ed.), *Computational models of learning* (pp. 55-88). Berlin:

Springer-Verlag.

Ohlsson, S. (1988a). Computer simulation and its impact on educational research and practice. *International Journal of Educational Research, 12*(1), 5-34.

Ohlsson, S. (1988b). Mathematical meaning and applicational meaning in the semantics of fractions and related concepts. In J. Hiebert & M. Behr (Eds.), *Number concepts and operations in the middle grades* (Vol. 2, pp. 53-92). Reston, VA: The National Council of Teachers of Mathematics, Inc., & Hillsdale, NJ: Erlbaum.

Ohlsson, S. (in press). Towards intelligent tutoring systems that teach knowledge rather than skills: Five research questions. In E. Scanlon & T. O'Shea (Eds.), *New directions in educational technology*. London: Springer-Verlag.

Ohlsson, S., & Langley, P. (1988). Psychological evaluation of path hypotheses in cognitive diagnosis. In H. Mandl & A. Lesgold (Eds.), *Learning issues for intelligent tutoring systems* (pp. 42-62). New York: Springer-Verlag.

Ohlsson, S., Nickolas, S.E., & Bee, N.V. (1987). *Interactive illustrations for fractions: A progress report* (Tech. Rep. No. KUL-87-03). Pittsburgh, PA: University of Pittsburgh, Learning Research and Development Center.

Ohlsson, S., & Rees, E. (1988). *An information processing analysis of the function of conceptual understanding in the learning of arithmetic procedures* (Tech. Rep. KUL-88-03). Pittsburgh, PA: University of Pittsburgh, Learning Research and Development Center.

Post, T.R., Wachsmuth, I., Lesh, R., & Behr, M.J. (1985). Order and equivalence of rational numbers: A cognitive analysis. *Journal for Research in Mathematics Education, 16*(1), 18-36.

Reiser, B.J., Anderson, J.R., & Farrell, R.G. (1985). Dynamic student modeling in an intelligent tutor for LISP programming. *Proceedings of the Ninth International Joint Conference on Artificial Intelligence* (pp. 8-14). Los Angeles, CA: Morgan Kaufmann.

Resnick, L.B. (in press). Treating mathematics as an ill-structured discipline. In R. Ch.•:les & E. A. Silver (Eds.), *Research agenda for mathematics education: Teaching and assessment of mathematical problem solving*. Hillsdale, NJ: Erlbaum.

Resnick, L.B., & Omanson, S.F. (1987). Learning to understand arithmetic. In R. Glaser (Ed.), *Advances in instructional psychology* (Vol. 3, pp. 41-95). Hillsdale, NJ: Erlbaum.

Self, J. (1985). A perspective on intelligent computer-assisted learning. *Journal of Computer Assisted Learning, 1,* 159-166.

Self, J.A. (1988). Bypassing the intractable problem of student modelling. *Proceedings of Intelligent Tutoring Systems* (pp. 18-24). Montreal, Canada: Universite de Montreal.

Siegler, R.S. (1978). The origins of scientific reasoning. In R.S. Siegler (Ed.), *Children's thinking: What develops?* (pp. 109-149). Hillsdale, NJ: Erlbaum.

Silver, E. (1986). Using conceptual and procedural knowledge: A focus on relationships. In J. Hiebert (Ed.), *Conceptual and procedural knowledge: The case of mathematics* (pp. 181-198). Hillsdale, NJ: Erlbaum.

Smith, D.A., Greeno, J.G., & Vitolo, T.M. (1989). A model of competence for counting. *Cognitive Science 13*(2), 183-211.

Tatsuoka, K.K. (1984). *Analysis of errors in fraction addition and subtraction problems* (Tech. Rep.). Urbana IL: University of Illinois, Computer-based Education Research Laboratory.

Thurston, H.A. (1956). *The number-system*. New York: Dover.

VanLehn, K. (1986). Arithmetic procedures are induced from examples. In J. H. Hiebert (Ed.), *Conceptual and procedural knowledge: The case of mathematics* (pp. 133-179). Hillsdale, NJ: Erlbaum.

VanLehn, K. (1987). Learning one subprocedure per lesson. *Artificial Intelligence: An International Journal, 31*(1), 1-40

VanLehn, K. (1988). Student modeling. In M. C. Polson & J. J. Richardson (Eds.), *Foundations of intelligent tutoring systems* (pp.55-78). Hillsdale, NJ: Erlbaum.

VanLehn, K. (1990). *Mind bugs. The origins of procedural misconceptions*. Cambridge, MA: MIT Press.

# 3

## DIALOGUE AND TEACHING STYLES*

### MARK T. ELSOM-COOK

### 1. INTRODUCTION

This chapter discusses the role of knowledge about interaction in intelligent tutoring systems. In particular, it examines the idea of a *style of teaching*, and discusses the implications which teaching styles have for the form of interaction between student and machine: The first section discusses the reasons for studying teaching styles, the second and third describe the teaching knowledge of two existing systems which embody models of interaction. Subsequent sections relate this to work on dialogue and propose a set of components which must exist in a tutoring system if it is to support the kinds of interaction described here.

### 2. WHAT ARE WE TRYING TO DO?

There can be a variety of reasons for studying intelligent tutoring systems. The most obvious is to attempt to build a device which satisfies an educational need. In this case, we do not mind whether our system is human-like or not, provided that it is an effective educational tool. This is

*This chapter owes much to discussions with Sally Douglas, Allan Collins, George Kiss, Claire O'Malley, and Mike Baker.

similar to the more general position taken in "hard" artificial intelligence which suggests that, provided a program exhibits "intelligent behavior", the mechanisms by which this is achieved are of no concern. This is not such a clear-cut position in the case of intelligent tutoring systems, because our systems necessarily interact with human beings, so they must, at some level, have human-like properties. This is particularly true in the field of student modelling. It is not clear that a psychologically implausible student model can be constructed. Although it seems clear that we must examine human teaching, since humans are the only examples of teaching systems which are available for study, this does not imply that our tutoring systems should be constrained to human-like interaction. While taking human interaction as the base of study, we must continually consider the "space of possible educational interactions" which may involve forms that cannot be executed by a human teacher.

A second reason for studying intelligent tutoring systems (or, more generally, AI and education) may be the desire to understand better what is meant by education, and to help expand educational theory in such a way that human teachers can improve their educational interactions. This can be done independently of whether we use the knowledge acquired to implement human-like computer-based teachers. What is the contribution that AI makes to education theory? A number of researchers (e.g., Peters, 1966; Bruner, 1966) have divided an educational theory into two components. The first is an educational philosophy which provides the goals and values to be espoused by a particular educational theory. The second is an educational psychology which, given the goals and values, explains what we should do in order to achieve those aims and provides a model which should explain why doing those things is effective. It is in this latter part of an educational theory that AI can serve a purpose.

Psychology (especially cognitive psychology) has been strongly influenced by the use of the computational metaphor. Before this was available, it was difficult to express theories about information processing systems in a precise enough form to enable detailed comparisons. Attempts at mathematical models of psychological theories were of limited success. The advent of the computer in general, and AI in particular, provided a language within which information processing systems could be discussed. Information processing and its implications for the architecture of the human processing system could be discussed using the language of computing. More than this, a computer program permits us to build a precise formal model to represent a theory. This model is executable, is (in some sense) complete, and provides concrete form for the predictions of the model. Combining the information processing ideas with more traditional cognitive psychology has led to the new field of cognitive science. This field has changed the way we think about the mind.

From the perspective of education theory, we can expect the computer to have a similar impact for similar reasons. The study of the psychological component of the theory is amenable to the same computationally based techniques which have changed the way that psychological theories are represented. AI can provide tools to express educational theories in a more precise form, to decide criteria for testing those theories, and to compare the predictions of the theories. Since the education theories which we are discussing involve explaining appropriate educational processes and the way in which these processes operate; we expect the theories to incorporate models of teaching and learning, as well as more general claims about the architecture of the mind and the implications that this has for education. Given an educational theory on this scale, which is embodied in an AI-based approach, one outcome that we would expect is a runnable, predictive model of educational processes that can teach in a similar way to a human teacher.

This implies that we must engage in cognitive science, whatever the ultimate goal of our tutoring system. We need to know how individuals acquire, represent, and use knowledge. We must seek to understand the mechanisms by which this process can be facilitated. The work reported in this chapter is intended to approach one particular question: What do we mean by teaching? It is based upon the assumption that teaching is a specific case of more general strategies of interaction between humans.

Tutoring systems often focus on issues of student modelling or domain representation. Why should such an emphasis be placed on interaction here? The reason is that the interaction is the only observable information we have about teaching processes. Building student or domain models which are sophisticated but cannot be effectively used to their full potential in the interaction is a pointless exercise, since there is an infinite set of such models. The claim being made here, and expanded upon by Elsom-Cook (1990a) is that we should explore interaction as the primary aspect of tutoring systems, and that work on domains or student models should be driven by the needs identified in the study of interaction.

## 3. IMPART: AN EDUCATIONAL DIALOGUE MECHANISM

IMPART (Elsom-Cook, 1984) is a tutoring system for Lisp constructed around the discovery learning paradigm. It embodies a model of interaction based upon cognitive models of dialogue in humans. In particular, it attempts to combine focus-based and functional approaches.

A focus-based approach to dialogue (e.g., Grosz, 1977; Reichmann, 1978) attempts to describe the way in which topics move over the course of an interaction. It is based around the use of *context spaces* associated with particular topics. These focus spaces can be *open, closed,* or *active.* An active context space is one in which the topic is currently the topic being discussed in the dialogue. An open context space is one in which the topic has been active but is no longer so. An open space can be reopened. A closed context space describes a topic which is considered completed. For it to be discussed again, it must be reintroduced as though it was a new topic.

To illustrate this, consider a conversation about whether or not to go and see a film. Suppose the participants begin discussing the merits of the particular film in order to make their decision. At this point, the active context space is the merits of the film, while the context space containing the decision about whether to go to it is open. That is, it is not what is currently being discussed, but it can be returned to. If a decision is made to go to the film, and the conversation passes on to dicuss where to eat beforehand, then the previous two spaces will be closed.

Work on focus-based approaches has concentrated on analyzing dialogues and has attempted to find rules marking topic changes. These rules are essentially descriptive, however.

Function-based approaches (e.g., Levin & Moore, 1978; Power, 1979) model the function of segments of dialogue in a way which is independent of content. It has its foundations in work on adjacency pairs (Schegloff & Sacks, 1973), and led to the definition of *dialogue games*. Dialogue games are segments of dialogue designed to achieve a particular goal. They can be embedded within one another to produce larger structures of interaction.

IMPART combines these approaches in a demon-like mechanism similar to the issue recognisers in WEST (Burton & Brown, 1982). Each topic in the system is represented by an active demon called a *topic controller*, which has a number of procedural and declarative attachments. These controllers repeatedly make bids for control of the interaction, and a *conversation controller* resolves and combines the bids to produce segments of dialogue. The topic controllers use dialogue games to communicate with the user, and the conversation controller can constrain the game choices to improve the coherency of the interaction. For the purposes of this chapter, the conversation controller is the most interesting component. Let us examine a plan for a segment of conversation and see how it is generated.

```
(evaluation impart (function impart (argument illustrate action-probe) (value
illustrate)))
```

In this instance, the topic controllers *evaluation, function, value* and *argument* are communicating with the student. They been constrained to use a mixture of three games: *impart* (give information), *illustrate* (show a concrete example), and *action-probe* (ask the student to do something). The order and activities of the topic controllers are constrained using a set of heuristics. Some of these are given below:

- Introduce the topic which made the highest "importance" bid first.
- If a topic and a subtopic made high bids, introduce the major topic but constrain it to introduce the subtopic in context.
- If more than one topic uses the same subtopic, introduce the subtopic then the major topics.
- Do not use the same dialogue game more than twice in a segment.
- Illustrate a topic before imparting information about it.

IMPART used 20 such rules, but these give a reasonable flavor.

### 3.1. Strengths and Weaknesses

The primary strength of IMPART lies in the attempt to combine existing models of dialogue processes to generate a structured interaction. It has some longer-term plan of interaction which goes beyond the purely reactive (or single utterance) nature of many systems.

There are many weaknesses to IMPART. It is, in essence, an *engineering* approach to educational interaction. This is particularly noticeable in the heuristics for control given above. These rules do not even have the claim of being empirically derived in the way that those of Collins (Collins & Stevens, this volume) were. IMPART succeeded in separating out knowledge of the interaction in a way that made it possible to change it independent of the rest of the system, but it made no contribution to formalizing educational knowledge about interaction.

## 4. DOMINIE: MULTIPLE STYLES AND A STRATEGY

DOMINIE (Elsom-Cook & Spensley, 1987) is a tutoring system which embodies a number of distinct teaching styles and an overall strategy. A major goal behind the system was to try to represent a number of different teaching strategies explicitly. The criteria for success do not require the styles to be educationally or psychologically valid. At this stage of development it is sufficient that the strategies be distinguishable and (if possible) recognizable. By *distinguishable* I mean that the styles should produce different behaviors from each other. For a strategy to be *recognizable*, it should have some observable features in common with the paper description of the characteristics of that style.

DOMINIE teaches a student to use a computer application. It can teach any application which can reasonably be regarded as a procedural task in which a major goal can be repeatedly divided into subgoals which can be achieved by carrying out some actions upon the computer. An individual task is represented as a plan composed of these goals and subgoals. Examples of appropriate tasks include the customization of office automation systems, the maintenance of electronic telephone exchanges and the maintenance of system accounts on a mainframe. It is less appropriate for tasks such as learning to use a database package, since the procedural decomposition model is not necessarily appropriate in these cases.

The system embodies eight teaching styles, and chooses between them during the course of interaction with a particular student. We will only discuss three of the styles here. The third will be discussed in detail to give a feel for the extent to which educational knowledge has been formalized in the system. Following this we will proceed to a brief discussion of the strategy for selecting between styles.

## 4.1. Cognitive Apprenticeship

There has been a lot of interest recently in a teaching technique known as *cognitive apprenticeship* (Collins & Brown 1987). This is based on the idea that cognitive skills can be learned in the way that crafts were learned from an expert in that craft. The apprentice commences by watching the expert in action and asking questions. As time passes, the expert allows the apprentice to perform small parts of the whole task. These parts will gradually increase in size until the pupil is able to perform the whole of the task in question. The claim for cognitive apprenticeship is that this technique operates beyond the level of manual skill acquisition. Problem solving, reasoning, and other cognitive processes are claimed to be amenable to this approach. This approach relies on the expert having reasoning techniques which are meaningful to the pupil. In the case of a computer-based tutor, the computer must reason using glass-box (psychologically valid) techniques if it is to attempt to teach in this style.

As far as DOMINIE is concerned, it is a working assumption that the reasoning which it uses (i.e., the goal structures generated by the planner) are meaningful to the users. Since these structures are input by experienced human users, this is a reasonable assumption, but one which is to be investigated in field trails.

The tutor must select an appropriate part of the domain and teach it to the student, using a mixture of demonstrations and exercises for the user. In selecting an area to teach, our assumption is that the area should be slightly beyond the current state of knowledge of the pupil (as inferred from the student model). There should be enough material to give the exercise a structure and purpose, but not so much that the pupil is overwhelmed. In terms of our plan tree this is represented by choosing to teach a goal within the tree for which all sub-subgoals (if they exist) are already known to the pupil, but the majority of the subgoals are not. DOMINIE would actually teach such a goal by demonstrating it (which includes a demonstration of the subgoals). The tutor then explicitly breaks the goal into subgoals, and for each subgoal demonstrates it and then asks the pupil to carry out the same subgoal. If any of the subgoals are already known to the user, the tutor simply asks for them to be carried out (rather than demonstrating them). Finally, the tutor demonstrates the overall goal again and asks the pupil to perform the whole task. At any point during this process the pupil can ask for an explanation in terms of the role of this action within the overall plan, or the domain concepts with which this plan is associated.

## 4.2. Successive Refinement

Successive refinement is a top-down approach to teaching. It derives from the work of A.N.Whitehead (1932). The basic principle is that a good teacher should be able to explain a topic at a number of levels of detail, always providing an interaction at a level which is meaningful to the pupil in his or her current state of knowledge. In particular, a domain which contains an overwhelming number of details should be taught initially at a very general level, telling a coherent story but omitting the full ramifications of the topic. This provides the pupil with an overview and a systematic framework into which subsequent teaching of the domain can be fitted. As the pupil becomes more sophisticated, a more powerful model of the domain may be taught. This is likely to involve explicitly highlighting erroneous simplifications which the tutor made for pedagogical purposes and actively supporting the construction of new, restructured models of the domain.

It has recently been pointed out (Collins, personal communication, November 1988) that there are three well-defined methods mixed together here. One is the restructuring approach, based on offering simple models which make incorrect predictions and are subsequently replaced with models that are better but involve a different view of the domain. A second is to offer the student a model which can make general predictions in restricted parts of the domain and can be refined by extending it without changing the basic conceptualization (this is the approach taken by Fredrikson & White, 1988, for example). A third is the framework approach—providing the student with a comprehensive, general, but very weak overview of the domain into which details can be slotted. This latter is really a motivational approach, attempting to get students to learn details by knowing where they are going. It is this third method that was intended in this implementation.

DOMINIE selects the highest level untaught goal in the plan. It then uses information about the concepts associated with each goal in that tree to generate *weighted subnets* of the declarative knowledge in the system. These nets identify relevant concepts and assign them an importance in terms of the current plan. (This process is described in more detail in Spensley & Elsom-Cook, 1987.)

Starting from the highest procedural goal, the tutor presents the major concepts associated with that goal and briefly summarizes the subgoals and actions which are involved in achieving the goal. On subsequent passes the subgoals are presented in a similar fashion. This process is repeated recursively through the plan tree. The level of explanation given at each point depends on the importance of the concepts within the weighted subnets and the level of understanding of the concepts and procedures which the pupil already has.

## 4.3. Discovery Learning

The nature of discovery learning remains a subject for debate. Some educationalists see such learning as implying a completely free activity on the part of the pupil. At the other extreme the pupil may have the impression of discovering new material for himself or herself, but the task is actually carefully structured by a teacher who knows in advance the sequence of discovery which the pupil will make. In our model of this style, a teacher is necessary to set up an appropriate environment in which the learning can take place, and to provide guidance to the pupil when requested or when the pupil is in difficulty. A major part of the teacher's action is to assess the current state of knowledge of the pupil, and to select a task for the pupil to explore which is slightly beyond the current state of his or her knowledge, but not so much so as to be too difficult for him or her to achieve. Choosing such a task can be extremely complex and may involve finding similar situations in which the learner has made an appropriate cognitive leap, or identifying knowledge which the learner can bring to bear on the task. In our case we only attempt to model the selection of one type of area appropriate to discovery learning: that is, an area which is new to the student but which has a structure analogical to something which the student has already learnt.

Having chosen an area, the tutor should monitor the student working in that area. If the student gets into difficulty or asks for help, then the tutor should provide it. In general this help could take any of a number of forms. Since we are restricting ourselves to analogical reasoning the help can be similarly restricted. The tutor offers guidance by a sequence of progressively more detailed hints which give information about the analogy with previous knowledge. In terms of our knowledge representation this is fairly simple. An appropriate area for discovery learning by analogy is one in which the student knows most of the skills involved in a task, but does not know some part which is analogical to somthing previously learned. In our usage two goals are analogical if they involve the same procedure in different problem contexts with different parameters. The first level of hint which the tutor offers is identifying the context in which the analogous procedure arose. Subsequent hints identify individual parameters in the two contexts.

Let us now examine the actual rules within DOMINIE which embody this particular strategy:

1. In order to find an appropriate area to teach, search the plan tree for the current task in a top-down, breadth-first manner, search at a given ply being from left to right.
2. A segment of the plan is appropriate if it is untaught and it is analogous to a goal which is already known.
   a. Two goals are considered analogous if they are represented by different parameterizations of the same planning procedure.
3. Present the problem to the student then do "discovery assessment."
4. To present the problem to the student, present an introduction to the strategy and then offer the problem context.
   a. Presenting a strategy involves displaying motivating text and an explanation of what the student should do. If it is the first time the student has used the strategy, present a detailed explanation; otherwise, present a short summary.
   b. Presenting a context involves presenting the goal of the problem and the reason that goal is relevant to the overall task.
5. To carry out discovery assessment, ask the student to demonstrate the procedure and monitor the student performance.
6. At any time while monitoring performance the student can ask for a hint or a demonstration of the correct next step.
7. If the student asks for a demonstration, only give one if all the hints have been used.
8. If the user asks for a hint, then...
   a. If the user tried an action associated with a procedure but omitted an action associated with the preconditions of the procedure, then remind the user what the procedure is and state the omitted precondition.
   b. If the user is in one branch of a disjunct and has executed an action from the other branch, then tell the user the critical post test which should determine the branch to choose.
   c. Otherwise, if this is the first time the user has asked for a hint, then identify the context of the analogy.
   d. Otherwise, identify a parameter of the procedure and give its old value.
9. Monitor student performance by generating a solution to the problem from the planner and seeing if it matches the student actions.
   a. If the match is complete, increase confidences in the student model

and present the student with a summary of what he or she did.
  b. If the student moves away from the correct solution, decrease
     confidence in the student model and offer the hint menu.

The rules divide into two sections: rules 1 and 2 are concerned with what
to teach, while rules 3–9 are concerned with how to teach by this method.
This division of decisions occurs in all the styles. Choosing what to teach has
two components: the first (rule 1) tells us how to look for something to
teach, while the second (rule 2) tells us how to identify an appropriate area
when we find it. Again, this division is common across all styles. The
remainder of the rules are fairly self-explanatory and differ for each style. We
have found no common patterns here. The sort of differences embodied can
be seen by comparing monitoring as defined in the above case with
monitoring in the practice strategy. In discovery learning, monitoring
involves updating the student model and only offering advice if the student
requests it, no matter how far the student deviates from the correct course of
action. In the practice case, monitoring is conducted by a mechanism akin to
Anderson's "model-tracing" (Anderson, 1982), in which any deviation from
the correct solution is immediately remediated.

## 4.4. Strategy Selection

Given the eight strategies embodied in the system, the tutor must decide
which is most appropriate at a given point. The primary decision the tutor
takes when it considers a strategy change is the balance of teaching and
assessment in its activity. Obviously, the tutor wants to present new material
to the student, but it also has goals of ensuring that the student has
understood the material and checking that its model of the student is still
accurate. The system therefore starts by teaching when it has a new pupil. This
is based on the assumption that the pupil knows nothing about the area
which is being taught. As the interaction progresses, the gap between material
taught and material assessed widens. When this factor has become sufficiently
large, the tutor will switch to a strategy which increases the amount of
assessment.
  Within this decision about teaching or assessment is a decision about the
general area on which the tutor will focus. The two are linked together and
result in a compound decision which encompasses teaching new material,
reteaching old material, and assessing or reassessing the student's understanding. The system then has a set of heuristics to give an order of preference to
the possible styles. These rules are intended to embody a strategy of choosing
the least interventionist method which is applicable.
  Once these decisions have been made, the system uses local rules (like those

given above) to find an appropriate subarea to teach, using the preferred style. It is possible that no appropriate area can be found within this topic. In that case, the style is obviously inapplicable in this situation, and the tutor will try and use the next preferred style on the list.

### 4.5 Strengths and Weaknesses

DOMINIE succeeded in capturing eight different teaching styles at a level of detail which allowed them to be distinguished, and where an observer could see the relationship of a given style to the paper description. It also provided a mechanism which switches between these styles in a reasonable manner. The whole system has been successfully field-tested in several countries. Is this therefore the answer? Do we simply need to refine the rules representing the styles and incorporate more rules for other styles? The answer is (of course) no.

The rules given produce a reasonable behavior, but there are several reasons why they are inadequate. We will consider the question of strategy. It is apparent that human teachers do not switch between styles in the extreme manner of DOMINIE. Rather, they pursue one style, even when it is failing, and try to repair the failures. Is this simply because teachers can only remember one thing at a time? What we have omitted entirely from the discussion is any consideration of why the rules achieve something, and until we do this, of course, we cannot consider their relationship to the learner. To have a strategy which reasons about the styles, the styles must be captured as something more than simply descriptions of behavior. We need a model that explains those styles and, preferably, a model from which those styles and their variants can be derived. The use of rules has been helpful in marking out the range of things to be studied when examining teaching knowledge, and in showing what can be done, but to really capture appropriate interaction processes we must go beyond this and discuss goals, intentions, reasoning processes, and deeper models of interaction. The purpose of the next section is to raise and discuss some of these issues.

## 5. IMPLICATIONS OF TEACHING STYLE FOR DIALOGUE MECHANISMS

### 5.1. Dialogue Models and Teaching Plans

Some approaches to modeling dialogue were discussed above. These models have now effectively been superseded by combined theories of focus and function (e.g., Grosz & Sidner, 1986) and by models of speech acts as derived from deeper goals (e.g., Cohen & Levesgue 1987; Appelt, 1982) The dialogue games approach gave one level of analysis of a dialogue, but ultimately it was a descriptive tool. It did not explain where the goals for the games came from, or how they mapped into specific sequences of utterances. Both were simply accepted as "conventional." More recent systems have become much more formal, commonly using S5 logics and possible world semantics (e.g., Appelt, 1982). The overall view is that a dialogue model must take as its starting point the goals, intentions, desires, wants, and so on, of the participants (see Beveridge & Rimmershaw, this volume). Current models assume that the generation process is one of moving from a goal to an utterance by generating a plan in terms of intentional structure. This plan is generated by reasoning about the way the world should be, once the goal is achieved, and trying to ensure that an utterance constrains there to be such truth in all possible worlds. A major advantage of this approach is that it does offer us explanatory power at all levels, although, to explain low-level detail such as the exact form of an utterance, our planner must have stronger ideas than currently exist about the interaction of multiple goals.

The recognition process in dialogue is seen as the reverse of the generation process described here. A speaker receives an utterance and must try from this to infer the plan, and hence the goal, which the speaker must have had. How the speaker deals with this goal once recognized passes into the realms of theories of agenthood. These are discussed in the next section.

## 5.2. Theories of Agents

In earlier discussions we have emphasized the need for our tutor to reason explicitly about its actions, and to take into consideration the state of the pupil. Both of these issues are approached in work on theories of agents. The goal of this field of research is to try and define what it is that makes an information processing system an "agent" as opposed to being a reactive system which simply does what it is told. Agents are regarded as entities which are capable of taking actions rationally and autonomously in some world. We will examine one theory which goes beyond this viewpoint and attempts to discuss agents as social, interacting entities. This is clearly the situation which we are trying to achieve with a tutoring system.

Kiss (1988) centers his theory of agents on the idea that an agent must possess attitudinal states. He then posits that agents are "capable of taking many different kinds of attitudes to the world, and through the manipulation and utilization of these attitudes are capable of pursuing their interests." Kiss is concerned with the underlying nature of consciousness and the architecture of intelligent systems. For the purposes of this chapter we will review some of the major points which he makes without detailed exposition or justification.

In discussing computer agents interacting with users, Kiss modifies the idea of autonomy to deal with the restricted class of agents which are autonomous subject to constraints imposed by the interests of the user. This is precisely the class of systems which we require for an ITS. Kiss identifies processes of conflict and cooperation as key aspects of these agents and proposes a mechanism based upon deciding commitments to actions (or goals or other attitudinal states).

In the current version of the theory, three classes of attitude are identified: cognitive, conative, and affective. The cognitive attitudes are knowledge and belief (the distinction being that knowledge is definitely true in the world, whereas beliefs are held to be true by a given agent). The primary conative attitudes are wants and intentions. A *want* is an attitude towards some proposition or state. An *intention* is an attitude towards an action, specifying a (possibly conditional) commitment by the agent to carry out that action. Affective attitudes express values of other attitudes or states in terms of liking or disliking.

The agent is viewed as a system which is continuously evaluating potential actions with respect to its system of values, making commitments to action, and carrying out those actions. Actions can be of three types: deliberative, basic, and reflex. *Reflex* actions are immediate responses to situations, *deliberative* actions are parts of the reasoning process, and *basic* actions are things which may result from that process, but have no substructure. These actions do not necessarily occur in the world. For example, deciding to take a decision is an action.

The evaluative mechanism must be able to select between attitudes and states. This is achieved by positing a value system within each agent. The theory specifies the way in which states can acquire a value through their hedonistic attributes. These values, in combination with cost assessments (the amount of work required to achieve a state) allow us to create a value for the want associated with that state. The values of a particular sort of attitude form a partially ordered set. If one item has a higher value than another in this set, then the agent is said to have a *preference* for the first over the second.

This model provides us with a framework in which to express the reasoning and decision-making processes of a tutor. In interacting with a student, the tutoring system will extend its own attitudinal system with attitudes about the students system and values. There is no implication that the attitude system of the agent must be exact, or that it must be consistent.

By thinking of our tutor in terms of this model of agents, we gain several advantages. One advantage is that we can talk about intentions and wants in a manner that allows us to provide more detailed models of the reasoning involved in a decision by the tutor. The terms that we use, and their relationships, can be justified in terms of a deeper model of the architecture of agents, but we can worry about how these components are used together rather than seeking to explain the underlying theory. A third advantage is that the agent theory provides a very general model of action which we can use to integrate the features of the planning approaches and the situated action approaches into a single uniform framework.

## 5.3. Situated Action and Opportunistic Tutoring

Some recent work on human–computer interaction (Suchman, 1987) has questioned the role of planning in cognitive science in general, and models of interaction in particular. Suchman presents a caricature of AI planning work, shows how this sort of planning is inappropriate for interaction models, and offers the alternative of *situated action*. Unfortunately, this is also a caricature of an extreme position. The mechanisms of interaction must actually lie between these two extreme positions. Nevertheless she makes a number of important points which must be taken into account.

Suchman (1987, p. 27) offers the following definitions of the two extremes.

> On the planning view, plans are prerequisite to and prescribe action, at every level of detail. . . . The alternative view . . . is that while the course of action can always be projected or reconstructed in terms of prior intentions and typical situations, the prescriptive significance of intentions for situated action is inherently vague.

The essential contrast that she expresses is between action which is completely planned in detail in advance of execution, and actions which occur in response to a concrete context. She points out that, in general, plans like this cannot be generated prescriptively, and that they can be an artifact imposed in a posthoc manner by the observer of an interaction. She points out that we cannot anticipate all eventualities and therefore cannot plan for them. In terms of situated action, the action (or utterance) derives its significance from the context in which it occurs, without necessarily being used to identify the preexisting plan of the agent performing the action. She is deliberately vague about the nature of this context, suggesting it includes purposes and possibly an agenda. This vagueness is not a limitation of the approach, she claims, but an inherent part of the nature of interaction. She claims of her approach that

> it recommends that we turn our focus from explaining away uncertainly in the interpretation of action to identifying the resources by which the inevitable uncertainly is managed. (Suchman, 1987, p. 69)

In justification of this she hints at the frame problem in interaction, but, more importantly, talks about the inexactness of our inferences about intention. We cannot, in general, infer another agent's intentions exactly, and, more importantly, we do not need to. An intention is only inferred to the level of detail necessary for action. If, for example, an agent has a strong goal of pleasing another agent, then the first agent only needs to satisfy himself or herself that a request from the second agent is not impossible and will not harm the first agent. No more detailed analysis of intention is necessary. Suchman also points out that much of dialogue is repair (or elaboration), in which an utterance which failed to express an intention adequately to result in action is refined by collaborative problem solving between the two individuals.

In Suchman's case study of interaction (with an expert help system) there is unfortunately an additional confusion which makes the implications for interaction less clear. In most of the book, she has been discussing plans for dialogue. In the case study the plan to which she refers is the plan for achieving the task. These two plans are somewhat different. The task plan corresponds to the dialogue plan in cases such as that of Grosz's (1977) work, where a single expert who knows "the right way" to perform the task is interacting with a novice. In Suchman's case there are two novices, and considerable ambiguity in the way in which the help system expresses the plan. (It is interesting to compare this with DOMINIE, which uses essentially the same representation of the domain.) One further point which Suchman makes is that the computer and humans in this case cannot have a shared context, because not all the things which are accessible to the human are accessible to the computer. In conclusion, Suchman points out three major issues arising from this asymmetry between human and machine: (a) How can we extend machine access to actions and context? (b) How can we make the machine's limitations on access clear to the user? and (c) Can we provide the machine with computational alternatives for things to which the user has access.

Given this quick summary of the points which Suchman makes, what can we draw from this work for our educational interaction mechanisms? Her issues about the inadequacy of complete, prespecified plans are clearly correct, but not of great interest, since AI planning work has never (to my knowledge) made any claims that planning in the real world is anything like that. We accept that people produce partial plans, plans which specify concrete actions or exist in an abstract, partially instantiated form. Recent work on joint planning and execution, and metaplanning, leads to a more flexible view of the planning process into which Suchman's requirements can be incorporated.

Perhaps the most important outcome of this work is the idea of uncertainly of intention, and the vagueness of the idea of context. Both of these, I would claim, point to the way in which planning techniques must be incorporated with the idea of situated actions. The plan, or set of plans (there is no reason to assume an individual is working on a single plan at any given time) provide the context, for a single agent, in which action occurs. This context is necessarily different for each agent, though there are some commonalities. We must not think of a plan, but of an active planning process being carried on through the course of the interaction. The current states of the set of plans are our context, and the situated actions, which may not be executed as part of a plan but are necessarily related to plans, contribute not only to plan execution, but to the metaplanning process. This architecture is discussed in more detail in Section 6.

### 5.4. Educational Research on Interaction

Both the above approaches offer us information about the nature of interaction in general, but they make no proposals specific to the educational interaction. It would seem that the place to look for such information is the educational literature on interaction. This raises the issue of whether AI and education research can derive any benefit from previous work in education. This point is discussed further by Elsom-Cook (in press), but here we will focus on one aspect of the issue: levels of analysis.

There has been a large amount of work on educational interaction in the classroom, less on small group interaction, and virtually none on one-to-one educational interaction. Let us set aside this distinction for the moment and assume that it is all relevant to one-to-one interaction with the computer. What can be derived from looking at this literature? Unfortunately, most of this work is descriptive and statistical in nature. It tells us that a teacher spends 40% of his or her time responding to student-initiated activity (or whatever) but offers no help in understanding the processes and mechanisms involved. Similarly, the nonquantitative work, based on sociological and anthropological approaches, is of limited value for the types of models and theories which we wish to construct in AI and education. The analysis is at the wrong level of detail for our purposes. This is not to suggest that educational research should be conducted at a level which is directly formalizable in AI terms. If we were to wait for this state of affairs, we would have to stop asking most educational questions for some time to come, since current AI methods can only describe a small number of educational processes and activities. The problem of levels of description is not that educational research is conducted at the wrong level, but that the gap between this level and the detailed level needed for AI approaches is too great to bridge.

The questions which are asked and answered by the literature on educational research are often meaningless from the perspective of AI. If a study reports on the effectiveness of a variety of teaching styles, then teaching style must be defined in such a way that it can be expressed formally before the results of the study can even be examined to discover their relevance to AI and education.

An example of a piece of work on interaction in the educational literature that does appear to be relevant to AI issues is that of Bellack, Kliebard, Hyman, and Smith (1966). It was intended as a statistical, descriptive study of classroom language use, but in the final chapter it provides some "rules of the language game of teaching." While again being essentially descriptive, these rules do at least provide a framework for talking about the educational issues. They raise some detailed questions which can reasonably be explored using an AI methodology. The rules describe classroom behavior in terms of four types of language move: soliciting, responding, reacting, and structuring. The rules tell us, for example, that the teacher reacts (i.e., comments upon a pupil utterance, as opposed to responding to it) far more often than the pupil does. More strikingly, the pupil does not engage in 'rating' the teacher utterances (e.g., "I agree but..."), whereas the majority of teacher reactions are ratings of the pupil. This at least gives us a place where we can begin to ask questions from the AI viewpoint. Why was this difference in reacting behavior found? Is it specific to a particular teaching style? If so, what is it about that style which makes this distribution of reacting appropriate? What effect does the reaction by the teacher have on the cognitive state of the student? Why is it that teachers rarely react negatively, even if the pupil has said something wrong? In such circumstances the teacher normally reacts in a positive way, but with qualification.

The main point I wish to make here is that we must obviously look at education if we are to find out about educationally specific goals. It is not clear, however, whether we can derive the information we need from existing work. There is a large gap to be bridged in terms of levels of description. If that gap cannot be bridged, then it is necessary for AI and Education to include repetitions of previous research at finer levels of detail.

## 6. COMPONENTS OF A PROPOSED DIALOGUE SYSTEM

The general model proposed in this section involves considering interaction as a planning process in which multiple plans are being created simultaneously and are, at a given time, at a variety of levels of abstraction and completeness. These plans can predict actions, but can also be used as a context in which to evaluate actions which they did not predict, and the actions themselves can change the planning process. Planning is not regarded as a process to be completed with a resulting end product which is executed. Planning is dynamic and never-ending. The system can invoke actions without ever generating a complete plan.

To make this clearer, consider the following architecture. A dialogue history consists of a set of utterances generated by the two (we will restrict ourselves to two for present) participants in the interaction. A dialogue model is an abstraction over the dialogue history, representing the current state of the dialogue, both in terms of possible subsequent behaviors by both participants, and in terms of (historical) justifications for those behaviors. A model of an agent is an abstraction over the dialogue model together with knowledge about the world and previous states of the agents. An agent in a dialogue has a model of the other agent and of itself. These models are necessarily inexact. It can, however, contain both knowledge and belief. Plans represent the set of possible expansions of the goals, intentions, wants and desires within an agent. A metaplanning process controls the choice of plans to expand upon and may change the category of the plan (e.g., a desire may become a goal if it is believed to be achievable). Actions can occur because they are predicted by a plan (even if the plan is only partially instantiated) or because the system has a belief that the action is appropriate in the context of the set of plans. The metaplanning process is itself affected by the actions each agent performs.

To make this framework more complete, the following sections will discuss these components in more detail.

## 6.1. Goals, Wants, and Intentions

A first requirement of our interaction mechanism is that it must be flexible enough to reflect the states of the agents involved in the interaction. By this I mean, not just the cognitive states, but also the conative and affective states. This must be the fundamental level of the representation upon which all else is built. It is also important that these states are represented symmetrically (as far as possible) for the two agents (we will continue to think about one-to-one interaction for the present). The teacher must take account of the state of the student in deciding what to do next, but also compare this with the teacher's own state. If conflicts of goal arise between the agents, then the teacher should attempt to resolve these by reasoning about the two agents and initiating negotiation where appropriate. This can only be done if the agents are effectively represented in the same way. This level of representation is also important from the perspective of justification. Our teacher must always be able to justify its behavior at a given time. Referring back to our model of education theory, the part amenable to AI study is that which follows from the given goals and values of a particular educational approach and leads to a model explaining what to do in terms of ways to achieve those goals. I would therefore claim that an initial set of attitudes is the base level of our interaction mechanisms for intelligent tutoring. Other beliefs, wants, and desires may be generated during the interaction, but they are elaborations of this base set.

It is not being claimed that we have to wait for a complete theory of agenthood before we can build interaction models. We can state that something is a belief or want and then try to understand how to use it. We do not need to be able to explain the fundamental nature and origins of beliefs and desires in order to make use of them. I would suggest that the following components should be incorporated into the system:

- beliefs...attitudes about propositions or states [e.g., believes (tutor, believes(student,not(is-list(NIL))))]
- wants...states which the tutor (or student) desires to achieve [e.g., wants(tutor, believes(student, is-list(NIL)))]
- commitments...an intention to achieve a state, or carry out an action [e.g., commited(tutor,believes(student, is-list(NIL)))]
- preferences...the relative ordering of two attitudes or states [e.g., prefers(tutor, believes(student, is-list(NIL), believes(student, is-atom(NIL)))]

More justification and explanation of these components, as well as a discussion of the way in which they are used, can be found in Elsom-Cook (1990b).

## 6.2. Planning for Simultaneous Satisfaction of Multiple Goals

In the previous section we described a set of goals, and so on, which must be combined to produce behavior. To date, dialogue work has taken the view that a single goal is used as the root for a plan which determines the dialogue. This is an obvious simplification in a number of ways. For example, suppose we have asked someone a question, and he or she gets an answer wrong. From this we can acquire a goal of correcting the misconception. But do we say "No," "That was a good try, but...," or "Wrong, you idiot"? Each of these will satisfy the stated goal, but some will be appropriate in some situations, and some in others. Which is appropriate is determined by other goals and beliefs of the teacher, such as maintaining the motivation of the pupil. In general, then, we can regard an action as contributing to the achievement of one or more plans, and each plan may lead to satisfaction of one or more goals (if it is completed).

This raises a second issue, about the types of goals. We have effectively assumed that there is a single type of goal—that which is established and can be completed, after which it will cease to exist. Some goals are generated, satisfied, and disappear in this way (e.g., buying a watch). Some can be satisfied, but will recur at a later time (e.g., not being hungry). Some goals do not have a well-defined state of achievement but are used as criteria for assessing action (e.g., being rich and famous). Our planning mechanisms must deal with all these goals, and with levels of abstraction of goal varying from highly abstract ideas such as "make the student independent" to very concrete ones such as "say no."

Given this complexity of goal forms, and the idea that many goals may be tied together by a plan, we are no longer able to talk about plans achieving their goals (except in special cases). Instead, we must return to the idea of getting as close as possible to as many of the goals as possible. Obviously this involves "satisficing" all the goals and then attempting to get additional benefits on individual goals. For example, in the above case of reporting on a student's incorrect answer, the goal of responding is a transient goal that must be completed, while the goal of maintaining student motivation is one that (let us say) can be satisficed by not actually decreasing student motivation. In these terms, all three utterances satisfy the goal of responding, but the insulting comment would not satisfice the motivational goal. Either of the other two responses would therefore be acceptable, but the one with positive reinforcement will be preferred, because it takes us closer to our motivational goal.

Another issue for the planner implied by the interaction problem is that the planning must take into account the goals of both agents. Suchman (1987) bemoaned the lack of symmetry in human–computer interaction, and it is even more important in the educational setting. An effective educational interaction relies on negotiation between teachers and pupils (often implicitly) in order to satisfy the goals of both. Several researchers have been examining this problem in tutoring systems recently, notably Petrie-Brown (1990) and Baker (1990). Our interaction planner must deal with goals from both agents consistently, and must have principled reasons if it chooses to prefer the goals of one agent to those of another.

Finally, as has been emphasised in the discussions of DOMINIE and IMPART, the planner cannot operate simply by manipulating syntactic rules. It must be able to justify its behavior, which in turn implies a semantic model of the planning process. This is necessary in any case for principled metaplanning.

## 6.3. Plan Monitoring

One of the most important points from Suchman's (1987) work which must be taken into account is the inexactness of the ability to infer the intentions of another agent, and the necessity of repair as a process that allows agents to jointly determine the meaning of utterances to a level adequate to continue the interaction. This necessarily implies that the agents have beliefs about the effects of their actions, and that these beliefs are used in an evaluative manner. In the architecture described here, these effects are predicted from the set of plans being maintained by the system. These predictions may be inexact.

The existence of such predictions, however, also implies the existence of some monitoring component which seeks evidence that the effects have been achieved (or possibly assumes they have, while seeking evidence that they haven't). For this component, we can derive useful information form the literature on real-world planning produced by the AI community working on problems of robotics. This is not the complete answer to the problem, however, since these techniques rely on being able to derive exact knowledge in a given situation. To apply these ideas to interaction, where the changes in the other participant may not be directly visible, it is necessary to combine them with the uncertain modelling and inferencing techniques discussed earlier.

## 6.4. Opportunism

Many of the criticisms which Suchman offers of AI planning can be answered with the use of opportunistic planning systems, for example, Hayes-Roth, Hayes-Roth, Rosenschein, and Commavata (1979). The system described in that paper makes use of a blackboard architecture and a set of planning specialists to facilitate multidirectional planning. Plans can be created (or partially created) both top-down and bottom-up. A local behavior is established in the context of an intended plan and can affect that plan even though the plan itself is not complete. Another important component of the system, from our point of view, is the facility to metaplan. The planner can establish models of planning and evaluation criteria to be achieved in a particular context, and can support the simultaneous following of multiple plans. To support such opportunistic processes adequately, it is proposed that the following criteria should be applied to the design:

- Actions performed by the tutor are carried out in the context of one or more currently active plans. This does not mean that the plan must be completed in order to perform the action, but that the tutor has either expanded the plan sufficiently to predict that particular action, or that *the tutor has a belief that that action will contribute to the achievement of one or more plans.*
- Any action performed by either tutor or student feeds back into all partially instantiated plans via a metaplanning mechanism. This implies an evaluation function for the effect of an action with respect to a particular plan, even if that action is not predicted explicitly by that plan.

- In order for the metaplanning to function with partial plans it is necessary to introduce the concept of work into the planner. There are two forms of work: *execution work* and *planning work*. The former refers to an estimated cost of execution for a given plan (and should be calculable even on incomplete plans in a heuristic manner). The latter refers to an estimation of the further effort required to instantiate the plan.

## 7. CONCLUSIONS

In this chapter I have attempted to justify the importance of studying interaction in intelligent tutoring systems. I have illustrated the interaction mechanisms of two systems which embody teaching knowledge at some level. By discussing the limitations of these systems I have raised some issues that require basic research. Following this, some areas which can contribute to this research were outlined, and the components of a sophisticated mechanism for handling educational intraction were discussed. This discussion dealt with the architecture in general terms and highlighted the difficult problems involved in developing each of the components.

## REFERENCES

Anderson, J.R. (1982). Acquisition of a cognitive skill. *Psychological Review, 89.*

Appelt, D.E. (1982). *Planning natural language utterances to satisfy multiple goals* (SRI Tech. Note 259).

Baker, M. (1990). Arguing with the tutor. In M.Elsom-Cook (Ed.), *Guided discovery tutoring.* London: Paul Chapman Publishing.

Bellack, A.A., Kliebard, H.M., Hyman, R.T., & Smith, F.L. (1966). *The language of the classroom.* New York: Teachers College Press.

Bruner, J. (1966). *Towards a theory of instruction.* Cambridge, MA: Harvard University Press.

Burton, R.R., & Brown J.S. (1982). An investigation of computer coaching for informal learning activities. In D.Sleeman & J.S. Brown (Eds.) *Intelligent tutoring systems.* London Academic Press.

Cohen, P., & Levesque, H. (1987). Persistence, intention and commitment. In G.Georgeff & A.Lansky (Eds.), *Reasoning about knowledge and action.* Los Altos, CA: Morgan Kaufmann.

Collins, A., & Brown, J.S. (1987). Cognitive apprenticeship: Teaching students the craft of reading, writing and arithmetic. In L.B.Resnick (Ed.), *Cognition and instruction.* Hillsdale, NJ: Lawrence Erlbaum Associates.

Elsom-Cook, M.T. (1984).*Design considerations of an intelligent tutoring system for Lisp.* Doctoral thesis, Warwick University.

Elsom-Cook, M.T. (in press). Aims and methods in AI and education: Some issues. In E. Scanlon & T. O'Shea (Eds.), *New directions in advanced educational technology.* London: Springer-Verlag.

Elsom-Cook, M.T. (1990a). Guided discovery tutoring. In M.Elsom-Cook (Ed.), *Guided discovery tutoring.* London: Paul Chapman Publishing.

Elsom-Cook, M.T. (1990b). Formal description of a teaching dialogue. In M.Elsom-Cook (Ed.), *Guided discovery tutoring*. London: Paul Chapman Publishing.

Elsom-Cook, M.T., & Spensley, F. (1987). Using multiple teaching strategies in an ITS. In *Proceedings of Intelligent Tutoring Systems*. Montreal, Canada: Universite de Montreal.

Fredrikson, J.R., & White, B.Y. (1988). Intelligent learning environments for science education. In *Proceedings of the First International Meeting on ITS* (IMITS-88). Montreal, Canada.

Grosz, B.J. (1977). *The representation and use of focus in dialogue understanding*. Doctoral thesis, University of California at Berkeley.

Grosz, B.J., & Sidner, C.I. (1986). Attention, intentions and structure of discourse. *Computational Linguistics, 12*(3).

Hayes-Roth, B. Hayes-Roth, F. Rosenschein, S., & Cammarata S. (1979). Modelling planning as an incremental opportunistic process. In *Proceedings of Sixth IJCAI*. Los Altos, CA: Morgan Kaufmann.

Kiss,G.R. (1988). *Some aspects of agent theory* (HCRL Tech Rep.). Milton Keynes, UK: The Open University.

Levin, J.A., & Moore,J.A. (1978). Dialogue games: Metacommunication structures for natural language interaction. *Cognitive Science,11*.

Peters, R.S. (1966). *Ethics and education*. London: Allen and Unwin

Petrie-Brown, A.M. (1990). Freedom of speech. In M.Elsom-Cook (Ed.), *Guided discovery tutoring*. London: Paul Chapman Publishing.

Power, R. (1979). The organisation of purposeful dialogues. *Linguistics,17*.

Reichmann, R. (1978). Conversational coherency. *Cognitive Science, 2*.

Schegloff, E., & Sacks, H. (1973). Opening up closings. *Semiotica,8*.

Spensley, F.M., & Elsom-Cook, M.T. (1987). *DOMINIE: Teaching and assessment strategies* (CITE Tech. Rep. 37). Milton Keynes, UK: Open University.

Suchman, L. (1987). *Plans and situated actions*. Cambridge: Cambridge University Press.

Whitehead, A.N. (1932). *The aims of education*. Benn

# 4

## LEARNER MODELING IN COLLABORATIVE INTELLIGENT EDUCATIONAL SYSTEMS*

GEOFF CUMMING AND JOHN SELF

Our purpose is to argue that conceptions of intelligent tutoring systems (ITSs) need to change in response to enriched ideas of the learning that can be supported by a computer. We refer to *intelligent educational systems* (IESs), which will offer comments and advice to the user considered as collaborator in learning, rather than direction to the user considered as pupil. Learner modeling in the collaborative IES can be a shared activity, with the learner model even being open to inspection and change by the learner. The conversational interaction of system and learner is likely to have a number of strands, with a jump to an alternative strand being used when an impasse occurs. Building such IESs will need the study of collaborative and conversational aspects of human tutoring interactions.

First, consider user models in general. Any device intended for human use embodies a model of its user. For example, the size and shape of a screwdriver handle betray assumptions about characteristics of likely users. The model may be of classes of user, as with normal screwdrivers, or of a single user, as when I insist on a screwdriver shaped to my own hand. The model may be constant over time or, in the case of devices capable of modifying themselves,

*Support for this research has been provided for Geoff Cumming by the Australian Research Grants Scheme, and for John Self by the U.K. Science and Engineering Research Council Grants D/16079 and D/63055.

85

may be dynamic: it may always be changing to fit better the current state of the user.

A user model is a special case of a model of a device's environment. Craik's (1943) fundamental contribution to the foundation of cybernetics was to point out that a machine could best interact with its surroundings if it could use an internalized abstraction of relevant aspects of its environment. The idea of both systems and people using internal models to guide interaction has come to pervade psychology. Humphrey (1986) went so far as to argue that the evolutionary purpose of consciousness is to allow us to have a model of our own mental and social life, so that we can use this as a model of other humans, and so be able to interact with them more effectively.

User models are, therefore, pervasive. User models for individuals must continue to have a central place in research on intelligent educational systems, because individualization is the key to supporting effective learning, and a system can generate individualized responses only if it has information about the user, in other words a learner model.

The research questions in learner modeling that arise from the above are:

What should be modeled?
What detail is necessary?
How closely tailored to individual learners does the model need to be?

We seek guidance on these questions by considering conventional ITSs, and ways of advancing beyond present methodologies. This leads to the proposal for collaborative IESs, the learner modeling requirements of which are different and possibly easier to satisfy.


## 1. LEARNER MODELS IN TUTORING SYSTEMS

Hartley (1973) included a learner model in what has become the classic identification of the components of an IES: knowledge of the domain, a learner model, and knowledge about teaching.

Self's (1974) analysis of learner modeling identified the learner's current knowledge of the domain as being just a subset of what the system needs to know about the learner. In most subsequent work, however, domain knowledge has dominated ITS research (Wenger, 1987). The learner model has typically been represented as an overlay of the domain knowledge or, in a further refinement, has included distorted or erroneous versions of domain knowledge, corresponding to the learner's misconceptions. Such a learner model thus comprises a dynamic model of the individual learner's current domain knowledge (Clancey, 1986). In addition, some aspects of an entire class of learners were modelled implicitly, in a static way, by the system's teaching rules and user interface.

Such a tutoring system has been intended to convey domain knowledge to a learner. It reflects the classic approach to ITS design: the idea of one-way knowledge transmission, or *knowledge communication* (Wenger, 1987), is appropriate.

## 2. THE CARICATURE TUTORING SYSTEM

We could go further and describe a caricature ITS as one with a straightforward, authoritarian tutoring style guided by simple teaching rules, and a learner model based on domain knowledge. The need to represent the domain within the limited knowledge formalisms currently available means that the domain would need to be well defined and have a simple structure. It would probably comprise procedural skills and be related to mathematics, physics, computer programming, or the use of some computer application package.

Criticisms of the caricature system address its teaching style and the skills it imparts. For example, Ridgway (1988) argues that, first, the glamor of computers, if associated with such impoverished tutoring, could lend legitimacy to a narrow, passive view of the learner's role, and so hamper advances in educational practice. Second, the procedural skills taught by the caricature system are likely to be:

1. seen as superficial by those who emphasise understanding, metacognition, and personal growth as educational goals; and
2. the skills that are most amenable to being rendered redundant by the advent of computer-based tools.

It remains true that good drill-and-practice CAI in well-structured domains can lead to gains on traditional educational tests (Kulik, Kulik, & Cohen, 1980), and that some computer tutoring of procedural skills does seem effective (Anderson, Boyle, & Reiser, 1985). The danger is that such skills training may be seen as more than a small part of education and, further, that such successful computer approaches may limit our thinking about how the computer might best be used to promote attainment of richer educational goals.

It is also true that the caricature does injustice to many of the early tutoring systems (Barr & Feigenbaum, 1982), which did experiment with a range of styles of interactions with the learner, including mixed initiative questioning (SCHOLAR), Socratic dialogue (WHY), coaching (WEST), and case-based discussion (GUIDON).

In summary, even though a caricature ITS may give learning gains in its limited area, the approach is unsatisfactory because it is confined to shallow, well-defined domains and provides only a restricted style of instruction. More perniciously, it may promote impoverished views of the nature of education.

## 3. ADVANCING BEYOND THE CARICATURE

Several developments now necessitate advance beyond the caricature view of a tutoring system: Some come from research on tutoring systems, and some from study of human expertise—both its nature, and how it can be developed. In addition the possibility of learners having scope for more initiative must be explored.

### 3.1. Difficulties Revealed by Research on Tutoring Systems

To give good comments, an IES should be able to offer explanations ranging from the local and small ('Use the back-arrow key.'), to the broad and conceptual ('Think of integration as the inverse of differentiation.'). This is partly a question of choosing an appropriate *grain size*, and partly that of choosing the best *view* of the issue to use as the basis for an explanation. *Grain size*, which varies from small to large, micro to macro, local to global, refers to the scale of conceptualization of the domain. Choosing the best view, by contrast, refers to choosing among alternative types of conceptualisations: in the RECOVERY BOILER TUTOR simulation of a complex industrial plant (Woolf, 1988), for example, one view is in terms of physical pressures and flows, while another view may refer to a control systems model based on feedback loops. In the GUIDON tutor concerned with infectious diseases (Clancey, 1987) one view may be based on pharmacology, another on epidemiology. We bring together the need to choose an appropriate *grain size* and an appropriate *view* for an explanation by referring to the *basis* on which it will be formed.

Attempts to specify how the best basis can be chosen for an explanation have identified (a) the need for multiple representations of domain knowledge; (b) the difficulty of choosing what basis is most suitable at a particular moment; and (c) the need for consideration also of the basis for expression of misconceptions. We consider these points in turn.

The main lesson of GUIDON and NEOMYCIN (Clancey, 1987) was that it is very difficult to build a domain knowledge base sufficiently able to provide the explanations needed to develop good understanding. A rich diversity of explanations requires, in turn, a correspondingly rich representation of the domain; a standard rule-based expert system does not suffice.

Clancey argues that wanting to support a good range of explanations means that multiple representations of domain knowledge are needed.

This however, exacerbates the problem of choice. GUIDON could readily generate explanations that would keep the user occupied for several hours on a single case study, but it is difficult for the system to choose the small portion of output which best meets the learner's current needs. What would be the basis for the explanation that is most effective for the learner at that time? Being able to support such choice puts complex demands on the learner model. Beyond what the learner currently knows in the domain, and the learner's preferences, it would seem necessary to know something of the learner's current hypotheses and goals.

Hartley and Smith (1988) describe a similar choice problem: the EURO-HELP system attempts to judge which questions the user could most usefully ask at a particular time, and presents them in a menu. Users, however, typically browse past many questions before selecting one. This difficulty of system choice arises even though the domain is relatively small and does not have a deep or complex structure.

The third problem identified above concerns attempts to model learner misconceptions in discrepancy or *bug* terms. The classic bug or malrule approach (Brown & Burton, 1978) may try to distinguish performance *slips* from genuine misconceptions, but otherwise attempts to describe errors at one grain size. Misconceptions can, however, be described in any of a number of different bases, even for seemingly simple arithmetic skills (Ridgway, 1988). Payne and Squibb (1987) also found the malrule approach inadequate for accounting for a large collection of children's algebra errors. No degree of abstraction could be found which enabled them to identify malrules which were applied in the systematic way that the malrule approach suggests, leading them to conclude that the distinction between *slip* and *bug* is not clearcut, and that account needs to be taken of the effect of partially formed conceptual knowledge on procedural skills.

Sleeman (1984) presented evidence that misunderstandings in the domain of algebra need to be described from a number of different views. More recently (Sleeman, 1987; Sleeman et al., this volume), he has rejected a malrule approach after finding that remediation based on diagnosis using a single set of malrules is not more effective than simple reteaching. His conclusion relies on the accepting of a null hypothesis, so is weak, and may arise from an uncertain rationale for remediation. It does, however, raise further doubt about any bug analysis that relies on just one view of all errors, and at a single grain size.

## 3.2. Learning as Progress towards Expertise

Rich learning has always been regarded as having many facets, and as being more than mere information accretion. Contemporary study of human expertise identifies corresponding diversity, so that a simple, appealing, and practically useful way to specify rich learning is to describe it as progression towards expertise. Taking such learning as the goal and considering the study of human expertise together give a foundation for specifying IESs that go beyond the caricature discussed above.

### 3.2.1. Multiple Representations in Human Expertise..

The performance of an expert, even if it seems fast and automatic, can draw on a wide variety of strategies and conceptualizations that are domain specific and very effective. Learning—advancing from novice towards expert status—requires, therefore, the development of additional, more effective conceptualizations. And so, to provide explanations matched to a learner's current view of the domain, an IES needs to incorporate representations of each successive conceptual level, or mental model, to be developed by the learner.

This conclusion, which concurs with the multiple representations view discussed earlier, underlies the design of QUEST (Frederiksen & White, 1988). This system is based on a sequence of domain representations, ranging from a simple qualitative novice view to a detailed quantitative representation that would typically be one of the mental models of the field available to an expert.

As an example of a detailed description of expert abilities, consider Schoenfeld's (1985) identification of four components of mathematical expertise:

1. Resources: facts, skills, procedures, memory for particular problems seen before.
2. Heuristics: not merely the well-known Polya (1945) collection, but specializations of these to the domain; "consider a special case" would, for example, have different, more specific, versions in geometry, and in various fields of algebra.
3. Control: the ability to manage resources, to monitor what is being done, to decide when to shift tack, to judge the prospects of some particular approach.
4. Beliefs: a mathematical world-view; expectations as to what is required and acceptable, attitudes to various broad approaches, for example, the building of a formal proof.

In the expert, these components are closely intertwined but all identifiable. Schoenfeld presents evidence that good mathematical training needs to pay attention to all four aspects of expertise. In particular, components 2, 3, and 4 are essential and need to be addressed explicitly. These components, especially 3, are strongly related to metacognition, and so Schoenfeld's approach accords well with current educational thinking that, first, metacognition is vital and, second, that the best way to promote it is to discuss, model, and practice it explicity.

*3.2.2. Apprenticeship: Multiple Learning Strategies..* The inference for IES design that should be drawn from Schoenfeld's analysis is that multiple representation of the domain must be complemented by a range of types of learning activities. Collins, Brown, and Newman (1987) adopt the term *cognitive apprenticeship* to link the need for a diversity of learning approaches with the idea of learning as progress towards some type of expertise. The *teaching knowledge* component in the classic description of a tutoring system needs, therefore, to be construed very broadly. To avoid the unwanted, narrow connotations of words such as *teaching, tutoring,* and *coaching,* and to emphasize that we wish to encompass the full range of types of comment useful to a learner (including tutoring, advising, explaining, demonstrating, answering, suggesting, giving exposition, and remaining silent), we proudly introduce a new verb to the English language: *to mentor,* which, like Humpty Dumpty, we will use to mean just what we choose it to mean.

Aspects of expertise that vary as widely as those identified by Schoenfeld certainly need a variety of mentoring strategies. In addition, choice of mentoring approach should no doubt be influenced by learner style and preference: learning is likely to be more effective if the method is matched to the individual learner. It has proved difficult to establish clear gains in effectiveness by such matching, but there are encouraging findings (Snow, Federico, & Montague,1980). Elsom-Cook (this volume) is exploring possibilities, and the prospect remains extremely attractive.

The study of human expertise therefore suggests that a good IES should support multiple mentoring strategies and, in concurrence with tutoring research considered earlier, incorporate multiple views of its domain. These conclusions can also be regarded as special cases of two very broad conclusions from AI research. First, currently available formalisms are inadequate to support the richness of knowledge representation that is needed if the performance of AI programs is to be improved. Second, and more fundamentally, human learning, like human intelligence, is even more subtle, complex, and impressive than was imagined in the early days of Al.

## 3.3. Learner Initiative

Using multiple mentoring strategies implies that the learner takes a share of the initiative. The emphasis above on metacognition, and on fostering its development by discussing it and practicing it explicitly, suggests that the learner should have a large amount of control over the learning interaction. Current interest in learner control and personal knowledge construction has ancient roots but, following Papert's (1980) persuasive advocacy, has recently gained a strong following in educational computing. Especially in the context of Logo and microworlds—small modeling environments—learner control has been advocated, not only as more worthy in principle, but as the only way for a learner to achieve ownership and deep understanding of knowledge

It is, however, challenging to put fine sentiments about learner initiative into effective practice. Evaluations of the use of Logo (Carmichael, Burnett, Higginson, Moore, & Pollard, 1985) and Prolog (Cumming & Abbott, 1988) emphasize the difficulties of achieving learner control in practical educational settings. It is essential to note, with Papert (1980, p. 32), that learners need guidance, inspiration, and support if learner freedom is not to become chaos and disillusionment. In addition, as mentioned earlier, it remains true that CAI and other highly structured and directive approaches to instruction can be effective, judged by traditional educational measures. At least in some limited settings, control of learning sequence by a simple mathematical model is more effective than sequence selection by the learner (Atkinson, 1972). Structured, directed learning cannot be dismissed out of hand.

It is easy to draw a stark contrast between the caricature ITS that tells the learner exactly what to do, and the wished-for imaginative, self-starting, and empowering use by a learner of Logo or some other modeling tool. There seems a vast gulf between two irreconcilable world views of education. Some welcome attempts, however, have recently been made to bridge the gulf: Sleeman (1985) discusses the two traditions and looks forward to a constructive rapprochement between tutoring systems and the ideas of the Logo school. Lawler and Yazdani (1987) do at least bring together papers representing the two approaches, even if not all the authors would see rapprochement as imminent. Is it possible for a learner to have room for initiative yet still benefit from structured teaching?

## 4. THE ADVISING, COLLABORATIVE IES

### 4.1. From Instruction to Advice

Even a simple first-principles analysis suggests that there need be no conflict between the desire for learner control and the need for learner guidance. The important realization is that offering suggestions need not require taking control. Provision of comments, even very detailed advice, need not presuppose that control is with the tutor or computer system. Conversely, the fact that the learner has the initiative does not imply that exploration has to be random. An interested learner will seek out and accept advice, and may well do so in a way that gives good learning.

In these terms, Papert's analysis has not sufficiently recognized the need for guidance, while traditional ITS approaches have undervalued scope for learner enterprise. From the point of view of IES development, the vital realization is surely that judicious offering of individually tailored advice does not require control to lie with the computer system.

The importance of metacognition and the attractiveness of learner initiative encourage every effort to realize effective systems in which the learner is often in charge. The IES builder should think, not in terms of specifying an individually chosen path for the user, considered as the object of instruction, but of offering well-chosen advice to the user, considered as collaborator in learning (Self 1988). It remains to be explored how sweeping the consequences may be of this seemingly slight shift from *feedback* and *instruction*, which hint at directive teaching, to *comment* and *suggestion* which do not.

We find, the classical approach to tutoring systems difficult and limited. On the one hand it is hard to choose and formulate the comment that is most suitable at any particular moment; on the other it is unacceptable that the IES should fully set and control the course of the learning interaction. Might both problems be ameliorated at the same time?

In other words, the goal is not simply the transmission of any single view of the domain, but the acquisition of the broad range of abilities that comprise expertise in some field. The IES should therefore draw on a wide range of both knowledge and mentoring activities. Further, we see the learner as explicitly wanting to work towards expertise, and the job of the IES as being a supportive collaborator, offering judicious advice. Can we describe feasible IESs that would support a range of learning activities, and prompt considerable initiative by the learner? What learner model would such a system require?

## 4.2. Metacognition and Interpreting Advice

We suggest that the switch from ITS-as-instructor to IES-as-collaborator is crucial for two reason: It should change the learner's expectations about the system, and it should also change the learner's way of interacting with it. A learner adopting the role of tutee, who passively receives instructions, is likely to regard the system as reliable and insightful. Less-than-ideal output would therefore be likely to lead to puzzlement and rejection. On the other hand, a learner who regards the system as a helpful partner in a joint but uncertain learning enterprise should have a more forgiving attitude to puzzling responses from the system. System output would be regarded as advice or commentary, rather than instruction, and the learner would feel responsibility for interpreting what the IES was suggesting, and for choosing what next input to the system would best advance mutual understanding. The new IES should be more modest but also may be more effective than the classic ITS.

The collaborative IES may, therefore, bring two benefits. First, because the user is not expecting infallibility, demands on the accuracy and individual relevance of system response are reduced. The learner will be able to work with any of a range of responses that are more or less appropriate. Second, the user will work at building a richer model of the system itself to assist in comprehending system output. Building such a model, and working to achieve collaborative understanding of the subject of the learning interaction, together call on the learner to use metacognition and higher-level control processes: having the learner do this in the domain of interest is itself an important goal.

This is not to say that an obtuse IES is better, because it makes the learner work harder to achieve insight, thus learning more in the process! Rather, the IES needs to offer multiple paths forward so that the learner is encouraged to take the initiative to side-step any impasse and find an alternative route to understanding.

## 4.3. Respecting the Learner's Abilities

A further way to regard the role suggested here for initiative and metacognition by the learner is in the context of earlier analyses. Burton and Brown (1982) reported that children using the WEST coach would deliberately set out to try to make the coach interrupt: They had moved up to a metalevel and were trying to build a mental model of the coach and its intervention strategies. Clancey (1987) reported that students sometimes chose a response with the aim of "finding out what the system would say." Howe and du Boulay (1979) noted that users of drill and practice CAI often exploit the system to ease the task, usually bypassing topic area learning in the process. At the simplest level, for example, a child might seek error inputs that lead, perhaps after three attempts, to output of the correct answer.

In all of these cases the researchers were noting that learners can choose to take the system itself as the object of study. The learners are showing initiative, but this does not necessarily result in learning in the intended domain. Similarly, teacher driving in the classroom (Ridgway, 1988) occurs when children work at a metalevel: They investigate and exploit the teacher's way of operating, and may use this knowledge to duck the assigned leaning task. Ridgway (1988) suggests that opening a tutoring system to investigation by the learner could make good educational use of the learner's ability to treat a system as the object of study.

A collaborative IES would respect the learner by recognising such capabilities for initiative and inventiveness. The IES should draw on these learner abilities by prompting the learner to use them within the intended domain. The outcome would be, ideally, that the learner's metacognitive abilities are enhanced, the learning interaction enriched, and the classical ITS problems eased as well. The suggested role of metacognition also places emphasis on what the learner can do—on positive abilities—rather than, as in classic bug approaches, on the learner's shortcomings (Self, 1988).

The proposed concept of an IES may also be described in terms of where the intelligence is seen as being. In the caricature ITS the developer's task is to represent symbolically in the tutoring system sufficient about the learner and the domain to be able to present somewhat intelligent tutoring to the learner. The learner is the object of modeling, is "out there," and is seen as the problem to be solved.

By contrast, Norman (1988) argues for a view of intelligence that sees the context in which a person undertakes a task as playing an essential role in the person's remembering and reasoning. The environment, including the tools available, will strongly influence what the user does, what mental models the user develops, and, generally, the quality of thinking. Providing a rich context for learning activities is therefore a prime goal for IES design.

The analysis of Winograd and Flores (1986) goes even further by maintaining that intelligence cannot be encapsulated in any program, but has meaning only in terms of a system in intimate interaction with its environment. Their analysis would see the collaborative IES, not merely as a possibility worth considering, but as a necessary approach, if computers are to be fully exploited in education. Their analysis need not be accepted in full to offer support for the view of an IES as part of an interactive partnership with the learner. The intelligence is not within the computer system, but is a property of the interaction between system and user. The aim of the IES designer is, above all, to recognize and draw on the abilities and initiative of the learner.

### 4.4. The Locus of Initiative

If an IES is to be collaborative it will be important to consider carefully how responsibility for directing the learning interaction is shared between the system and the learner. This is a more complex question than simply asking, "Which party is in control?"

If I engage a human expert to teach me, I may decide to submit to the expert's detailed instruction and do exactly as I am told. The expert has local, momentary control of my learning activities, but at a global level I can take the initiative to change the nature of the interaction, or to end it altogether.

By contrast, consider a teacher who tries to promote discovery learning by encouraging children in a class to explore and take initiative. The children are urged to take immediate and local control, but the teacher retains global control; learners may find it difficult to cope with even the local scope for initiative or, conversely, may feel that, lacking global control, they have been given only the illusion of control.

These examples show that immediate control in a learning interaction must be distinguished from global, or metalevel, control. In addition, degrees of control, and also collaboration or the sharing of initiative, must be recognized. We see the collaborative IES as offering the learner a large measure of global control, and as supporting a range of possibilities for local decision making. This arrangement would allow such plausible scenarios as that suggested by Riel, Levin, and Miller-Souviney (1987): At first the system should be largely in (local) control but, as learners acquire expertise, they should be encouraged to take more (local) initiative. To the extent that the IES offers advice that earns acceptance by the learner, who has global control, a feeling of collaboration can be developed.

The proposal of Riel et al. (1987) also accords well with Vygotsky's idea (Wertsch, 1985) that a learner has a *zone of proximal development* (ZPD) within which a problem can be solved, if hints, cues, or some suitable support are given. When working close to the far edge of the ZPD the learner has most scope to use and to develop metalevel skills—Schoenfeld's 2, 3, and 4 abilities—and also to make best use of the opportunity to take control. A novice's ZPD is small, and there is only limited scope for the learner to make good use of control. With the development of expertise, of metalevel abilities especially, the ZPD grows and there is more scope for the learner to benefit from having control.

The general questions of what constitutes scope for initiative, who decides where the initiative is to lie, and how the initiative might be shared are important questions for the development of collaborative IESs. They require more detailed analysis than they have so far received in education.

## 4.5. Sidestepping Impasses

An advantage claimed for the new IES is that any output of the systems, although intended to be individually appropriate at that moment, is not fully committing or critical, because, if the user is puzzled, he or she can query the output, or seek restatement, or try a different approach to the question. The requirement is therefore that such a variety of responses by the user must be supported by the system: the user must always be able to call for a side-step and an alternative approach. Both the user and the IES need to have the scope to back away and try a reformulation whenever either indicates an impasse.

Operating in this way should not only allow the learner to cope with system output that is somewhat capricious, but also to develop control and metacognitive abilities.

## 4.6. Multiplicity of Representations

The requirement that impasses can be side-stepped means that multiple paths must be available. Interaction with a collaborative IES might, at one minute, concern fine detail of some domain material; at the next, a different view of the same material; then a general strategic approach. In each case the system needs to be able to call on some appropriate form of domain information, corresponding information from the learner model about the learner's current understanding, and a suitable type of mentoring strategy.

The emphasis is therefore not on the full complexity and richness of any single representation of the domain or learner understanding, but on supporting multiple representations, each good enough to be of some practical use. Multiplicity is required in each of the three components of an IES—domain knowledge, learner model, and mentoring strategies—so that an alternative basis for an explanation or presentation to the learner can be chosen when an impasse occurs.

Considering mentoring in particular, a number of current IES projects are investigating the support of multiple strategies within systems with a microworld flavor. Feurzeig (1987), for example, describes a Logo-based system to support the learning of algebra. The development of skill at algebra manipulations, concepts, and problem-solving strategies are all addressed explicitly, with appropriate ways for the learner to interact with the system being provided in each case. Similarly, Scardamalia, Bereiter, McLean, Swallow, and Woodruff (1988) describe *computer-supported intentional learning environments* (CSILEs) which provide a variety of ways for a learner to interact with rich knowledge bases. These and other projects emphasize a powerful user interface, learner control, and good tools to help the user explore the domain knowledge. Such projects are very much in the spirit of the collaborative IES proposed here, although in general they have not yet addressed learner model considerations in detail.

In the remainder of this chapter we discuss further aspects of IESs in the light of the collaboration-and-advice proposal, and consider in particular the implications for learner models.

## 5. LEARNER MODELING IN THE COLLABORATIVE IES

What learner model would an advising, collaborative IES require? The discussion above suggests that multiple representations would be needed, corresponding to multiplicity in domain representation, so that alternative avenues of investigation by the learner can be pursued. The possibility of side-stepping impasse means, however, that no single representation need claim to be fully accurate and comprehensive.

Many traditional learner model concerns and techniques remain relevant. Use of some overlay approach to represent the learner's current domain understanding, and some discrepancy technique for current misconceptions seem logically necessary. The system needs information about the user's current goals. Machine learning techniques to help maintain the learner model also remain relevant. These methods have, however, proved troublesome and limited. To be an advance, the collaborative IES needs to allow additional approaches, as well as reducing the demand for accuracy of any single aspect of the learner model. We mention first two preliminary points.

## 5.1. Limiting the Learner Model Task

Any learning tool is used by a learner in a context and with a purpose. Even if acquiring expertise depends on a richness of learning possibilities, the IES need not provide every aspect: it may address only some of the learning goals, and it may be designed for use in company with other learners, or with a teacher, or with some other device or information source. The setting and way in which an IES may best be used have been relatively little studied, but, as usual, the computer should be used just for what it does better, and any limitations on the role assigned to the IES are likely to simplify the learner modeling task. Considering learning to be collaborative, and expecting the learner to take initiative, makes it natural to draw in other resources alongside the IES when that would help.

Given that the aim of a system is to improve learning, there is no point in modelling an aspect of the learner unless (a) having modeled that aspect, we can make use of this extra information to change subsequent behavior of the IES; and (b) these change do lead to better learning. In other words, the learner model need only provide what the mentoring component can make good use of. Building a learner model may be quite different from building a full cognitive simulation.

## 5.2. The Inspectable, Modifiable Learner Model

We consider the user to be an active, responsible agent, taking initiative in learning activities. The learner model need not, therefore, be a hidden, secret dossier, but can be open and inspectable by the user. If at least part of the learner model can be represented in comprehensible form, the learner can not only see what view the IES currently has of him or her but may be able to change aspects of the model. Engaging the user in collaborative development of the learner model—providing this continues to represent the user's state—is thus equivalent to, and another way of thinking of, the educational task. For the learner, as well as the IES, the learner model records progress so far, and gives a context for further work. In addition, a learner model that is open should allay the suspicion sometimes felt in the microworlds camp that simply having a learner model makes an IES paternalist, manipulative, or necessarily inhibiting of learner initiative.

*Plan recognition*, in which the system tries to second guess the user, could be replaced with a notion of *plan agreement* or *plan negotiation*, in which system and user also collaborate about this aspect of the interaction. Such a flexible arrangement should be best able to cope with the incomplete, nested, and frequently changing plans typical of humans in exploratory situations.

The learner model has, logically, three types of information available from the learner: learner behavior on learning tasks, learner behavior on diagnostic tasks specifically set by the IES to get information relevant to the learner model, and comments from the learner or answers to questions specifically about learner model things, for example, preferences of the learner for various types of activity. In a collaborative IES, asking the user directly may be the simplest and best way to build and maintain many aspects of the learner model. For example, the learner may be the best judge of the success of some activity.

Learner modeling, as well as the basic learning enterprise, thus becomes a joint task for user and system. There is an analogy with a human tutor who reveals and discusses the learner model by saying things like "You seem to have grasped P, but don't realize that Q ...". The learner comments or disagrees, and an agenda for further learning activities is set.

This human tutor analogy of the inspectable learner model suggests that it will be worthwhile to investigate what models human tutors build of their students, and how these models are used, shared, and changed in the course of the learning interaction. A tutor and student who discuss what they see to be the learner's current stage of understanding are engaged in the collaborative development of a learner model as advocated above. This discussion may be used to plan activities likely to advance the learner's understanding, and may itself serve to enhance understanding.

## 5.3. The Basis of Representation, and Learner Modeling

Our analysis has called for multiplicity in learner modeling as well as domain representation. In Section 3.1 multiplicity was specified as referring to grain size, and also to the view taken of the domain. The learner-modeling issues that are most important are likely to vary markedly according to the basis (in the sense of Section 3.1) of domain representation.

Consider, for example, the immediate surface details: having excellent system and interface design supplemented by a good integrated help facility should reduce the need for ambitious intelligent tutoring on such specifics. Note that many ITS projects have chosen UNIX applications, or similarly opaque command-driven systems, as the domain to be tutored. By contrast no one has apparently seen the need to build an ITS for Macintosh applications of comparable power: the good interface design largely removes the need for complex tutoring or learner modeling of surface detail.

The "immediate detail" referred to may be dismissed as being merely part of the computer interface, rather than domain content. However, this distinction is not always easy to maintain: computing domains have been chosen for many tutoring projects, and, as well, direct manipulation interfaces (Hutchins, Hollan, & Norman, 1985) now give a more fundamental merging of subject matter and interface. In these interfaces the user sees representations of objects which appear, and which may be controlled, in a way that matches a good mental model of the domain as closely as possible. Good design of how the domain content is presented for manipulation by the learner means that discovering how to use the interface should give useful domain learning as well.

As a second example, consider a basis for representation that is far from the fine surface detail: the strategies and broad conceptions typical of experts. The corresponding aspect of the learner model will need to focus on expert strategies rather than the traditional domain database. In the RECOVERY BOILER TUTOR (Woolf, 1988), for example, the emphasis in building the coach was on the investigation and troubleshooting procedures used by human experts. The knowledge engineering effort was not, therefore, mainly on domain knowledge, but as well included study of the methods used by experts in the domain. The learner model also needed to include strategies.

The above contrast of surface detail and expert strategies illustrates differences in the learner modeling requirements in the two cases. In a collaborative interaction we would expect continual swapping around among these two, and many other, bases for the discussion between learner and system. Noting the contrast between a system-learner conversation concerning surface details, and one about broad strategies, led us to think of the learning interaction as consisting of a number of conversations. Often there seem to be conversations interweaved concurrently, and strands of conversation are broken off and replaced when impasses occur.

In Cumming and Self (1990) we take further the notion of conversations, and identify a predominant pattern, in which there is an interaction at a *task* level—the learner carries out some activity—while at a higher level the system and learner carry on a *discussion* level conversation in which they evaluate, plan, and reflect on activity at the task level. Describing the collaborative learning interaction in terms of conversations also leads to some suggestions as to how the study of human tutoring may assist IES development; we turn to this now as the final issue discussed here.

## 6. CONCLUSIONS AND RESEARCH IMPLICATIONS

We have suggested the use of the term *intelligent educational system* to avoid any presumption of a one-way, authoritarian style of tutoring, and have used the term *mentoring* to cover the full range of possible learning and teaching interactions between learner and system. We have argued that a collaborative view of the learning interaction is compatible with both scope for learner initiative and some structure in the guidance offered by the system.

The collaborative IES proposal has arisen from problems identified in previous ITS research, from enriched ideas about desirable goals for learning, and, in particular, from the attractiveness of encouraging learner initiative. What lines of research will assist the development of collaborative IESs?

Most fundamentally, a better understanding is required of the cognitive and social processes of learning. Study of selected aspects of human tutoring is needed. There is also the attractive possibility that study of the way learners interact with collaborative IESs will advance understanding both of specific aspects that will be immediately applicable to IES development, and of basic learning processes.

### 6.1. The IES as a Research Setting

An individual learner—or perhaps two or three learners—interacting with a computer system designed to support learning gives an outstanding research setting. The researcher's control, in the experimental design sense, is excellent, detailed data collection is straightforward, and characteristics of individuals can be studied. Study of many aspects of learning is warranted in this setting and should contribute broadly to educational understanding. Two aspects of particular interest here are individual differences in learning styles and preferences (see Section 3.2 above), and the encouraging and supporting of learner initiative (see Section 4.4).

### 6.2. The Study of Learner–Teacher Collaboration

Development of collaborative IESs needs study of several aspects of human tutoring. Most basically it will benefit from study of how two human participants in a learning interaction make a sequence of exchanges in the search for communication. Negotiation of understanding is the theme of the chapter by Beveridge and Rimmershaw (this volume). We might expect considerable changing among conversational strands as the participants seek a basis for understanding. This can be contrasted with the interaction and detailed interpretation at a single level that the classic malrule approach is based on.

Study of communication through conversation is the study of dialogue and discourse (Carlson, 1983; Grosz, 1978). It is important for the development of good collaborative interactions with IESs, despite Wenger's (1987) argument that the study of human one-to-one tutoring may be of only limited use to IES research, because humans have so much shared context and background, and great skill in inferring meaning and intent of utterances.

We speculate that observation of many human–human learning interactions would show great variety and apparent capriciousness as the participants swap among conversational strands, and also considerable inefficiency, with misunderstandings left unresolved. We have not found in the education literature detailed analyses of teaching interactions to support this view, but we would expect to see the interaction jump about from fine detail of the task, to motivation, to strategy, to distant analogy, to planning, to demonstration, to nearly irrelevant chat. Many loose ends would be left dangling, even as overall understanding increased.

Any fragment of the interaction with a collaborative IES might therefore often resemble the interaction with some traditional tutoring system or computer application. Globally, however, the most salient feature of the interaction would be a jumping around, both among conversational strands and as to who is taking the initiative. Being able to participate in such an interaction would ideally allow an IES to prompt greater engagement by the learner, to give constructive, successful learning, and to do this despite its abilities with any single conversational strand being less than comprehensive. Taking seriously this view of learning clearly must influence strongly the nature of the learner model to be developed and the types of study of human learning that would be most informative.

## REFERENCES

Anderson, J.R., Boyle, C. F., & Reiser, B. J. (1985). Intelligent tutoring systems. *Science, 228*, 456-462.

Atkinson, R.C. (1972), Optimizing the learning of a second language vocabulary. *Journal of Experimental Psychology, 96*, 124-129.

Barr, A., & Feigenbaum, E. (Eds.). (1982). *The handbook of artificial intelligence* (Vol. 2). Los Altos, CA: Morgan Kaufmann.

Brown, J.S., & Burton, R.R. (1978) Diagnostic models for procedural bugs in basic mathematical skills. *Cognitive Science, 2*, 155-191.

Burton, R.R., & Brown, J.S. (1982). An investigation of computer coaching for informal learning activities. In D. Sleeman & J. S. Brown (Eds), *Intelligent tutoring systems* (pp. 79-98). New York: Academic Press.

Carlson, L. (1983). *Dialogue games: An approach to discourse analysis.* Boston: Reidel.

Carmichael, H., Burnett, D., Higginson, W., Moore, B., & Pollard, P. (1985). *Computers, children and classrooms: A multisite evaluation of the creative use of microcomputers by elementary school children.* Toronto, Canada: Ontario Department of Education.

Clancey, W,J. (1986). Qualitative student models. *Annual Reviews of Computer Science, 1,* 381-450.

Clancey, W.J. (1987). *Knowledge-based tutoring: The GUIDON program.* Cambridge, MA: MIT Press.

Collins, A., Brown, J.S., & Newman, S.E. (1987) . Cognitive apprenticeship: Teaching the craft of reading, writing and mathematics. In L. B. Resnick (Ed.), *Cognition and instruction: Issues and agendas.* Hillsdale, NJ: Erlbaum.

Craik, K.J.W. (1943). *The nature of explanation.* Cambridge, England: Cambridge University Press.

Cumming, G., & Abbott, E. (1988). Prolog as a medium for learning in the classroom: Assessing a board range of computer-based activities. In F. Lovis & E.D. Tagg (Eds.), *Computers in education* (pp. 317-321). Amsterdam: North-Holland.

Cumming, G., & Self, J. (1990). Intelligent educational systems: Identifying and decoupling the conversational levels. Instructional Science, *19,* 1-17.

Feurzeig, W. (1987). Algebra slaves and agents in a Logo-based mathematics curriculum. In R.W. Lawler & M. Yazdani (Eds.), *Artificial intelligence and education* (Vol. 1, pp 27-54). Norwood, NJ: Ablex Publishing.

Frederiksen, J.R., & White, B.Y. (1988, June). Intelligent learning environments for science education. *Proceedings of Conference on Intelligent Tutoring Systems-88* (pp. 250-257) Montreal.

Grosz, B.J. (1978). Discourse Knowledge. In D. E. Walker (Ed.), *Understanding spoken language. Section IV: Discourse knowledge* (pp 229-344). Amsterdam: North-Holland.

Hartley, J.R. (1973). The design and evaluation of an adaptive teaching system. *International Journal of Man-Machine Studies, 5,* 421-436.

Hartley, J.R., & Smith, M.J. (1988). Question answering and explanation giving in on-line help systems. In J. Self (Ed.), *Artificial intelligence and human learning: Intelligent computer-aided instruction* (pp 338-360). London: Chapman & Hall.

Howe, J.A.M., & du Boulay, B. (1979). Microprocessor assisted learning: Turning the clock back? *Programmed Learning and Educational Technology, 16,* 240-246.

Humphrey, N. (1986). *The inner eye.* London: Faber.

Hutchins, E.L., Hollan, J.D., & Norman, D.A. (1985). Direct manipulation interfaces. *Human-Computer Interaction, 1,* 311-338.

Kulik, J., Kulik, C., & Cohen, P. (1980). Effectiveness of computer-based college teaching: A meta-analysis of findings. *Review of Educational Research, 50,* 525-544.

Lawler, R.W., & Yazdani, M. (1987). (Eds). *Artificial intelligence and education* (Vol.1). Norwood, NJ: Ablex Publishing corp.

Norman, D.A. (1988, August). *Computer simulation of intellectual performance: The problem of disembodied intellect.* Paper presented at XXIV International Congress of Psychology, Sydney.

Papert, S. (1980). *Mindstorms: Children, computers, and powerful ideas.* New York: Basic Books.

Payne, S.J., & Squibb, H.R. (1987). *Understanding algebra errors: the psychological status of mal-rules* (Tech. Rep. No. 43). Laucaster, England: Centre for Research on Computers and Learning, University of Lancaster.

Polya, G. (1945). *How to solve it.* Princeton, NJ: Princeton University Press.

Ridgway, J. (1988). Of course ICAI is impossible . . . worse though, it might be seditious. In J. Self (Ed.), *Artificial intelligence and human learning: Intelligent computer-aided instruction* (pp 28-48). London: Chapman & Hall.

Riel, M.M., Levin, J.A., & Miller-Souviney, B. (1987). Learning with interactive media: Dynamic support for students and teachers. In R. W. Lawler & M. Yazdani (Eds.), *Artificial intelligence and education* (Vol.1, pp. 117-134). Norwood, NJ: Ablex Publishing.

Scardamalia, M., Bereiter, C., Mclean, R., Swallow, J., & Woodruff, E. (1988). *Computer supported intentional learning environments.* Toronto, Canada: Ontario Institute for Studies in Education.

Schoenfeld, A. H. (1985). *Mathematical problem solving.* New York: Academic.

Self, J. A. (1974). Student models in computer-aided instruction. *International Journal of Man-Machine Studies, 6,* 261-276.

Self, J. A. (1988). Bypassing the intractable problem of student modelling. *Proceedings of Conference on Intelligent Tutoring System-88* (pp. 18-24). Montreal.

Sleeman, D. (1984). An attempt to understand students' understanding of basic algebra. *Cognitive Science, 8,* 387-412.

Sleeman, D. (1985). AI and education: Two ideological positions. *Quarterly Newsletter of the Society for the Study of Artificial Intelligence & Simulation of Behaviour, 55-56,* 26-31

Sleeman, D. (1987). Some challenges for intelligent tutoring systems. *Proceedings of the International Joint Conference on Artificial Intelligence,* Milan.

Snow. R. E., Federico, P.A., & Montague, W.E. (Eds.). (1980). *Aptitude. learning and instruction* (Vol. 1). Hillsdale, NJ: Erlbaum.

Wenger, E. (1987). *Artificial intelligence and tutoring systems.* Los Altos, CA: Morgan Kaufmann.

Wertsch, J. V. (Ed.). (1985). *Culture, communication, and cognition: Vygotskian perspectives.* Cambridge, England: Cambridge University Press.

Winograd, T., & Flores, C. F. (1986), *Understanding computers and cognition: A new foundation for design.* Norwood, NJ: Ablex Publishing.

Woolf, B. P. (1988). Representing complex knowledge in an intelligent machine tutor. In J. Self (Ed.), *Artificial intelligence and human learning: Intelligent computer-aided instruction* (pp 3-27). London: Chapman & Hall.

# SECTION II

---

# EMPIRICAL STUDIES OF TEACHING FOR ITS DESIGN

# 5

# TUTORIAL PLANNING SCHEMAS*

## DAVID LITTMAN

## 1. INTRODUCTION: MOTIVATION AND GOALS

Intelligent tutoring systems (ITS) are enjoying increased attention from both researchers and educators because of their intrinsic interest and their potential for providing uniformly high-quality tutoring in diverse educational settings. With the increased popularity of ITS, the problems that must be solved to ensure their success in complex domains has become a focus of research (Anderson, Boyle, Farrell, & Reiser, 1984; Clancey, 1979; Littman, Pinto, & Soloway, 1987). In distinction to simple domains, where students learn relatively straightforward skills such as arithmetic operations or rules for spelling words, complex domains such as computer programming require the student to acquire a large amount of knowledge and to master a large number of skills. As an example, Soloway, Spohrer, and Littman (1987) provide a discussion of a small portion of the knowledge and skills that students must acquire in an introductory programming course.

In order to study the problems entailed by building ITSs for complex

*I would like to express my thanks to Elliot Soloway for his never-failing support of my work. As well, I would like to thank Peter Goodyear for giving me the oppportunity to present this paper at the 1988 CERCLE Workshop, in Ullswater, England, and the participants of the workshop for their constructive criticisms and many stimulating discussions. Finally, I express my sincere appreciation to the main reviewer of this chapter, whose misconceptions about both the goals and the content of the research have led me to write a better final draft.

domains, the Cognition and Programming Project of Yale University and the University of Michigan has been developing the components of an ITS for introductory programming. To date, PROUST, a diagnostic component that is able to identify the nonsyntactic bugs in Pascal programs written by students in introductory programming classes, has been built (Johnson, 1985). MARCEL, the student model component, is currently nearing completion (Spohrer, 1988). The chapter addresses a major issue that has been the focus of our work on the tutorial component of the ITS. It is the third and final major component, and the one responsible for determining what to do to help the student and how to deliver this help.

The major issue that arises for a tutor trying to help a student with a complex task, whether the tutor is human or not, is the problem of deciding how to manage a tutoring session to help a student who has made multiple errors. For example, Figure 5.1 shows Program 1, a real, typical program written by a student in an introductory Pascal programming course in response to the Rainfall Assignment (Johnson, 1985). This program contains nine errors, or bugs. When the student brings this program to a tutor, the tutor must solve three problems before it is possible to begin tutoring effectively. Each of these three tutoring problems requires the tutor to reason about each of the student's bugs:

> *Tutoring Problem 1: Whether to tutor each bug*—some bugs are critical: others are too trivial, or too hard, to tutors; others offer opportunities for determining the student's skill level.
>
> *Tutoring Problem 2: When to tutor each bug*—bugs seem to "fit more naturally" into the tutoring plan at some points than they do at other points.
>
> *Tutoring Problem 3: How to tutor each bug*—some bugs can simply be pointed out to the student; others require that the tutor build up to them.

Addressing these three problems in the case of the nine bugs in Program 1 can lead to a combinatorial explosion. Tutoring Problem 2 requires the tutor to decide what *order* to tutor the bugs in and how to *group* the bugs together according to, for example, common causes or remedies. The combinatoric difficulties arise as follows: The ordering decision presents the tutor with 9!, or 362,880 alternatives. Deciding how to group *and* order the bugs for tutoring gives rise to over 20,000,000 alternatives. Suppose further that there are four strategies potentially appropriate for each bug. Then the number of alternative combinations of orderings, groupings, and strategies reaches into the large numbers [((4 ** 9) 20,000,000) is approximately 5,200,000,000,000]. Thus, the tutor's difficulties in deciding how to tutor multiple bugs arise precisely because of the large number of alternative possible ways to organize the tutoring of multiple bugs. Clearly a human tutor does not, and a machine

```
PROGRAM  NOAH (INPUT , OUTPUT);
CONST
SENTINEL = 99999;
VAR
RAINFALL, AVERAGE, RAINDAYS, TOTALRAIN : REAL;
BEGIN
(* PROMPT FOR  AND READ IN FIRST VALUE *)
WRITELN ('PLEASE TYPE IN THE FIRST VALUE');
READLN;
READ (RAINFALL);
(* INITIALIZE THE VARIABLE *)
BUG 1: Assignment of 0 to RAINFALL Clobbers Input of RAINFALL
RAINFALL ;= 0; HIGHEST := 0;
BUG 2: Missing Initialization of RAINDAYS
(* READ IN NUMBERS UNTIL 99999 IS READ *)
(* ENTER DATA IN ONE DAY AT A TIME *)
WHILE RAINFALL <> 99999 DO
BEGIN
(* CHECK FOR HIGHEST RAINFALL *)
IF RAINFALL > HIGHEST THEN
HIGHEST := RAINFALL;
(* INCREMENT COUNT VARIABLES  DEPENDING ON RAINFALL VALUE *)
IF RAINFALL < 0 THEN
WRITELN ('ENTER ONLY POSITIVE NUMBERS')
ELSE
BUG 3: No Counter For Rainy Days -- RAINDAYS Increments Each Time
RAINDAYS :=  RAINDAYS + 1;
BUG 4: No READ(RAINFALL) In Loop
END;
BUG 5:  Update of TOTALRAIN Below Loop
BEGIN
TOTALRAIN := RAINFALL + TOTRAIN;
END;
(* COMPUTE THE AVERAGE RAINFALL *)
BUG 6: Divide By Zero Guard Missing
BEGIN
AVERAGE := TOTALRAIN/RAINDAYS;
END;
(* PRINT OUT THE RESULTS *)
WRITELN;
WRITELN('THE PROGRAM READ IN ', RAINDAYS :0:2, 'RAINY DAYS');
BUG 7:  Wrong Variable Output
WRITELN('THERE WERE   ', RAINFALL :0:2, 'RAINY DAYS IN PERIOD');
BUG 8: No Guard for Undefined Average
WRITELN('THE AVERAGE WAS ', AVERAGE :0:2, 'INCHES PER DAY');
BUG 9: No Guard for Undefined Maximum
WRITELN('THE MAXIMUM WAS ',  HIGHEST :0:2, 'INCHES');
```

Figure 5.1. Sample Buggy Rainfall Program.

tutor cannot, generate all possible alternative treatments of a student's multiple bugs and pick the ''best'' from among them. And even if a tutor *did* generate all the alternative plans, or even some subset of them, by what criteria would the tutor select one over the others?

The problem of managing multiple bugs has several possible solutions. Two of them, developed by other investigators whose work is considered briefly below, attempt to minimize the impact of multiple bugs on the tutoring process. The approach described in the chapter, on the other hand, takes the view that the issue of multiple bugs is a significant one for tutoring in complex domains and therefore treats it as a full-fledged planning problem that requires the tutor to bring a large amount of domain specific knowledge to bear on the process of developing a viable tutorial plan. The next section briefly describes the two approaches taken by other researchers to the problem of multiple bugs. In addition, a brief synopsis is presented of my initial research on this topic. This initial work has been reported elsewhere. The focus of the chapter follows this description of the current status of efforts to manage the problem of multiple bugs. The focus here is on one aspect of plan generation for multiple bugs, namely schematic knowledge that represents what tutorial plans for multiple bugs should be like.

## 2. PREVIOUS WORK ON MULTIPLE BUGS

This section briefly reviews efforts to manage multiple bugs. First, two well-known approaches to managing multiple bugs are described. The initial work I performed to identify the knowledge used by tutors when they formulate tutorial plans for managing multiple bugs is then described.

### 2.1. Other Investigators

The problem of multiple bugs can be treated with several straightforward approaches. Two approaches, that of the Anderson group and that of the BBN group, capitalize on different aspects of the domains for which they have built ITSs.

*The Anderson Group.* In the simplest approach to the problem of multiple bugs, the tutor simply prevents the student from making multiple bugs and tutors each bug immediately, as it occurs; this is the approach taken by the tutoring systems built by John Anderson and his colleagues (Anderson et al., 1984). The advantage of preventing multiple bugs is clear: The problem of deciding which bug to tutor does not even arise. The tutor's only task is to decide which strategy to use with the student. In spite of the obvious advantages of preventing multiple bugs, there are some potential disadvantages. First, it may simply be impossible to diagnose individual bugs as they are created. In complex domains, such as computer programming, it may not be possible to determine that a bug *is* a bug at the time that the student produces the buggy code. It may be possible to do so for very small programs, that is, those less than 15 lines long, but for programs as large as 40 lines, it is generally impossible. In such cases it is frequently necessary to permit the student to generate more code before it is possible to conclude that the original code is buggy. Of course, in the process of generating the additional code, the student may create more bugs, leading immediately to the problems of multiple bugs.

Second, it may actually be good for students to make several bugs and then receive tutoring on them as a group. For example, there are common patterns of bugs in students' programs (Spohrer & Soloway, 1985). It seems plausible that, in many of these bug-pattern situations, tutoring all the bugs in the patterns is better than tutoring each bug separately.

*The BBN Group.*.   A second approach to multiple bugs relies on the view that some domains have intrinsic structure that makes it possible to use a few general heuristics to order and group multiple bugs for tutoring. This is the approach taken in the WHY Socratic tutor for teaching knowledge about weather patterns, which can be viewed as consisting of causal scripts that relate, for example, temperature change (a cause) to evaporation of water (an effect) (Stevens, Collins, & Goldin, 1982). When it tutors, WHY tries to address misconceptions about general issues and prior causal events before tackling problems with more specific issues and later causal events. The advantages of these simple heuristics are clear. Unfortunately, in many complex domains, and computer programming is one, it is hard to see what would be the analogue of causal scripts. It might be proposed that programming plans constitute the components of such scripts, but the wide variety of combinations that can be made of the same plans to solve the same problem means that there is no intrinsic structure that restricts the way in which pieces in the domain go together. Thus, few complex domains can be seen as having the kind of intrinsic, script-like structure that allows a few heuristics to suffice for managing the tutorial planning problems presented by multiple bugs in the weather domain.

## 2.2. My Work

Research on tutorial planning in the domain of computer programming has shown that human tutors engage in sophisticated, knowledge-intensive planning to avoid the combinatorial solution when deciding how to tutor a student who has made multiple bugs. Previous papers have described some of the knowledge that human tutors use to generate tutorial plans in multiple bug tutoring situations. For example, this research has shown that, to generate a tutorial plan, tutors reason extensively about why the student made the bugs, which bugs are critical to tutor, which goals are desirable to achieve in tutoring the bugs, and so on. This initial work has shown that (a) tutors engage in extensive tutorial planning when confronted by multiple bugs; and (b) they bring a great deal of knowledge to bear on the tutorial planning process as they confront the three tutoring problems (Littman, Pinto, & Soloway, 1985, 1986, 1987).

In this initial work, however, the approach has been descriptive. That is, although much of the knowledge has been identified that human tutors bring to bear on the three tutoring problems, for example, which bugs are critical, no account has been given of the knowledge tutors use to generate particular tutorial plans, for example, address critical bugs *first*. In essence, several kinds of knowledge have been identified that tutors use when they address the three tutoring problems; for example, they know what bugs are critical bugs and what strategies are appropriate for tutoring particular problems, but, to date, how tutors use this knowledge in generating tutorial plans has not been characterized. The main goal of the remainder of the chapter is to begin to describe this kind of knowledge. First, a construct underlying the model of tutorial planning, namely *tutorial planning schemas* (TPS), is described. Next is a discussion of the space of these schemas. Then TP, a computer implementation of the tutorial planner, is described. Finally, some main conclusions from, implications of, and future directions for this research are presented.


## 3. KNOWLEDGE THAT GUIDES TUTORIAL PLANNING

This section focuses on three main issues that have been central concerns in the effort to develop a model of tutorial planning. First, the class of tutorial planning schemas that appear to guide tutorial planning in multiple bug situations is identified. Then, one such planning schema is considered in detail with the goal of showing how it would produce a tutorial plan for the bugs in Program 1. In describing how this plan is generated, empirical evidence is presented that tutors employ such schemas. Following this description of the input–output behavior of the tutorial planning schema, the knowledge that the schema employs to generate a tutorial plan is characterized. Thus, the bulk of this section is intended to show how tutorial planning schemas are used by tutors to address the three tutoring problems engendered by multiple bugs.

## 3.1. Schemas That Guide Tutorial Planning

Analyses of the tutorial planning behavior of human tutors have revealed that they frequently follow script-like schemas as they develop their tutorial plans for tutoring multiple bugs. These script-like schemas do not appear to be tied to particular bugs—indeed, they appear to be relatively independent of the content of the domain, for example, programming.

Tutorial planning schemas consist of ordered subgoals that a tutor must achieve to produce a viable tutorial plan. Each of the subgoals of the TPS identifies a task in the process of constructing the tutorial plan; the ordering of the subgoals constrains the order in which the tutor attempts to achieve the subgoals. As it happens, it is the nature of the subgoals of a TPS, and especially the ordering of the subgoals, that allow the planning process to avoid the potential combinatorial difficulties raised by the three tutoring problems. An extended example showing the structure and behavior of a TPS will show why.

## 3.2. A TPS Analyzed: Planning Around Hard Bugs

This section shows how a particular TPS, "Planning Around Hard Bugs," operates on the bugs in Program I to produce a tutorial plan which consists of (a) an ordering and grouping for the bugs, and (b) strategies for tutoring the bugs. Thus, this example shows how using the TPS solves the three tutoring problems. The presentation of the operation of the TPS proceeds in two main steps.

First, the ordered subgoals of Planning Around Hard Bugs are identified and motivated in the context of a human tutor formulating a plan to manage the multiple bugs in Program 1: The plan generated by the TPS is the same as the plan generated by the human tutor. Second, a subset of the subgoals is selected, and the knowledge required to solve them is identified—a complete description of the knowledge required to achieve all the subgoals can be found in Littman (1989).

*3.2.1. The Subgoal Structure Of Planning Around Hard Bugs.* Figure 5.2 shows the subgoals of Planning Around Hard Bugs, identifies the types of bugs referred to in the subgoals, and presents quotes from a tutor who used the TPS to formulate a plan for the bugs in the Program 1; these quotes are intended both to support the psychological reality of the subgoal structure of the TPS and to give a feeling for what, e.g., a *hard* bug is. For example, the first subgoal, Find Hard Bug, tells the tutor that the first task in formulating a plan for the bugs, in, e.g., Program 1, is to isolate the hard bug, a bug

---

| Subgoals of "Planning Around Hard Bugs" | Empirical Support |

---

Subgoal 1:  Find Hard Bug                                    "harder to understand ..."
                   Hard Bug: Hard to tutor                 "Bug 5, the other major bug ..."
Subgoal 2:  Find Interfering Bugs                        "... easy error to make but hard to fix "
                   Interfering Bug:                          "Bug 4 ...missing reads in loops confusing."
Subgoal 3:  Select Strategies For
                   Interfering Bugs and Hard Bugs      "I would say in English what loop is doing, "
Subgoal 4:  Find Lead-in Bugs                            "... use 3 ...gently ease into Bug 5 ..."
                   Lead-in Bug:                             "idea of using Bug 3 is to lead up to Bug 5"
Subgoal 5:  Select Strategies For Lead-In Bugs      "running through it (loop) by hand ...
                                                                        to show him the workings of a loop"
Subgoal 6:  Find Groups of Remaining Bugs          "Other bugs ... small and easy for students
..."
          Remaining Bugs:
Subgoal 7:  Order Groups of Remaining Bugs                    SEE QUOTE BELOW
Subgoal 8:  Select Strategies For Groups of          "(Student should) go rewrite the program
          Remaining Bugs                                  independently ... (he'll) fall into them."

---

Figure 5.2. Subgoals of Planning Around Hard Bugs & Evidence For Them.

---

Runtime Action 1:  Work on  Interfering Bugs     (Bug 4)
Runtime Action 2:  Work on Lead-in Bugs           (Bug 3)
Runtime Action 3:  Work on Hard Bug                (Bug 5)
Runtime Action 4:  Work on Remaining Bugs       (Bugs 1, 2, 6, 7, 8, 9)

---

Figure 5.3. Order of Run-time Actions In Planning Around Hard Bugs.

which, for reasons discussed in the next section, is hard to tutor. As the tutor's quotations, "harder to understand" and "... the other major bug," show, the concept of hard bug comprises, at least, the idea of how difficult it is for the student to understand the bug. In essence, the driving force behind Planning *Around* Hard Bugs, and the reason that it is called Planning Around Hard Bugs, is that it imposes the constraint that as many as possible of the student's bugs contribute to the tutoring of the hard bug. Thus, during *planning* the tutor first identifies the hard bug [1] and then builds the tutoring plan so that it facilitates tutoring the hard bug. The order of events in the *execution* of the tutoring plan builds up to the hard bug by tutoring other, strategically selected, bugs first, as Figure 5.3 shows [2]. The next section illustrates how the TPS operates on the bugs in the program shown in Figure 5.1 to produce a tutorial plan.

---

[1] We deal only with the case of one hard bug; Littman(1989) handles the more general case of several hard bugs.

[2] A discussion of the implementation schemas for tutoring plans can be found in Littman (1989).

### 3.2.2. *"Planning Around Hard Bugs" At Work On Program 1.* As
Figure 5.2 shows, this TPS has two distinct types of subgoals, *bug* selection subgoals (subgoals 1, 2, 4, and 6) and *strategy* selection subgoals (subgoals 3, 5, and 8). Notice that these subgoals are interweaved. The TPS constrains the selection of strategies for the bugs that are not hard by taking into account the strategy that is most appropriate for tutoring the hard bug. The quotations enclosed in parentheses are taken from Figure 5.2 and represent part of the evidence culled from the tutor's protocol for the psychological reality of the TPS. Execution of the main subgoals for Program 1 proceeds as follows:

*Subgoal 1:* Find Hard Bug—The tutor selects Bug 5, the misplaced update of TotalRain, because it is hard for the student to understand it("harder to understand").

*Subgoal 2:* Find Interfering Bugs—The tutor selects Bug 4, the missing update of the loop control variable, RAINDAYS, because it is confusing and hard to fix ("hard to fix" and "missing reads in loops confusing").

*Subgoal 3:* Select Strategies For Interfering Bugs and Hard Bugs—The tutor selects mental simulation of the loop, with the constraint that the tutor will guide the simulation to direct the student's attention ("say in English what the loop is doing").

*Subgoal 4:* Find Lead in Bugs—The tutor intends to use Bug 3, which he has interpreted as a missing guard on the counter for rainy days, as a way to ease into Bug 5, because both bugs are caused by unintended behavior of the main loop ("use 3 ... gently ease into 5").

*Subgoal 5:* Select Strategies For Lead-In Bugs—The tutor selects mental simulation because it focuses attention on the behavior of the loop ("running through loop by hand ... to show him the workings of a loop").

Finally, the tutor recognizes that there are some bugs "left over" but says that the student will stumble on them by himself. As the tutor says, "he (the student) has enough to worry about for now."

It is important to understand that the order of *identifying* bugs and strategies imposed by the subgoals of "Planning Around Hard Bugs" is not the same as the order in which those bugs are *tutored.* Figure 5.3 shows the order in which the bugs identified by "Planning Around Hard Bugs" are tutored. Notice that the hard bug is tutored *after* the interfering bugs and the lead-in bugs, though it is *identified* at planning time before the latter two types of bugs.

The tutor's main tutorial goal, as shown by the quotation in Figure 5.2 associated with the subgoal of finding the hard bug, is to tutor the misplaced update of the TotalRain variable. The tutor believes that the student thinks that the scope of a WHILE loop is defined as any consecutive sequence of BEGIN-END blocks. This is a fairly serious misconception. In the student's program, the update of TotalRain occurs only once, after the final execution of the WHILE loop. The tutor believes that it is unlikely that the student intended that TotalRain be updated only once; hence, the tutor concludes that the student has a misconception about the scope of the loop. Given that the tutor wants to tutor Bug 5, he has the problem of figuring out how to introduce Bug 5 in a smooth manner.

As the final tutorial plan shown in Figure 5.3 illustrates, the tutor has created a "tutorial path" to the hard bug. That is, rather than jumping right in and tackling the hard bug, the tutor tries to lay some groundwork by addressing other carefully chosen bugs first. First, the tutor works on Bug 4, the bug that produces an infinite loop that interferes with the student's ability to see the action of the loop. Next come two lead-in bugs, Bug 3, which serves to focus the student's attention both on the loop and on the mental simulation of the main loop, the strategy that the tutor wants to use for Bug 5, the hard bug. The tutor has selected the strategy of mental simulation for the hard bug so that he can focus the student's attention on the central aspect of the behavior of the loop, namely its scope. The hard bug is thus tutored third, after the groundwork has been laid by tutoring the interfering bug and the lead-in bug. Finally, the tutor lets the student go off to work alone, having decided that the student has plenty to work on and will probably encounter the remaining bugs, most of which are "housekeeping" bugs, as the main body of the program is corrected.

In sum, the execution of Planning Around Hard Bugs solves the three tutoring problems. Instead of being forced to search an immense space of possible plans for managing the nine bugs in Program 1, the TPS guides the tutor in deciding (a) which bugs to tutor, (b) when to tutor them and which to tutor together, and (c) how to tutor them. Obviously, the tutor that uses planning Around Hard Bugs, whether human or machine, must have a great deal of knowledge about students, programming, and bugs, to be able to execute it. The next section gives a feel for how the knowledge identified in earlier work is brought to bear by the tutor in executing Planning Around Hard Bugs.

### 3.3. How Knowledge Is Used To Achieve Subgoals of Planning Around Hard Bugs

This section identifies some of the major types of knowledge used by two subgoals of Planning Around Hard Bugs: Subgoal 1, Find Hard Bugs; and Subgoal 2, Select Strategies for Interfering Bugs.

*Subgoal 1:* Find Hard Bugs—Littman et al. (1987) identified several types of knowledge that tutors use when they formulate tutorial plans. One of the knowledge types that supports the tutorial planning of all the tutors is bug criticality. Bugs can be critical to tutor for several reasons. One chief reason is that they result from deep misconceptions. Additional reasons for a bug being critical to tutor range from being necessary preconditions for a subsequent component of the tutorial plan to providing necessary knowledge preconditions either for tutoring subsequent bugs or for correctly completing a later homework assignment.

As described above, the tutor identified Bug 5 as a hard bug because it was caused by a serious misconception about the scope of WHILE loop. It is this knowledge about causes of bugs, and especially which bugs can result from particular misconceptions, to which Planning Around Hard Bugs appealed to fulfill the first subgoal, Find Hard Bugs, and resulted in the selection of the update of TotalRain below the loop as the bug around which to construct part of the tutorial plan. Littman et al. (1987) present an extensive discussion of the complexities of bug criticality.

*Subgoal 3:* Find Interfering Bugs—This subgoal identifies Bug 4, the missing [Readln (Rainfall)] and cause of an infinite loop, as a bug that is likely to interfere with the student's ability to understand why the program behaves as it does. The selection of the tutorial strategy for Bug 4 is based on two main sources of knowledge, one that depends directly on the selection of Bug 5, the Hard bug, and one that depends on the type of Bug 4, namely, missing update of loop control variable.

The selection of the tutorial strategy for Bug 4 depends on the hard bug, because when a hard bug is selected for tutoring, the tutor identifies tutorial activities that can facilitate the tutoring of the hard bug. These activities, called *facilitating preconditions,* are associated directly with particular kinds of difficult bugs, and bug types, and represent information about what debugging skills the student should be familiar with, what the behavior of the program should be like (e.g., no infinite loops), and so on. Facilitating preconditions are part of the mechanism that places constraints on constructing parts of the tutorial plan that are intended to facilitate tutoring the hard bug. This is one of the major reasons that "Planning Around Hard Bugs" requires that the selection of the hard bug, around which the tutorial plan is to be built, is the first task in building the plan.

To select a tutorial strategy for Bug 4, the interfering bug, the tutor determines whether any facilitating preconditions can be satisfied by tutoring it. The tutor discovers that if the student were to be familiar with mental simulation of the loop, tutoring the hard bug would be facilitated. The tutor then consults a second source of knowledge, one that represents information about which tutorial strategies are optimal, acceptable, or unacceptable for tutoring particular, very common, bugs. Bug 4 is a common bug; the tutor finds that mental simulation is, in fact, an optimal strategy for helping students with bugs that cause infinite loops, and therefore chooses mental simulation of the loop as the tutorial strategy for Bug 4. In this way, the hard bug constrains the selection of the strategy for Bug 4, which in turn facilitates tutoring the hard bug.

In sum, satisfaction of the subgoals of tutorial planning schemas is knowledge intensive. Even though the subgoals can be stated quite simply in the abstract, tutors use large quantities of domain specific knowledge (e.g., which strategies are appropriate for tutoring particular bugs?) to achieve the subgoals. Indeed, this description of the knowledge applied to achieve Subgoal 1 and Subgoal 3 understates the amount of knowledge actually required to achieve them. Furthermore, the remaining subgoals in Planning Around Hard Bugs also require large amounts of domain knowledge, and Planning Around Hard Bugs is only one of several in a space of tutorial planning schemas.

## 4. THE SPACE OF TUTORIAL PLANNING SCHEMAS: A BRIEF TOUR

The current state of research on tutorial planning has not yet produced an exhaustive enumeration of all tutorial planning schemas (TPS). Nonetheless, because tutorial planning schemas appear to be important for tutorial planning, rather than refrain from addressing the topic of the space of tutorial planning schemas altogether, this section describes two additional TPSs and indicates how each would be chosen by a tutor. Additional analysis of the space of TPS and the problem of selecting an appropriate TPS is described in Littman (1989).

Tutors often help students whose programs do not have any serious bugs, such as Bug 5 in Program 1. In cases like this, tutors often use whatever bugs the student has made as a springboard to teach one of several kinds of knowledge or skill. In these circumstances the tutor constructs a tutorial plan based on an assessment of the student's current knowledge and what the student needs to know.

Two important topics of tutorial interactions between students and programming tutors are (a) the skills of debugging and program testing, and (b) the acquisition of new plans to achieve goals for which the student already knows a plan. For example, tutors often use missing guards on calculations and output variables to teach students both the importance of testing their programs and methods for generating appropriate test data. In the case of missing boundary guards, tutors try to teach the importance of considering, and developing test data for, boundary cases such as those in which the user of a program does not enter any legal values. Building a tutorial plan around these concepts and skills follows a TPS called *Using Bugs For Skill Refinement*.

A second kind of help that tutors give students whose programs do not contain serious bugs revolves around teaching students new ways to solve old problems. For example, tutors sometimes use the student's WHILE loop solution to the Rainfall Problem to teach the student how to solve the same problem with a REPEAT-UNTIL loop. Elsewhere an argument was made that teaching students alternative ways to solve the same problem greatly improves their chances for developing more generalized programming skills (Soloway et al., 1987). Tutors integrate practice with heuristics for deciding which plan is most appropriate with developing the new plan for solving the "same" problem. Tutors appear to be guided in formulating a plan for teaching students such material just as they are when the student makes hard bugs. The TPS that guides development of such a tutorial plan is called *Using Bugs For Variation Exploration*.

In brief, tutors appear to have available several different TPS to formulate a tutorial plan to help a student who has made several bugs. Some TPS focus on helping the student with particular bugs and their causes, for example, Planning Around Hard Bugs, and others focus on *using* the student's somewhat innocuous bugs to improve the student's knowledge and skills, as do the two described in this section. The important issues of the nature of the rules for selecting appropriate TPS, and the form of rules for implementing them, are a focus of current research on tutorial planning.

## 5. IMPLEMENTATION

This section briefly describes TP, the program that produces tutorial plans in multiple bug situations. A more detailed description of TP is given in Littman (1989).

TP is written in Coral Common Lisp running on a MAC II and currently consists of approximately .5 megabyte of source code. Figure 5.4 gives a high-level view of the architecture of TP. The figure shows the three primary components of TP. Each component is indicated by the underlined words along the left side of the figure.

- *INPUT:* The input to TP consists of two subcomponents: (a) a list of descriptions of the student's bugs, and (b) TP's knowledge base, which contains knowledge about students, the domain (of programming), bugs, and teaching. The knowledge about teaching is represented primarily as rules for constructing tutorial plans, as the figure suggests.
- *PROCESSING:* TP's processing is controlled by a rule applier which executes the rules stored in the knowledge base that are appropriate

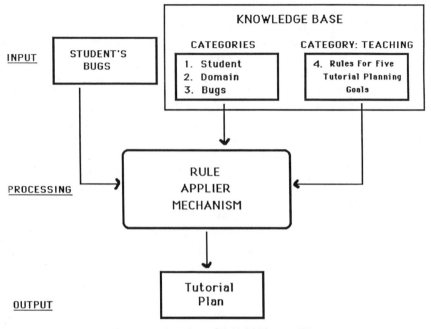

Figure 5.4. Overview of Tutorial Planner, TP.

for each tutorial planning subgoal. A separate set of rules is responsible for achieving each of the subgoals of a tutorial planning schema.

- *OUTPUT:* TP's output is the tutorial plan for multiple bugs. The
  tutorial plan specifies groups of bugs, how much attention to give to
  each bug, the order in which to tutor bugs, the objectives to be
  achieved in the tutoring session, and the strategies to be used to
  achieve the objectives.

During tutorial planning, a straightforward goal queue control mechanism
controls the attempt to achieve each tutorial planning goal. Separate groups
of rules represent the knowledge required to achieve each tutorial planning
subgoal. The rules consult declarative knowledge about the student, bugs,
tutorial objectives, and tutorial strategies as they attempt to achieve their
corresponding subgoals.

The achievement of subgoals produces side effects. Some of the side effects
generate constraints that are used in the processing of subsequent subgoals,
for example, constraints on strategy selection for interfering bugs. Other side
effects add tutorial goals to the tutorial plan.

The output of TP is the tutorial plan in which the bugs are grouped and
ordered, and strategies are identified for each bug. The tutorial plan is then

passed on to a tutorial plan executor. The plan executor is responsible for carrying out the tutorial plan, detecting run-time failures, and recovering from failures. The plan executor is discussed in Littman (1989).

In short, TP uses a straightforward rule-based goal queue architecture to build a tutorial plan for multiple bugs. The tutorial plan specifies the actions to be taken by the tutorial plan executor. The tutorial plan is passed to the plan executor which uses the tutorial plan to direct the tutoring session.

## 6. CONCLUSIONS, IMPLICATIONS, AND FUTURE DIRECTIONS

In conclusion, this chapter has described efforts to construct a process model of human tutorial planning in complex domains. The main focus was on planning in the domain of novice programming, and it was demonstrated that, even for relatively straightforward programs, the problem of multiple bugs presents significant challenges to a tutorial planner. The analyses of the planning activities of human tutors confronted with multi-bug, novice computer programs has led to the identification and description of abstract schemas that appear to guide the tutorial planning process. These planning schemas, which are named tutorial planning schemas, provide a potentially powerful mechanism by which tutorial planners can avoid the combinatoric impossibilities of exhaustively searching the space of tutorial plans for multiple bugs and then selecting the "best" plan. The potential for using TPS in ITSs is demonstrated by TP, the program which uses TPS to produce tutorial plans in multiple bug situations.

There are many implications of the current work. One important issue is the mutual dependence of domain-*specific* knowledge and domain-*general* knowledge in constructing tutorial plans. The main implication of this work for the issue of domain specificity in tutorial planning appears to be that effective tutorial planning in complex domains requires the carefully managed integration of knowledge about the domain with knowledge about abstract planning principles of the type that TPS embody. The current work suggests that the hopes of developing a purely abstract tutorial planner, or conversely the hope of devising a tutorial planner that has no knowledge of abstract planning principles, are both unlikely to be met in practice. Once a "certain level" of complexity is reached, and there is not yet at least upper-bound on that level of complexity, tutorial planners will have to use both domain specific and domain-general knowledge to generate tutorial plans that mirror the performance of good human tutors.

In the future, this work on tutorial planning will be developed in three directions. First, the tutorial planner itself must be strengthened with respect to the number of abstract planning schemas it knows about, the knowledge it has about the programming domain, and the manner in which it brings both kinds of knowledge to bear on tutorial planning tasks. Second, the tutorial planner will be integrated with a bug finder, such as PROUST, a student modeler, such as MARCEL (Spohrer, 1988), and a tutorial manager, which can execute and monitor the tutorial plans generated by the planner. This integration will produce a working ITS for the programming domain which can be used both to teach students and to perform research on good and bad tutoring strategies. Thus, when such a working ITS has been built, it can be extensively tested with students to identify and build on its strengths and to eliminate its weaknesses.

Third, and finally, because the interaction of domain-specific knowledge with domain-general knowledge appears to be such a key issue in building ITSs for complex domains, tutorial planning in other domains, such as proof construction in geometry, should be explored to develop a more articulate model of the interaction of domain-general and domain-specific knowledge in one-on-one tutoring in complex domains.

## REFERENCES

Anderson, J., Boyle, C., Farrell, R., & Reiser, B. (1984). *Cognitive principles in the design of computer tutors* (Tech. Rep.). Pittsburgh, PA: Advanced Computer Tutoring Project, Carnegie-Mellon University.

Clancey, W. (1979) Tutoring rules for guiding a case method dialogue. *International Journal of Man-Machine Studies, 11,* 25-49.

Johnson L. (1985) *Intention-based diagnosis of errors in novice programs.* Unpublished doctoral dissertation, Department of Computer Science, Yale University, New Haven, CT.

Littman, D., Pinto, J., & Soloway, E. (1985) Observations on tutorial expertise. In *Proceedings of IEEE Conference on Expert Systems In Government.* Washington, DC: IEEE.

Littman, D., Pinto, J., & Soloway, E. (1986) An analysis of tutorial reasoning about programming bugs. In *Proceedings of 1986 National Conference on Artificial Intelligence* (AAA186). Philadelphia, PA: AAAI.

Littman, D., Pinto, J., & Soloway, E. (1987, May) *The knowledge required for tutorial planning: An empirical analysis.* Paper presented at Third Annual Conference of Artificial Intelligence and Education. Pittsburgh, PA.

Littman, D. (1989). *Tutorial planning in complex Domanis.* Unpublished doctoral dissertation, Department of Computer Science, Yale University, New Haven, CT.

Soloway, E., Spohrer, J., & Littman, D. (1987) *E Unum Pluribus: Learning to generate alternative designs* (Tech. Rep. No. 564). New Haven, CT: Department of Computer Science, Yale University.

Spohrer, J. (1988). *A cognitive model of novice program generation.* Unpublished doctoral dissertation, Department of Computer Science, Yale University, New Haven, CT.

Spohrer, J., & Soloway, E. (1985). Putting it all together is hard for novice programmers. *Proceedings of IEEE International Conference on Systems, Man, & Cybernetics.* Tucson, AZ: IEEE.

Stevens, A., Collins, A., & Goldin, S. (1982). Misconceptions in students' understanding. In D. Sleeman & J. Brown (Eds.), *Intelligent tutoring systems.* New York: Academic Press.

# 6

## TUTORING AS INTERACTION: DETECTING AND REPAIRING TUTORING FAILURES*

### SARAH A. DOUGLAS

Any of the systems and contingencies implicated in the production and reception of talk—articulatory, memory, sequential, syntactic, auditory, ambient noise, etc.—can fail. Aspects of the production and analysis of talk that are rule-governed can fail to integrate. In short, the exchange of talk is indigenously and exogenously vulnerable to trouble that can arise at any time.

—E. Schegloff
(From "The relevance of repair to syntax-for-conversation." In T. Givon (Ed.), *Syntax and Semantics,* 1979)

## 1. INTRODUCTION

Much intelligent tutoring system research has been devoted to understanding and modeling the learner's knowledge acquisition process. Typically, this involves the implicit theory, which we might call the *knowledge transfer* theory, that knowledge is a commodity transferred to the student by some behavior of the tutor, including language production. The tutor "infers" the acqui-

*This research is funded by FIPSE grant #84.116C from the U.S. Department of Education. I am indebted to Russell Tomlin, David Novick, Susan Olivier, and Sharon Collins for many hours of videotape analysis, computational modeling, discussion and insights of interpretation.

123

sition of that knowledge by observing the student's performance. If the student's performance does not confirm proper knowledge, then the student is seen to have a "misconception" due to either interference from prior knowledge or a failure to properly acquire the transferred knowledge, e.g. inattention. Designing the interface requires eliminating error by anticipating all possible error situations, including faulty design of the curriculum presentation, and all possible misconceptions on the part of the student. The knowledge transfer theory concentrates on evolving to perfection the design of an ITS product through analysis of the knowledge base itself.

This chapter explores an alternative theory of tutoring, what Wenger (1987) calls *knowledge communication*. If we take the notion of communication seriously, we commit to the concept of *interaction*. Interaction involves at least two agents and focuses more on the process than the product. I will assert and demonstrate empirically in this article that the process of human–human communication commonly fails during tutoring. Following common practice, failures are classified into either performance failures called *slips*, or reasoning failures called *bugs*. Bugs can be further classified into either *insufficient planning* failures or *inherent knowledge model* failures. I hypothesize that insufficient planning failures are caused by the demands of complex concurrency of planning, execution, and execution monitoring. Model failures exist because we must constantly assume and infer the knowledge of another interacting agent. Since failure is common, human communication has evolved highly sophisticated and robust techniques for the detection and repair of failure rather than its elimination. I will examine in detail how tutors and students cope with communication failure and how it specifically affects the control and content of tutoring.

These ideas apply to all systems composed of knowledge-based agents, including human–computer tutoring systems. Knowledge and knowledge communication are inextricably intertwined. In a knowledge communication theory, agents don't simply transfer knowledge. Instead, they provide each other with communication elements (i.e., language) which represent problematic issues of otherwise transparent activity occurring in a physical and social context (Suchman, 1987). If we overlook the process of communication failure and repair in an ITS, we may find ourselves trying to solve the impossible problem of anticipating and programming all possible situations of knowledge misunderstanding. Embracing the ideas presented in this chapter relieves us of the burden of perfecting our teaching by perfecting an omniscient knowledge representation that always has a complete and consistent student model. In its place we can concentrate our efforts on detecting and repairing trouble as indicated in the *form* of communication. Concentrating on the form gives us hints about what is misunderstood and how.

## 2. THE DOMAIN STUDIED

Since 1985 Russell Tomlin in the Linguistics Department and I at the University of Oregon have been studying the possible computer simulation of teaching beginning oral communication skills for second (natural) languages. Oral communication skills—the abilities to comprehend and produce oral discourse—are crucial in nearly every educational, business, and scientific setting of language use. Yet how oral communication skills develop remains a difficult theoretical and practical problem, and traditional language teaching approaches regularly fail to help many learners.

From the point of view of language teaching theory our project draws on two important and innovative approaches to second language learning and teaching: the *communicative* and the *comprehension* approaches. Proponents of the communicative approach argue that successful language learning occurs when the student is provided the opportunity to solve nonlanguage problems using the developing second language (Widdowson, 1978; Krashen & Terrell, 1983). They criticize traditional language teaching for focusing too much effort on the conscious discussion and manipulation of rules of language usage, and not enough effort on the acquisition of the second language through efforts to use that grammar to solve actual communication problems. This philosophy integrates well with the general spirit of ITS inherited from Newell and Simon's (1972) approach to intelligence, artificial or natural, as a problem-solving process.

Proponents of the comprehension approach argue that second language learning is enhanced when beginning stages of language learning are devoted to developing the ability to understand the second language. Obligatory oral production is delayed until the student is able to understand easily utterances in the second language. In contrast, standard language instruction mixes two complex, asymmetric cognitive activities, comprehension and production, in two different modalities, sound and sight. This places tremendous cognitive load and consequently stress on the beginning language learner. Allowing the student to develop competency in only one area, oral comprehension, later accelerates student performance when oral production, reading, and writing are introduced (Asher, 1969; Postovsky, 1977, 1979; Winitz, 1981; Winitz & Reeds, 1973).

Our project embraces both of these complementary approaches to language learning and teaching. The instructional system we have created involves the student in solving communicative problems interactively with the system. The student participates in problem-solving simulations which allow manipulation of objects in a physical scenario or microworld. Information about the problem to be solved as well as information about the microworld is given in the second language. Metalevel commentary by the tutor is also in the second language. The teaching intervention in these simulations can vary from highly directed to coaching to purely student-controlled exploration.

## 3. PROTOCOL STUDIES

In order to understand more fully the teaching task that we were modelling, we conducted a series of empirical studies of human tutor–student interactions using the communicative/comprehension approach. Our motivation in studying how human tutors worked with human students was to answer questions which are fundamental to the process of designing an ITS.

1. What does the tutor teach, e.g., the curriculum?
2. What kinds of problems does the tutor generate?
3. How does the tutor diagnose student misconceptions?
4. How does the tutor remediate misconceptions?
5. What is the control strategy of the tutor?

The major difficulty that we faced was that the tutoring approach, namely spontaneous natural language within a loosely structured problem-solving task, explicitly discourages the tutor from extensive curriculum construction and rote-like teaching and speaking. The goal is for the tutor to produce "natural" language appropriate to the situation. This does not imply that tutors had no global goals or loose agenda of issues. This they seemed to have. However, they lacked a text, syllabus , or prior experience with the tutoring task. They were encouraged to spontaneously organize the teaching task as they saw fit. We saw variances in the global organization of teaching which varied by overall teaching experience, experience in teaching just this task, and student performance.

### 3.1. Procedure

The tutoring situation we studied, which we call *Flatland,* involved a mainly tutor-directed set of identification and movement tasks intended to teach the linguistic function of referring to objects in a physical context. During a tutoring session the tutor and student sat facing each other across a small table. The tutor had eight cardboard objects, each varying by shape (square or circle), color (red or blue), and size (large or small). In keeping with the spontaneous, situated method of the communicative approach, the tutor was given only very general goals for the teaching session: Teach the student how to identify these objects by shape, color, size, or spatial relation (above, below, left of, right of, between). A typical task might be "This is the small blue square. Show me, which one is the large blue square?'' (identification by a deictic, or pointing task) or ''Pick up the small red circle and put it to the left of the large blue circle.'' (identification by change-of-state task).

Seven videotaped protocols were taken of two different tutors who work at the American English Institute at the University of Oregon. One tutor is highly experienced and is considered one of the foremost world experts in this particular teaching method. The other tutor had 6 months of experience using this technique. They were both native English speakers, and the language to be taught was English. Recording of the more experienced tutor's work produced five protocols, while that of the novice tutor produced two. The students were primarily of either Oriental or Arabic first-language origin and were enrolled in a beginning course of study at the Institute. They knew virtually no English and had no prior familiarity with this problem domain.

## 3.2. Macro analysis

After collecting the protocols, we were faced with the problem of how to analyze the data in order to answer our major questions. We needed a classification system of constituent types for codifying the events. Lacking any other system, we decided to analyze the rhetorical organization of the teaching discourse. There is quite a bit of precedent for this approach, as it attempts to capture the notion of speaker intention through a set of linguistic acts. Sinclair and Coulthard (1972) studied language in the classroom and proposed a hierarchical categorization of discourse units organized by level of abstraction. The highest level is the *lesson,* followed by *transaction, exchange, move,* and *act.* The act corresponds most closely to the syntactic clause. Their model proposes 21 act types which can be variously combined into five move types according to specified rules. Exchanges are then comprised of moves, also according to specified structures. The model derived is thus a structural context-free form of classroom discourse.

Two applications of the Sinclair-Coulthard model described in the literature, Burton (1981) and Coombs and Alty (1985), take the basic Sinclair-Coulthard model and apply it to other domains. Burton looked at casual conversations. Coombs and Alty looked at conversations between computer center advisors and computer users. Both of these applications alter the original model to account for different observations in the particular domain studied by adding or subtracting types at the levels.

In addition to the work by Sinclair and Coulthard a similar attempt was made by Grimes (1975) to categorize rhetorical predicates. McKeown (1985) modeled these directly in a program for computer generation of natural language in response to database queries. Neither the categorization by Grimes nor that adopted and slightly modified by McKeown will suffice for the tasks which we are modeling. This is primarily because the classification does not include actions in the world such as a directive to the hearer ("Now take the small blue circle and put it on the right of the large red square."), but are limited to descriptive language. The difficulty is not simply adding more rhetorical predicates, but adding a complementary set of rhetorical actions.

Other computer implementations of discourse generation (Reichman, 1985; Woolf & McDonald, 1984) adopt similar categorizations of constituents and use grammars implemented as transition nets to model the rules relating constituents. The work by Woolf and McDonald (1984) is particularly interesting in that it attempts to manage the discourse of an ITS for Pascal programming. The rhetorical organization is hierarchical consisting of three levels: pedagogic, strategic, and tactical. Each level successively refines the actions of the tutor. Later work by Woolf and Murray (1987) uses a transition network of predicates which describe the state of the tutoring discourse, such as "pose problem" or "teach by example," and conversational actions which the tutor can take to change the state of the discourse situation.

All of the above models propose a structure for discourse that is largely independent of the pragmatics of the particular context. Thus, the history of the discourse, the student (hearer) model, and the tutor's (speaker's) intentions are informally implied. The models are able to define a set of rules that determines well-formedness, i.e., *whether* a particular sequence of acts will occur, but are unable to explain *why* a particular sequence of rhetorical acts occurs at a particular time in the discourse. This makes them very difficult to apply to other domains where new descriptive categories might occur, as well as leaving the analyst unsure how to apply the categorization.

Given these dissatisfactions, we chose to develop our own approach to analysis. Our major motivation was to link the rhetorical organization of the discourse to the details of the usual components of an ITS system, its data structures (tutoring goals, curriculum, and student model), and processes (problem generation, diagnosis, and remediation). From a methodological perspective, this analysis is completely post hoc and interpretive. It does not test whether these mental states and processes actually exist in these tutors.

We decided on a hierarchical classification with the lesson as the basic context, followed by the exercise, and terminating with the episode. (See Table 6.1.) The lesson is organized around the teaching goals and curriculum. Each lesson is broken down into a number of exercises which are the structuring of the curriculum by topic. In the case of our domain, this can be represented by a partially ordered graph in which the first exercise is the identification of object(s) by either color, size, or shape as individual attributes; then the identification of object(s) by composite attributes; and finally the identification/movement of an object by its location relative to another object. (See Table 6.2.) This ordering follows the syntactic complexity

**Table 6.1. Protocol Analysis Classification.**

Lesson
    Exercise (by curricular topic)
        Episode
            Introduction
                Introduce topic
            Closure
                Close topic
            Testing/Diagnosis
                Problem generation
                Affirmation demonstration
            Demonstration
            Repairs
                Descriptive referral
                Repetition
                Physical demonstration
                Opportunistic remediation
                Meta-Level Comments
            Emotional Reinforcement
                Acknowledge
            Reassurance
                Reassure

of direct reference in the utterances: noun ("the square") > noun with adjective modifier ("the red square") > noun with phrase modifier ("the red square to the left of the small blue square"). It also follows the semantic complexity: entity > attribute > 2 entity relation > 3 entity relation.

The third level comprises the episodes of the tutor's discourse. These episodes are grouped into eight general classes, including repair episodes, which we will examine in more detail later in this paper. Each episode was defined by a set of criteria, a classification rule, used later to identify episodes in the protocol. The criteria always specify the intentions (usually teaching

**Table 6.2. Overall Tutoring Organization Showing Partial Order of Exercise Introduction (Frequency counts for 7 protocols).**

|  |  | Attributes | | | Spatial Relations | | |
|---|---|---|---|---|---|---|---|
|  |  | shape | color | size | vertical | horizontal | medial |
| Order Introduced | 1st | *4* | 2 | 1 |  |  |  |
|  | 2nd | 2 | *4* | 1 |  |  |  |
|  | 3rd | 1 | 1 | *5* |  |  |  |
|  | 4th |  |  |  | *5* | 2 |  |
|  | 5th |  |  |  | 2 | *5* |  |
|  | 6th |  |  |  |  |  | *6* |

*Note:* Bold italics highlights the most frequent.

goals) of the tutor, the assumed state of the student's knowledge, the context and focus of previous discourse, the context of the physical environment, and the expected effect on the student, For example, the episode type *problem generation,* requires that (a) teaching goals are to teach the concept and it is legal in the partial ordering of the curriculum,(b) the tutor does not know whether the student knows the concept,(c) discourse context is appropriate (i.e., can't generate a new problem if in the middle of a repair), (d) object configurations are legal, and (e) the expected result is for the student to take an action.

After all seven protocols were broken down into both exercises and episodes, we did several things. First, we analyzed the frequency and amount of time for each type of episode. We did this for each protocol, each tutor, and overall. Second, for each protocol, tutor, and overall, we analyzed the transitions between episodes. Our inspiration was the Problem Behavior Graph of Newell and Simon (Newell & Simon, 1972; Ericsson & Simon, 1984) and the work in transition networks for discourse management by Woolf et al. (1984, 1987). This allowed us to get some sense of overall control and a stylistic comparison between tutors and individual student sessions. It also provided an analysis of the overall percentage of effort. Table 6.3 illustrates a transition matrix for all protocols. As an example of the qualitative analysis possible, the reader can observe that problem generations are very frequently followed by repetitions of the problem. The analyst can hypothesize that the tutor seemed to get feedback from the student that the initial problem statement was not fully understood, thus necessitating its repetition. Repetition is a common linguistic device when feedback is conveyed by hesitation in performing the task, a quizzical look, and so on.

### 3.3. Microanalysis

Finally, we selected a number of episodes for more detailed analysis. Examples of each of the episode types were chosen, as well as all of the episodes of tutor failure and repair. The selected episodes were modeled as a production system in order to find consistent justifications for the interpretations we were making about tutor and student behaviors. Since we as observers can only infer the mental states of others, formalization offers a verification of our inferences.

This detailed analysis involved the coding of the verbal actions (lexical as well as phonological aspects) of both tutor and student, nonverbal actions (pauses, gaze, and gestures), and mental states. The grammar for coding the transcript is shown in Table 6.4. Each episode classification rule (see Section 3.2 above) was formalized as a set of production rules that modeled the goals

Table 6.3. Overall Tutoring Organization Showing Episode Transitions (Frequency counts for 7 protocols).

| Episode Type | Intro | Close | Pg | AD | Dem | DR | Rep | RD | OT | Met | Ack | Res |
|---|---|---|---|---|---|---|---|---|---|---|---|---|
| Introduction | | | | | | | | | | | | |
| Introduce topic (Intro) | | | 5 | | 3 | 16 | | | | | | |
| Closure | | | | | | | | | | | | |
| Close topic (Close) | 2 | | 17 | | 4 | | | 1 | | | | |
| Testing/Diagnosis | | | | | | | | | | | | |
| Problem generation (PG) | 4 | 17 | | | 3 | 3 | 123 | 2 | 4 | 40 | 1 | 1 |
| Affirmation demonstration (AD) | | | | | | | 8 | | | 6 | | |
| Teach by Demonstration (Dem) | 2 | 3 | 18 | 1 | | | 1 | 1 | | 16 | | |
| Repairs | | | | | | | | | | | | |
| Descriptive referral (DR) | | | 5 | 1 | | | | 1 | | | | |
| Repetition (Rep) | 2 | | 97 | 6 | 6 | | | 5 | 6 | 4 | 1 | 4 |
| Physical demonstration (RD) | | | 2 | | 2 | 3 | | | | 1 | | |
| Opportunistic teaching (OT) | | | 6 | | | | 3 | | | | | |
| Metalevel Comments (Met) | | 1 | 26 | 4 | 15 | 2 | 1 | | | 1 | | |
| Emotional Reinforcement | | | | | | | | | | | | |
| Acknowledge (Ack) | 3 | | 6 | | | | | | | | | |
| Reassurance | | | | | | | | | | | | |
| Reassure (Res) | | 1 | 4 | | | | 1 | 1 | | | | |

*Note:* Similar tables were computed for each protocol and totaled by each tutor. This allows a stylistic comparison between tutors and individual student sessions, as well as an analysis of overall percentage of effort.

of the teacher, the student model, the current physical context, and expected results. The curriculum was represented as a partial order and determined the choice of teaching goals. (See Table 6.2.) Context gives the object configuration on the table as the state of the world. This factor circumscribes, to a certain extent, the moves available to the tutor. The student model was essentially a differential model, representing only the state of the student's comprehension of curriculum concepts within the context of the lesson. Fairly simple rules can be associated with building up this student model, for example:

R1: (S requested to perform task) & (S Performs task correctly) →
    (S knows (action AND referents))
R2: (S requested to perform task)& (S performs task incorrectly) →
    (S ~ know aspect in which S performed incorrectly)

**Table 6.4.  Microanalysis Coding Grammar.**

```
<illocutionary-act> :: =          <request-act>  |  <assert-act>  |
                                  <change-of-state-act>  |  <deictic-ref>
<request-act> :: = request(Actor, <illocutionary-act>)
<assert-act> :: = assert(Actor, <value> (<illocutionary-act>  |
                                  <state>))
<change-of-state-act> :: = know(Actor, <illocutionary-act>  |
                                  <state>) |
                           take(Actor, <state>) |
                           put(Actor, <state>)|
                           has(Actor, <state>)
<deictic-ref> :: = physically-refer-to(Actor, <state>)
<state> :: = prop(<referent>,property) |
             spacial-rel(<relation>, <referent>)
<referent> :: = name(Obj) | descriptor(Obj) | deictic-ref(Obj) |
             anaphora(Obj)
<value> :: = True | False | Ambiguous | Unknown
<relation> :: = Above | Below | Right-of | Left-of | Between | Under
<meta-act> :: = demarcate-focus-boundary(Actor) |
             reassure(Actor,Hearer)
```

*Note:*  In the grammar constants are denoted with upper-case names, e.g., Actor. Terminals are not shown since they are essentially all the lexicon of words and actions used in the protocols. Object configurations are from the student's perspective.

R3: (S identifies A) & (A orthogonal[1] to B) →
       (S knows (A&B))
R4: (S requested to perform task) & (S ~ performs task)→
       (S ~ know (action OR referents))

Readers interested in more of the technical issues concerning the coding, theoretical assumptions about mental states such as intentions, and the computer modeling, can consult Novick (1988).

For example, suppose we wish to explain the following discourse:

Tutor: "Now, take the small red circle"
            <pause>
Student: <takes the card and moves it to the side of the table>
Tutor: "and put that below the large red circle."
Student:       <hesitates>
Tutor: "Below the large red circle."
Student: <pushes the small red circle to below the large red circle>

This segment consists of three episodes denoted by the three separate acts of the tutor with corresponding nonverbal responses by the student. The

---

[1]*Orthogonal* here means the opposite value of a concept, i.e., large vs. small.

tutor's first two acts are diagnostic, and the third is a repetition of the previous referent phrase. What is immediately apparent is that the episodes must be coded at a level below the sentence and clause, usually at the phrase or even single lexical item level. A second observation is that many of the interaction cues are nonverbal—consisting of hesitations, intonations, physical actions, etc. Frequently, we observed that tutors broke the sentences into diagnostic units such as the above so that the complexity of identifying where the misconception occurs is reduced. Tutors observed all student actions intently *during their performance* to ascertain if trouble was imminent. The coding of the first utterance from the example above is shown in Figure 6.1. As can observed, this coding is quite tedious.

## 4. TYPES OF TUTORING FAILURE AND REPAIR

Approximately 40% of all episodes in these protocols are tutor repairs. (See Table 6.3.) Tutors spend about 30% of their time repairing their failures. However, there are some failures which are never detected. We counted at least 10 episodes of tutor failure which the tutors failed to repair. Expert and novice tutors made about the same number of failures, but the expert was markedly better at detecting and repairing them.

These failures are not unusual in human behavior. Card, Moran, and Newell (1983), in their study of expert human text editing, concluded that, though error behavior is far from infrequent or inconsequential, in experts the detection and correction of errors is mostly routine. They observed errors in 36% of the tasks under study and found that errors doubled the time to perform the tasks in which they occurred.

The types of failure that we compiled fall nicely into two categories, slips and bugs. The term *slip* comes from the compendium of data on verbal "slips of the tongue" phenomena, but was extended by Norman (1981) to include nonlinguistic failures. A slip is defined by Norman (1981, p.1) as "a form of human error defined to be the performance of an action that was not what was intended." *Bugs* are the remaining failures, which result from failure in formation of intention. Inappropriate goal determination, faulty knowledge, and inability to recognize context shift fall into this category (Brown & Burton, 1978).

### 4.1. Slips

Slips are performance as opposed to planning failures and were relatively infrequent (10% of the total). For example, tutors sometimes cannot remember what they just said. This is often a particular word or concept:

Utterance: "Now, take the small red circle" <pause>

Initial Context:

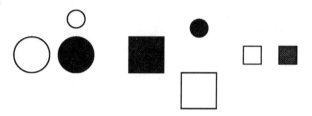

(In focus: small blue circle and large red circle from the previous utterance)

Curriculum: Teach(spatial-rel(Below))
Goal:  know(T,know(St,spatial-rel(Below,descr(SRC),descr(LRC))))
    OR know(T,~know(St,spatial-rel(Below,descr(SRC),descr(LRC))))
Subgoal pursued:  know(T,know(St,prop(descr(SRC), Small Red Circle)))
    OR know(T,~know(St,prop(descr(SRC), Small Red Circle)))

Tutor's Illocutionary Act:  request(T,take(St,prop(descr(SRC), Small Red Circle)))

Student Model:  know(T,know(St,prop(descr(SRC), Small Red Circle)))
    (assumed for this example having been confirmed earlier)

Tutor's Intended (Perlocutionary) Effect:  take(St,prop(descr(SRC), Small Red Circle))

Episode Class: DIAGNOSIS                    (Student Model & Curriculum & Goals)
Subclass: PROBLEM GENERATION        (Intended Perlocutionary Effect)

Apply rule R1:  (St requested to perform task) & (St performs task correctly) Æ (St knows (action AND referents))

State of Student Model after rule application:  know(T,know(St,prop(descr(SRC), Small Red Circle)))  AND know(T,know(St,take(St,<state>)))

*Note:* Black objects are "red"; white are "blue". C is Circle, S is Square, L is Large, S is Small, B is Blue, R is Red; T is Tutor, St is Student.

Figure 6.1. Coded microanalysis example.

"and put it between . . .did I say 'between'? "Given the apparent simplicity of the language generation, why do slips occur in these protocols?

Another cause of slips is the conflict in tutors between their normal use of the language and the restricted subset they must use in a lesson. It is very difficult to restrict performance of routinized behavior. It requires a great deal of consistency in word choice which in fluent discourse would rarely be demanded. For example, tutors frequently taught *above* as a relation and then later used *over*. Either word choice, used alone, would have been reasonable, but when the words were used together, the students became confused and the tutors had a hard time understanding this.

Language also has mechanisms which establish a context of referential objects; these objects may have priority over the immediate utterance. Thus we observed a tutor establish a focus of attention on an object and then refer to it with an obviously incorrect noun phrase. Since the student responded to what had to be meant (!) rather than what was said, the tutor never noticed the discrepancy between what was said and what the student did.

## 4.2. Bugs

Most failure in the protocols was classifiable as bugs. Out of 215 tutor failures classified (including 10 not repaired), 90% were bugs. For our tutors, bugs constitute failures to diagnose properly a student's knowledge, selection of inappropriate teaching strategy, misjudgement about the difficulty of the curriculum and its sequencing, and often a failure to coordinate what is said (as an intention of what is to be taught) with what is in the context.

Examples of these tutoring bugs abound. Tutors constructed tasks and failed to notice that the context was inappropriate until they had already uttered it. We call these *insufficient planning* bugs. They were the most frequent tutor failure we observed (approximately 80% of the bugs). For example, one tutor said "Point to the square" when there were two on the table and "Take the circle "when there was no circle. The novice tutor didn't anticipate the complexity of diagnosing a student misconception in a simple movement task and presented it before confirming the student's knowledge of the component elements. A major cause is the difficulty of the task. Language tutors have limited time for planning and revision. They must concurrently attend to the response of the student while creating the next tutoring action. At any moment, depending on the behavior of the student, they may have to alter their plan mid-course. We discovered many monitoring strategies that tutors use to detect quickly trouble in the student's understanding of what has been said. Thus the complex interleaving of plan formation, plan execution, and online monitoring creates *insufficient planning* bugs.

Although the above bugs reflect difficult failures, the most pernicious bug is *model failure,* where assumptions about states of knowledge are wrong. For example, imagine a situation where there are congruent states of knowledge:

T = Tutor; S = Student

(1)    T believes that p;
(2a)  T believes that S believes that p;
(3a)  S believes that p;

(4a)  S believes that T believes that p.

However, it might be the case that the states of knowledge are incongruent:

(3b replaces 3a)  S believes that q;
(4b replaces 4a)  S believes that T believes that q.

It is the tutor's task to detect and repair or bring about a congruent state of knowledge again:

(2b replaces 2a)  T believes that S believes that q;
(5 added)         T believes that S believes that T believes that q.

It is sometimes the case that both p and q can be right, caused by the ambiguity of the situation or the language. For example, tutors often did not anticipate the ambiguity of point of view in spatial relations, i.e, "on the left" as *your* left versus *my* left. In normal conversations this occurs regularly. Both people can be talking about two different things and yet appear to be talking about the same thing. How then can the tutor diagnose this failure? I will return to this topic again when I discuss the problem of detection and repair of failure in detail.

## 4.3. An Extended Example

In order to understand more fully some of the issues in tutor failure and repair, an extended example, shown in Figures 6.2–6.5, will be used. The detailed coding has been omitted for sake of readability. This example is taken from the expert tutor working with a Japanese learner. (As is often the case with this teaching approach, the tutor does not speak the student's native language.) The tutor and student had been working together for approximately 1.5 minutes. The tutor has decided that the student can discriminate deictically (e.g., by pointing to) the individual objects by color, shape, and size and a combination of features in response to requests like "Show me the small blue square." She now wants to test knowledge of spatial relations by a movement task.

This protocol segment has been divided into four exercises. In Exercise #1 the tutor starts by testing the student to verify that the referent "small blue square" is known (lines 1–5). Then the student performs a very confusing (to the tutor) series of actions in response to the tutor's request to put one object "under" (lines 6–17) another. All of these actions occur very quickly, and the tutor comes to the conclusion that the student might understand the word *below* better than *under*. This motivates Exercise #2 in which the tutor

01:34 [Tutor places the objects in this configuration.]

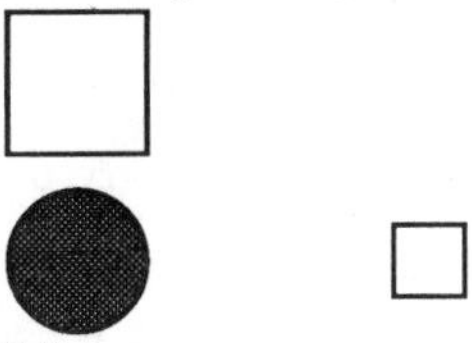

1)      TUTOR: "Show me the SBS."
2)      STUDENT: [quizzical look]
3)      TUTOR: "Show me the SBS."
4)      STUDENT: [points to the SBS]
5)      TUTOR: "Okay."
6)      TUTOR: "Move ... take the LRC."
7)      STUDENT: [takes LRC in hand]
8)      TUTOR: "Uh-huh."
9)      TUTOR: "and put it under the BS." [tutor has SBS in focus and uses anaphoric]
10)     STUDENT: [leaves LRC below the SBS]

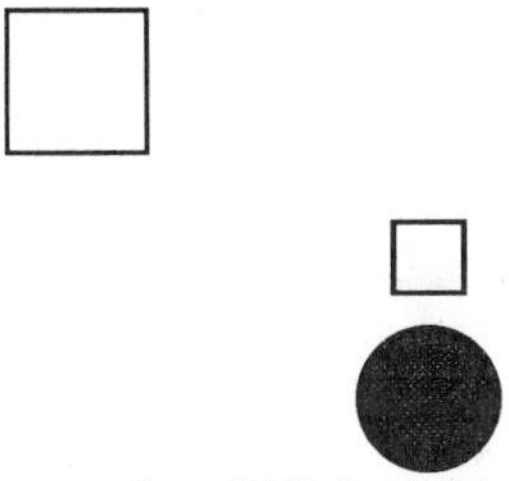

11)     STUDENT: [moves SBS to previous LRC slot (which is below the LBS)]

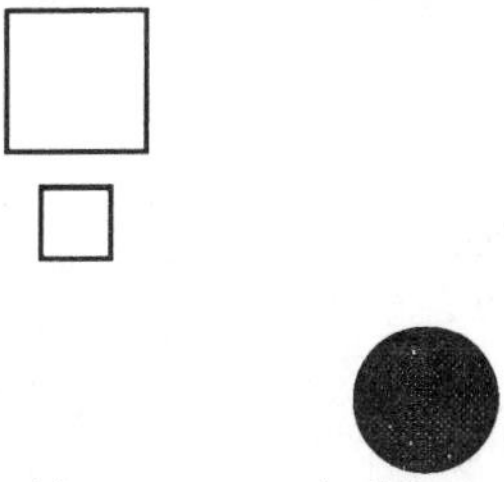

12)     TUTOR: "UhhHmm..." [ambiguous as to whether positive or negative feedback]
13)     STUDENT: "Under....under" [touches LBS then SBS]
14)     STUDENT: [slides SBS to the center of the table]
15)     TUTOR: "Wait, wait one minute."
16)     STUDENT: [physically places LRC on top of SBS. looks at her and laughs.]
17)     TUTOR: "Ah-hah, that's very nice." [Laughs, gestures]
18)     STUDENT: [removes LRC and moves SBS back to slot below LBS]
19)     TUTOR: "Okay good, okay."
20)     TUTOR: "Let's start again." [Exchanges SBS with LRC.]
*Note:* Black objects are "red"; white are "blue". C is Circle, S is Square, L is Large, S is Small, B is Blue, R is Red.

Figure 6.2. Extended example, Exercise # 1.

137

1)   TUTOR: "Let's start with this one, the SBS." [points to SBS]
2)   TUTOR: "Now, take the LR, take the LRC,"
3)   STUDENT: [takes LRC]
4)   TUTOR: "and put it below, put it below the BS, below the BS."
5)   STUDENT: [picks up SBS places it on top of LRC]
6)   TUTOR: "Okay, okay don't worry, don't worry."
7)   STUDENT: [exchanges SBS and LRC.]
8)   TUTOR: "Almost, almost." [Laughs]
9)   STUDENT: [puts LRC back in slot.]

*Note:* C is Circle, S is Square, L is Large, S is Small, B is Blue, R is Red.

Figure 6.3. Extended example, Exercise # 2.

1)   TUTOR: "Let's try again." [moves the object back.]
2)   TUTOR: "Here we've got the, okay, SBS."
3)   TUTOR: "Now, take the LRC."
4)   TUTOR: "Put the LRC, the LRC, _below, the LRC _below the SBS."
5)   STUDENT: [points to LRC, then the SBS. picks out LRC and puts it to the
     left of the SBS.]
6)   TUTOR: "Oh....kay, okay. Now this, this is, this is on the left, that's on
     your left, that one's on the left."
7)   TUTOR: "So below" [picks up LRC] "and yeah, under, below." [puts it
     below SBS]
8)   TUTOR: "Okay." [places LRC back in the slot.]

*Note:* C is Circle, S is Square, L is Large, S is Small, B is Blue, R is Red. The _
symbol designates verbal stress.

Figure 6.4. Extended example, Exercise # 3.

[All objects are placed at the side of the table again with SBS in center.]

1)   TUTOR: "First, take the SBS."
2)   STUDENT: [takes SBS in hand]
3)   TUTOR: "Okay."
4)   TUTOR: "Now, take the LRC and put it below the SBS."
5)   STUDENT: [takes LRC in hand and places it below the SBS]
6)   TUTOR: "Good, okay, okay."

*Note:* C is Circle, S is Square, L is Large, S is Small, B is Blue, R is Red.

Figure 6.5. Extended example, Exercise # 4.

tries the same test with the word *below*. The student still misunderstands. In
Exercise #3, the tutor decides to demonstrate the spatial relation with the
world *below* by analogy with *left* using the same two objects as in Exercise #1.
In Exercise #4 she tests the student with the relation using *below* and the same
two objects. The student mimics her behavior exactly. The tutor then decides
that the problem is resolved and the student understands. The remainder of
the protocol (not shown in Figure 6.5) confirms this understanding.

This sequence is representative of the complexity of tutoring failure that we
observed. There is one slip where the tutor self-corrects *move* to *take* (Exercise

#1, line 6) without any apparent feedback from the student. But most failures are bugs. For example, an ambiguous use of "blue square" (Exercise#1 line 9) causes the student to confuse the two blue squares. The tutor had assumed that the small blue square was in discourse focus. However, the major tutor bug is much more complicated and is a type of model failure. Rather than assuming a two-dimensional plane surface for the spatial relation "under" as the tutor expects, the student interprets it as three dimensional, i.e, "underneath" (Exercise #1 line 14–17). This masks another tutor bug. The tutor fails to notice that the student reverses the two referents (Exercise #1 line 11 and 16). The reversal of the two referents would be possible in Japanese, where the subject/object role in a relation are marked by particles. English requires word order to specify these roles.

In Exercise #2 these two issues are still confused. The tutor uses the word *below* but the student still interprets it three-dimensionally. She gives negative feedback to the student about his action (line 6), but the student interprets it as the need to reverse the two referents (line7). The tutor still fails to see that the student has reversed the relation between the two referents. After tutoring by demonstration in Exercise #3 and testing in Exercise #4, the student not only learns that the words *under* and *below* are used two-dimensionally in this context, but English syntax (word order) specifies which objects are marked in the relation.

## 5. DETECTION OF FAILURE

In the extended example above, we are struck by the microscopic level of detail that the tutor uses to interpret her own success or failure in communicating with the student. Thus one strategy aiding detection is that the tutor repeatedly breaks the presentation into small units so that detection of failure is simplified. It is important to stress that the form of the communication may be just as crucial as the content. In particular, we observe the tutor monitoring many nonverbal actions of the student while the tutor speaks: hesitations, gaze, and gesture. Some research on communication (Mehrabian,1972) has suggested that, in judging deception, a case where model congruence is intentionally pretended, vocal information contributes 38% of the information and facial expression 55%. Verbal information is only 7%. These data suggest that human interaction is highly attuned to the observation of the process of communication, particularly of nonverbal information.

All language interaction is essentially collaborative. Cues that indicate communication failure are given and detected by both speaker and hearer. Speakers can detect their own failure. Self-detection can occur in at least two ways. The first is that the speaker imagines the act of hearing her own utterances. This can account for anticipating ambiguities on the part of the hearer. The second way is that the speaker can review her own memory of what she has just said and debug it. The incidence of self-correction in the protocols demonstrates this phenomenon.

Speakers can also detect that trouble has occurred from cues given by the hearer. Nonverbal cues consisted of confused facial expression, hesitation in performance, and hesitation in turn-taking. Verbal cues often consisted of the repetition of a confusing word or expression with a question intonation. In these tutoring protocols we observed most of the detection strategies documented by Clark and Wilkes-Gibbs (1986) in their study of referring. Model failures are particularly difficult to detect because of inherent ambiguities in communication. It frequently took quite a few interactions for the tutor to realize that the student was in trouble.

Not only is the speaker's detection of trouble important for speaker repair, but there is an equivalent detection by the hearer of the speaker's detection of trouble. This is apparent from the speaker's false-starts and interruptions, use of metalanguage, intonation, gestures, and nervous laughter. This is important information for the hearer, since it suggests certain conventional actions for control of the conversation. For example, if the hearer detects that the speaker is in trouble, there is a deference to the speaker's retention of the turn.

## 6. REPAIR STRATEGIES

There is a preference in interaction for self-repair by the speaker or whoever is the active agent until the turn is passed (Schegloff, Jefferson, & Sacks, 1977). In the protocols we examined, turn-taking definitely existed, although the student was not a ''speaker'' in the normal sense of the word. The notion of turn-taking is fundamental to all interaction, and its control is very complex (Novick, 1988). Students often aided the tutor in making repairs. They would sometimes fill in or complete the task according to their assumptions of what they thought the tutor intended. This further stresses the collaborative and interactive nature of knowledge communication.

The tutor, upon detecting trouble, had three major repair strategies.[2] In the first strategy, which we call *correct and repeat,* the tutor would repeat the request or other utterance modifying only the corrected part. Figure 6.6 illustrates such a repair.

Similarly, after a failure was detected and a repair made, the next activity would often maintain the focus of attention of the student on the same

---

[2]These are more global tutoring strategies than the rhetorical types of repair episodes in Table 6.1.

04:51 [From previous exercises the objects are in the following arrangement at the center of the table. The tutor is directing the student in placement of objects and working on "small" and "large".]

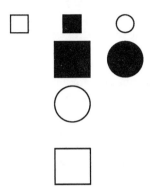

1)      TUTOR: "The _small red circle below the _large red...
1)      TUTOR: [Notices that the large red square already has an object below it.]
2)      TUTOR: "Sorry, the large _blue square."
3)      STUDENT: [Places SRC below the LBS.]

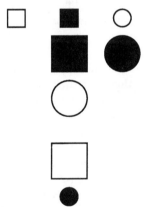

*Note:* Black objects are "red"; white are "blue". C is Circle, S is Square, L is Large, S is Small, B is Blue, R is Red. The _ symbol designates verbal stress. Orientation is from student's perspective.

Figure 6.6. *Correct and repeat* strategy.

objects. This second type of repair we call *repair reinforcement*. Maintenance of the context of interaction and focus of attention is crucial, since, when failure occurs, it is often impossible to know what is wrong. In a detailed analysis of protocols, 25 had the strategy which we call *repair reinforcement*. Repair reinforcement is when the repaired referent is used, not only in the current problem generation, but in the following as well. Figure 6.7 illustrates an example of repair reinforcement. In this example, the repaired referent "large red square" is used in the next exercise. Repair reinforcement occurs usually after the first 10 minutes. It serves to maintain focus of attention on that referent and verify that the student's performance is not confused by the teacher's repair discourse. It illustrates the opportunism that failure can create in tutoring.

In the third type of repair, *shift context and reconfirm,* the tutor was forced to abandon the repair. She would then usually make a major context shift and retest knowledge previously believed known. This strategy is that of last resort because of the required investment in tutoring energy.

The most common repair strategy of tutors for slips was *correct and repeat.* Students had no difficulty comprehending that there had been a problem, probably given by the tutor's verbal intonations and the mismatch of the original utterance to what was context. We also saw tutors take advantage of their slips to teach or diagnose a concept out of the planned sequence. ("The large red ... no, well okay. Large red circle below the small blue square.") In other words, the preference to maintain context was stronger than teaching a particular example. Thus failure promotes an opportunism for correction that creates local curriculum sequence differences. Tutors also ignored slips they had made. We do not know if this was intentional.

Repair of bugs was much more difficult than slips. *Insufficient planning* bugs were most frequently repaired by a *correct and repeat* strategy. The correction often involved the substitution of the opposite value of the attribute. For example in Figure 6.7 we see the tutor substitute *large* for *small.* This helps maintain the context and clearly involves less effort in problem solving. We see this as a simple generate and test problem solving method.

*Model failure* bugs were most frequently repaired by *repair reinforcement* and *shift context and reconfirm* strategies. Since these are the most serious failures, their repair necessitates a shift in context and return to common ground. Tutors often lapsed into metalevel discourse, which was incomprehensible to the student but which signaled that something was wrong. When encountering great difficulty in teaching a concept, both tutors prematurely terminated teaching and moved on to another topic. Later they returned to it successfully. We noticed that the complete failure of an initial diagnostic strategy in the first protocol of the novice tutor resulted in a radical rearrangement of the tutoring activities to resemble more closely that of the expert tutor. A particularly difficult repair for tutors was *model failure* bugs caused by the point of view ambiguity of left and right, and above and below. Halfway through the teaching episode, the tutor realized that the examples had all been reversed. (Since the tutor sat across from the student, she had inadvertently taught left as *her* left.) The tutor attempted a repair by getting up and sitting next to the student and then repeating the tasks.

Exercise #1

Initial Context:

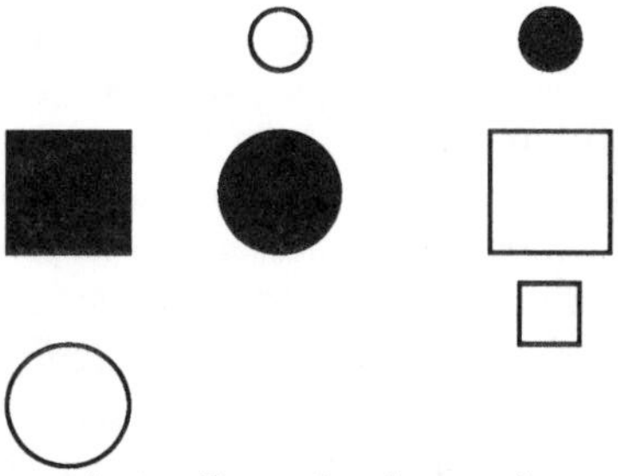

TUTOR: "Now, move the small, no, the _large red square"
STUDENT: [picks up LRS]
TUTOR: "and put that between the small blue and small red circles."
STUDENT: [puts LRS between SBC and SRC]

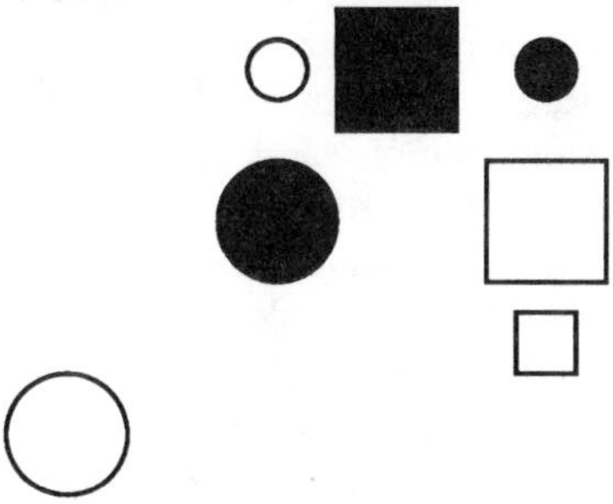

Exercise #2
TUTOR: "Large blue circle above large red square."
STUDENT: [puts LBC above LRS]

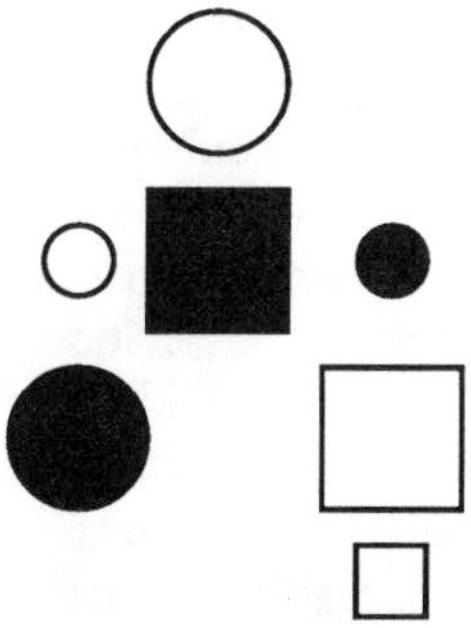

*Note:* Notice that "large red square" is repeated in Exercise #2. Black objects are "red"; white are "blue". C is Circle, S is Square, L is Large, S is Small, B is Blue, R is Red. The _ symbol designates verbal stress. Orientation is from student's perspective.

Figure 6.7. *Repair reinforcement* strategy.

## 7. COMPUTATIONAL IMPLICATIONS FOR INTELLIGENT TUTORS

There are some interesting control issues which spring from the problem of failure and repair that we observed in these protocols. Classical ITS control appears to have few strategies modeled on the kind of interaction which we observed in these protocols. Classical control is determined by the structure of the curriculum, student modeling issues, and a high-level tutoring task cycle, i.e., problem generation, diagnosis, and remediation (cf. Woolf & McDonald, 1984). These are determined by the structure of the knowledge representation isolated from its communication. What we observed in these protocols is more opportunistic control (bottom-up and data-driven) incorporating trouble repair strategies such as *repair reinforcement* and *shift context and reconfirm*. Curricula must be structured as partial orders to allow this flexibility. Repair, including repair reinforcement, tends to require control which maintains a focus of attention within the tutoring context. When trouble occurs in communication, it is always the case that the repair action ruptures the normal ongoing activity and establishes a recursive repair context. Returning to the ongoing tutoring is often a delicate and difficult task, since it may be difficult to determine context boundaries. We believe that there are many perceptually observable activities which tutors use to create context shifts. We need to understand these better.

A second interesting issue we observed with computational implications is the balancing of planning versus execution versus monitoring. ITS are rarely built with dynamic planners integrated into the system (but see Peachey & McCalla, 1986). Human tutors appeared to plan under real-time constraints, and achieve multiple goals. Slips and bugs are no doubt created because of these demands (Birnbaum, 1986). In general, we saw tutors use very opportunistic styles of planning. The kind of opportunism observed in repair involves the ability to suppress currently active goals and recognize goals which are not currently active but could be achieved. As Birnbaum observes (1986), it requires much more flexible indexing systems with fast pattern matching—drawing, perhaps, on the kind of rich typificatory knowledge possessed by experienced teachers (cf. Calderhead, this volume).

Finally, if human–human interaction is any guide, we need to pay attention to more microlevel feedback from the interface—attending to the duration of pauses, the path of mouse selections, or the short verbal feedback signifying the questioning of a referent, for example. I believe that many of these are domain independent and reflect our general knowledge about communication. More intensive study of human conversation could prove very useful. Some of the collaborative processes that speakers and hearers use to detect and repair misunderstandings are just beginning to be studied (Clark & Wilkes-Gibbs, 1986; Cohen, 1985). In the longer range, our research is developing theoretical computational models of interactive communication (cf. Novick, 1988). These concepts, which are basic to symbolic human interaction and not just natural language, may help us to build better models of the complex interaction process between tutor and student.

One caveat is that our systems are without visual input which often carries crucial information for face-to-face interaction (Suchman, 1987). One question we can ask is, "How do human tutors adapt to situations without visual access to the student?" Protocol studies we have just completed using the same tutoring task and audio access only may give us some answers to this question (Tomlin, Douglas, & Novick, 1989; see also Kamsteeg & Bierman, this volume).

## 8. CONCLUSIONS

Are these tutoring failures peculiar to this particular domain of natural language discourse? The tutoring situation modeled here approximates very closely the type of human–computer interactions that is common today— verbal instruction from the tutor, and pointing and movement requested of the student. Indeed, the observations made in this chapter are common to any interaction between knowledge-based systems, whether human or machine. All such interactions occur within a context where reference must be established and maintained. Allocation of attention becomes important. It is impossible for any programmer to anticipate all future interactions between the program and a human, or to guarantee that the program will perform without failure. Because tutoring must occur in real-time, it may be computationally impossible to derive an exact solution in many tutoring cases. Then too, the world may not be completely known in advance. Thus, the machine tutor, like the human, may be forced to adopt actions which are more susceptible to planning insufficiency bugs. Finally, no tutor has access to the complete state of knowledge of the student. And no human communication is without ambiguous interpretation. Model failures are inescapable.

Although the position I am taking here may appear radical, it is founded on the hard lessons of our ITS experience. We know that errors cannot be eliminated completely from an interface. Thus we must accommodate the problem and build systems which are robust in detecting trouble and inventing repair. In essence I have turned the normal relationship between the interface and the rest of the tutoring system around. In a knowledge communication system the interface or discourse manager, may be the most crucial component—the vulnerable Achilles heel in building effective intelligent tutoring systems.

# REFERENCES

Asher, J.J. (1969). The total physical response approach to second language learning. *Modern Language Journal, 53,* 3-17.

Birnbaum, L. (1986). *Integrated processing in planning and understanding.* Unpublished doctoral dissertation, Department of Computer Science Yale University, New Haven, CT.

Burton, M. (1981). Analysing spoken discourse. In M. Coulthard, & M. Montgomery (Eds.), *Studies in discourse analysis.* London: Routledge and Kegan Paul.

Brown, J.S., & Burton, R. (1978). Diagnostic models for procedural bugs in basic mathematical skills. *Cognitive Science, 2,* 155-192.

Card, S., Moran, T.P., & Newell, A. (1983). *The psychology of human-computer interaction.* Hillsdale, NJ: Erlbaum.

Clark, H., & Wilkes-Gibbs, D. (1986). Referring as a collaborative process. *Cognition,22,* 1-39.

Cohen, P.R. (1985). The pragmatics of referring and the modality of communication. *Computational Linguistices, 10,* 97-146.

Coombs, M.J., & Alty, J.L. (1985). An application of the Birmingham Discourse Analysis System to the study of computer guidance interactions. *Human-Computer Interaction, 1,* 243-282.

Ericsson, K.A., & Simon, H.A. (1984). *Protocol analysis: Verbal reports as data.* Cambridge, MA: MIT Press.

Grimes, J.E. (1975) *The thread of discourse.* The Hague, Netherlands: Mouton.

Krashen, S., & Terrell, T. (1983). *The natural approach.* San Francisco, CA: Alemany Press.

McKeown, K.R. (1985). *Text generation: Using discourse strategies and focus constraints to generate natural language text.* Cambridge, England: Cambridge University Press.

Mehrabian, A. (1972). *Nonverbal communication.* Chicago, IL: Aldine-Atherton.

Newell, A., & Simon, H.A. (1972). *Human problem solving.* Englewood Cliffs, NJ: Prentice-Hall.

Norman, D.A. (1981). Categorization of action slips. *Psychological Review, 88,* 1-15.

Novick, D.G. (1988). *Control of mixed initiative discourse through meta-locutionary acts: A computational approach.* Unpublished doctoral dissertation, University of Oregon. (Available from University Microfilms and as Tech. Rep. CIS-TR-88-18, Department of Computer and Information Science, University of Oregon).

Peachey, D.R., & McCalla, G.I. (1986). Using planning techniques in intelligent tutoring systems. *International Journal of Man-machine Studies, 24,* 77-98.

Postovsky, V. (1977). Why not start speaking later? In M.Burt (Ed.), *Viewpoints on English as a second language.* New York: Regents.

Postovsky, V. (1979). Effects of delay in oral practice at the beginning of second language learning. *Modern Language Journal, 58,* 229-239.

Reichman, R. (1985). *Getting computers to talk like you and me.* Cambridge, MA: MIT Press.

Schegloff, E.A., Jefferson, G., & Sacks, H. (1977). The preference for self-correction in the organization of repair in conversation. *Language, 53,* 361-382.

Sinclair, J. McH., & Coulthard, R.M. (1972). *Toward an analysis of discourse.* London: Oxford University Press.

Suchman, L.A. (1987). *Plans and situated actions: The problem of human-machine communication.* Cambridge, England: Cambridge University Press.

Tomlin, R., Douglas, S.A., & Novick, D.G. (1989, February). *The microanalysis of individual tutorials: The first hour.* Paper presented at the Ninth Second Language Research Forum, University of California at Los Angeles.

Wenger, E. (1987). *Artificial intelligence and turoring systems.* Los Altos, CA: Morgan Kaufman.

Widdowson, H.G. (1978). *Teaching language as communication.* Oxford, England: Oxford University Press.

Winitz, H. (Ed.). (1981). *The comprehension approach to foreign language instruction.* Rowley, MA: Newbury House.

Winitz, H., & Reeds, J. (1973). Rapid acquisition of a foreign language by the avoidance of speaking. *International Review of Applied Linguistics, 11,* 295-317.

Woolf, B., & McDonald, D.D. (1984, September). Building a computer tutor: Design issues. *IEEE Computer,* pp. 61-73.

Woolf, B., & Murray, T. (1987). *Discourse transition networks for intelligent tutoring systems.* (Tech. Rep.). Amherst, MA: University of Massachusetts, Computer and Information Science Dept.

# 7

## COGNITIVE AND INTERACTIONAL ASPECTS OF CORRECTION IN TUTORING*

BARBARA A. FOX

## 1. INTRODUCTION

As intelligent tutoring systems have grown in power, there has been an increasing desire for more robust interfaces which can manage such necessary tutoring tasks as correction, intervention, redirection, and the like. Until now, systems which have tried to model these tasks have done so on the basis of researcher intuition or a few psychological experiments. The research presented here begins to remedy this situation by providing detailed evidence, from videotaped human–human tutoring sessions, regarding effective strategies for correction, tutor intervention (what I have called *assistance),* and a variety of other topics in tutorial dialogue. The findings discussed here should be taken as critical areas for exploration in the development of future intelligent tutoring systems.

The present chapter explores the interactional and cognitive processes involved in correction and tutor assistance in a set of tutoring sessions. As we will see in Sections 2 and 3 these two facets—interactional and cognitive—of correction and assistance are really flip sides of one another: tutors and

*The research reported in this chapter is part of a larger project on human tutorial dialogue supported by a contract from the Office of Naval Research. Thanks go to Mannuel Arce, Susan Chipman, Manny Schegloff, and Lucy Suchman for their comments on an earlier draft of the chapter.

students interact in a way that is cognitively beneficial to the student, and the cognitive processes needed are in turn at least partially determined by the interaction between tutor and student. In a sense, interaction and cognition live together in an ecological system and thus have "evolved" such that their characteristics are intertwined.

The remainder of this section of the chapter provides an overview of the project within which this work is situated. Section 2 describes the interactional aspects of correction (including tutor assistance). Section 3 outlines some of the cognitive processes involved in correction, and Section 4 presents some ideas for future systems.

## 1.1. Overview of Project

The research within which the present chapter is situated seeks to gain an understanding of some of the processes of human tutorial dialogue, including conversational repair, tutor intervention, and linguistic encoding of communicative strategies. It also seeks to characterize the effect on these processes of manipulating several variables, such as mode of communication (i.e., face-to-face vs. terminal-to-terminal), subject matter of instruction, and expertise level of the student. This work is meant to provide an empirical foundation for the enhancement of design principles for tutorial components of intelligent tutorial systems and knowledge-based help systems.

In addition, the research attempts to characterize the differences between human–human tutorial dialogue and human–computer tutorial dialogue, so that a realistic picture of the dialogue requirements on current intelligent tutorial systems can emerge.

## 1.2. Human–Human Dialogue and Intelligent Tutoring Systems

As intelligent tutoring systems grow and become more robust, they will need to enter into increasingly extensive natural language dialogues with users. As a result, these systems will need complex natural language interfaces; in particular, they will need sophisticated models of how to carry on natural dialogue.[1]

---

[1] Hayes (1983) puts forth an interesting perspective on the relationship between human conversation and the kinds of dialogue we should expect between people and computers:

> In brief, we believe that direct simulation of human conversation will not play an important role in user-friendly interfaces until speech processing has made sufficient technical advances to allow spoken language to be used freely and in conjunction with pointing, but that the study of human communication will continue to be relevant to

Because of this need to model human dialogue, the study of human–human instructional dialogue is a critical step in the further development of intelligent tutoring systems, in that such research will provide the theoretical foundation on which working systems can be built. That is, this project is based on the belief that the best tutorial systems will arise out of a fine interplay between what would be theoretically ideal (based on what humans actually do) and what is practically possible (based on what the current technology allows). The focus of this portion of the project is on the former; we examine naturally-occurring tutorial interactions (as one type of instructional interaction which is closely related to the problem at hand and readily observable in a university environment) in the context of furthering our understanding of how people learn and teach through extended dialogue.

The theoretical background for this particular approach to human–computer interaction is captured in the following quote from John Seely Brown (n.d.):

> A dialogue involves constant conversational repairs between two people. When someone doesn't understand what I've just said, I must try to diagnose not only what, but why, he didn't understand and then accordingly repair what I said. It is basically an adjusting process that goes on between the two of us communicating . . . .We have been misled into thinking that natural language, per se, is so powerful. Instead, I think it is the *dialogue process* that is so powerful, e.g. the notion of conversational *repairs* that occur between two people. If we can understand this process and how to capture it in man-machine communication, we will have made a major breakthrough on the perceived friendliness of machines.

Brown makes two crucial points in this statement: one, the study of human–human dialogue will form a fundamental part of the development of robust human–computer interfaces; and two, even though human–computer dialogue may differ on the surface in extreme ways from human–human dialogue, at least some (if not most) of the basic underlying processes of human–human dialogue must be captured in a human–computer interface if it is to be user friendly. Thus, even if users communicate with computers in a way that suggests they believe the computers to be less than adequate communicative partners, some of the processes of natural human–human dialogue will still be apparent. In spite of the potential differences, then, between human–human dialogue and human–computer dialogue, the study

---

interactive computer interfaces of all kinds. (p.230)

I agree with this statement, and I would emphasize that what we need to model from human conversation is critical communicative processes, not all of human communication or human conversation.

of human–human interaction will provide necessary insight into design principles of human–computer interfaces.

In addition to the theoretical support for the study of human–human dialogue offered by Brown's statement, there has been a precedent in AI research for the approach proposed here, in the work of Grosz (1977), Reichman (1985), Hobbs (1976), and others. In these studies, findings from human–human interactions were effectively modeled in computer systems. The widespread recognition of this work throughout the cognitive sciences indicates that it has added significantly to our understanding of human cognitive processes in general, as well as to the robustness of intelligent systems. It is clearly a fruitful avenue of research to pursue.

Nonetheless, it is important to recognize that human–computer instructional dialogue will differ in critical ways from human–human instructional dialogue. Our research in part seeks to explore the nature of the differences between human–human instructional dialogue and human–computer instructional dialogue in order to determine what the current dialogue demands on tutorial systems are. By studying both types of dialogue, it will be possible to reach a balance between what is theoretically ideal and what is currently required to achieve an optimal model of dialogue for intelligent tutorial systems.

## 2. INTERACTIONAL ASPECTS OF CORRECTION

### 2.1. Organization of Tutoring Interaction: Correction and Tutor Assistance

The main focus of this research to date has been understanding the process of a subcomponent of repair, namely correction, including the process of tutor intervention, or, as we prefer to think of it, tutor assistance. We have chosen to start with this large area because of its significance to a wide range of topics, including the role of the student in creating the learning environment, differences between child and adult learners, the use of interactional and linguistic resources to accomodate a less than normal situation (i.e., an otherwise competent adult in a noncompetent role), questions in natural language processing, and issues in interface design.[2]

While modeling the *cognitive* processes involved in correction is clearly a necessary task in the design of more robust user interfaces, especially in the area of ITS, it may at first seem somewhat less critical to model the *interactional* processes involved. While this view is certainly understandable,

---

[2] For a complementary perspective on repair, see Douglas, this volume.

given the vast differences in interactionality between humans and computers, nothing could be further from the truth. First, as we will see in Section 3, it is impossible to separate entirely the cognitive processes to be modeled from the interactional ones. Second, we know that human tutors are still more effective than computer tutors (Resnick, personal communication, 1986), and so we must assume, at least for now, that the strategies used by human tutors to accomplish things like correction are effective, and thus worthy of being modeled. Some systems, for example, the systems developed (following the ACT* theory) by Anderson and others (e.g., Anderson, Boyle, Farrell, & Reiser, 1984), already assume a model of the interactional aspects of correction based on intuitions about what is psychologically effective for students. The research presented here aims to provide an empirical foundation for such models, by examining how tutors and students actually do carry out such necessary tasks as correction.

We have found that the best way to understand correction (including tutor assistance) is to examine the overall structure of the tutoring sessions; in other words, correction is best studied within the sequential organization of the interactions themselves. The full structural details of each interaction are beyond the scope of the present chapter; below I provide only enough description to motivate the analysis of correction.

The sessions divide themselves into two groups: the first group is characterized by the student working through problems in a textbook (in one case the student brought in a set of problems from the text that she had been having difficulties solving); the second group is characterized by something more of a lecture format, wherein the tutor talks about domain concepts and demonstrates how to solve problems. This description is an oversimplification of the sessions, but it is sufficient for our purposes here.

When students work through a problem with a tutor, they very often verbalize what they are doing, step by step. For example, in the following excerpt, the student doesn't just write down the steps as he works through them—he talks about what he is doing as he does it (see Appendix for a list of notational conventions):

S:   So:, ah:m (1.0) this, okay, secant, of theta, I know
     eqs- equals three:. Now, so but- my equation here is
     (0.4) secant squared theta. So what I want to say is
     .hh the square root, (0.6) of secant, (0.5) squared
     theta. .hh would equal three:. .Right?

Why do students produce this ongoing commentary? They do it to display to the tutor how they have understood the problem and how they understand what they are currently doing to solve the problem. So every student utterance of this sort is a display of understanding. As with any understanding, the student's understanding of a particular step in a problem can match or not match the interlocutor's understanding, so that any such display of understanding calls for a confirmation (or disconfirmation) from the tutor, by which the tutor displays that the student's displayed understanding matches her own (see Labov & Fanshel, 1977, for a related point). A confirmation agrees with the student's understanding; a disconfirmation disagrees with it.

Now, it is known from past research (Pomerantz, 1975) that agreements come very quickly after the utterance they agree with, while disagreements are somewhat delayed. In these tutoring sessions we have found that, when the tutor agrees with the student's displayed understanding, her signal of confirmation comes quickly after the student's turn, as in:

S:  Mkay. .hh And I know it's negative, just to follow your
    thought process, because I know that the sine is positive.
T:  Mhm

S:  And this (draw it out). (0.3) And the double bond goes away
T:  Right

whereas, if the tutor disagrees with the student's understanding, the delivery of the disagreement is somewhat delayed (and in some cases what might be described as "hesitant"):

S:  And it's going to change when I put this in- there, right?
                    (1.7)
T:  I don't think so.

S:  So that triple bond is like ess pee three?
       (1.1)
T:  Ah:: no:, that- a triple would be an ess pee.

So here is the first point about correction: Tutor correction (or indication of a problem with the student's understanding) is delayed with regard to the relevant student utterance.

Furthermore, it follows from this and past work on disagreements (Pomerantz, 1975) that, when a student has produced a display of his or her understanding and there is no immediate response from the tutor, the student can anticipate that the tutor is going to disagree with his or her understanding; students in this situation will very often rephrase their statement as a question, thereby *inviting* correction from the tutor:

S:  Okay, just for review for my sake. .hh a cosecant
    is .hh uh:m, one over the tangent.
                    (1.3)
S:  Am I correct?

T:        N:o.

S:        And it's going to change when I put this in- there, right?
            (1.7)
T:        I don't think so.
    [
S:        Does the capacitance change?
            (0.5)
T:        I think the charge changes.

Students can also use this "predisagreement" silence to try by themselves
to correct whatever may be wrong with their understanding:

S:  I use this one for that one, 'cause I don't think I had
     a dialectric
            (0.6)
S: wait, no, I do:
            (0.9)
T: ts 'cause you have paraffi//n
S: Paraffin.
T: That's the whole point about the paraffin.

S: ey: is minus one, and bee is zero.
            (1.5)
S: No, bee is one.

If the student's understanding does not match the tutor's understanding,
then there are three options listed below:

1. the student can correct himself or herself
2. the student can invite correction
3. the tutor can initiate correction

A note is in order at this juncture regarding my use of the word *match*. I
do not mean for this to imply that the tutor has an abstract understanding
which she compares with the student's to find discrepancies; if this were the
case, and the tutor were sophisticated enough and the student novice
enough, then everything the student said would have to be corrected,
inasmuch as a sophisticated understanding of some domain is apt to be
radically different from a novice's (my own understanding of a phoneme, for
example, is not what I would bring to bear in tutoring beginning linguistics
students). It must be, then, that the tutor takes into account the task at hand
(for example, solving a textbook problem), and the kind of understanding
that one could expect from a novice, to determine what counts as "wrong"
for the purposes of their particular interaction. Developing this context-based

notion of correctness for use in computer systems is an essential area for future research.

The student and tutor go on in this way, displaying and repairing their understandings until the student gets stuck.[3] Here again there are several alternative responses that either participant could make, assuming that the student is displaying overt signs of "being stuck" (and not, for example, "thinking").

Notice first that the situation of a student being stuck (and showing being stuck) creates a potential conflict. In our everyday interaction, if we see someone having difficulty in some way, it is preferred for us to offer help before that help is requested (Pomerantz, 1975). I do not mean that it is personally or psychologically preferred for us to offer help in this situation; indeed, we may be in a hurry, or not like the person, or have something else we'd rather be doing. Rather, it is preferred socially and structurally, so that, if we are not going to offer help, we must provide an excuse for not doing so, or pretend we didn't see the trouble, etc. Preference organizations of this sort are independent of the momentary preferences of individual participants.

So it is possible that, in tutoring interactions, the preferred response to the student's difficulty would be for the tutor to in some way offer help. But, as we have seen, there is a conflicting preference organization which indicates that participants should be allowed to repair their own trouble (Schegloff, Sacks, & Jefferson, 1977).

The tutors in this study display an orientation to both kinds of preferences (for a similar finding with regard to compliment responses, see Pomerantz, 1978). Tutors do provide assistance, but they do so in such a way that students are given the opportunity to unstick themselves, both before the assistance is provided and while the assistance is emerging. Consider the following exchange:

> S: and they want to know what the tangent is.So.
> I have one over cosine of theta equals three.
> (0.8) And I have the sine of theta over cosine
> of theta (1.0) hmm:. (0.8) .hh Okay, so I guess
> I somehow have to: (0.8) tangent of theta is going
> to be: (0.4) sine of theta over cosine of theta.
> (2.0) One over cosine of theta,// so (0.3) three.
> T: Mkay. Now,

---

[3] In some case the student avoids getting stuck by indicating before the difficult step that this next step was exactly the reason he or she needed help with this problem:

> S: And kay is the: constant that, I know that (0.5) and
> um (1.2) eff, that's what I had a problem with, was eff

This strategy only works if the student has worked the problem before coming to see the tutor.

S: Okay
T: ts looking up here, ju//st at what =
S: Aha
T: = they've done, (0.4) .hh cause I can tell, we're
    headed in the wrong direction.
S: Ye:ah, they used to con-they use // one of the
    pythagoreans.
T: One plus (0.6) tangent squared e-quals the secant squared
                                             [
S:                                                 secant squared.

The student in this case is going around in circles—he has repeated by now several times that tangent equals sine over cosine—without finding a new way to look at the problem. The tutor thus intervenes, but not without giving the student a fair opportunity to figure out the answer for himself. Furthermore, the assistance is produced in such a way that the student can collaborate in the redirection, as he in fact does with his last lines. Here again, correction/assistance is momentarily withheld to give the student a chance to fix the problem himself. The withholding time is not long, however, and a student who wishes to be given a longer opportunity to work the problem out for himself or herself must specifically request such an "extention":

S: Now, .hh let's see, when we said tangent of theta
    was less than zero .hh u::hm the tangent was
        (0.7)
S: give me a second. The tangent was sine over cosine.
T: Mhm

Correction/assistance of this sort thus is slightly delayed but is still offered without being "overtly" requested.

Tutors regularly provide assistance for the student if the student has produced one step in a chain of reasoning but apparently does not see the inference(s) which should be drawn for the next step:

S: Ey plus cee equals zero.
    (0.3)
T: Right, so that tells // you
S: Ey equals cee.
    (0.4)
T: Minus cee.

S: So it's got to be: in our fourth quadrant.
T: Right.
    (1.4)

S: Aha. (0.8) Aha, o//kay.
T: Which means?
S: Then I have to come back down here and I'm- you're
   asking me to choose a sign, righ//t?
T: Right
S: .hh Okay.
T: For your cosine.


The conflict between tutor providing help and student working through
the trouble himself or herself is overtly displayed in the following passage.
The fragment starts with the student trying to determine the quadrant for the
tangent given in the problem; he first gets into trouble by giving the wrong
formula for cotangent. The tutor provides help, and then the two appear to
play a very tame kind of tug of war to see who is going to do the next steps
of the reasoning. They subtly try to wrestle a few turns from one another,
culminating in the student finally saying "let me see if I can figure that out."


S: I have to place it in a quadrant, is what you're telling
   me, right?
T: Mhm
   .

   .
   .
S: I would say: (.) uh, a cotangent, in terms of ex wai, (0.3)
   is let's see, one over the uh-
   cotangent is one over the uhm, (0.7) hold on
   a sec, (LAUGH) uh: cotangent is one over the sine.
      (0.4)
T  N:o
   .

   .
T: Cotangent is one over the tangent.
S: Now, if I'm thinking in terms of ex and wai, though, (0.8) fo:r (0.8) the
   sake of the quadra//nts>
T: It would be cosine over sine.
      (0.8)
S: Right =
T: =Which is ex over wai.
S: Okay
   .

   .
T: And the cosecant//is-
S: Co- cosecant, it's that's the one over the sin//e right
T: One over sine.
   .

T: Which means that your ex value is positive.
    (0.2)
S: Right.
T: Which puts you in:
    (0.5)
S: 'kay, .hh let's see if I can figure that out.
T: Okay.

Quite often especially in more conceptual domains (such as physics), tutor assistance is provided in the form of a question whose answer will serve as a resource for getting the student unstuck if the student sees how the answer is a resource. This strategy has two parts: the first part requires that the student be able to answer the question, and the second requires that the student see how that answer is a resource for continuing the problem. Since both of these processes may end up involving correction, and since correction is dispreferred, this strategy is undertaken very cautiously and with a heavy degree of support from the tutor. Consider the following.

S: eff. that's what I had a problem with, was eff, they said
    (3.1) if (0.5) if the electric force between them is
    equal to the weight>
        (0.4)
T: ts Okay.
S: So: I tried to look at the wei:ght,
        (0.9)
T: And all's they give you is the ma:ss.
        (0.2)
S: and it- yeah: (0.7) Oh, that's what it was, it
    was the mass.
        (0.8)
T: Yeah:.
        (1.0)
S: Oh:, I s//ee. I want weight.
T: You wrote down mass.
        (0.3)
→ T: Yeah, what's the difference between weight and mass.
S: I used to know this let's see
        (1.7)
T: I think, (0.8) I think what it is (0.8) is that,
    (0.5) n- what is uh, when you do (0.6) uh:,
    gravity problems. =
S: = Right.//It's that-
→ T: What do you always do?
        (1.2)

S:   You have to multiply it by the-=
T:   =by gee.=
T:   =Gee. Right.

.

.

.

S:   So I need to multiply this time (0.8) gee.
T:   Right.


There are two tutor assistance questions in this passage, marked by arrows in the margin. The second question is of course meant as a resource for answering the first question, which the student shows difficulty answering. Notice that the tutor gives the student a fairly long space in which to answer the question. When she shows that she is not able to answer, the tutor does not directly provide the answer. Rather she asks a further question, whose answer and import will enable the student to answer the first question. The student and tutor work together to produce the answer to the second question, at which point it is relevant for the student to indicate that she sees the import of the question for the problem they are trying to solve. In fact, the student eventually sees how the answer is a resource and goes on to the next step of the problem. It is critical to note in this passage that the tutor always provides a safety net around the student, so that, if she shows signs of not being able to answer the question, the tutor offers a resource for answering. If the student shows signs of not seeing the import of a question for the problem at hand, then the tutor steers the student towards seeing the connection. All of this is kept in balance with not correcting or redirecting the student before she has had the opportunity to do those things herself.

Tutors also ask questions before the student has gotten stuck, often to help frame the problem, and the solution.[4] In the following passage, for example, the tutor checks to see if the student understands the kinds of units—and therefore the appropriate formulae—the problem involves:


T:   (STARTS READING THE PROBLEM) A one ohm wire.
     Okay, what's ohms
           (1.4)
S:   It's resistance


----

[4] This framing is reminiscent of Vygotsky's concept of *scaffolding* (see Cole, 1978), by which the teacher in an apprenticeship situation structures a task such that it is always within the learner's abilities: as the learner's abilities increase, the teacher gradually removes the *props* which have made the task approachable, until finally the learner can perform the task without assistance. See also Collins, Brown, and Newman (1986).

T: Okay. Is drawn out to three times its original length.
   What is the resistance now.

The response to these questions is carefully monitored, as with all tutor questions, to make sure that the chances of the student producing an appropriate answer are maximized. If the student has difficulty answering the question, the tutor will provide clarification, hints, and so on, as in the following example:

T: What is the speed of a three hundred and fifty
   ee vee electron.Okay.
        (1.2)
T: So the main thing he:re, I mean, when you look at that,
   what is electron volts, what kind of a
S: It'//s ahm.
T: what are we talking about.
        (1.5)
S: Isn't it- the charge of an electron times?
        (0.9)
T: Right.// but what is it-what is that. Is it-=
S: The voltage?
S: =It's s:maller
        (0.2)
S: I//t's
T: No- okay, I'm n- I'm a I'm a I'm not asking
   a specific enough question, U:hm, (1.1) Uh
   (0.3) is this units of length
?
        (0.9)
S: Oh, no it's uhm
        (1.9)
S: It's voltage, isn't it?
[the tutor goes on to redirect the student until she sees
that the answer is energy]

For the sessions in which the tutor does most of the talking (both about general procedures and concepts and about solving problems for the student), the student can display his or her understanding by finishing the tutor's utterances, as in:

T: So this is really the integral of ex (0.8) the who- e-
   ex goes in the whole time=
                [
S:              Right
T: =.hh plus the remainder one over ex.

S:                       [
                             one over ex. Yeah

T:   In order for this to become basic,
       (1.2)
S:   It'll I have to lose a=
T:   =it'I I have to lose a hydro//gen
S:   hydrogen

In fact, the tutors often capitalize on collaborative completion as a means of finding out what the student understands by starting an utterance, with a slightly rising intonation, cueing the student to finish the utterance appropriately:

T:   So I need to: do what.
       (2.0)
T:   Multiply on the inside by
        (0.1)
S:   half
T:   one half to get rid of that. (0.8) And so on the outside
     I'm going to be:
       (1.3)
T:   multiplying by
       (1.7)
S:   a factor of two, yeah
               [
T:               two

This strategy, which uses statement syntax to elicit information from the student, neatly avoids the problem of correcting a wrong answer from the student—if the student provides an inappropriate completion for the utterance, the tutor can provide the "correct" answer as if she were merely finishing her own sentence.

T:   Integral of ex gives us ex squared over two One
     over ex gives
        (0.4)
S:   One ex
       (0.5)
T:   Natural log
       (0.4)
S:   Absolute value of ex

The tutor can also incrementally add clues to the partial utterance if the student fails to finish the utterance at the first opportunity:

T:   .hh Second thing> i:s
            (1.0)
T:   to>
            (1.7)
T:   fa//ctor>
S:   factor the denominator.

In this passage, the student is unable to complete the tutor's utterance until he hears the first syllable of *factor*; as soon as he is equipped with that clue, he is able to produce the appropriate completion. This strategy provides the tutor with a kind of metric for judging the student's understanding, inasmuch as each opportunity to complete the utterance that is passed is some indication of how well the student is keeping up (see Fox, 1987, for a detailed discussion of this phenomenon).

In some rare cases, the tutor can even end up completing her own utterance entirely, if the student fails to provide a completion:

T:   the main thing with the exponential function.
       (1.8) you have (0.2) ee to the ex (1.4) and its
       derivative is
            (2.3)
T:   ee to the ex ( )

The utterance-completion strategy tends to be used mostly for working on a step of a problem (usually a problem being solved out loud by the tutor in front of the student). For more conceptual issues, or more tactical issues, the tutor will often ask a question, with the syntactic form of an interrogative:

T:   Is there something we can put in here, to wipe this
       part out?=
S:   =Well that one will go to zero, yeah.
T:   Yeah ( // )
S:   The ex equals zero.

Here, as with the tutor questions discussed above, the issue of correction is prominent. This format is overtly a question, which of course makes an answer from the student socially appropriate. Both parties work to avert an incorrect answer from the student. They manage this in an intricate way: the silence that grows after the tutor's question is carefully monitored for signs that the student either will or will not be able to answer the question. The student participates by displaying signs of working on a calculation, for example, or by displaying signs of confusion or lack of comprehension. The tutor participates by looking for these signs and responding appropriately. For example, if the tutor has asked a conceptual question and the student responds by "staring blankly" at the textbook, the tutor is likely to provide assistance before the silence has grown beyond 2 seconds; on the other hand, if the tutor asks the student what the outcome of a particular calculation is, and the student responds by displaying signs of "working on it," the tutor may allow the student a fairly long silence, usually lasting until the student either answers the question or displays further signs of being stuck. Eye movement, facial expression, body posture, position of pencil, and non-linguistic verbal cues (such as sighs, inbreaths, clicks) are all used and monitored during this particularly sensitive time.

There are three central outcomes of this interaction: (a) the student answers the question (usually correctly); (b) the student asks a question about some portion of the problem or question, the tutor answers, and the student then answers the original question; or (c) the tutor provides assistance—in the form of clarification, hint, a more leading question—and the process starts again, most often until the student answers. In a few rare cases, the tutor provides the answer itself, but this occurs only after the student has passed several opportunities to answer. The most striking outcome of this whole process, of course, is the low rate of incorrect student answers—I found only 12 incorrect answers produced after tutor questions, out of a total of 97 possible answer slots. This low rate is seen as an achieved outcome of the processes described above, rather than a natural fact of, say, the student's IQ or knowledge of the subject matter.

## 2.2. Summary of Correction Strategies

Above we saw that tutors withhold correction and even assistance until the student has had an opportunity to initiate correction on his or her own. In some cases this strategy is effective in getting the student to produce a correction, but in other cases the student is unable or unwilling to produce a correction; in these cases, the tutor takes on, in some instances with the overt collaboration of the student, the task of correction or assistance. How the trouble is handled depends on where in its sequence it is produced.

There are four main positions in which the tutor engages in correction, or initiation of correction. In the first case, the student has produced a display of understanding which is in some way incorrect; the tutor withholds correction and in this space the student, anticipating disagreement from the tutor, invites correction. The tutor responds with a correction.

S:   Because secant squared of theta is square root of
           (0.8)
S:   Can I do it that way?
S:   S- can I say three minus one?

    [
T:  Mm::
T:  No, you want to say three squared. Because the secant is three.

The second position is the case of a wrong answer produced after a tutor question. The tutor in this situation regularly initiates correction, and the student attempts self-correction.

    T:   Did the area change?
          (1.0)
    S:   Wouldn't the area be the same?
          (0.9)
    T:   We only have the same amount of copper.
    S:   Yeah.
    T:   Well think of taking silly putty.
    T:   Like a block of silly putty like this> and you
         pulled it out? What would ha//ppen?
    S:   It's the same.
          (0.2)
    T:   It would get long and skinny, though.

Notice that, in this case, when the correction was not invited by the student, the tutor does not overtly correct the student; rather the tutor tries to redirect the student's thinking. The behavior of the tutor is thus clearly sensitive to the context of utterance of the problem.

The third position follows an utterance or set of utterances by the student which usually exhibit(s) that the student is stuck. In this position, the tutor regularly initiates correction and allows the student the opportunity to actually accomplish the final correction:

    S:   tangent of theta is going to be: (0.4) sine of theta
         over cosine of theta. (2.0) One over cosine of
         theta, // so, (0.3) three.
    T:   Mkay. Now,
    S:   Okay
    T:   ts looking up here, ju//st at what =
    S:   Aha
    T:   =they've done, (0.4) .hh Cause I can tell, we're
         headed in the wrong direction.
    S:   Ye:ah, they used to con- they use one of the pythagoreans.

((Student working problem: 10.8))
    T:   .hh Where did this minus sign come from.
    S:   .hh It's minus ex. This minus ex shouldn't be here.

The fourth position is the rarest, and involves the student producing an utterance—usually in conjunction with working a step of a problem—that completes a tutor prompt. In this case, the tutor initiates and accomplishes correction by simply producing the rest of her original utterance, with the correct piece of completing material serving as the correction (which gives something like an embedded correction). These instances all involve low-level calculations which the student has produced while working a problem.

> T:  One over ex gives
>         (0.4)
> S:  One ex.
>         (0.5)
> T:  Natural log.

We can see from these examples that where an error arises very much affects how it is handled by the tutor and the student. Thus, in order to model the kinds of strategies employed in tutoring, we need models of conversational structure in tutoring, such as those presented above.

## 3. COGNITIVE ASPECTS OF CORRECTION

In Section 2 we saw the interactional considerations relevant to correction and tutor assistance. In this section we examine some of the cognitive processes which must underly correction, to see if we can shed some light on the kinds of processes an intelligent system must be capable of to manage correction.

For the purposes of this discussion, let us use the following passage as a testbed. In this passage, the tutor asks a question, gets an incorrect answer, points out that it is incorrect, and then initiates the process for finding the correct answer.

> S:  I use this equation, and what I need to find the speed?
>         (0.4)
> T:  Right. And velocity (0.4) Do you know the difference
>      between velocity and speed?
>         (2.4)
> S:  Velocity is the distance times time
>         (1.7)
> S:  Speed is uhm
>         (2.9)
> T:  No, distance is- velocity isn't distance times//time.
> S:  It's not?
> T:  uh-uh

       (0.7)
T:  Think of it=
S:  =Huh
T:  .hh You go: six hundred miles per hour.
S:  Oh, that's uhm (0.4) that's the speed?
       (0.8)
T:  Yeah. .hh And velocity and speed are the same thing.
       (0.3)
T:  Except the thing is, is that- velocity is a vector.
     And speed is just a number.

  .

  .

  .

T:  That equation's still wrong.
S:  Is it?
T:  Yeah, think of miles per hour.
       (1.5)
T:  So what is that.
S:  Over time=
T:  =Right.
       (1.1)
S:  Okay.
       (0.9)
T:  The one you might be thinking of is- distance is velocity
     times time.
       (1.3)
S:  Oh, that's got to be it. He did that in class today.
       (0.2)
T:  Yeah, velocity times time.

  .

  .

T:  But that's really easy just to (carry) to the side,
     all of a sudden

There are two issues being dealt with in this passage: the relationship between velocity and speed, and the correct equation for velocity. When the student starts to answer the initial question, she shows that (a) she has gotten the equation for velocity wrong; and (b) she thinks there is a difference in equations between velocity and speed. She is thus wrong on two counts, and the tutor must guide her out of both errors.

The tutor begins by trying to correct the equation for velocity. She starts off by saying that the equation for velocity is not what the student has written down and then gives an example (of velocity) in vernacular formulation from which the student can deduce the correct formula for velocity (distance over time). The student misinterprets this utterance; she hears "six hundred miles per hour" as a vernacular formulation of *speed*—which in fact it is—and therefore not as a resource for correcting her equation for velocity (since she clearly still thinks that velocity and speed are different in some fundamental way). The tutor then repairs this misconception by informing the student that velocity and speed are the same. This information should allow the student to go back, using the formulation of speed, to correct for herself her equation for velocity. She fails to do this, so the tutor comes in (after giving the student a chance to fix the problem herself) with "that equation's still wrong." The tutor once again offers an English version of the formula for velocity, and this time, with a bit more prompting, the student is able to correct her equation. Notice that the last lines in the passage are the tutor indicating to the student how her error arose; as the tutor describes it, the student followed a very natural kind of process—taking the same equation and switching two of the terms in a reasonable but mathematically incorrect way:

$$d = vt \qquad v = dt \quad \text{(should be } v = d/t\text{)}$$

What processes enable the tutor to carry out the correction in this passage? At least four components must be acknowledged:

1. The tutor must be able to interpret the utterance, or set of utterances, requiring correction.
2. The tutor must be able to determine that the interpretation displayed by that set of utterances requires correction.
3. The tutor tries to understand the path by which the student was led to the error or misconception.
4. The tutor must be able to articulate a new direction for the student so that the "error" can be discovered and corrected by the student. This new direction must be designed such that it takes into account the exact error made (and its underlying misconceptions), and, if possible, the path which led to the error.

In the passage under consideration, for example, the tutor recognizes that "velocity is the distance times time" is meant as a formula for velocity, which is part of the answer to the tutor's first question. Furthermore, the tutor recognizes that this formula is incorrect and that its being incorrect represents a stumbling block for solving the problem at hand. And finally, and most interestingly, the tutor formulates a redirection, based on maneuvering the student away from the particular error she made—she gives an example velocity which does not conform to the formula given by the student. She also tries to articulate the path which led to the error.

Modeling these four processes, which are only the most obvious aspects of correction, remains an extremely difficult task, one whose seriousness has not been adequately acknowledged in the ITS literature. While there is an abundance of work on finding the "bugs" in students' domain knowledge, there has been very little work done on how tutors determine whether something is (a) incorrect for the purposes of the ongoing problem solving; and (b) deserving of correction during the tutoring (see Sleeman et al., this volume). Furthermore, given that most intelligent systems operate with canned text, it is difficult to see how the fourth process could be modeled at all, since it requires careful design of the redirecting utterances to take into account the *specific* error made by the student. Since the range of student errors cannot be determined in advance, it is of course impossible for a system using canned text to tailor its "utterances" to steer a student away from every possible errorful conception.

The difficulties grow considerably if we also consider correction of communicative problems, in addition to correction of domain knowledge. In order to perform these kinds of corrections (or repairs), the tutor must engage in behavior which will be even more troublesome for computer systems to emulate:

1. The tutor must be able to interpret the utterance, or set of utterances, requiring correction (or repair).
2. The tutor must be able to recognize that the interpretation displayed by that set of utterances requires repair.
3. The tutor must be able to see what in the preceding discourse could have led to the interpretation requiring correction and how it could have led to it.
4. The tutor must be able to re-articulate the source of trouble such that the new formulation takes into account the path which led to the "errorful" interpretation (and eliminates it as a viable interpretation).

It is safe to say that no system currently in use could manage these four processes. In particular, the last two steps—tracing the path which led to the misinterpretation, and reformulating the trouble source—seem beyond the capabilities of current systems. These processes involve not an abstract domain of knowledge—such as physics or chemistry—but rather a history of the preceding discourse, the ability to find alternative interpretations, based on another's utterances, of one's own verbal behavior *and* the ability to redesign one's own utterances to rule out undesired interpretations and guide the hearer towards the desired interpretation. These are extremely sophisticated processes which demand an extensive familiarity with possible relationships between syntactic/semantic structure and discourse structure—natural language understanding in the very deepest sense of the phrase—and an entirely different kind of cognitive flexibility than computers have displayed up to now. The issue of interpretation, and multiple interpretations, is crucial here—more specifically: what kinds of utterances in what kinds of contexts lead to what kinds of interpretations? We need to begin addressing these issues seriously if are to capture the power of the process of correction.

It is extremely important to point out here that the processes as formulated above are at once cognitive and interactional. That is, while the processes themselves must take place "in the mind," the goals motivating these processes are clearly interactional, and their product—for example, a correcting utterance—is a piece of interaction, fitted to the context of utterance. Thus there is no way to formulate cognitive processes, at least the kind having to do with human discourse, independently of interaction.

## 4. CONCLUSION

In addition to the implications for modeling correction and tutor assistance, the work presented here brings a new emphasis to the role of the student in the learning process (although see Woolf, 1984; Oberem, 1987; Miyake, 1986; and Cumming & Self, *this volume* for suggestions in roughly the same direction). In particular, it should be clear from this work that, given the opportunity, learners play a critical role in the structure and substance of a tutoring session. It is essential, then, that ITS systems allow for maximum learner participation, in particular by instituting mechanisms for enabling learners to signal states—confusion, lack of understanding, etc.—to invite correction when appropriate, and of course to ask questions when necessary. These requirements put pressure on systems to be able to interpret student behavior, including such potentially ambiguous behavior as silence. This kind of interpretation can only be done if the system can create and maintain a dynamic model of the structure of the dialogue so far.

It is important here to stress a view of tutoring as an accomplishment achieved by both parties, a cooperative endeavor. Any outcome of the tutoring process (e.g., a low rate of student error, or an interaction which is more tutor guided in some places and more student guided in others) should be seen and analyzed as a product of the work of both parties.

This work also brings a slightly different perspective to unguided, discovery learning as an inherent part of tutoring. According to most of the literature in AI (e.g., see most of the papers in Sleeman & Brown, 1982), mistakes are valuable for students—from their mistakes, and especially from traces of their mistakes (see Collins & Brown, 1988), students learn to identify their own misconceptions and to see how such misconceptions could have arisen. I— and most of the tutors and students in the project—would agree that mistakes and unfocused discovery have their place in the learning process. But I think we would want to disagree with this perspective as a characterization of *tutoring,*; at least as that activity is organized by human participants (it is precisely for this reason that some scholars in the field are careful to distinguish between *coaches* and *tutors*.) In our study, tutors and students worked together closely to produce a secure but not overly constraining safety net around the student, so that student errors, and in particular tutor correction of student errors, are kept to a minimum. These two different philosophies of learning may simply represent two stages in the process—at first it may be helpful for the student to work mainly alone, floundering and bungling at will, until he or she knows what kinds of problems he or she is having trouble with, or where he or she often gets stuck, and can bring these problems in for more guided instruction. I think they may both need to be accommodated by robust systems. But it is important to stress the degree to which the tutor provides assistance, after as little as a few seconds', difficulty. In fact, only one tutor–student pair we observed accommodated any great degree of bungling, and this occurred only because the student stated at the beginning of the session (and also at several points during the session) that he liked to "flail" around for a while and the tutor agreed that that was an acceptable strategy for their particular interaction. In other words, tutors will only let a student engage in rather unfocused discovery if the student has specifically requested that as a strategy, and, of course, if the tutor agrees to it. Bungling and flailing are not the default values in the tutoring we observed.

On the other hand, even though the kind of learning I have observed in this project is guided, it does not constrict the autonomy of the student—far from it. The student is always given the opportunity to repair his or her own errors and to check on his or her own understanding before the tutor steps in. Granted, the opportunity may consist of 0.4 of the tutor withholding correction or initiation of correction, but given the pace of face-to-face interaction, even this apparently slight bit of silence is sufficient to allow both parties to see whether the student is going to perform correction or initiate repair himself or herself. In this way, tutoring provides both for autonomy and independent study effort and for the supportive safety net of a knowledgeable tutor.

## APPENDIX: NATIONAL CONVENTIONS IN TRANSCRIPTS

The following notational conventions are used in the transcripts.

| | |
|---|---|
| // | point at which current utterance is overlapped by the next utterance produced by another speaker. |
| (0.0) | Numbers enclosed in parentheses indicate length of silence. |
| Underlining | indicates stressed syllables |
| : | lengthened syllable |

|   |   |
|---|---|
| - | Glottal stop cutting off a word |
| = | indicates a relationship between two utterances in which there is not the usual beat of silence between them. |
| ? | rising intonation |
| (( )) | non-linguistic action |
| ( ) | unintelligible stretch |
| hh | audible outbreath |
| .hh | audible inbreath |
| (hh) | laughter within a word |

## REFERENCES

Anderson. J., Boyle, C.F., Farrell R., & Reiser. B. (1984). Cognitive principles in the design of computer tutors. In *Proceedings of the Sixth Annual Conference of the Cognitive Science Society* (pp. 2-9). Hillsdale, NJ: Erlbaum.

Cole, M. (Ed.). (1978). *Mind in society*. Cambridge, MA: Harvard University Press.

Collins. A., & Brown, J.S. (1988). The computer as a tool for learning through reflection. In H. Mandl & A. Lesgold (Eds.), *Learning issues for intelligent tutoring systems*. New York: Springer-Verlag.

Collins. A. Brown, J.S., & Newman, S. (1986). *Cognitive apprenticeship: teaching the craft of reading, writing and mathematics* (BBN Rep. No. 6459).

Fox, B. (1987). *Interaction as a source of diagnostic information in human-human tutoring*. Unpublished manscript

Grosz, B. (1977). The representation and use of focus in dialogue understanding. *SRI Technical Notes, p. 151.*

Hayes. P. (1983). Introduction. *International Journal of Man-Machine Studies,19*, 229-230.

Hobbs. (1976). *A computational approach to discourse analysis*. New York: City University of New York.

Labov, W., & Fanshel, D. (1977). *Therapeutic discourse*. New York: Academic Press.

Miyake, N. (1986). Constructive interaction and the iterative process of understanding *Cognitive Science,10*, 151-177

Oberem, G. (1987). *ALBERT:A physics problem-solving monitor and coach.* Paper presented at Third International Conference on Artificial Intelligence and Education, Pittsburgh, PA.

Pomerantz, A. (1975). *Second assessments: a study of some features of agreements/disagreements*. Unpublished doctoral dissertation, University of California, Irvine.

Pomerantz, A. (1978). Compliment responses: Notes on the cooperation of multiple constraints. In J. Schenkein (Ed.), *Studies in the organization of conversational interaction* (pp. 79-112). New York: Academic Press.

Reichman, R. (1985). *Getting computers to talk like you and me*. Cambridge, MA: MIT Press.

Sacks, H., Schegloff, E., & Jefferson, G. (1974). A simplest systematics for the organization of turn-taking. *Language, 50, 696-735.*

Schegloff, E., Jefferson, G., & Sacks, H. (1977). The preference for self-correction in the organization of repair in conversation. *Language, 53*, 361-382.

Sleeman, D., & Brown, J.S. (Eds.). (1982). *Intelligent tutoring systems*. New York: Academic Press.

Woolf, B. (1984). *Context-dependent planning in a machine tutor*. Unpublished doctoral dissertation, University of Massachusetts, Amherst.

# 8

# AN OVERVIEW OF RECENT STUDIES WITH PIXIE*

DEREK SLEEMAN
ROBERT D. WARD
EAMONN KELLY
ROSEMARY MARTINAK
JOYCE MOORE

## 1. INTRODUCTION

PIXIE is an Intelligent Tutoring System that attempts to diagnose student errors in domains represented by task sets, good rules, and malrules.

This chapter provides an overview of the four major aspects of the PIXIE project during the period 1984–1987, namely: field work undertaken to determine how teachers diagnose and remediate in introductory algebra; a set of experiments to determine the relative effectiveness of *model-based remediation* (MBR) and reteaching; systems work carried out to remedy previously noted shortcomings of PIXIE; and an experiment to determine whether PIXIE can be used to enhance teachers' diagnostic skills.

Despite the considerable advances which have taken place in cognitive psychology, and in particular in information-processing psychology, in the last two decades, the field does not have a prescriptive theory of instruction. Consequently, cognitive and instructural psychology are essentially still empirical sciences, although they have a growing corpus of knowledge to guide decisions. Several cognitive psychologists now view the field of

---

*Helpful comments and insights have been provided by Professor R.D. Hess (Stanford, School of Education) and Professor K. Lovell.

Most of this work was carried out with support from ARI/ONR contract number MDA-903-84-k-0279, at Stanford University and the University of Aberdeen.

intelligent tutoring systems (ITSs) as offering an important test bed for psychological theories (Anderson, Boyle , Farrell, & Reiser, 1984); certainly these systems have the important characteristic of producing a reproduceable environment. The lack of overall theory has led this research group to be particularly rigorous with field testing of its systems. This, as we shall see, has been a sobering exercise for the team, but we, hope, a valuable one for the field as a whole!

Given an accurate model of a student's performance in a domain (algebra), the focus of this project has been, how does one build an effective remedial system? The overall design assumed that remediation would be based on information in the student model, and that such a remedial system would be highly effective. It was then proposed to further fine-tune this remediation to tailor it to the student's individual aptitudes and learning styles. Indeed, we hoped to implement a truly adaptive intelligent tutoring system, namely one that would address the aptitude-treatment interaction issue (Cronbach & Snow, 1977). It was tacitly *assumed* that:

MODEL-BASED REMEDIATION would be superior to RETEACH-ING.

where model-based remediation provides specific comments on students' errors before reteaching the correct procedure, and reteaching simply shows students the correct procedure (without addressing specific errors).

In the early 1980s, due to the influence of the BUGGY work (Brown & Burton, 1978) and the carry over of the programming debuggy analogy, the prevailing wisdom of ITS research was that:

- diagnosing a student's error was much more complex than (subsequent) remediation; i.e., remediation followed trivially once one had an accurate student model.
- highlighting a student's specific error(s) would create cognitive dissonance which would then make the student receptive to hearing the "truth."
- by and large it was expected that many student errors would be stable; i.e., students would have (reasonably) stable models of the task domain.

This project has produced experimental evidence which challenges the assumptions listed above and which supports the idea that students' errors vary over time and in duration.

Brown and VanLehn (1980) suggest that the metaphor of the computer bug may have been misleading, and that bug instability is a phenomenon which the field needs to take seriously, Sleeman (1985) noted that there were different types of errors present in a population of algebra students, and that many students seem to follow a pattern of maturation during their understanding of a topic:

UNPREDICTABLE – > CONSISTENT USE of MAL-RULES – > CORRECT

The layout of the chapter is as follows: Section 2 describes the studies undertaken to investigate how teachers diagnose and remediate student errors in algebra, and includes a brief description of the remedial subsystem that was subsequently added to PIXIE to produce the RPIXIE program.[1] Section 3 describes a series of experiments undertaken to probe the effectiveness of the remedial subsystem. Specifically, we investigated its effectiveness in comparison to simple reteaching. Section 4 describes some modifications carried out to the PIXIE system to make it a more effective tutor. Section 5 describes an experiment in enhancing teachers' diagnostic skills. Section 6 reports the overall conclusions of the research, and Section 7 sets out an ambitious program of work which follows from this study and its conclusions.

## 2. FIELD STUDIES OF TEACHERS CARRYING OUT DIAGNOSIS & REMEDIATION

In order to begin to identify the constituents of effective diagnosis and remediation of linear algebraic equations, (e.g., solving for x in equations such as $5x + 6 = 3 - 2x$), and how this relates to the design of intelligent tutoring systems, two substantive and two supportive studies of "master teachers" were undertaken. In the first study, 4 experienced teachers were shown a series of task–answer pairs which had been incorrectly worked by pupils, and asked to suggest a diagnosis and a suitable remediation. Although there was often a common error in each of the several sets of tasks presented, this was not pointed out to the teachers. Only one of the four teachers looked for a common error; the others were happy to make suggestions on a task-by-task basis. The teachers suggested remediation for approximately 50% of the errors, it being notable that, when multiple errors were suggested, the teachers often proposed remediation for only one of them (the most important error?). Further, procedural forms of remediation (i.e., where algebra is taught as a sequence of operations without reference to possible representative meaning) were suggested more than twice as frequently as conceptually based forms of remediation.

In the second study an experienced mathematics teacher was observed

---

[1]When we refer to PIXIE, we mean the system for diagnosing errors. RPIXIE has an additional subsystem which attempts to remediate the diagnosed errors.

tutoring eight students, based on the diagnosis provided for each student by the PIXIE system. This teacher's remediation was also essentially procedural, but it did have two striking and unexpected features. Firstly, this teacher, having been told that the student was doing flipped division (i.e., transforming tasks of the form $5x = 3$ to $x = \frac{5}{3}$) would probe this diagnosis by means of a series of simpler equations to determine the reason for this. For instance, did the student know how to write 5 divided by 3? Did he or she know how to cope with improper fraction? Or was he or she simply lacking a general procedure to solve tasks of this form? Having carried out this further probing and diagnosis, the teacher would then proceed to give the student procedurally based remediation. (Because of the way in which these diagnoses had been confirmed, we refer to this as *causal-based remediation*.) Secondly, the teacher presented his remediation in a very tentative way; taking great care to point out to the student the steps he had followed correctly, and the reasonableness of the errors made. This teacher was a model empathetic tutor.

The first supporting study was a series of interviews with three Irish mathematics teachers; the interviews covered how they taught and remediated algebra bugs. All supported the need to teach algebra (and one suspects most of mathematics) procedurally, on the grounds of effectiveness and time-constraints. Further, these teachers also stressed the need *not* "to demolish a student's confidence by pointing out a series of errors."

For the second supporting study, we held a workshop for algebra teachers in the San Francisco area to discuss the teaching and remediation of algebra. This again pointed to the centrality of procedural teaching.

As a result of these studies we concluded that it was common to teach algebra procedurally. It was therefore decided to implement a remedial system which had that form. (It was decided not to implement the more complex causal-based remediation approach.)

The philosophy behind the remediation was that it would be beneficial to highlight each error, and to explain the error and what should have been done. Finally, to reinforce these points the task was reworked *correctly*, with a commentary on each of the steps. Throughout this document, this will be referred to as *model-based remediation* (MBR), an alternative name being *error-based remediation* (Figure 8.1). Another commonly used mode of remediation available within RPIXIE is *reteaching*, illustrated by the part of the protocol below the line in Figure 8.1.

Figure 8.1 illustrates interaction with the RPIXIE system during the series of experiments described in Section 3. The system developments described in Section 4 were carried out in parallel with this experimental work and therefore had not been completed at the time the instructional experiments were conducted.

An Example of a Student Interaction with PIXIE (Model-Based Remediation)

(This protocol is slightly edited)

```
    Solve (f = Finished, q = Quit early)
    7x = 2 * 2
S: 7x = 4
S: f

    Simplify further 7x = 4
S: x = 4
S: f
```

Thank you,
but you didn´t get that one right. We will now look at that task
again.

Here we are considering the task 7x = 2 * 2

Did you work out the task something like this?:

```
    7x = 2 * 2
    7x = 4
    7x/7 = 4
    x = 4
    Please type YES or NO: y (Student replies)
```

It seems that you changed 7x = 4 to something like 7x/7 = 4

This is WRONG. Do NOT only divide ONE side by the coefficient.    You
should divide both sides of the equation by the coefficient to change
7x = 4 to 7x/7 = 4/7

------------------------------------------------------------------------

Now let me show you how you SHOULD have worked the whole task

```
    7x = 2 * 2          multiply 2 numbers

    7x = 4              divide both sides of the equation by the
                        coefficient

    7x/7 = 4/7          divide

    x = 4/7             Finished
```

FIGURE 8.1.

# 3. THE SERIES OF EXPERIMENTS ON THE RELATIVE EFFECTIVENESS OF THE SEVERAL REMEDIAL TREATMENTS

As noted in the introduction, the relative effectiveness of different forms of
remediation was the central issue in this research. The intention was to build
a highly adaptive, intelligent tutoring system. As a first step in this process,
we attempted to verify the hypothesis that MBR was superior to reteaching.
Subsequent experimentation was to establish the optimum conditions for
students with differing aptitudes.

Essentially, we could find no evidence supporting the greater effectiveness of MBR for algebra when taught procedurally (or, more specifically, not for our target populations). The rest of this section discusses in some detail the main points of the experiments conducted to investigate this issue. Sleeman, Kelly, Martinak, Ward, and Moore (1989) reports this series of experiments in detail.

After a series of pilot studies to verify that students were able to use the RPIXIE system easily, we ran our first formal experiment. This, and the subsequent studies, followed a pretest–intervention–posttest design. For a class of 24 13–14-year-old pupils who were below average in mathematics, it was found that, although MBR and reteaching both produced positive gains, MBR was *not* better than reteaching. This was a surprising result.

However, as only 30% of students' errors were diagnosed by the system, the two conditions may have been, in effect, educationally equivalent, because, when RPIXIE was unable to arrive at a diagnosis for an error, it simply showed the student the correct way to work the problem; i.e., it simply retaught the topic. This result led us to believe that the issues of diagnosis and remediation were much more subtle than initially suspected, and therefore we decided to replicate the study using *human* tutors. However, this second study still gave essentially the same result. It was then hypothesised that these results may have occurred because the treatments had not created adequate cognitive engagement, or that, alternatively, PIXIE's corrective comments, targeted at those part(s) of the task the student had worked incorrectly, were failing to create the expected cognitive dissonance. A third experiment was therefore conducted with four treatment groups, namely, MBR, MBR + Cognitive Engagement (here the student was asked to reteach to the tutor the correct procedures), MBR + Cognitive Dissonance (here the student was required to substitute his or her incorrect solution back into the original equation, thereby demonstrating that the solution was wrong), and reteaching. Again there were no significant differences between treatments.

This result led to a further range of hypotheses; specifically, to suppose that many errors are in fact unstable; that is, the same student given a comparable task on different occasions, would work the task differently. Indeed, a retrospective analysis of the last experiment, showed that only 18%–26% of errors made on the pretest were present on the *same items 1 week later* during the tutorial. (Note that this is a very stringent requirement for stability of errors; a more lenient criterion is introduced below.)

The fourth experiment in the series was explicitly designed to investigate the issue of stability. A test containing 51 items was developed—17 sets of three comparable items. This measure was given twice at a week's interval. The intent of this study was to identify errors that were stable over time, and then to provide human tutoring on those errors. On this occasion, for an

Table 8.1. *Tutored stable errors*—numbers of students making particular errors (with the numbers of errors they made in parentheses).

|  | MBR | | RETEACH | | CONTROL | |
| --- | --- | --- | --- | --- | --- | --- |
| ERROR TYPE | Pretest (mean) | Posttest | Pretest (mean) | Posttest | Pretest (mean) | Posttest |
| 1 Bracket | 4(17) | 4( 8) | 4(19) | 3( 9) | 4(30) | 4(26) |
| 2 Precedence | 3(11) | 2( 7) | 4(14) | 2( 6) | 5(20) | 5(19) |
| 3 Computational | — | — | 2( 6) | 2( 3) | 4(30) | 3(17) |
| 4 Change side not sign of x-term | 1( 5) | 0 | 2(20) | 1(11) | 1( 3) | 1( 4) |
| 5 Subtract coeff | 1(34) | 0 | 1(35) | 0 | 2(25) | 2(28) |
| 7 Add neg sign | 1( 3) | 0 | 1( 3) | 1( 2) | 1( 3) | 1( 5) |
| 10 Inv Division | 1(29) | 0 | — | — | — | — |
| 11 Minus before wrong number | — | — | 1(12) | 0 | 1(12) | 1(11) |
| 12 Subtract a Multiplier | — | — | 1( 3) | 1( 3) | — | — |
| TOTALS: | 11(99) | 6(15) | 16(112) | 10(34) | 18(123) | 17(110) |
| % ERRORS REDUCED: | | | | | | |
| student-errors | 45% | | 38% | | 6% | |
| total-errors | (85%) | | (70%) | | (11%) | |

error to be classified as *stable*, it had to occur at least twice in both pretests, although not necessarily in similar items. By this criterion there were 19 stable errors accounting for 70% of all errors. Twenty-four students with stable errors were then assigned randomly to one of three conditions, namely MBR, reteach, or the control group. Both the MBR and reteach groups were tutored individually for a 50-minute period; the control group took only the two pretests and the posttest. Only nine of the stable errors recurred during tutoring, and Table 8.1 shows the occurrences of these errors within the three groups of subjects. Even taking stable errors alone, there were still significantly fewer errors on the posttest for the treatment groups when compared with the control group, and again both treatment groups were comparable.

The data suggest that errors are fairly stable from Pretest-1 to Pretest-2, but decrease substantially in the posttest, presumably due to the effects of tutoring. Once an error had been tutored, it tended not to reappear in the same tutorial session. Tutoring also appeared to suppress attentional errors.[2] The results suggest that, although some errors are unstable, tutoring is effective at remediating stable errors, but again MBR is *not more effective than reteaching.*

Several additional experiments were run with RPIXIE which generally supported the result that MBR and reteaching were very comparable. One additional finding was that students appeared to make more unstable errors using RPIXIE than on analogous tasks with a human tutor.

---

[2]Errors caused by lack of attention to the task (e.g., adding or omitting signs).

These results will now be interpreted within the framework of the assumptions listed in the introductory section. Explicitly, the results from our experiment will be related to each of these assumptions.

### Assumption 1: Diagnosing a student's error is much more complex than remediation.

Even if a diagnosis has been made correctly, remediation involves conveying that information to the student in a way that is intelligible. Much of our social knowledge is about communication, such as phrasing a request so that it will appear attractive to the hearer. Remediation is no less subtle; the teachers in our study (Section 2) seemed to understand that. (Unfortunately, RPIXIE did not!)

*Conclusion.* Those of us who have been enamored with the technicalities of inferring student models have overlooked the complexities inherent in subsequently communication the remediation. (Note: This is not to say that diagnosis is a simple matter.)

### Assumption 2: Highlighting a student's specific error(s) would create cognitive dissonance.

This set of experiments clearly established that, for this topic and teaching approach, reteaching and model-based remediation were each better than no treatment at all, but that reteaching and model-based remediation were comparable. This initially surprising result suggests that, for this topic and students, *CAI would have been just as effective as ICAI* (as, of course, CAI programs are quite capable of storing pre-worked solutions to tasks)

*One* interpretation of the fact that students did equally well on reteaching as on MBR is that the students in the reteaching group were self-correcting. That is, they compared their incorrect working with the correct form, and generally inferred their own errors. This could be one reason why immediate feedback is so important for learning (Lewis & Anderson, 1985). (If the *critical* component is the provision of virtually instant feedback, then this would explain why the feedback provided by teachers on exercises a week or so after the event is also not very effective.) This interpretation is consistent with other experiments on "passive" versus "active" instruction, and is consistent with the literature on metacognition (Brown, 1978).

### Assumption 3: Many student errors would be stable.

The identification of stable and unstable errors supports the error-types suggested by Sleeman (1985). That is, one should expect to find students with a *range* of types of errors, including:

- strongly held, consistent malrules.
- related "families" of malrules which are applied "randomly."
- passing attentional errors (like adding/omitting signs).
- guessing because the tutor or the program demands an answer.[3]
- mental slips and casual (typing) errors.

This analysis has considerable implications for remediation. Clearly, one might wish to highlight and discuss in detail a known stable error, but a detailed discussion of a pure guess might be counterproductive, as it might help "cement" the incorrect form. The diagnosis and remediation of different types of errors is both a complex and a subtle process, and one which has yet to be properly addressed by ITSs. The version of RPIXIE used in these experiments lacks the sophistication of being able to make a "global" diagnosis of a student's error pattern. This may however, be an important issue. Section 4 discusses a pilot system which produces more global diagnoses, i.e., diagnoses which "explain" a series of errors—possibly which occurred in various task-sets. How to phrase remedial comments, as we have seen, is of vital importance.

We further hypothesized that, had the students been taught conceptually, rather than procedurally, then there would have been a greater chance of them forming a more meaningful mental model of the domain, and thus exhibiting more stable errors. We were unable to find any secondary school that taught algebra conceptually, so this hypothesis remains untested.

The implications of the series of diagnostic/remedial experiments are discussed in some detail in Section 6.


## 4. SYSTEMS WORK

During the course of the 3-year project, an extensive amount of systems work was carried out (Sleeman, 1987; Moore & Sleeman, 1988). This was driven by the studies of master teachers reported in Section 2, and by the analysis of different error sources reported in Section 3 and by Sleeman (1985). (Note these developments were completed after the experimental work described in Section 3.) Below, work of principally educational importance is mentioned:

- The PIXIE shell has been modified so that it is possible to tutor (i.e., diagnose and remediate) in several subject areas. This gives the capability of having found a consistent precedence bug in algebra

---

[3]After the 1981 experiment, a facility was added to PIXIE to allow students to QUIT any task, so as to avoid this situation.

(e.g., $4 + 5x = 19 \Rightarrow 9x = 19$) to have the student tutored on arithmetic precedence, i.e., tasks of the form $3 + 4*5$.

- PIXIE had the ability to infer alternative models consistent with the student's answer. However, RPIXIE only proposed MBR if it had inferred only a *single* model; when it had several possible models, it simply retaught the task. The remedial system has been improved so that it *selects*, for presentation to the student, remedial models which are consistent with the student's intermediary workings. By using the student's intermediary workings the set of models can often be *greatly* reduced; this reduced subset is now presented to the student by the enhanced system.

- A subsystem has been implemented which produces a more global analysis of a student's performance on a wide range of tasks. Previously, the most commonly used mode of the RPIXIE system produced a diagnosis (and if needed remediation) which was specific to a particular task. This was too myopic a view. The current subsystem when it is shown a student analysis record of the following form:

$$5x = 15 \Rightarrow x = 3 \text{ and } 5x = 7 \Rightarrow x = 2$$

suggests that it is probable the student can correctly solve tasks of the form $ax = b$ when b is divisible by a, but not when b is indivisible by a. This subsystem also suggests sets of tasks that should be used in tutoring such a student.

Similarly, given the following student performance:

$$5x + 3 = 11 \Rightarrow x = 8/5 \text{ and } 5x + 3x = 11 \Rightarrow x + x = 11 - 3 - 5$$

this subsystem would suggest that the student can successfully solve tasks of the form $ax + b = c$, but not those of the form $ax + bx = c$, suggesting that the student does not know how to combine x-terms.

- Various software aids have been produced for the developer of new knowledge bases. These include a program which generates tasks for discriminating between alternative possible models. Another package checks for syntax errors and certain semantic inconsistencies in knowledge bases (e.g., entities being referenced but not defined.)

- We have implemented a system, called INFER*, to infer new malrules from protocols, given additional background knowledge and some focusing heuristics. Additionally, we have implemented a system, MALGEN, which applies perturbatious to correct rules, and filters out "variants" which violate certain metaconstraints. For details of these approaches see Sleeman (1982) and Sleeman, Hirsh, Ellery, and Kim (1990).

## 5. AIDS FOR HELPING TEACHERS BE BETTER DIAGNOSTICIANS

We have developed a version of the system called TPIXIE.[4] This drew some of its inspiration from the BUGGY program (Brown & Burton, 1978), which presents trainee teachers with incorrectly worked subtraction tasks and then asks them to suggest additional tasks, and to indicate how the student who produced the erroneous answer, if consistent, would work them. The major difference between BUGGY and TPIXIE is the domain of application.

A pilot study with the system in California, using trainee teachers as subjects, suggested that experience of working with TPIXIE led to improvements in their algebra error diagnosis skills. However, the trainee-teachers suggested that the example-set be changed so that more difficult tasks would be encountered earlier in the session (Schneider, Kelly, Blando, Martinak, Sleeman, & Snow, 1986).

A further experiment with an enhanced TPIXIE system was conducted in Aberdeen with a larger sample of trainee-teachers (Kelly, Sleeman, Ward, & Martinak, 1987). The encouraging trend of the pilot study was confirmed. The subjects on TPIXIE were significantly better at diagnosing algebra errors on the posttest than those in the control group. However, further replication using a refined methodology and test instrument is required before firm conclusions can be drawn.

If, as Section 3 suggests, Reteaching is as effective as MBR, then there is *less* point in training teachers to be good diagnosticians than we had previously thought. Nevertheless, one could make the case that being aware of possible student errors would make them better classroom teachers.

## 6. CONCLUSIONS

Listed below are the conclusions drawn from this series of related studies:

- Virtually all teachers encountered in this study in American, English, Irish, and Scottish schools taught algebra procedurally (Section 2).
- Model-based remediation and reteaching using humans as tutors are both more effective than no tutoring (Section 3).
- Model-based remediation and simply reteaching are equally effective when the tutoring is carried out by humans. This leads to the hypothesis discussed in Section 3 that the students in the reteaching

---

[4]TPIXIE is a variant of PIXIE which presents the trainee teacher with a student's incorrectly worked tasks, and asks the teacher to demonstrate an understanding of the error by working further tasks in the same incorrect way.

group were self-correcting, and the conclusion that, for some domains and some student populations, *CAI would be as effective as ICAI* (Section 3).

- In the final study, a significant number of students had stable errors which accounted for approximately 70% of errors recorded. There appeared to be a bigger proportion of unstable errors when students solved analogous tasks with RPIXIE (Section 3).
- There is further evidence that students make a wide variety of types of errors (from "hard" bugs to careless—typing—errors), and that students hold beliefs of varying strengths about these error types (Section 3; see paragraph on Assumption 3).
- The PIXIE system has been further enhanced, so that it should be more humanlike in its tutoring—having the ability to tutor in several domains and to form "global" diagnoses. These facilities now need to be thoroughly field tested (Section 4).
- It appears to be possible to train teachers to diagnose error patterns in examples wrongly worked by students (Section 5).

As a result of these studies, two clear questions have evolved, which should be answered before it is sensible to build an intelligent tutoring system for a particular domain:

- Can human tutors demonstrate that MBR is more effective than reteaching in that domain?
- Are student errors in the proposed domain stable?

## REFERENCES

Anderson, J.R., Boyle, C.F., Farrell, R., & Reiser, B. (1984). Cognitive principles in the design of Computer Tutors. *Proceedings of the 6th Annual Conference of the Cognitive Science Program* (pp.2-9). Pittsburgh, PA: Carnegie-Mellon University.

Brown, A.L. (1978). Knowing when, where and how to remember: A problem of metacognition. In R. Glaser (Ed.), *Advances in instructional psychology* (Vol. 1 pp.77-165). Hillsdale, NJ: Erlbaum.

Brown, J.S., & Burton, R.R. (1978). Diagnostic models for procedural bugs in basic mathematical skills. *Cognitive Science, 2,* 155-192.

Brown, J.S., & VanLehn, K. (1980). Repair Theory: A generative theory of bugs in procedural skills. *Cognitive Science, 4,* 379-426.

Cronbach, L.J., & Snow, R. E. (1977). *Aptitudes and instructional methods.* New York: Irvington.

Kelly, A.E., Sleeman, D., Ward, R.D., & Martinak, R. (1987). *TPIXIE: A computer program to teach diagnosis of algebra errors.* (Tech. Rep. No. AUCS/TR8710). Aberdeen, Scotland: Department of Computing Science, University of Aberdeen.

Lewis, M.W., & Anderson, J.R. (1985). Discrimination of operator schemata in problem solving: Learning from examples. *Cognitive Psychology, 17,* 26-65

Moore, J.L., & Sleeman, D. (1988). Enhancing PIXIE's tutoring capabilities. *International*

*Journal of Man-Machine Studies, 28,* 605-623.

Schneider, B., Kelly, A.E., Blando, J.A., Martinak, R., Sleeman, D., & Snow, R.E. (1986). TPIXIE: Towards improved diagnosis of algebra error patterns by teachers. *Proceedings of Annual Meeting of the American Psychological Association.* Washington DC.

Sleeman, D. (1982). Inferring (mal)rules from pupil's protocols. In *Proceedings of the 1982 European AI Conference,* pp. 160-164. (Republished in *Proceedings of the International Machine Learning Workshop,* Illinois, June 1983).

Sleeman. D. (1985). Basic algebra revisited: a study with 14-year-olds. *International Journal of Man-machine Studies, 23,* 127-149.

Sleeman, D. (1987). PIXIE: A shell for developing Intelligent Tutoring Systems. In R. Lawler & M. Yazdani (Eds.), *AI & Education* (Vol.1, pp. 239-265). London: Chapman & Hall.

Sleeman, D., Hirsh, H.B., Ellery, I. & Kim, In-Yung. (1987). Expanding domain theories: Two case studies in student modeling. *Machine Learning, 5,* 11-37.

Sleeman, D., Kelly, A.E., Martinak, R., Ward, R.D., & Moore, J. (1984). Studies of diagnosis and remediation with high school algebra students. *Cognitive Science, 13,* 551-568.

# 9

# TEACHER THINKING, LEARNER THINKING: THINK-ALOUD PROTOCOL ANALYSIS IN TUTORING SYSTEMS RESEARCH*

PAUL KAMSTEEG
DICK BIERMAN

## 1.INTRODUCTION

At the Psychonomics Department of the University of Amsterdam, one of the research groups is called 'Knowledge Acquisition in Formal Domains.' Research in this group focuses on how people solve problems, for example, in the domain of physics, and on how they learn to do so. One of the main research methods used is think-aloud protocol analysis. There is reason to believe that think-aloud protocols reflect the ongoing mental processes with a reasonable lack of distortion (Breuker, Elshout, Van Someren, & Wielinga, 1986). Therefore, analysis of such protocols can and should result in a model of the problem-solving behavior in the respective domain.

In practice this approach implies a continuous cycle of analysis and model construction, where protocols are analyzed within the framework of the current model and where differences cause further refinement and adaptation of the model. Models may be implemented as computer programs using artificial intelligence techniques. Evidently, a computer program which claims to be a model of an advanced problem solver should be able to solve the problems too, and the 'mental trace' of such a program should correspond with the trace of the human problem solver in as far as this can be deduced

*The research reported in this chapter was partially funded by the Dutch Foundation for Educational Research (SVO) as projects 1039 and 7015.

from the protocol. In the same vein a good model of a novice problem solver should make the same errors as its human counterpart.

A computer model for an advanced solver [1] of simple problems in the domain of thermodynamics (or rather, gas laws and heat theory as applied to gases) was developed within our research group in the early 1980s (Jansweijer, Konst, Elshout, & Wielinga, 1982). A typical example of the problems it is able to solve is the following:

> *A container which is closed with a piston contains an ideal gas. The volume is 2 litres and the pressure is 120 kPa. By moving the piston slowly outwards the volume is increased to 3 litres. The temperature is kept constant. What is the pressure now?*

The 'problem solver' was used as the seed for a research project in which we aimed to develop a computer coach for the same domain. The goal of this project was not so much a fully fledged operational ITS for practical use, but a limited prototype for research purposes. More specifically, the computer coach should be able to monitor and teach a "program of actions and methods" (Mettes & Pilot, 1981), that is, an efficient sequence of problem-solving steps leading to the solution. Its architecture would have to allow for relatively easy changing of educational strategies, and the tutorial interventions of the computer coach should be based on some explicit dynamically adjusted model of the cognitive state of the learner.

A computer coach may be seen as a model of an ideal [2] individual teacher. On the one hand, this means we may not only look at teachers' *behavior* as a template for *what* our computer coach is supposed to do, but also use protocols of teachers' *thinking* as indications of *how* it should do it. On the other hand, since a teacher in general is an advanced problem solver by profession, the computer coach should be able to solve the problems, too. As mentioned before, at the start of this computer coach project we already had a system that could solve problems in a psychologically plausible way. So it seemed reasonable to expect that the implementation of other parts of the system would not cause too many problems. This expectation turned out to be overly optimistic. What actually happened was that we had to devise a new method of knowledge elicitation in order to be able to proceed with the project. This knowledge elicitation method can be considered to be an important product of the project, since it appears to be a new avenue in research into teachers' thinking (A complete report on the computer coach project is given in Bierman & Kamsteeg, 1987.)

---

[1] Rather a very obedient novice who is solving the problems exactly according to the rules.
[2] Ideal, in the sense of being completely consistent and having a perfect memory.

## 2. THE MUSPA METHOD FOR KNOWLEDGE ELICITATION

Specialists' (empirical or intuitive) knowledge is rather heuristic by nature and is seldom found in written form; moreover, this knowledge usually appears to be difficult to elicit by means of post hoc interviews. A much used technique to get at this type of knowledge is asking experts to solve problems while thinking aloud. Wielinga et al. have designed a special methodology (called KADS—Knowledge Acquisition, Documentation, and Structuring) and a procedural support system for knowledge elicitation along these lines (see, e.g., Wielinga & Breuker, 1984).

Likewise, the expertise relating to individual tutoring is not described in full anywhere. Even global knowledge about this subject is hard to find (Kamsteeg, 1984). Educational theories are usually phrased in overall, theoretical terms and are rarely operationalized in terms of teacher actions (Knoers, 1973). Furthermore, most theories implicitly assume a context of classroom education. Hence, from the viewpoint of individual coaching, they overemphasize organizing and managing tasks, and underemphasize individual diagnosis and interaction. An exemplary quote in this respect is the following, by Ausubel, Novak, and Hanesian (1978, p. 50): "the teacher's most important and distinctive role in the classroom is still that of director of learning activities". In fact, barring a single exception dedicated to a specific domain (Mettes & Pilot, 1981; Mettes & Roossink, 1982), there is no detailed prescriptive theory of education in problem solving, although several authors express the need for theories of this kind (Reif, 1980; Shuell, 1980).

But, contrary to other domains of expertise, in the area of tutoring the specialist knowledge of an individual teacher cannot be elicited directly through the method of think-aloud protocol analysis, since the teacher thinking aloud would interfere drastically with the individual teaching he or she is engaged in simultaneously. Therefore, we have chosen to use the MUSPA method.

The multiple source protocol analysis (MUSPA) method is actually the combination of two well-known traditional methods.

The first one is known as the 'Wizard of Oz' method, after the American tale. In this method, in an early implementation stage of a computer system (generally as early as the specification stage), system developers confront one or more 'representative' future user(s) of the system with a pseudo-version of it. The functionality of the pseudo system is actually supplied by a human at another terminal who simulates the responses of the to-be-developed system. As in the tale, the system is a hoax: the main characters (users) believe they are interacting with an inhuman wizard (the computer system), but in fact this wizard is just an ordinary person.

Within the MUSPA approach this 'Oz' method is combined with a second method, the recording and analysis of think-aloud protocols. Protocols are obtained from both the person who simulates the system (in our case an expert teacher) and the user (in our case the learner). Furthermore, the written interaction between the two is stored. These three protocols are consequently merged into a single protocol of the session (hence, the name multiple source protocol analysis). The study of such protocols provides information about the diagnostic and tutorial knowledge used by the human teacher, and also about the actual effect of the tutorial actions that are based on that knowledge. As a bonus, it points to aspects of the interaction filtered out[3] by the interface, which might cause misunderstandings between the teacher and the learner separated by this narrow-bandwidth communication channel.

A fundamental aspect of this approach is the sequencing of the knowledge elicitation process in three discrete stages. Each stage results in the elicitation of knowledge which is implemented in the system in the next stage. At the final stage there is enough knowledge to have the system function more or less independently of human help. In that stage experimental sessions will result in refinement of the knowledge base. Thus the educational task, initially performed by the human teacher, is gradually taken over by the system. The computer coach is therefore an essential instrument in the process of its own creation. During this gradual development of the system the teacher's task shifts from thinking aloud to 'criticizing aloud.'

**MUSPA—Stage 1: The Computer Coach Does Not Exist At All**

In the initial stage the teacher and the learner communicate through alphanumeric terminals (Figure 9.1).

The learner performs the actual problem-solving tasks using paper and pencil. Paper copies of the set of problem texts and of a list of procedural hints are provided. A typical protocol fragment is given in Figure 9.2.

Each line of the protocol starts with a number indicating the time from the start of the session. The source of the interaction is indicated with a T(eacher) or a P(upil). Note that in this protocol the teacher needs 3.5 minutes to select a proper problem. From the think-aloud protocol it appears that this delay is due to the fact that this teacher doesn't know anything about this learner. His[4] considerations in choosing problem 5 reflect didactic principles which might be implemented in the next stage of the development of the computer coach.

---

[3]Since the teacher and the learner communicate through the computer, certain communication methods (such as facial expressions) are impossible. In this respect the interface functions as a filter which only passes part of the interaction.

[4]Where we use the words 'he', 'him,' etc., instead of 'he or she', 'him or her', etc., this relates to a specific male teacher. All teachers in our experiments were males.

Figure 9.1. MUSPA Stage 1.

| TIME | SOURCE | INTERACTION |
|------|--------|-------------|
| 03.30 | T: | OK, YOU MAY START WITH PROBLEM 5 |
| 05.00 | T: | COULD YOU TELL ME ONCE IN A WHILE WHAT YOU ARE DOING OR WHEN YOU NEED HELP? |
| 06.00 | P: | COULD YOU GIVE ME THE FORMULA OF THE MOL? |
| 07.30 | T: | YOU'VE GOT SOME HINTS ON PAPER. DID YOU ALREADY NOTE WHAT THE 'SYSTEM' IS? |
| 09.00 | P: | WHAT KIND OF 'SYSTEM' DO YOU MEAN? |
| 10.00 | T: | HAVE ANOTHER GOOD LOOK AT THE HINTS AND EXECUTE HINT 1 AND 2. WHEN YOU'RE READY PLEASE SAY SO. |
| 12.30 | P: | I FINISHED THAT |
| 12.31 | T: | WHAT KIND OF OBJECT DID YOU DRAW? |

Figure 9.2. MUSPA—Stage 1, protocol fragment (only the interaction part is shown).

A recurrent theme in the protocols produced in this stage is the teacher's lack of information with regard to what the learner is doing.[5] Teachers were especially frustrated by not knowing what notes and sketches the learner was making. On the basis of these findings, a number of learner–machine interface criteria were formulated, the most important being that the learner should be able to make notes and sketches in a natural way on the machine itself. After implementation of this interface, the 'electronic scratchpad' (Bierman & Anjewierden, 1986), the second stage of the MUSPA-sessions started.

### MUSPA—Stage 2: The Interface Is Implemented

In this stage there is no educational knowledge implemented, but the interface is ready. Thus the learner experiences the system in its intended final form. Next to the alphanumeric communication terminal the teacher now has a graphic terminal which enables him or her to view the graphic manipulations of the learner on the electronic scratchpad (Figure 9.3). A typical protocol from this stage is given in Figure 9.4.

An analysis of this and other stage 2 protocols shows considerable consistency in the intervention strategy of the teacher. When the learner deviates from the ideal (norm) path, a sequence of increasingly specific hints

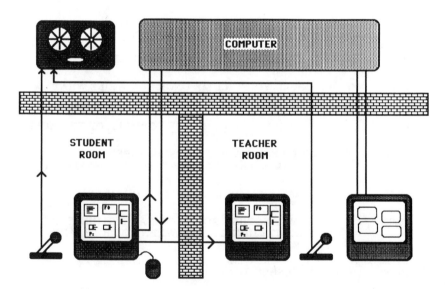

Figure 9.3. MUSPA Stage 2, experimental situation with implemented interface.

---

[5]Because of this lack of information, the teacher was forced to probe the learner rather extensively. These probes sometimes unwittingly function as hints.

| TIME | SOURCE | INTERACTION |
|------|--------|-------------|
| 02.09 | P: | TO THIS END I WILL USE THE FIRST LAW |
| 02.38 | T: | WOULDN'T YOU FIRST ANALYZE THE SITUATION? |
| 03.33 | P: | THE PRESSURE CHANGES<br>THE TEMPERATURE IS CONSTANT<br>THE VOLUME CHANGES |
| 03.54 | T: | I ALSO MEAN A DRAWING |

Figure 9.4. MUSPA—Stage 2, protocol fragment (only the interaction part is shown).

appears to be given. For example, in this protocol the teacher first asks, "Wouldn't you first analyze the problem? [before jumping to selection of a formula - PK/DB]" and later on, when this hint did not have the right effect, the teacher suggests more explicitly, "I also mean a drawing."

A hint generator was implemented in which this kind of educational strategic knowledge was embedded. This hint generator makes use of a partially ordered hierarchy of increasingly specific (intermediate) solving structures. For instance: A solution consists of a problem description followed by a solvable set of equations followed by an answer. In turn, a problem description consists of a drawing, a set of givens, an asked, etc. The abovementioned teacher interaction is simulated in the hint generator by noticing, when the learner produces a certain intermediate result prematurely, which earlier intermediate results (at the most specific level) the learner has omitted. Consequently, a hint is given for the highest intermediate solving structure superseding at least the first missing intermediate result. If, after this hint, the learner still omits necessary solving steps, the next more specific solving structure is hinted. E.g., in the situation of Figure 9.4, where the pupil forgets to make a drawing, the hint generator would first hint: "Your solution is not yet done. You should still complete your problem discription" and when this did not have the required effect "Your problem description is not done. You should still make a drawing."

In the same way a superficial diagnoser was constructed. All modules of the computer coach now had sufficient knowledge to work alone without having to rely on knowledge provided by the human coach. Although the knowledge was sufficient to have a stand-alone computer coach, it was still very superficial. This initiated stage 3.

**MUSPA—Stage 3: The Computer Coach Is Born.**

The sessions in this stage are intended to elicit knowledge to refine the implemented knowledge. This is done by asking the teacher to pay attention to considerations and actions of the system that he or she does not agree with. In other words, he or she is requested to criticize the system. To this end, the teacher is enabled to overrule the system's proposed tutorial actions. In order to enable this task to be done, a representation of the computer coach's data processing is shown on the terminal. This is schematically portrayed in Figure 9.5; in reality, the windows alternate on the computer screen.

There are three windows, representing the functioning of the interface, the diagnosis, and the tutorial modules, respectively. Apart from this information the terminal indicates which part of the norm-trace is matched against the actual learner behavior. The cognitive steps of the system are represented in the form of IF (condition) THEN (action) rules. Both the conditions and the actions are shown on the teacher screen. If the tutoring component decides to perform an interaction, this proposed action is shown to the teacher, and the system halts to offer the teacher the opportunity to modify, cancel, or replace this action with his or her own intervention. The interaction protocol in this stage 3 therefore has three participants: the learner, the human coach, and the computer coach. A typical example is given in Figure 9.6. In order to comprehend what is going on, we have added to this protocol information about the learner's solution activity (inserted between square brackets).

Note that the human coach decides to give a positive reinforcement ("ok, go ahead") and to this end rejects the null-action proposed by the system. Also it can be observed that the human coach gives an (implicit) hint about the meaning of the phrase *problem feature*. The computer coach is not able to

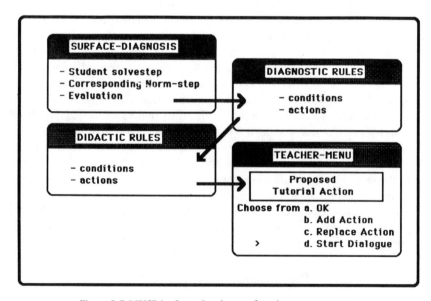

Figure 9.5 MUSPA—Stage 3, schema of teachers trace screens.

| TIME | SOURCE | INTERACTION |
|------|--------|-------------|
| 00.19 | S: | HELLO....HERE IS YOUR (HYBRID) TEACHER. LET'S START! |
| 01.51 | S: | SEARCHING FOR SUITABLE PROBLEM. ONE MOMENT PLEASE... |
| 02.08 | S: | HERE COMES YOUR PROBLEM. GOOD LUCK. |
| | | [pupil makes drawing containing trivial error] |
| 11.55 | T: | OK GO AHEAD <<OUT>> |
| | | ["V1 is 2 liter"] |
| 17.41 | S: | OK, BUT YOU DIDN'T FINISH THE PROBLEM YET: YOU SHOULD FINISH THE PROBLEM SKETCH. |
| | | ["P1 is 120 kPa"] |
| 21.22 | S: | OK, BUT YOU DIDN'T FINISH THE PROBLEM SKETCH YET: YOU SHOULD WRITE DOWN THE PROBLEM FEATURES. |
| | | ["T1 is T2"] |
| 26.09 | T: | GO AHEAD <<OUT>> |
| | | ["closed system"] |
| 27.32 | S: | YES, GO AHEAD |
| | | ["V2 = 3 liter"] |
| 29.44 | T: | GO AHEAD <<OUT>> |
| | | ["pressure diminishes"] |
| 31.44 | S: | YES, GO AHEAD |
| | | [pupil chooses formula: Boyle's law] |
| 35.29 | T: | IS THIS FORMULA VALID FOR ALL GASES? <OVER> |
| 37.13 | P: | NO, ONLY FOR IDEAL GASES, SO IT'S OK TO USE IT HERE <OVER> |
| 38.44 | T: | LOOK AT THE PROBLEM AND EXTEND YOUR PROBLEM SKETCH WITH THESE KIND OF FEATURES <<OUT>> |

Figure 9.6. MUSPA—Stage 3, protocol fragment (only the interaction part is shown).

generate this hint from its present knowledge base. Thus further knowledge should be inserted to incorporate similar interventions.

## 3. EXPLORATIONS USING MUSPA

As implied in the previous section, in each MUSPA stage a (rather modest) experiment was performed. In this section we would like to discuss some of the tentative results, specifically those that relate to the use of a learner model (as it is inferred from previous interactions with the learner) and the teaching history by our teachers. These dynamic long-term databases are usually regarded as the sine qua non of ITSs. If we regard ITSs as, in a sense, models of human individual tutors, we should find evidence of using learner model and teaching history in the think-aloud protocols of our teachers.

Note, however, that our use of the term *learner model* in this analysis is restricted to relatively long-term storage of problem-related cognitive idiosyncrasies. That is, results of on-the-spot diagnosis based locally on the learner's current solve step are *not* considered to indicate the use of a learner model (however they may or may not result in *updating* the pupil model for later use), and therefore are not included in this analysis. Neither do we include emotional and personality traits in this analysis. In short, we view as indications of (cognitive) pupil model use those occasions where a teacher *remembers* something about the learner and uses this in deciding on a diagnosis and/or feedback. Some authors have a considerably wider conception of learner modeling than this (for an overview, see, e.g., Self, 1988).

The first experiment, pertaining to the first MUSPA stage, was set up to clarify the interface requirements. Its data were primarily used to this end, and no inspection was done as to indications of using learner model or teaching history. This experiment is therefore not discussed further.

Based on data from the second experiment, a prototype computer coach was constructed. This was quite shallow, yet performed reasonably in diagnosing deviations from the normative problem trace and giving adequate feedback regarding these deviations. This prototype never was intended to treat conceptual mistakes (see introduction); consequently, no in-depth diagnosis was performed—that is, the deeper cause of mistakes was not inferred.

Although this prototype maintains a learner model, it only makes sparing use of it. This appears to be more than can be said about the teacher in our second experiment. On inspection of the think-aloud protocols from this teacher (211 minutes in total) there are only a few references to what might be a learner model. Evidence of actually *using* the learner model in diagnosing an action or deciding on some form of feedback are even more sparse, as are references to the teaching history (e.g., using knowledge about previous interactions with the learner). In counting the occurrences where aspects of learner model or teaching history were mentioned, they were classified into the following five categories:

1. Global learner assessments (e.g., "this seems to be a good/average/weak learner");

2. Mentioning a more or less specific suspected aspect of the learner's factual or declarative knowledge (actually, this is often hard to distinguish from just assessing a solution step. There should be some mention of a relatively stable learner *trait*, e.g., "this learner doesn't know the difference between . . ." instead of "in this step the learner confuses . . .");

3. References to previous solution steps of the learner or previous interactions between teacher and learner, not directly relevant—local—to the current situation (e.g., "in the previous problem the learner made the same mistake as now");

4. Remarks (possibly in the form of a prediction) based on a *generalized* learner model (e.g., "normally, learners tend to forget that . . .");

5. Specific predictions about solve steps of the current learner (e.g., "I foresee that the learner will fail to . . .").

The protocols collected in the second experiment consisted of 66 minutes of interaction in the MUSPA stage 1 setup—A—(as a control), 31 minutes with the same learner in the stage 2 setup—B—, and 114 minutes interaction with a second learner in the stage 2 setup—C—. Our counts are summarized in Table 9.1.

It appears that category 5 is not really a seperate category after all (insofar as this can be stated on the basis of four observations). At least for this teacher, a prediction about a future solution step of a particular learner always appears to be a kind of combination of a global learner assessment (cat.1) and a generalized prediction (cat.4): "being a level X learner, this learner probably will . . ." In the next experiment (with another teacher) this category is hardly found at all; the one time that it is, it consists of the same type of combination.

The figures in Table 9.1 are actually overly optimistic (i.e., too high), since the count was very lenient: Repetitions of the same remark were counted as seperate instances, and a number of dubious instances were included in the count. Moreover, when the teacher makes a remark concerning an aspect of

**Table 9.1. Occurrences of References to Long-term Data, Exp. 1.**

| Type of statement | Session | | | |
| --- | --- | --- | --- | --- |
| | A | B | C | Total |
| Category 1 (global assessments) | 6 | 3 | 1 | 10 |
| Category 2 (specific 'traits') | 4 | 2 | 3 | 9 |
| Category 3 (references to history) | 1 | * | * | 1 |
| Category 4 (generalized learner model) | 6 | 1 | * | 7 |
| Category 5 (specific predictions) | 2 | 2 | * | 4 |
| TOTAL OVER CATEGORIES | 19 | 8 | 4 | 31 |

a possible learner model, this does not necessarily mean that this aspect is actually *stored* in some kind of (long-term) learner model. The existence of such a learner model only shows unequivocally when it is *used* in performing a diagnosis or deciding on a tutorial action (i.e., when an aspect of the learner model is *retrieved*). Of course, references to the *teaching history* always mean retrieval.

On a total of 66 interactions on the teacher's side, indications of actually *using* learner model or teaching history were found 10 times: four times each a generalized learner model and a global assessment were used, one occurrence may be interpreted as using a specific aspect of a learner model but could also be based on a current diagnosis, and one occurrence is a reference to the teaching history.

It seemed this teacher did not make much use of learner models or traces of teaching histories. When he did use such data, they were almost always of a global nature (global assessment, general learner model). The tutoring process seemed to be driven, not so much by specific characteristics of the current learner, as by typical difficulties in the problems to be solved, which were categorized in some kind of hierarchy. That is, there is one set of typical mistakes that novice learners make, another that more advanced learners make, etc. This teacher tries to pick problem types in which only difficulties at the current level of the learner may arise. Of course, he also tries to foresee those difficulties.

Possibly this tutoring strategy was used in this experiment because the teacher did not have time to form any extended long-term databases, in view of the short time span of the interaction with any individual learner. Each learner was only tutored for a total of 1 1/2 to 2 hours, in which only two to four problems were tackled.

Therefore, in our third experiment (MUSPA stage 3), we asked a different teacher to tutor one learner over an extended period of time. We collected protocols of five sessions with the same teacher–learner combination; the total duration of these sessions was 327 minutes. The same categories of references to learner model or teaching history were used as in the previous experiment. This time we counted even fewer instances (in a greater period of time—see Table 9.2).

Utterances which might be interpreted as actually *using* such data were found three times, all three pertaining to cat. 2, in a total of 110 interactions on the part of the human–computer conglomerate teacher,[6] 44 of which were produced by the human teacher.

---

[6]Remember that, in this MUSPA stage, part of the tutoring is done by the computer coach. But since the human teacher has to criticize the computer program and to intervene when necessary, he or she is supposed to approve of the interactions made by the computer.

This teacher appears to use a tutoring strategy roughly equivalent to that used by the previous teacher—based on typical errors and global learner assessments—though less outspoken. This teacher more often gives the learner the benefit of the doubt (or, in other words, uses more of a laissez faire strategy). Treatment, and even definitive diagnosis, of suspected knowledge gaps or misconceptions is delayed until it is certain that there is something wrong. Long-term data are rarely referred to, but this teacher mentions relatively more *specific* aspects of a learner model (cat. 2) than the previous one. Usually these pertain to solution steps the learner is supposed to have mastered by now.

## 4. CONCLUSIONS

The MUSPA methodology appears to be a valuable tool, not only in the context of educational research, but more generally for the elicitation of knowledge in the context of an ongoing dialogue. This is because the dialogue is not disturbed by the thinking aloud of the participants, and because intended outcomes of certain interactions (as stated by one party, e.g., the teacher) can be checked for their actual effect (as it appears from the learner's thinking aloud). Furthermore, the cyclical approach, with an ever-increasing involvement of the computer system, offers an increasingly better interpretation model of this dialogue and its underlying knowledge. Finally, the confrontation of the human teacher with this computer coach, which is to some extent a model of himself or herself, offers a natural way to elicit criticism (or reflection) of the already implemented parts of his or her own knowledge. The whole cyclical approach appears to be the qualitative equivalent of the empirical cycle (De Groot, 1970), which is well known from the empirical (quantitative) sciences.

With regard to the use of learner models by individual (human) tutors, of course we can not conclude that these two teachers (much less teachers in general) hardly use elaborate learner models or traces of teaching histories. The experiments were too modest. Moreover, the scarcity of references to these long-term data in the think-aloud protocols does not necessarily reflect an equally scarce use by the teachers: Learner model and teaching history may play a role on an intuitive level outside of the teachers' awareness.

However, what we feel entitled to do is cautiously to express a warning against too great an emphasis on learner models and interaction traces in ITS design, especially since these are very complex and therefore time-consuming matters. Maybe a relatively simple learner model, coupled with a catalogue of typical errors and used with direct feedback in a relatively modest style (e.g., "You may have a problem with <A>, <B>, or both; do you want explanation?''), is to be preferred above an advanced complex learner model, which is very time-consuming to implement, at least in applications for a semantically rich domain.

To this end, we think that we need to know more about how learners react to didactic events (i.e., how they learn). This statement at first sight might seem to conflict with our (tentative) warning against too much emphasis on advanced learner modeling. But actually, it indicates a shift in focus: instead of trying to find out how a teacher might form an image of a specific learner, it concentrates on whether (and how) learners in general can benefit from relatively untailored direct feedback. Therefore our present research focuses on learner thinking instead of teacher thinking. Specifically, we try to bridge some of the gap between the 'LOGO—discovery learning' approach to education and the 'intelligent tutoring' one. In our view, a simulation environment can be a valuable medium to perform a socratic dialogue in; that is, it can be a good vehicle for remediating misconceptions. As such, it might to good effect be incorporated in, and monitored by, an ITS.

In the long run, we envisage hybrid ICAI systems which are based on three or four different paradigms for three different aspects of education.

First, expository teaching based on conventional CAI, possibly enriched by learner initiated exploration in the domain knowledge base (e.g., via 'hypertext'), by hands-on experience in a real or computer-simulated domain environment and by exposure through other media.

Second, practice by coached problem solving in the domain. In more than trivial domains this should be based on an 'intelligent tutoring' approach; that is, the system should be able to solve the problems itself (preferably in several ways) and to diagnose the learner's problem-solving behavior. But, as has been argued, we do not think a very complex learner model is necessarily called for.

Third, remediation of occurring misconceptions and incorrect models on the part of the learner, based on relatively guided discovery in a 'computer-simulated laboratory.'

## REFERENCES

Ausübel, D.P., Novak J.D., & Hanesian H. (1978). *Educational psychology, a cognitive view* (2nd ed.). New York: Holt, Rinehart & Winston.

Bierman, D.J., & Anjewierden, A.A. (1986). The use of a graphic scratchpad for students in ICAI (pp. 68-71). *Proceedings of the 27th ADCIS Conference*. New Orleans.

Bierman, D.J., & Kamsteeg, P.A. (1987). *A computercoach for thermodynamics* (SVO-grant 1039 final report). Amsterdam, Netherlands: University of Amsterdam.

Breuker, J.A., Elshout J.J., Someren M.W. van, & Wielinga B.J. (1986). Hardopdenken en protokolanalyse [Thinking aloud and protocol analysis]. *Tijdschrift voor Onderwijsresearch, 11(5)*, 241-254.

De Groot, A.D. (1970). *Methodology*. The Hague: Mouton.

Jansweijer, W.N.H., Konst L., Elshout J.J., & Wielinga B.J. (1982). PDP: A protocol diagnostic program for solving problems in physics. *Proceedings of the 5th European Conference on AI* (pp.278-280). Paris.

Kamsteeg, P.A. (1984). *Kennis van docenten bij individuele coaching* [Knowledge of teachers in individual coaching] (Department of Psychonomics Memo 25.6.84.421). Amsterdam Netherlands: University of Amsterdam.

Knoers, A.M.P. (1973). Instructiemethoden [Instructional methods]. In J.A. van Kemenade (Ed.), *Bijdragen uit de onderwijswetenschappen*. Alphen aan den Rijn, Netherlands: Samsom.

Mettes, C.T.C.W., & Pilot A. (1981). Linking factual and procedural knowledge in solving science problems: A case study in a thermodynamics course. *Instructional Science, 10,* 333-361.

Mettes, C.T.C.W., & Roossink H.J. (1982). *Terugkoppelen bij het maken van vraagstukken* [Feedback for problem solving] (OC-rapport 48). Enschede, Netherlands: University of Twente.

Reif, F. (1980). Theoretical and educational concerns with problem solving: bridging the gap with human cognitive engineering. In D.T. Tuma & F. Reif (Eds.), *Problem solving and education, issues in teaching and research*. Hillsdale, NJ: Erlbaum.

Self, J. (1988). Student models: what use are they? In P. Ercoli & R. Lewis (Eds.), *Artificial intelligence tools in education*. Amsterdam: Elsevier North Holland.

Shuell, T.J. (1980). Learning theory, instructional theory and education. In R.E. Snow, P.A. Federico, & W. E. Montague (Eds.), *Aptitude, learning and instruction, volume II: Cognitive process analyses of learning and problem solving*. Hillsdale, NJ: Erlbaum.

Wielinga, B.J., & Breuker J.A. (1984). Interpretation of verbal data for knowledge acquisition. *Proceedings of the 6th European Conference on AI* (pp.41-50). Pisa, Italy.

# 10

## A COGNITIVE THEORY OF INQUIRY TEACHING*

### ALLAN COLLINS AND ALBERT L. STEVENS

### 1. INTRODUCTION

We have been studying transcripts of a variety of interactive teachers. The teachers we have studied all use some form of the case, inquiry, discovery, or Socratic method (Anderson & Faust, 1974; Davis, 1966; Sigel & Saunders, 1979). The topics they are teaching range over different domains: mathematics, geography, moral education, law, medicine, and computer science. But we think it is possible to abstract common elements of their teaching strategies, and to show how these can be extended to different domains. In this way we think it is possible to identify the most effective techniques that each of these teachers has discovered, so that they can be made available to anyone who wants to apply these techniques in his or her own teaching (Collins, 1978).

In a related paper (Collins & Stevens, 1982), we have attempted to specify a formal theory to describe the goals and strategies of the teachers we have been analyzing. In this chapter we instead want to pick the most striking *techniques* they are using, and show how these can be applied across widely disparate domains.

The theory of instruction we are developing in these two papers is at base a *descriptive theory* in the terms of Reigeluth (1983, chapter 1). We are trying to describe expert performance, in the current tradition of cognitive science (e.g., Chase & Simon, 1973; Larkin, 1979; Simon & Simon, 1979). By focusing on experts, the descriptive theory becomes a *prescriptive theory* as well. That is to say, a descriptive theory of expert performance is in fact a prescriptive theory for the nonexpert performer.

Our theory of inquiry teaching is *domain independent*. That is not to say that this is the only useful kind of analysis of expert teaching. There is much to be gained from careful examination of the kinds of misconceptions students have in different domains (e.g., Brown & Burton, 1978; Stevens, Collins, & Goldin, 1979) and of the specific methods suited to teaching a particular domain (e.g., VanLehn & Brown, 1980). But at the same time, task analysis can be used to abstract the significant generalizations about teaching that cut across domains. Comparison across diverse domains makes it possible to see what teachers are doing in a more general way, and forces insights into teaching that might not otherwise be noticed.

Our theory of inquiry teaching is cast in a framework similar to that used by Newell and Simon (1972) to describe human problem solving. It contains three parts:

1. The goals and subgoals of teachers.
2. The strategies used to realize different goals and subgoals.
3. The control structure for selecting and pursuing different goals and subgoals.

Teachers typically pursue several *goals* simultaneously. Each goal has associated with it a set of strategies for selecting cases, asking questions, and giving comments. In pursuing goals simultaneously, teachers maintain an *agenda* that allows them to allocate their time among the various goals efficiently (Collins, Warnock, & Passafiume, 1975; Stevens & Collins, 1977). The theory therefore encompasses goals, strategies, and control structure.

## 1.1. Terminology Used in the Theory

Many of the teaching strategies we describe serve to communicate the teacher's understanding of the causal structure of a domain to a student. Thus we need a way to notate a causal structure. One way of representing causal dependencies is in terms of an *and/or graph* (Stevens & Collins, 1980). Figure 10.1 shows such a graph for the causal dependencies derived by a student in a dialogue on growing grain in different places (Collins, Warnock, Aiello, & Miller, 1975). Each place that was discussed functioned as a *case* in the terminology of the theory. In the figure, rice growing is the *dependent variable* and is treated as a function having two possible *values:* Either you can grow rice or you cannot. In other sections of the dialogue, wheat growing and corn growing were discussed as alternative dependent variables. Unlike

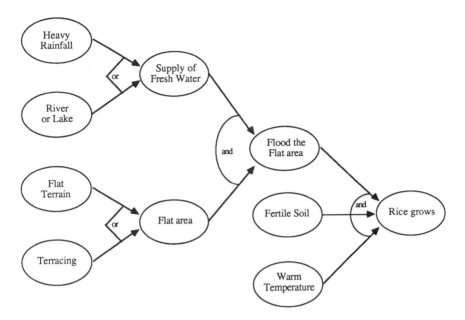

Figure 10.1. A student's analysis of the causal factors affecting rice growing.

grain growing, which the student treated as a threshold function, many dependent variables are treated as continuous functions (e.g., a place is colder or warmer), where there is a continuous range of values.

During the course of the dialogue, the student identified four principal *factors* affecting rice growing: fresh water, a flat area, fertile soil, and warm temperature. These were configured as shown in the diagram. These factors (or *independent variables*) are linked to rice growing through *chains* with various *intermediate steps*. In fact, any step in a chain can be considered as a factor.

Given a set of factors and a dependent variable, a *rule* is any function that relates values of one or more factors to values of the dependent variable. A rule can be more or less complete depending on how well it takes into account all the relevant factors and the entire range of values of the dependent variable. For example, a rule about rice growing might assert that growing rice depends on heavy rainfall and fertile soil. Such a rule is obviously incomplete with respect to the minitheory shown in Figure 10.1. A *theory* specifies the causal structure interrelating different rules. In complex domains like rice growing and medicine, no theory is ever complete.

Given the dependencies in the diagram, it is apparent that a factor like heavy rainfall is neither *necessary* nor *sufficient* for rice growing. It is not necessary because obtaining a supply of fresh water (which *is* a necessary factor) can also be satisfied by irrigation from a river or lake. It is not sufficient because other factors, such as a warm temperature, are required. When prior steps are connected into a step by an *or*, any of the prior steps is sufficient and none is necessary. For example, either heavy rainfall or a river or a lake is a sufficient source for fresh water, but neither heavy rainfall nor a river nor a lake are necessary. In contrast, when prior steps are connected into a step by an *and*, all of the prior nodes are necessary and none is sufficient. For example, fresh water is necessary to flood a flat area, but it is not sufficient. Any variable not included as a factor in the diagram is effectively treated as *irrelevant* to the theory.

## 1.2. Independent and Dependent Variables in Different Domains

Table 10.1 illustrates how the terminology applies to teaching strategies in different domains. We believe that these teaching techniques can be applied to virtually any domain. In Table 10.1 we are not trying to list all possible independent and dependent variables, nor are we ruling out other possible assignments; these are merely meant to indicate the most common assignments that teachers make.

Let us briefly explain these examples:

1. In arithmetic, a student solves problems in order to learn how to handle different operations, numbers, variables, and so on. Because of the procedural emphasis in arithmetic, it is the domain that fits our terminology least well.

2. In art history, the teacher attempts to teach students how different techniques, uses of texture or color, structural interrelationships, and so on, create certain effects on the viewer.

3. In law, historical cases are used to teach students how different variables (historical precedents, laws, aspects of the particular case etc.) affect legal outcomes.

4. In medicine, the goal is to teach students how to diagnose different diseases, given patterns of symptoms, their course of development, and the patient's history and appearance.

5. In geography, most variables are treated both as independent and dependent variables on different occasions. For example, average temperature is a dependent variable with respect to the first-order factors, latitude and altitude, and general second-order factors, distance from the sea, wind and sea currents, tree and cloud cover, and so on. But, in turn, temperature is a factor affecting dependent variables such as population density, products, land types, and so on.

6. In moral education, teachers try to teach rules of moral behavior by considering different situations with respect to the actions and motives of the participants.

Table 10.1. Elements that Function as Cases, Independent Variables, and Dependent Variables in Different Disciplines.

| Discipline | Cases | Independent Variables | Dependent Variable |
|---|---|---|---|
| Arithmetic | Problems | Numbers, operators, variable assignments | Answers |
| Art history | Pictures, sculptures | Techniques, relation of parts | Effects on viewer |
| Law | Legal cases | Laws, past rulings, facts of case | Court decisions |
| Medicine | Medical cases | Symptoms, history, course of symptoms | Diseases |
| Geography | Places | e.g., latitude, altitude, currents | e.g., climate |
| Moral education | Situations, events | Actions, rules of behavior | Fairness |
| Botany | Particular plants | Shapes, leaf and branch structure | Type of plant |

7. In botany, one learns what configurations of the shape, branches, leaves, and so on, go with what plant names.

Whether a variable is treated as a dependent or independent variable depends on what the teacher is trying to teach. It does not depend on the direction of causality. What functions as a dependent variable is merely what one tries to make predictions about in the real world.

## 1.3. Data Analyzed

The dialogues we have analyzed range over a variety of subject-matter domains and take place in a variety of situations. Some are with individual students and some with groups of students. The students range in age from preschoolers to adults. In some cases the teacher has a well worked-out plan for where the dialogue will go; in others, the teacher does not. We can illustrate the variety by describing briefly each of the dialogues we have analyzed, which we have listed in Table 10.2.

1. In arithmetic Professor Richard Anderson of the University of Illinois systematically varied different variables in problems of the form $7 \times 4 + 3 \times 4 = ?$ until the student discovered the shortcut to solving them based on the distributive law (i.e., $(7 + 3) \times 4$).

2. In geography Anderson compared different places to get the student to see that average winter temperature depends on distance from the ocean as well as latitude.

3. In moral education Anderson compared the American revolutionaries to draft resistors to force the student to consider what factors make rebellion right or wrong.

4. In one dialogue Professor Max Beberman of the University of Illinois had junior-high students figure out the pattern underlying the wrong answers in an arithmetic test ($5 + 7 = 57$, $1/2$ of $8 = 3$), where the answers were derived by manipulating the symbols (i.e., numerals) rather than number concepts. His goal was to teach the difference between numbers and their symbols.

5. In the other Beberman dialogue he got students to abstract the rules for addition of real numbers. He gave them problems to work on graph paper by drawing lines to the right for positive numbers and lines to the left for negative numbers.

6. In two dialogues on grain growing, Collins (the first author) questioned adults about whether different places grow rice, wheat, and corn in order to extract the factors that determine which grains are grown.

Table 10.2. Teachers, Students, Domains, and Topics in the Analyzed Transcripts.

| Teacher | Student | Domain | Topic |
|---|---|---|---|
| Anderson, R.C. | Junior-high girl | Arithmetic | Distributive law |
| Anderson, R.C. | Hypothetical student | Geography | Factors affecting temperature |
| Anderson, R.C. | Hypothetical student | Moral education | Morality of American revolutionaries |
| Beberman, M. | Junior-high students | Arithmetic | Numbers versus numerals |
| Beberman, M. | Junior-high students | Arithmetic | Addition of real numbers |
| Collins, A. | Adults | Geography | Grain growing |
| Collins, A. | Adults | Geography | Population density |
| Mentor | Hypothetical student | Medicine | Diagnosis of disease |
| Miller, A. | Adults | Law | Fairness of sentences |
| Schank, R. | Graduate students | Computer science | Types of plans |
| Socrates (Plato) | Slave boy | Arithmetic | Area of squares |
| Stevens & Collins | Adults | Geography | Causes of rainfall |
| Warman, E. | Preschoolers | Moral education | Who can play with blocks |
| Warman, E. | Preschoolers | Moral education | Character's morality in Peter Pan |

209

7. In two dialogues on population density, Collins asked why different places have more or fewer people to determine what factors affect population density.

8. Mentor is a computer system developed by Feurzeig, Munter, Swets, and Breen (1964). In its medical dialogues the student tries to identify a particular disease by asking the system about symptoms and test results. In turn, the system interrogates the student about his or her hypotheses.

9. In a television series Professor Arthur Miller of Harvard Law School conducted a dialogue with his audience on whether or not there should be mandatory sentencing, by considering what would be fair sentences for various hypothetical crimes.

10. In his computer-science class Professor Roger Schank of Yale asked students first to define a plan, then to form a taxonomy of different types of plans, and finally to analyze a real plan in terms of the taxonomy.

11. In the Meno dialogue, Socrates (Plato, 1924) uses systematic questioning to get a slave boy to figure out that the area of a square can be doubled by multiplying each side by $\sqrt{2}$.

12. In the Stevens and Collins (1977) dialogues, several adults were questioned about the factors leading to heavy rainfall or little rainfall in different places.

13. In a dialogue with a class of preschoolers, Eloise Warman tried to get the students to solve the problem that arose because the boys were always playing with the blocks, thus preventing the girls from playing with them.

14. In another dialogue, Warman questioned the children about the morality of different characters after the children had seen a film of Peter Pan.

We show excerpts from many of these dialogues as we discuss the various strategies that inquiry teachers use to get their students to solve different problems.

## 2. THE THEORY

Our theory of inquiry teaching has three parts: (a) the goals of teachers; (b) the strategies teachers use; and (c) the control structure governing their teaching. Each of these is discussed here.

### 2.1. Goals of Teachers

There are two top-level goals that teachers in inquiry dialogues pursue: (a) teaching students *particular rules* or theories; and (b) teaching students how to *derive rules* or theories. There are several subgoals associated with each of these top-level goals. The top-level goals and subgoals that we have identified are shown in Table 10.3.

The most frequent goal is for the student to derive a *specific rule* or theory that the teacher has in mind. For example, in arithmetic Beberman tried to get students to derive the rule for addition of real numbers, and Anderson the distributive law. In geography Anderson tried to get the student to understand how distance from the ocean affected temperature, and Stevens and Collins tried to get students to build a first-order theory of the factors affecting rainfall.

Along with trying to teach a particular rule or theory, teachers often try to elicit and *debug incorrect rules* or theories. The teachers want the student to confront incorrect hypotheses during learning, so that they will not fall into the same traps later. This kind of goal is evident in Beberman's dialogue, in which he tries to teach the difference between numbers and numerals; Socrates' dialogues, in which he traces the consequences of his student's hypothesis down to a contradiction; and in Anderson's dialogues on geography and moral education, in which he entraps students into revealing their misconceptions.

Another goal that frequently pairs with teaching a given rule or theory is teaching students how to make *novel predictions* based on the rule or theory. Simply knowing the structure of a theory is not enough; one must be able to operate on that structure to deal with new problems. For example, in mathematics Anderson gives harder and harder problems for the student to predict the answer. In geography Collins and Stevens start with cases that exemplify first-order factors and gradually move to more difficult cases to predict. Feurzeig et al. are trying to get students to diagnose novel cases. This goal emphasizes the ability to use the theory one has learned.

The other top-level goal of inquiry teachers is to teach students *how to derive* a new rule or theory. For example, Schank tried to get his students to

**Table 10.3. Goals and Subgoals of Teachers.**

1. Teach a general rule or theory (e.g., Beberman, Anderson, Collins).
   a. Debug incorrect hypotheses (e.g., Beberman on numbers and numerals, Socrates, Stevens & Collins, Feurzeig et al., Anderson on moral education and geography).
   b. Teach how to make predictions in novel cases (e.g., Beberman, Anderson in arithmetic, Warman, Collins, Feurzeig et al.).
2. Teach how to derive a general rule or theory (e.g., Schank, Warman).
   a. Teach what questions to ask (e.g., Schank, Warman).
   b. Teach what is the nature of a theory (e.g., Schank, Beberman, Stevens & Collins).
   c. Teach how to test a rule or theory (e.g., Anderson in geography, Schank).
   d. Teach students to verbalize and defend rules or theories (e.g., Warman, Miller, Schank).

formulate a new theory of planning, and Warman tried to get her preschoolers to devise a new rule for allocating blocks. Many of the dialogues had a similar aim.

One related ability is knowing *what questions to ask* in order to derive a new rule or theory on your own. For example, Warman teaches her preschoolers to evaluate any rule by how fair it is. Schank tries to get students to construct a theory by asking taxonomic kinds of questions. Feurzeig et al. emphasize considering different diagnoses before reaching a conclusion.

A goal that underlies many of the dialogues is to teach students what *form* a rule or theory should take. In Schank's case, the structure of a theory is a set of primitive elements, as in chemistry. In one of Beberman's dialogues he taught students the form of arithmetic rules,where variables replace numbers in order to be general. Stevens and Collins' (1977) notion of a theory of rainfall was hierarchically organized, process theory. The principal method for achieving their goal seems to be to construct rules or theories of the idealized type.

Occasionally in the dialogues the teachers pursue a goal of teaching students how to *evaluate* a rule or theory that has been constructed. For example, in teaching about what affects temperature, Anderson tried to get the student to learn how to control one factor while testing for another. After his students had specified a set of primitive plan types, Schank tried to get them to test out their theory by applying it to a real-world plan (i.e., becoming president). The strategies teachers use are specific to the kind of evaluation methods being taught.

Finally, it was a clear goal of both Warman and Schank to get their students to *verbalize and defend* their rules or theories. For example, it is clear why Warman's children were always interrupting to give their ideas: She was constantly encouraging and rewarding them for joining in. Similarly, Schank tried to get each student in the class to either offer his or her ideas, adopt one of the other's ideas, criticize one of the other's ideas, and so on. Both Warman and Schank stressed the questioning of authority in their dialogues as a means to push students to formulate their own ideas.

These are the top-level goals we have been able to identify so far. They are summarized in Table 3 earlier. In pursuing these goals, teachers adopt supporting goals of identifying particular omissions or misconceptions and debugging them (Stevens & Collins, 1977). Thus these top-level goals spawn supporting goals that drive the dialogue more locally. This is discussed more fully in the section on control structure.

## 2.2. Strategies for Inquiry Teaching

We have decided to focus on 10 of the most important strategies that inquiry teachers use. The 10 strategies are listed in Table 10.4, together with the

**Table 10.4. Different Instructional Techniques and their Practitioners.**

1. Selecting positive and negative exemplars (Anderson, Miller, Stevens & Collins)
2. Varying cases systematically (Anderson, Stevens & Collins)
3. Selecting counterexamples (Collins, Anderson)
4. Generating hypothetical cases (Warman, Miller)
5. Forming hypotheses (Warman, Schank, Anderson, Beberman)
6. Testing hypotheses (Anderson, Schank)
7. Considering alternative predictions (Feurzeig et al., Warman)
8. Entrapping students (Anderson, Collins, Feurzeig et al.)
9. Tracing consequences to a contradiction (Socrates, Anderson)
10. Questioning authority (Schank, Warman)

teachers who used them. Our plan is to show excerpts of the teachers illustrating each of these techniques, and then show how the technique can be extended to two other domains.

The domains we use to illustrate the techniques are mathematics, geography, moral education, medicine, and law. These domains cover radically different kinds of education: Mathematics exemplifies a highly precise, procedural domain; moral education and law exemplify domains in which loosely structured belief systems are paramount (Abelson, 1979), and geography and medicine exemplify domains in which open-ended, causal knowledge systems are paramount (Collins, Warnock, Aiello, & Miller, 1975).

*1. Selecting Positive and Negative Exemplars.* Teachers often choose positive or negative paradigm cases in order to highlight the relevant factors. *Paradigm cases* are cases in which the relevant factors are all consistent with a particular value of the dependent variable. This strategy was most evident in the geographical dialogues of Stevens and Collins (1977), but it is also apparent in Anderson's arithmetic dialogue, and Miller's law dialogues.

We can illustrate this strategy for geography in terms of selecting paradigm cases for rainfall. In the beginning of their teaching, Stevens and Collins chose positive exemplars such as the Amazon, Oregon, and Ireland where all the relevant factors had values that lead to heavy rainfall. They also chose negative exemplars like southern California, northern Africa, and northern Chile where all the relevant factors have values that lead to little rainfall. Only later would they take up cases like the eastern United States or China where the factors affecting rainfall have a more complicated pattern.

The method that Anderson used to select cases to illustrate the distributive law in arithmetic was based on the strategy of selecting positive exemplars. For example, the first problem he presented was $7 \times 5 + 3 \times 5 = ?$ He wanted the student to see that, because the 5 entered the equation twice, the problem could be easily solved by adding 7 and 3 and multiplying by 5. There are a number of aspects of this particular problem (and the subsequent problems he gave) that make it a paradigm case because: (a) 7 and 3 add up to 10, the 5 appears as the only significant digit in the answer; (b) the 5 appears in the same position in both parts of the equation; and (c) the 5 is distinct from the other digits in the equation. All these serve to highlight the digit the student must factor out.

In his work on discovery learning, Davis (1966) advocated a similar strategy for selecting cases. In getting students to discover how to solve quadratic equations by graphing them, he gave problems of the form: $X^2 - 5X + 6 = 0$, where the roots are 3 and 2, or $X^2 - 12X + 35 = 0$, where the roots are 5 and 7. The fact that both roots had the same sign was essential to getting the students to make the correct discovery; only when there are roots of the same sign is it readily apparent that the X coefficient is the sum of the two roots.

This same attempt to pick paradigm cases is apparent in Miller's law dialogues. In considering what should be a mandatory sentence for a crime, he considers worst cases, in which all the relevant factors (e.g., tough guy, repeat offender, no dependents) would lead a judge to give a heavy sentence, and best cases, in which all the relevant factors (e.g., mother with dependents, first offender) would lead to a light sentence. This exactly parallels the Stevens and Collins strategy in geography.

There are also two other strategies for picking positive and negative exemplars that we have named *near hits* and *near misses* after Winston (1973). *Near misses* are cases in which all the necessary factors but one hold. For example, Florida is a near miss for rice growing, because rice could be grown there except for the poor soil. Near misses highlight a particular factor that is necessary. *Near hits* are their counterparts for sufficient factors: cases that would not have a particular value on the dependent variable, except for the occurrence of a particular sufficient factor. For example, it is possible to grow rice in Egypt despite little rainfall, because of irrigation from the Nile. Near misses and near hits are important strategies for highlighting particular necessary or sufficient factors.

*2. Varying Cases Systematically.*    Teachers often choose cases in systematic sequences to emphasize particular factors that they want the student to notice. This is most evident in the dialogue in which Anderson got a junior high school girl to derive the distributive law in arithmetic. He started out giving her problems to work, like $7 \times 5 + 3 \times 5$ and $7 \times 12 + 3 \times 12$, in which the only factor that changed was the multiplier, which shows up in the answer (50 or 120) as the significant digits. He then gave problems in which he varied the addends systematically—$70 \times 8 + 30 \times 8$ and $6 \times 4 + 4 \times 4$—but preserved the fact that the multiplier formed the significant digits. Then he relaxed that constraint to examples like $11 \times 6 + 9 \times 6$, $110 \times 4 + 90 \times 4$, and finally $4 \times 3 + 8 \times 3$, so that the student would formulate the distributive law in its most general form. Anderson was systematically varying one factor after another in the problems he gave the student, so that the student could see how each factor in turn affected the answer.

We can illustrate this technique in geography by showing how teachers can systematically choose cases to vary the different factors affecting average temperature. First, the teacher might systematically vary latitude while holding other variables constant (e.g., the Amazon jungle, the Pampas, Antarctica), then vary altitude while holding other variables constant (e.g, the Amazon jungle, the city of Quito, the top of Kilimanjaro), then other factors such as distance from the ocean, sea, and wind currents, cloud and tree cover, and so on. The separation of individual factors in this way is precisely what Anderson was doing in arithmetic.

In moral education it is possible to consider what punishment is appropriate by considering cases in which the punishable behavior is systematically varied in different respects. For example, the teacher could systematically vary the malice of the intention, the severity of the act, and the damage of the consequences one at a time while holding each of the other factors constant.

Collins and Stevens (1982) point out four different ways this kind of systematic variation can occur. The cases already cited involve differentiation; in *differentiation* a set of nonfocussed factors is held constant, while the teacher shows how variation of one factor affects the dependent variable. Its inverse, *generalization,* occurs when the teacher holds the focused factor and the dependent variable constant, while varying the nonfocussed factors. The two other strategies highlight the *range of variability* of either the focused factor or the dependent variable: In one strategy the teacher holds the focused factor constant while showing how widely the value of the *dependent variable* may vary (because of variation in nonfocused factors); in the other strategy the teacher holds the dependent variable constant and shows how widely the value of the *focused factor* may vary. These four strategies allow teachers to stress various interactions between different factors and the dependent variable.

*3. Selecting Counterexamples.* A third method of choosing cases that teachers use in the dialogues we have analyzed is selecting counterexamples. We can illustrate two different kinds of counterexamples in the following short dialogue on growing rice from Collins (1977, p. 351):

AC:  Where in North America do you think rice might be grown?
S:    Louisiana.
AC:  Why there?
S:    Places where there is a lot of water. I think rice requires the ability to selectively flood fields.
AC:  OK. Do you think there's a lot of rice in, say, Washington and Oregon? (Counterexample for an insufficient factor)

S:     Aha, I don't think so.

AC:    Why?

S:     There's a lot of water up there too, but there's two reasons. First the climate isn't conducive, and second, I don't think the land is flat enough. You've got to have flat land so you can flood a lot of it, unless you terrace it.

AC:    What about Japan? (Counterexample for an unnecessary factor)

S:     Yeah, well they have this elaborate technology I suppose for terracing land so they can flood it selectively even though it's tilted overall.

The first counterexample (for an insufficient factor) was chosen because the student gave rainfall as a sufficient cause of rice growing. So a place was chosen that had a lot of rainfall, but no rice. When the student mentioned mountains as a reason why no rice is grown in Oregon, Japan was chosen as a counterexample (for an unnecessary factor), because it is mountainous but produces rice. As can be seen in the dialogue, counterexamples like these force the student to pay attention to different factors affecting the dependent variable.

One can see this same strategy for choosing a counterexample applied to moral education in the following excerpt from Anderson (in Collins, 1977, p. 356):

RA:    If you'd been alive during the American Revolution, which side would you have been on?

S:     The American side.

RA:    Why?

S:     They were fighting for their rights.

RA:    You admire people who fight for their rights. Is that true?

S:     Yes.

RA:    How about the young men who broke into the draft office and burned the records? Do you admire them? (Counterexample for insufficient factors)

S:     No, what they did was wrong.

What Anderson did was to pick a counterexample for an insufficient factor. He suspected that the student does not admire everyone who fights for his or her rights, so there must be other factors involved. This line of questioning forces the student to think about some of the different factors that determine the morality of an action.

We can illustrate the use of counterexamples in mathematics with an example from analytic geometry. Suppose a student hypothesizes on the basis of the graph for $x^2 + y^2 = 1$ (which yields a circle of radius 1) that the term on the right of the equation is the radius of the circle. Then the teacher might ask the student to plot the graph of $x^2 + y^2 = 4$. The student will find that this yields a circle of radius 2 rather than radius 4, and may infer that the radius is the square root of the term on the right. Learning to construct counterexamples is particularly useful in mathematics, where many proofs and intuitions rest upon this skill.

Two kinds of counterexamples were seen in the first excerpt from geography: a counterexample for insufficient factors, and one for unnecessary factors. There can also be counterexamples for irrelevant factors and incorrect values of factors (Collins & Stevens, 1982).

*4. Generating Hypothetical Cases.* In the dialogues of Eloise Warman on moral education and Arthur Miller on fairness of sentencing, these teachers often generate hypothetical cases to challenge their students' reasoning. Warman's use of the strategy was most apparent in a class discussion about a problem that arose because the boys (B) in the class were always playing with the blocks, thus preventing the girls (G) from playing with them. Two examples of Warman's use of the strategy occur in the following excerpt:

B:	How about no girls play with anything and boys play with everything.
EW:	OK. Let's take a vote. Boys, how about if you don't play with any toys here in school? Would you like that? (Hypothetical case)
B:	No
G:	Yea.
EW:	OK. David said something. What did you say?
B:	I would stay home.
EW:	He would stay home. OK. How about if we had boys could play with everything but blocks? (Hypothetical case)
B:	No. Rats.

What Warman does systematically is to illustrate the unfairness of the current or a proposed situation by reversing the roles as to who gets the advantage. Thus in the first hypothetical case she reverses the boy's proposed rule by substituting boys for girls. In the second hypothetical case she reverses the current situation in which girls do not get to play with the blocks. She reverses the polarity of some factor in the situation to force the students to see what factors will make things fairer.

A somewhat different version of this strategy is used by Miller in his television show "Miller's Court." In a show on sentencing, for example, he carried on a dialogue along the following lines with one man (M):

AM:	You believe that there should be mandatory sentences? What do you think should be the sentence for armed robbery?
M:	10 years.
AM:	So if a hardened criminal robs a bank of $1000, he should get 10 years in prison with no possibility of parole? (Hypothetical case)

M:    Yes that seems fair.

AM:   What if a poor young woman with children, who needs money to feed
      her kids, holds up a grocery store with an unloaded gun. Should she get
      10 years too? (Hypothetical case)

What Miller does is entrap the man into a confirmation of a harsh rule of
sentencing with one hypothetical case. His second case faces the man with the
opposite extreme (as did Warman's) in which the man's rule is satisfied
(armed robbery), but in which other factors override the man's evaluation of
the fairness of the rule. Bother Miller and Warman use hypothetical-case
construction to force their respondents to take into account other factors in
forming a general rule of behavior.

We can illustrate how this technique can be extended to geography with an
example. Suppose a student thinks rice is grown in Louisiana because it rains
a lot there. The teacher might ask, "Suppose it didn't rain a lot in Louisiana;
could they still grow rice?" In fact, irrigation could be used to grow rice. In
the Collins and Stevens' (1982) paper, we outline four different kinds of
hypothetical cases the teacher can construct; these parallel the four kinds of
counterexamples.

*5. Forming Hypotheses.*    The most prevalent strategy that teachers use is to
get students to formulate *general rules* relating different factors to values of the
dependent variable. We can illustrate these attempts in all three domains by
excerpts from Beberman, Anderson, and Warman.

In one dialogue Beberman was trying to get students to formulate a general
rule for addition of real numbers. To this end he gave students a procedure
to work through on graph paper to add a set of real numbers, by going right
for positive numbers and going left for negative numbers. After a while
students found a shortcut for doing this: They would add together the
positive numbers, then the negative numbers, and take the difference.
Beberman subsequently tried to get them to formulate this shortcut procedure into a few general rules for adding real numbers, which can be seen in
the following dialogue excerpt:

MB:   I want to state a rule here which would tell somebody how to add
      negative numbers if they didn't know how to do it before. Christine?

S:    The absolute value—well—*a* plus *b* equals uh—negative—

MB:   Yes, what do we do when we try to do a problem like that? Christine is
      on the right track. What do you actually do? Go ahead, Christine.

S:    You add the numbers of arithmetic 5 and 7, and then you—

MB:   I add the numbers of arithmetic 5 and 7; but how do I get the numbers
      of arithmetic when I'm talking with pronumerals like this?

We can illustrate the attempt to get students to formulate rules in
geography with an excerpt from Anderson (in Collins, 1977) on the factors

affecting average temperature. In an earlier part of the dialogue the student had been forced to the realization that there were places in the northern hemisphere that were warmer on the average than places to the south of them. The following excerpt shows Anderson's (in Collins, 1977, pp. 354-355) emphasis on hypothesis formation:

S:   Some other factor besides north-south distance must also affect temperature.
RA:  Yes! Right! What could this factor be?
S:   I don't have any idea.
RA:  Why don't you look at your map of North America. Do you see any differences between Montana and Newfoundland?
S:   Montana is in the center of the country. Newfoundland is on the ocean.
RA:  What do you mean by "in the center of the country"?
S:   It's a long way from the ocean.
RA:  Do you suppose that distance from the ocean affects temperature?
S:   I'm not sure. It would just be a guess
RA:  True! The name for such a guess is a hypothesis. Supposing the hypothesis were correct, what exactly would you predict?
S:   The further a place is from the ocean, the lower the temperature will be in the winter.

In her dialogue on who could play with blocks Warman never explicitly asked the children to formulate a new rule, but she stated the problem and encouraged them strongly whenever anyone offered a new rule for allocating the blocks. This can be seen in the following two short excerpts; in the first Warman rejects a proposed rule because it is the same as the current rule, and in the second she accepts the rule as the solution to the problem:

G:   I've got a good idea. Everybody play with blocks.
EW:  What do you think about that?
B:   Rats.
EW:  Isn't that the rule we have right now? That everyone can play with blocks.But what's the problem?
B:   I've got one idea.
EW:  Oh, Greg's got a good idea. (Reward rule formulation.)
B:   The girls can play with the big blocks only on 2 days.
EW:  Hey, listen we come to school 4 days a week. If the girls play with the big blocks on 2 days that gives the boys 2 other days to play with blocks. Does that sound fair? (Restate rule. Ask for rule evaluation.)
G:   Yea! Yea!

There are a variety of strategies for *prodding* students to formulate hypotheses about what factors are involved and how they affect the dependent variable. These are enumerated in Collins and Stevens (1982) as strategies for identifying different elements in a rule or theory.

   *6. Evaluating Hypotheses.*   Sometimes teachers follow up the hypothesis-formation stage by trying to get students to systematically test out their hypotheses. This strategy is seen more clearly in the Anderson and the Schank dialogues. Anderson tries to get the student to test his hypothesis by comparing temperatures in different places in the real world. Schank tries to get his students to test out their notions about what are the basic elements in planning by applying their taxonomy to a real-world problem, such as running for president. We now show how testing hypotheses can be applied to the three previous examples of hypothesis formation.

   We start with the Anderson (in Collins, 1977, p. 355) example, in which the student's hypothesis was that distance from the ocean affects average temperature. The dialogue continued as follows:

RA:   How could you test your hypothesis?
S:    By comparing temperatures of places different distances from the ocean.
RA:   Very good. Let's do that. Suppose we take St. Louis, Missouri. Which
      would be best to compare, Atlanta, Georgia, or Washington, D.C.?
S:    I'm not sure.
RA:   Why don't you look at your map? Maybe that will help you decide.
S:    I would pick Washington.
RA:   Why?
S:    Because it's at the same latitude as St. Louis.
RA:   Why is that important?
S:    Well, if Atlanta were warmer, I wouldn't know whether it was because it
      was nearer the ocean or further south.

What Anderson is doing here is teaching the student how to hold other variables constant when testing out a hypothesis. This is also one of the strategies used by teachers in the systematic variation of cases described earlier.

   After Beberman got the students to formulate several rules for the addition of real numbers, he could have had students test their rules by generating widely different examples to see if the rules as formulated could handle them. For example, one rule the class formulated was "If both $a$ and $b$ are negative, add the absolute value of $a$ and the absolute value of $b$ and give the sum a negative sign." There were such rules to handle different cases. To test out the rules he could get students to generate different pairs of numbers to see if the rules produce the same answers as the line-drawing procedure. In this case it is particularly important to make sure the rules work for special cases, such as when $a$ or $b$ equals zero.

   In the Warman excerpt in which Greg formulates a rule that boys get to play with the blocks on 2 days and girls on 2 days, Warman explicitly asks students to evaluate the rule for fairness. This in fact led later to one a amendment, that the girls get to go first because they have been deprived previously. Warman could have gone further in evaluating Greg's rule by asking the students to consider its fairness for all the people involved: boys, girls, teachers, particular children, and so on. If they had done this, they might have amended the rule further to let the child (or children) who was playing with the blocks invite one member of the opposite sex to play, because one of the boys had expressed a desire to play with one of the girls. They could have tested the rule even farther in this situation by trying it out for a day on which the boys got the blocks half the time and the girls half the time, to see whether the new rule worked.

There are different aspects to hypothesis evaluation, such as controlling variables or testing out special cases, that are important for students to learn. These can be brought out by getting students to systematically evaluate their hypotheses.

*7. Considering Alternative Predictions.* Hypothesis formation is concerned with identifying *different factors* and how they relate to values of the dependent variable. Thus Anderson was trying to get students to consider different factors that affect temperature and to specify a rule relating the factors to temperature. Sometimes, teachers, particularly in the Feurzeig et al. and Warman dialogues, try to get the students to consider different alternative values for the dependent variable.

We can see the teacher trying to get the student to consider alternative predictions in the following dialogue on medical diagnosis (Feurzeig et al., 1964, p. 751):

T: We've considered one possibility (i.e., pulmonary infarction). Do you have another diagnosis in mind?
S: No.
T: In that case I'd like to talk about viral pneumonia. The tachycardia, high WBC, elevated respiratory rate, shaking chills, bloody sputum, and severe pleural pain all lend weight to that diagnosis—right?

What the teacher is doing here is trying to get the student to consider how the values of the known factors fit with different possible values of the dependent variable. This forces the student to weigh different alternatives in making any predictions or judgments. This same strategy was applied by Collins in his dialogues on the factors affecting grain growing when he asked students to consider whether wheat or rice or corn could be grown in the same place.

An excerpt from Warman illustrates the same strategy applied to moral education. The excerpt is from a dialogue discussing the morality of the different characters in Peter Pan, which the children had just seen:

EW:   Are the Indians good in Peter Pan?
S:    Good.
EW:   Why are the Indians good?
S:    No. It's the Chief, because he catchẹd all of the boys.
EW:   So the Chief catches all the boys; so is the Chief good?
S:    Nope. He's bad.
EW:   He's bad? Is he always bad? Or is he good sometimes, or what do you
      think? That's a tough question. Is the Indian Chief always bad, or is he
      sometimes bad? What would you say?

Here Warman tries to get the children to consider different points on the morality continuum, in relation to where the actions of the Indian Chief fall on that continuum. Sometimes dependent variables have a discrete set of values as in medicine, and sometimes they are continuous variables, as in moral education, but in either case it is possible to get students to consider different possible values.

This strategy can be illustrated in mathematics with an example from geometry. Suppose the teacher wants the student to figure out what the regular polygon is with the most number of sides that can cover a plane surface. The student might have decided that four must be the answer, because you can cover a surface with triangles and squares but not with pentagons. The teacher might press the student to consider six, eight, and twelve as possible answers. Part of a mathematician's skill depends on being able to systematically generate other plausible solutions and to prove they cannot hold.

Encouraging students to consider other values of the dependent variable forces them into the more powerful methods of differential diagnosis or comparative hypothesis testing as opposed to the more natural tendency to consider only one alternative at a time. This is particularly important to prevent people from jumping to a conclusion without considering the best alternative.

*8. Entrapping Students.*   The teachers we have analyzed often use entrapment strategies to get the students to reveal their underlying misconceptions. This is most apparent in the dialogues of Anderson, Collins, and Feurzeig et al. We can illustrate the use of entrapment in the different domains by excerpts from three of the dialogues.

Anderson frequently uses a kind of entrapment strategy in which he takes the student's reasons and turns them into a general rule. One example of this occurred in the excerpt in which he formulated the general rule "You admire people who fight for their rights," and then suggested a counterexample. This strategy can be seen later in the same dialogue, when the student defended the American revolutionaries:

S: They were in the right. They didn't have any voice in the government. There was taxation without representation.
RA: So you would say that people do have a right to disobey laws if they don't have a voice in the government? (Formulate a general rule for an insufficient factor.)

Anderson's formulation of general rules can be applied not only to reasons based on insufficient factors, as in these two examples, but also to unnecessary factors, irrelevant factors, and incorrect values of factors (Collins & Stevens, 1981).

Another somewhat different kind of entrapment can be seen in the following dialogue excerpt from Collins (1977, p. 352):

AC: Is it very hot along the coast here? (points to Peruvian coast near the equator) (Entrapment into a prediction based on insufficient factors)
S: I don't remember.
AC: It turns out there's a very cold current coming up along the coast; and it bumps against Peru, and tends to make the coastal area cooler, although it's near the equator.

Here the teacher tries to entrap the student into a wrong prediction based on the equatorial latitude, which is an insufficient factor overridden in this case by an ocean current. Anderson (in Collins, 1977) also uses this kind of entrapment in his geographical dialogue when he asks "Which is likely to have the coldest winter days, Newfoundland or Montana?" The student is likely to guess Newfoundland because it is further north. Entrapment into incorrect predictions can also occur in different forms (Collins & Stevens, 1981).

Another kind of entrapment occurs in the medical dialogues of Feurzieg et al. (1964). This can be seen in the excerpt in which the teacher suggests that several symptoms lend weight to a diagnosis of viral pneumonia. In fact, all the symptoms mentioned either have incorrect values or are irrelevant to a diagnosis of viral pneumonia. Here the entrapment takes the form of a suggestion that particular factors lead to a given value of the dependent variable.

We can illustrate how entrapment might be used in mathematics by considering Socrates' dialogue with the slave boy in the Meno dialogue (Plato, 1924), in which Socrates tried to get the boy to figure out the area of a square:

Soc:  So the space is twice two feet?
Boy:  Yes.
Soc:  Then how many are twice two feet? Count and tell me.
Boy:  Four, Socrates.
Soc:  Well could there by another such space, twice as big; but of the same shape, with all the lines equal like this one?
Boy:  Yes.
Soc:  How many feet will there be in that, then?
Boy:  Eight.
Soc:  Very well, now try to tell me how long will be each line of that one. The line of this one is two feet; how long would the line of the double one be?
Boy:  The line would be double, Socrates, that is clear.

Here the boy is entrapped into a wrong hypothesis, that double the area is produced by a side double in length, in a manner similar to the previous geographical example. The entrapment would have been even stronger if Socrates had suggested, "Would the line of the double square be twice as long?" This is entrapment into an incorrect prediction, but other forms of entrapment are equally applicable with respect to mathematical rules or factors.

Entrapment is used to force the student to face difficulties that may arise later in other circumstances. By getting the student to reveal and correct misconceptions during learning, the teacher assures that the student has a deeper understanding of the subject matter.

*9. Tracing Consequences to a Contradiction.*   One of the ways teachers try to get students to correct their misconceptions is to trace the consequences of the misconceptions to some conclusion that the students will agree cannot be correct. This kind of approach is most evident in Socrates' Meno dialogue and Anderson's moral-education dialogue.

We can illustrate Socrates' use of this technique by picking up just after the slave boy had predicted that to double the area of a square, you must double the length of the side (the line segments are shown in Figure 10.2) (Plato, 1924):

Soc:  Then this line (ac) is double this (ab), if we add as much (bc) to it on this side.
Boy:  Of course.
Soc:  Then if we put four like this (ac), you say we shall get this eight-foot space.
Boy:  Yes.
Soc:  Then let us draw these four equal lines (ac,cd,de,ea). Is that the space which you say will be eight feet?

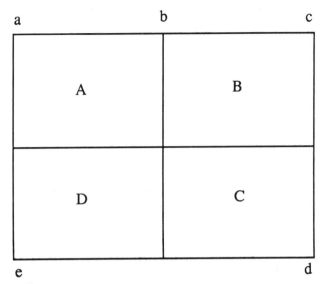

Figure 10.2. Diagram referred to by Socrates in the Meno dialogue.

Boy: Of course.
Soc: Can't you see in it these four spaces here (A,B,C,D), each of them equal to the one we began with, the four-foot space?
Boy: Yes.
Soc: Well how big is this new one? Is it not four times the old one?
Boy: Surely it is!
Soc: Is four times the old one, double?
Boy: Why no, upon my word!
Soc: How big then?
Boy: Four times as big!
Soc: Then, my boy, from a double line we get a space four times as big, not double.
Boy: That's true.

What Socrates did was to follow the chain of consequences until the slave boy recognized the contradiction.

Anderson (in Collins, 1977, p. 357) applied this same strategy in his dialogue comparing the Vietnam draft resistors to the American revolutionaries. In the segment shown there is a series of four questions in which he traces out several different consequences of the student's previous statements until the student finally finds a distinction that differentiates the two cases for him:

S: I don't think Viet Nam is such a good thing, but you just can't have individuals deciding which laws they are going to obey.

RA:  So, you would say the American revolutionaries should have followed the law.
S:  Yes, I guess so.
RA:  if they had obediently followed all the laws we might not have had the American Revolution. Is that right?
S:  Yes.
RA:  They should have obeyed the laws even if they believed they were unjust. Is that right?
S:  I'm not sure. I suppose I have to say yes.
RA:  In other words what the American revolutionaries did was wrong. That's true isn't it?
S:  No, damn it. They were in the right. They were fighting for their liberty. They didn't have any voice in the government. There was taxation without representation.

We can illustrate how this same technique can be extended to geography with an example from one of Stevens' and Collins' dialogues on the causes of rainfall in the Amazon. When asked from where the moisture evaporated that caused the heavy rainfall in the Amazon jungle, the student incorrectly answered the Amazon River. The implications of this could be traced with a series of questions such as:(a)Does most of the water in the river evaporate or flow into the ocean? (b) If most of the water flows into the ocean, won't the process soon dry up? The student will quickly be forced by this line of reasoning to see that most evaporation must occur from the ocean rather than from the river.

Tracing consequences in this way forces students to actively debug their own theories. This may prevent students from making similar mistakes in the future, and it teaches them to evaluate a theory by testing out its consequences.

*10. Questioning Authority.* A striking aspect of both the Schank and Warman dialogues is the effort these teachers make to get the students not to look to the teacher or the book for the correct answers, but rather to construct their own theories. This is a particularly important strategy to Schank's and Warman's goals of teaching students how to develop their own rules or theories.

We can illustrate how Schank and Warman apply the strategy with short excerpts from their class sessions. The segment from Schank shows him trying to get students to form a taxonomy of basic types of plans. He complains when he recognizes that the students are just repeating what they read in the book:

RS   Give me some categories of plans.
S2:  Bargain object. (laughter)

RS: Give me a better one than that. Anyway it's not a category, that's a plan.
S1: Plans to obtain objects. (Schank writes it down)
S4: Is there a reason why we want that category?
RS: No, I'm just looking for gross categories.
S2: Plans to establish social control over something.
RS: The two of you are agreeing that everything from the book is gospel. It's all right. Give me something new—I wrote those—invent something.

Warman comes to the same problem in her dialogue when she is trying to get her preschoolers to develop a new rule to decide who is allowed to play with the toy blocks in the classroom. The current rule is that anybody can play with anything, but the boys are dominating the use of the blocks, thus keeping the girls from them. The following excerpt shows her argument against deciding by authority:

EW: Do you think that it should be all right for only one person should get to make all the choices (sic) for who gets to play with blocks. Or do you think it should be something we all decide on?
G: I think it should be the teacher's.
EW: But why just the teacher's? It doesn't seem to work. We had an idea. We've been trying.

The questioning of authority is an important strategy for getting students to think like scientists, to get them to try out theory construction on their own, and to get them to question those things that may appear to be givens.

## 2.3. Dialogue Control Structure

The control structure that the teacher uses to allocate time between different goals and subgoals may be the most crucial aspect for effective teaching. An earlier attempt at a theory of the control structure was developed in Stevens and Collins (1977), based on tutors' comments about what they thought a student knew after each answer and about why they asked each question. The four basic parts of the control-structure theory are: (a) a set of strategies for *selecting* cases with respect to the top-level goals; (b) a student model; (c) an agenda; and (d) a set of *priority rules* for adding goals and subgoals to the agenda.

Given a set of top-level goals, the teacher selects cases that optimize the ability of the student to master those goals. There appear to be several overall strategies that the teachers apply in selecting cases:

1. *Selecting cases that illustrate more important factors before less important factors.* For example, in teaching about rainfall, Stevens and Collins

move from cases like the Amazon and Ireland that exemplify a
first-order theory to cases like eastern America or Patagonia where the
factors are more complex.

2. *Select cases to move from concrete to abstract factors.* Teachers tend to select
cases that emphasize concrete factors initially, in order to make contact
with the student's experience, and then move to cases that emphasize
more abstract factors.

3. *Select more important or more frequent cases before less important or less frequent
cases.* Other things being equal, a geography teacher will select cases like
the United States, Europe, and China, which are more important. A
medical professor will select the most frequent diseases and the ones
that are most important to diagnose.

When a case is selected, the teacher begins questioning students about the
values of the dependent and independent variables, and the rules interrelating
them. The answers reveal what the student does and does not know with
respect to the teacher's theory (Stevens & Collins, 1977). As the teacher gains
information about the student's understanding, factors in the teacher's
theory are tagged as known, in error, not known, and so on. This is the basic
student model.

The teacher's model of the student also includes a priori expectations of
how likely any student is to know a given piece of information in the theory
(Collins, Warnock, & Passafiume, 1975). As a particular student reveals what
he or she knows, his or her level of sophistication with respect to the teacher's
theory can be gauged. From this, an estimate can be made of the likelihood
that the student will know any given factor in the theory. This enables the
teacher to focus on adding information near the edge of what the student
knows a priori. The details of how this operates are given in Collins,
Warnock, and Passafiume (1975).

As specific bugs (i.e., errors and omissions) in the student's theory or
reasoning processes are identified, they create subgoals to diagnose the
underlying causes of the bug and to correct them. Often the questions reveal
multiple bugs. In such cases the teacher can only pursue one bug at a time.
Thus there has to be an *agenda* which orders the subgoals according to which
will be pursued first, second, third, and so on.

In adding subgoals to the agenda, there must be a set of priority rules. The
priorities we found in the earlier work (Stevens & Collins, 1977) were:

1. Errors before omissions.
2. Prior steps before later steps.
3. Shorter fixes before longer fixes.
4. More important factors before less important factors.

Errors take priority over omissions because they have more devastating consequences. Prior steps take priority because the teacher wants to take things up in a rational order, to the degree the order is not determined by the student's responses. Shorter fixes, like telling the student the right answer, take priority, because they are easier to complete. More important factors take priority, because of the order implied by the overall goals.

When more than one bug has been diagnosed, the teacher holds all but the one pursued on the agenda, in order of their priority. When the teacher has fixed one bug, he or she takes up the next highest priority bug, and attempts to fix that. Sometimes when trying to fix one bug, the teacher diagnoses another bug. If the new bug is of a higher priority, the teacher sometimes *interrupts* the goal he or she is pursuing to fix the higher priority bug. Thus in the dialogues, there is a pattern of diagnosing bugs at different times and holding them until there is time to correct them.

## 3. CONCLUSION

These techniques of inquiry teaching are designed to teach students to construct rules and theories by dealing with specific cases, and to apply these rules and theories to new cases. In this process the student is learning two kinds of things:(a) specific theories about the knowledge domain, and (b) a variety of reasoning skills (see Table 10.3). In some sense the inquiry method models for the student the process of being a scientist.

The kinds of reasoning skills we think the student learns from this process are: forming hypotheses, testing hypotheses, making predictions, selecting optimal cases to test a theory, generating counterexamples and hypothetical cases, distinguishing between necessary and sufficient conditions, considering alternative hypotheses, knowing the forms that rules and theories can take, knowing what questions to ask, and so on (see Table 10.4). In short, all the reasoning skills that scientists need arise in this model of teaching.

Furthermore the technique is exceptionally motivating for students. They become involved in the process of creating new theories or recreating theories that have been developed over centuries. It can be an exhilarating experience for the students.

In summary, by turning learning into problem solving, by carefully selecting cases that optimize the abilities the teacher is trying to teach, by making students grapple with counterexamples and entrapments, teachers challenge the students more than by any other teaching method. The students come out of the experience able to attack novel problems by applying these strategies themselves.

# REFERENCES

Abelson, R.P. (1974). Differences between belief and knowledge systems. *Cognitive Science, 3,* 370-385.

Anderson, R.C., & Faust, G.W. (1974). *Educational psychology:The science of instruction and learning.* New York:Dodd, Mead.

Brown, J.S., & Burton, R.R. (1978). Diagnostic models for procedural bugs in basic mathematical skills. *Cognitive Science, 2,* 155-192.

Chase, W.G., & Simon, H.A. (1973). The mind's eye in chess. In W. G. Chase (Ed.), *Visual information processing.* New York:Academic Press.

Collins, A (1977). Processes in acquiring knowledge. In R. C. Anderson, R. J. Spiro, & W. E. Montague (Eds.), *Schooling and the acquisition of knowledge.* Hillsdale, NJ : Erlbaum.

Collins, A. (1978, April). *Explicating the tacit knowledge in teaching and learning.* Paper presented at American Educational Research Association, Toronto, Canada.

Collins, A., & Stevens, A.L. (1982). Goals and strategies of inquiry teachers. In R. Glaser (Ed.), *Advances in instructional psychology* (Vol. 2). Hillsdale, NJ:Erlbaum.

Collins, A., Warnock, E.H., Aiello, N., & Miller, M.L. (1975). Reasoning from incomplete knowledge. In D. Bobrow & A. Collins (Eds.), *Representation and understanding: Studies in cognitive science.* New York:Academic Press.

Collins, A., Warnock, E.H., & Passafiume, J.J. (1975) Analysis and synthesis of tutorial dialogues. In G.H. Bower (Ed.), *The psychology of learning and motivation* (Vol. 9). New York:Academic Press.

Davis, R. B. (1966) Discovery in the teaching of mathematics. In L. S. Shulman & E.R. Keisler (Eds.), *Learning by discovery:A critical appraisal.* Chicago, IL:Rand McNally.

Feurzeig, W., Munter, P., Swets, J., & Breen, M. (1964). Computer-aided teaching in medical diagnosis. *Journal of Medical Education, 39,* 746-755.

Larkin, J. (1979). Information processing models and science instruction. In J. Lochhead & J. Clement (Eds.), *Cognitive process instruction.* Philadelphia, PA:The Franklin Institute Press.

Miller, A. (1979) Sentencing. Shown on *Miller's Court, WCVB, Boston on October 12.*

Newell A., & Simon, H.A. (1972). *Human problem solving.* Englewood Cliffs, NJ: Prentice-Hall.

Plato. (1924) *Laches, Protagoras, Meno, and Euthydemus.* (W.R.M. Lamb, trans.) Cambridge, MA: Harvard University Press.

Reigeluth, C. (1983). (Ed.). *Instructional design:Theories and models.* Hillsdale, NJ: Erlbaum.

Sigel, I.E., & Saunders, R. (1979). An inquiry into inquiry:Question-asking as an instructional model. In L. Katz (Ed.), *Current topics in early childhood education* (Vol. 2, pp. 169-193).Norwood, NJ: Ablex Publishing.

Simon, D.P., & Simon, H.A. (1979). A tale of two protocols. In J. Lochhead & J. Clement (Eds.), *Cognitive process instruction.* Philadelphia, PA: The Franklin Institute Press.

Stevens, A.L., & Collins, A. (1977). The goal structure of a Socratic tutor. *Proceedings of Association for Computing Machinery national Conference,* Seattle, WA.

Stevens, A.L., & Collins, A. (1980). Multiple conceptual models of a complex system. In R. Snow, P. Federico, & W. Montague (Eds.), *Aptitude, learning, and instruction:Cognitive process analysis.* Hillsdale, NJ: Erlbaum.

Stevens, A.L., Collins. A., & Goldin, S. (1979). Misconceptions in students' understanding. *International Journal of Man-Machine Studies. 11,* 145-156

VanLehn. K., & Brown, J.S. (1980). Planning nets:A representation for formalizing analogies and semantic models of procedural skills. In R. Snow, P. Federico, & W. Montague (Eds.), *Aptitude, learning and instruction:Cognitive process analysis.* Hillsdale, NJ: Erlbaum.

Winston, P. (1973). Learning to identify toy block structures. In R.L. Solso (Ed.), *Contemporary issues in cognitive psychology:The Loyola Symposium.* Washington, DC: Winston.

# SECTION III

## UNDERSTANDING TEACHING

# 11

# THE COGNITIVE SKILL OF TEACHING

GAEA LEINHARDT* AND JAMES G. GREENO

## 1. INTRODUCTION

We wanted to understand how it is that successful teachers do what they do. We observed teachers whose students had learned unusually well, and we compared these teachers' performance with that of novice teachers. Based on these observations, we propose a hypothesis about cognitive processes and knowledge that provides a basis for effective teaching.

Our hypothesis is based on the characterization of teaching as a complex cognitive skill. This skill requires the construction of plans and the making of rapid online decisions. The task of teaching occurs in a relatively ill-structured, dynamic environment. Goals and problem-solving operators are not specified definitely, the task environment changes in a way that is not always under the control of the teacher's actions, and information appears during the performance that is needed for successful completion of that performance. In these respects, teaching is similar to other tasks that have been studied recently such as medical diagnosis (Johnson et al., 1981;

*The research reported herein was supported by the Learning Research and Development Centre, from the National Institute of Education (NIE), U.S. Department of Education. The opinions expressed do not necessarily reflect the position or policy of NIE, and no official endorsement should be inferred.

The authors acknowledge the critical (in both senses) help of Carla Weidman and Cheryl Figura.

This chapter originally appeared in *The Journal of Educational Psychology*, 1986, 78(2), 75-95. Reprinted with permission of the American Psychological Association.

Lesgold, Glaser, Feltovich, & Wang, 1981; Pople, 1982) and chess (Chase & Simon, 1973; Wilkins, 1980) and is unlike the simpler tasks of solving puzzles (e.g., Newell & Simon, 1972) and performing specific procedures of calculation (e.g., Brown & Burton, 1978).

We consider skill in teaching to rest on two fundamental systems of knowledge, *lesson structure* and *subject matter*. The first is the knowledge required to construct and conduct a lesson. This knowledge is supported and partially controlled by significant knowledge of subject matter (the second area of knowledge) and is constrained by the unique circumstance or set of students (Leinhardt & Smith, 1985). The second is the knowledge of the content to be taught. Subject matter knowledge supports lesson structure knowledge in that it is accessed and used during the course of a mathematics lesson. Subject matter knowledge constrains lesson structures in that different types of content need to be taught differently. At one level, this is the expected difference between teaching math or another subject; at another level, it is the difference between teaching the introductory conceptual lesson in reducing fractions and the lesson on an algorithm for reducing fractions. Although we are aware of and are investigating these different knowledge bases, the current chapter focuses almost entirely on the lesson structure portion of instructional skill.

## 2. KNOWLEDGE FOR SKILLED TEACHING

We propose that a skilled teacher has a complex knowledge structure composed of interrelated sets of organized actions. We refer to these organized actions as *schemata*. They are applied flexibly and with little cognitive effort in circumstances that arise in the classroom.

The main feature of the skilled teacher's knowledge structure is a set of schemata for teaching activities. These schemata include structures at differing levels of generality, with some schemata for quite global activities such as checking homework and some for smaller units of activity such as distributing paper to the class. The idea that knowledge for skilled performance consists of schemata at different levels of generality was developed by Sacerdoti (1977). Sacerdoti's system constructs plans for performing tasks by choosing global schemata that satisfy general goals and then by choosing less global schemata that satisfy more specific goals and requirements of the higher level schemata. Sacerdoti's analysis, therefore, shows how a structure of schemata at different levels of generality provides a basis for performance in a complex cognitive task involving integration of high-level goals and actions with their lower level components. The idea has been useful in analyses of the cognitive processes of solving problems in high-school geometry (Greeno, Magone, & Chaiklin, 1979), in programming (Soloway, Ehrlich, Bonar, & Greenspan,

1982), and in the design of computer software (Polson, 1972; Polson, Atwood, Jeffries, & Turner, 1981). We apply it here in the analysis of the complex cognitive skill of teaching.

A characteristic of skilled performance is that many component actions are performed with little effort because they have become automatic through practice. We conclude that skilled teachers have a large repertoire of activities that they perform fluently. We refer to these activities as *routines* (Leinhardt, Weidman, & Hammond, 1987). For routines to be effective, the students as well as the teacher must have developed an organization of actions or schemata for the actions that are performed. Routines play an important role in skilled performances because they allow relatively low-level activities to be carried out efficiently, without diverting significant mental resources from the more general substantive activities and goals of teaching. Thus, routines reduce cognitive load and expand the teacher's facility to deal with unpredictable elements of a task.

We also hypothesize that the schemata for activities of teaching include structures that we call *information schemata*. In addition to conducting the current activity, a skilled teacher acquires and takes note of information that will be used in a later activity. The knowledge base for skilled teaching includes the kinds of information needed for the various activities of teaching, and provisions for acquiring that information are included in the schemata for activities in which the information is conveniently available. The information schema enables skilled teachers to deal with interactions between disparate goals and activities, a significant source of difficulty in complex domains. Theoretical analyses by Hayes-Roth and Hayes-Roth (1978) and by Stefik (1981) have shown how interactions can be taken into account in planning, either by recording relevant information on a kind of "cognitive blackboard" or with a system of "constraint posting" that uses knowledge of specific ways in which different activities are related. Processes described in these analyses permit information that is either expectedly or unexpectedly generated during actions to be saved, revised, and used for later actions.

## 3. PERFORMANCE OF TEACHING

We hypothesize that the conduct of a lesson is based on an operational plan that we call an *agenda*. The agenda includes the traditional "lesson plan." It also includes activity structures and operational routines that are specific versions of schemata in the teacher's general knowledge base. The agenda also includes decision elements that permit continuous updating and revision of the agenda itself.

The duration of a lesson often corresponds to a class period of 50 min, but in self-contained classes, many lessons are shorter or longer. Within a lesson there are subunits such as presentation of the subject matter and activity elements. We refer to the main segments of a lesson as *activity structures,* using a concept that has been prevalent in sociology and the sociology of education for some time, especially in the work of Bossert (1981), Stodolsky (1983), and Berliner (Berliner, King, Rubin, & Fisher, 1981) and in a different form from that of Good, Grouws, and Ebmeier (1983).

The agenda for a mathematics lesson includes several global activity structures such as checking homework, presenting new material, getting problems worked at the board, having independent seatwork done, and so on. Along with general features including goals and termination conditions found in the schemata, the activity structures include components that are chosen by the teacher for the specific lesson material, such as concrete examples and materials to be used in explaining mathematical concepts and in getting student performance up to a desired level of proficiency.

For a particular structure to "work," supporting routines need to be available. Routines are small, socially scripted pieces of behavior that are known by both teachers and students. For example, a routine for distributing paper is often initiated by the teacher walking across the front row of the room with a pad of paper and giving several sheets to each child in the front row. The first child in each column then takes one piece and passes the rest back through the column. This routine provides a quick and efficient way of distributing paper, a requirement that arises in several activity structures. Verbal routines also exist in the form of choral patterns of response or turn taking without repeated explanation. Intellectual routines exist in the form of turn taking in solving a new type of problem. "Watch and listen" and "Now you try to figure it out" are the unspoken guides to such actions (Leinhardt, 1983; Leinhardt et al., 1987).

Information that is important for decisions in some activity structures can be obtained easily during other activities, and skilled teachers take note of such information as part of their teaching performance. The activity of checking homework can be performed in a way that lets the teacher know who had difficulty and is therefore likely to lack understanding of a concept that is a prerequisite for learning later material. Skilled teachers also make use of an action that records which students had difficulty so that such information is available for later use.

According to this analysis, some important functions of planning and decision making are embedded in the performance of teaching a lesson. Thus, the agenda functions as a plan. Many items on the agenda are specified implicitly by the teacher's knowledge, rather than being worked out explicitly. Therefore, the conscious planning activity of teachers reflects only a small fraction of the planfulness that actually characterizes skilled teaching.

Skilled teaching requires decisions about whether to proceed with the next component of a lesson, based on students' readiness for new material and the likelihood that students will succeed in solving instructional problems, or involving selection of students to ask questions or give special help. For example, as a check on whether students understand and recall a relevant prerequisite vocabulary term or concept, a teacher may call on a weaker student because such a student is more likely than others to have misunderstood or failed to learn the concept. In our hypothesis, information needed for these decisions is obtained by skilled teachers in the process of conducting other activities. The information, therefore, is obtained as an incidental effect of satisfying other goals, rather than as a deliberate activity; however, it nonetheless provides the teacher with sensitive assessments of individual students' readiness and instructional needs.

## 4. EXAMPLE OF SEGMENTS

Having presented our hypothesis about the nature of teaching in general terms, we turn to a more detailed exploration of teaching. First, we lay out a series of *planning nets* for a sample of activity segments. These planning nets represent structures of actions and goals that are generated by the knowledge base that we hypothesize. The element that distinguishes this analysis from other analyses of educational events is that it combines easily observable activity elements with goals that are usually not explicitly described. The planning nets display examples of specific goals and actions that can be generated in actual performance with the knowledge base that we hypothesize.

In order for a teacher to function effectively, he or she must have an effective array of schemata that can be called on as the lesson progresses. Perhaps the most important schemata are those that support *presentation* of lessons. We hypothesize that there are several presentational schemata but that three are especially relevant: algorithmic, conceptual, and review. These include several common characteristics—a check for prerequisite knowledge states of students; a selection of the angle or approach of the lesson; a selection of exemplars; a monitor for student understanding and attention; and an exit for moving out of the presentation to the next element of the lesson. The algorithmic presentation must also contain knowledge for describing and performing the algorithm and for using whatever concrete representations will be included.

An action schema is a general representation of an action (at some level) that the individual can perform. The schema includes information that specifies one or more *consequences* of its action and *requisite conditions* that are required for the action to be performed. A *prerequisite* condition must be satisfied before performance of the action; a *corequisite* condition must be satisfied during performance of the action; and a *postrequisite* condition must be satisfied to complete the action. This representation of action schemata is based on Sacerdoti's (1977) formulation, with some additional features used by Greeno, Riley, and Gelman (1984) and by Smith, Greeno, and Vitolo (1983). Planning begins with a general goal, for example, to teach the material in a specified unit of the course. The planner has general procedures, including search for an action schema with a consequence that matches a specified goal. When such a schema is found, its requisite conditions have to be satisfied to include that action in the plan. Conditions may be achieved on the basis of subject matter knowledge or by using some feature of the classroom setting. Otherwise, conditions must be satisfied by setting goals for further planning, including search for additional action schemata.

The activity segments that we present here are three that occur quite frequently in lessons and that have structures quite different from one another: homework correction, lesson presentation, and guided practice. Many other lesson segments are also used quite frequently: tutorial, drill, and testing, for example. The three we have analyzed were chosen for their frequency and instructional significance. Homework correction is an ideal example of how one rather small lesson component (it lasts 2–5 min and is rarely mentioned by teachers, student teachers, or texts) can help achieve multiple goals. Lesson presentation is a central activity of teaching. Guided practice represents the critical transition to independence on the part of students.

As a first example of action schemata used frequently in homework correcting, consider the actions called ATTENDANCE, ORAL-CORRECT, and ORAL-SUMMARY:

ATTENDANCE:
consequence: homework status of all students is known
postrequisite: all students are checked
effect: students are monitored
effect: students about whom information is lacking are noted
ORAL-CORRECTION:
consequence: all items have been corrected
corequisite: answers are made available
postrequisite: all items are covered
effect: items causing difficulty are known (i.e., those items that many miss)
ORAL-SUMMARY
consequence: difficulty level of homework is known
postrequisite: all possible error combinations are covered
effect: children in difficulty are known (i.e.,those with multiple errors)

As another example, consider two actions called STATE-DEFINITION and CALL-ON-STUDENT, used frequently in presentation and described as follows:

STATE-DEFINITION
  consequence: definition is stated
  effect:little time is used
CALL-ON-STUDENT
  prerequisite: student probably knows definition
  consequence: student responds
  effect: students attend
  effect: more time is saved


Related to the CALL-ON-STUDENT schema is some causal knowledge that when a student responds to a question, the correct answer may be given; the probability of this varies, of course.

The planner considers schemata whose consequences match its current goal. For example, STATE-DEFINITION and CALL-ON-STUDENT will be considered when the goal is to have a definition stated. STATE-DEFINITION can be used to achieve that goal directly, and it uses only a small amount of time. The goal can also be achieved by CALL-ON-STUDENT, and the probability of success depends on which student is chosen. One effect of using CALL-ON-STUDENT is to increase the attention of the students, and if the teacher has time and increased attention is desirable, she or he can choose this schema instead of STATE-DEFINITION.[1]

Correction of homework can be a rather minor aspect of a lesson. We include it here because of its relevance to other parts of the lesson and to demonstrate how a planning net can be interpreted. Homework can be corrected in many equally effective ways. It can be passed in and marked by the teacher and passed back; it can serve as a lengthy review, with students putting problems on the board and discussing them; or it can be a public exchange of problems and answers. Activities such as homework correction and others like it do not occur every day, but when they do occur, the actions can have multiple effects, and poorly executed actions can have disruptive effects.

Figure 11.1 shows the planning net for an oral homework correction. The

---

[1]Some additional executive functions are independent of the level of planning that we are describing. For example, teachers must select the specific content and approach before moving into a teaching plan. We hypothesize that, while actually teaching, the teacher posts mental monitors that function throughout the lesson execution. These include maintaining attention, maintaining time flow, deciding whether to continue, watching for signals to abort the segment of the lesson (or in rare, but observed, cases the entire lesson), and posting stray pieces of student/lesson data. One can consider these as a series of questions that are addressed to the system on a regular basis: How are we doing on time (need to stretch or need to speed up?)? How are the weaker children doing? Is everyone "alive" or are they "dying" on me? We assume attention is given to these concerns from time to time and that information relevent to them is kept on a "cognitive blackboard" (Hayes-Roth & Hayes-Roth, 1978).

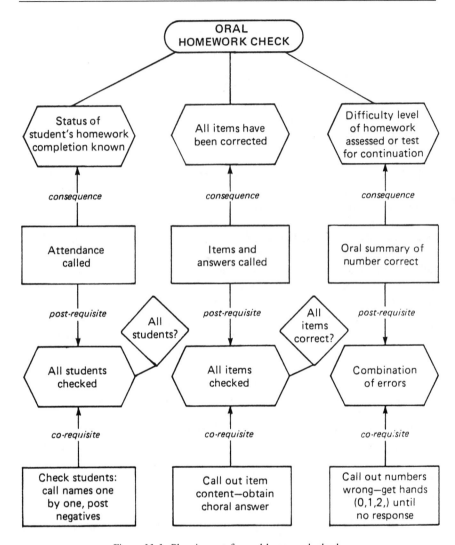

Figure 11.1. Planning net for oral homework check.

figure consists of a set of goals that are realized through a set of actions and other goals. Actions take place if the necessary prerequisites are satisfied, and they are completed or "exited" when the necessary postrequisites are achieved. Figure 11.1 shows the primary actions for homework in the context of goals and other actions. The top-level actions and their requisite conditions have already been described (attendance, oral-correction, oral-summary). The plan shows the series of goals that are the consequence of three rather simple actions: calling attendance and asking whether homework has been done or not; calling out items and obtaining their correct answers; and calling out numbers of items missed. By performing these actions the teacher places him- or herself in a position of knowing a great deal about the current knowledge level of the class, collectively and individually, and about difficulties that are likely to arise.

Figure 11.2 shows the first part of a presentation activity segment designed to communicate an algorithm. In presenting any segment of information to students, teachers need to determine that terminology to be used that has been covered in prior lessons is known. This goal is shown at the upper left of the figure and is accomplished by stating or reviewing all of the definitions. The teacher has two primary actions available for getting a definition stated. The actions are "student states definition" and "teacher states definition." If the teacher states the definition, he or she remains in control and is essentially going through the procedure of a lesson. There is no ambiguity or decision making required beyond that of presenting the correct term. The prerequisite is that the term is selected. The corequisite is that the students are attending. A consequence of stating the definition is that it tends to keep the lesson moving. It tends to be quicker than the alternative.

The second option of having a student state the definition has the advantage of student involvement. In order to have students define the terms, the students must be in a position to respond. Initially, students are in a position to listen or are attending or are presumed to be attending. The teacher has to engage in an action that alters that state from attending to responding. Depending on whether the teacher is calling for individual or choral response, the cues to change that state are calling a student's name or pausing significantly to get a choral response. If an individual student responds, the correctness of the student's statement has to be assessed. If it is correct, then the goal of having the definition presented has been met. If it is not correct, then decisions have to be made about whether time is available and whether other students are likely to present the information accurately. If time and another knowledgeable student are available, then another student can be called on. If time is not available or the teacher does not feel that another student can answer adequately, then the teacher cycles back up and uses the teacher statement.

The use of student action to achieve a teacher-based goal is an example of the dynamic nature of the classroom. When the teacher surrenders the control of action to a student, she or he has altered the probability of the correct action's taking place from near 1 to less than 1. The selection of a student is based on some prior causal knowledge the teacher has that the desired action will probably take place, but the uncertainty requires a test.

Another goal of presentation is to have the algorithmic portion of a lesson presented. The set of actions that support the goal of presenting an algorithm or procedure are STATE-ALGORITHM and DEMONSTRATE-ALGORITHM.

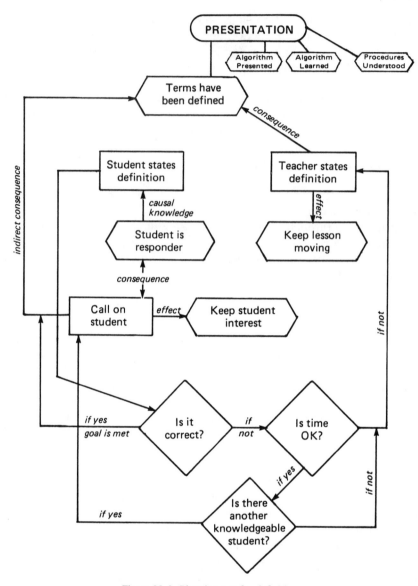

Figure 11.2. Planning net for definitions.

The planner will consider these actions when the goal is to present a new piece of mathematical procedure.

Figure 11.3 shows the planning net for the algorithm presentation portion of a lesson. At least two major actions can go on, either sequentially, simultaneously, or exclusively: (a) verbal description of the algorithmic

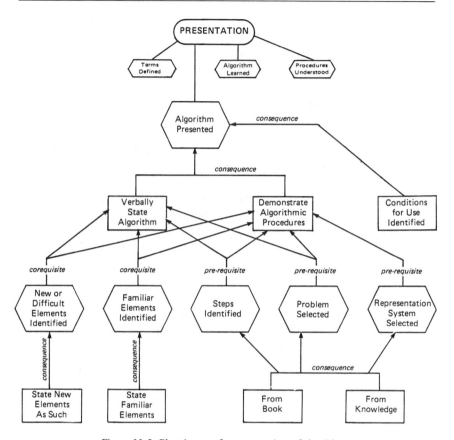

Figure 11.3. Planning net for presentation of algorithm.

procedures using an example or (b) demonstration of the algorithmic procedures. There can be demonstration without accompanying explicit verbal statements, just as there can be verbal description of the algorithmic procedure without a concomitant demonstration. The majority of algorithmic presentations, however, include both the verbal and the demonstrative portions. (Some reasons for this are discussed by Chaiklin, 1984.) In order to verbally describe the algorithm, the new or difficult elements must be identified. This can be done by presenting the new elements explicitly as such or by vocal emphasis. Another subgoal is to identify familiar elements, and this can be accomplished by stating that they are familiar. Prerequisites to verbally presenting or demonstrating the algorithm are identifying the steps of the algorithm and selecting problems. Identification of the steps of the algorithm can come from some general knowledge source or from a book. Constraints on this system are that the subskills are in place, the vocabulary is in place, and that one can maintain attention and maintain the pace.

Another goal of presentation is to have the algorithm learned (shown in Figure 11.4). The principal action for learning the algorithm is REHEARSE.

After defining terms and while presenting the elements of an algorithm, the teacher has the students rehearse. A postrequisite of rehearsal is that the algorithm is re-presented through several possible activities: board work, choral recitation, individual recitation, or by restatement. The first three of these actions have as a consequence that student attention is maintained. The actions for re-presenting the algorithm also require student selection and a testing of student accuracy like that shown for definitions in Figure 11.2. In addition to the accuracy tests for each type of student response, a test for the goal of learning the algorithm is necessary. Information for the test can be generated by learning the performance status of a range of students: strong, average, and weak. A portion of this information can come from the actions of having students at the board or having individuals recite. Finally, problems need to be selected that can be used for the re-presentation of the algorithm.

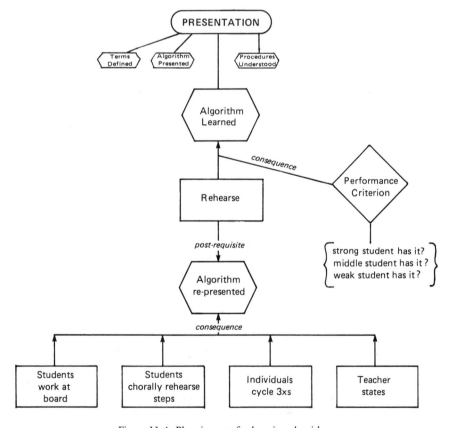

Figure 11.4. Planning net for learning algorithm.

It is possible under some conditions that a teacher will collapse the learning and presentation goals together.

A final action of presentation—explaining the algorithm—is shown in Figure 11.5. There are three possible goals: (a) to enhance learning, (b) to promote student understanding of procedures, or (c) to clarify individual or group confusion resulting from other actions. The action of explaining is related to the goal of understanding and can be set at any time during the review or presentation. Such a goal would emerge if and when student

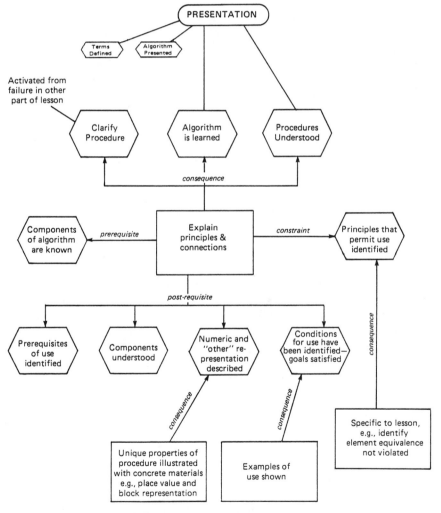

Figure 11.5. Planning for presentation for understanding of algorithm.*

*This model has been revised. See Leinhardt, 1987, 1989, in press.

performance indicated confusion. Thus, if performance indicates confusion then one should explain rationales behind procedures. Three subgoals drive the explanation: (a) reviewing the numeric representation and another system (e.g., blocks, pictures) so that the unique properties of the procedure can be identified and the flexibility of seeing the procedure work in another way can be developed (this also can strengthen linkage to the other system); (b) identifying conditions of use, namely, what doing this procedure produces in terms of goal satisfaction; and (c) explicating constraints that the algorithm satisfies, for example, maintaining equivalence, use of the identity property, use of the order property, and so forth.

In summary, we hypothesize that teaching is a cognitive skill that has features such as an agenda or master plan that usefully assembles goals and actions in the service of instruction. The agenda serves to organize the action segments of a lesson. We further hypothesize that lessons have activity segments, each of which can be characterized by its own plan. These plans contain both the action schema discussed previously and the goals, termination conditions, and/or tests for completion. Routines are a particular type of action schema—namely, shared, scripted, low-level elements of cooperative behaviors that are automatized and are indicative of successful classrooms. The cognitive skill of teaching also contains a system of information acquisition and retrieval that permits useful information to be noted at one level and used at another. We turn next to examples of expert and novice teachers and examine our theory in light of their actual performance.

## 5. OBSERVATIONS OF TEACHING

We now describe a research project in which successful, experienced teachers and novice teachers were observed and in which their activities were interpreted using the framework described previously. The goal of the research was to elucidate the activity structures and routines of skilled teachers by (a) describing what they are, (b) analyzing their frequency and duration, (c) analyzing the functions that routines serve for the cognitive processes of teachers, and (d) contrasting the activity segments of novices and experts.

### 5.1. Method

*Population.* The population used in this study was a group of "expert" teachers and a group of novices. Experts were identified by reviewing the *growth* scores of students over a 5-year period and selecting the classrooms that appeared within the highest 15% of each grade. Classrooms in which the *final achievement* was in the highest 20% were then chosen from among the high-growth classes. Of the 15 teachers identified, eight experts agreed to participate. All of the teachers taught in self-contained classrooms, and two taught an additional math section. The median class size was 28. Students in the classrooms came from families who ranged from lower class to lower middle class. One classroom was all white, two were all black, and two were integrated.

Novices were student teachers in their last semester of undergraduate training, chosen from a pool of 20 who were available. The four who were selected were considered to be the best students and were teaching fourth grade in two integrated middle-class schools. The most competent of the four was used for the detailed analysis presented here.

*Data Collection and Analysis.* Each teacher was observed during a 3 1/2-month period. Observations included about one-fourth of the mathematics classes the teachers taught during this period, nearly one-tenth of the classes taught during the school year. The pattern of observation was as follows: (a) observation of three classes with open-ended notes; (b) 1 week of observation of continuous classes, with an all-day observation taken once during the week; (c) 3 separate days of observation in which pre- and postinterviews were conducted that asked the teacher about his or her plans for that period; and (d) videotapes of three to five classes for which there were also preclass planning interviews and postclass interviews that included stimulated recall based on the videotapes of the classes. Further interviews with teachers about their own and their students' knowledge of mathematics were also conducted.

Two types of data were obtained: videotapes and transcriptions of notes and interviews. For each teacher, the notes were segmented into action records that listed durations, actions of student, action of teacher, and a name for the teacher's action. Each action was defined, and the definition was used as a basis for analyzing additional transcriptions or videotapes.

The total set of codable data for each teacher was used, and medians and ranges of time spent in each activity were calculated. For two experts and one novice we selected one tape for a more detailed interpretation of goals, activity structures, and routines. These tapes were selected for recording quality and teachers' comfort with the session. In analyzing these tapes, we also drew on information from the stimulated recalls, interviews, and other transcribed discussions with the teachers.

## 5.2. Results

*Activity Structures.* Ten categories[2] were used to describe the actions of expert teachers. The medians and ranges of durations for each of the 10

---

[2]*Presentation* refers to a teacher's uninterrupted explanation of new or very recently learned

**Table 11.1. Median Duration, Range, and N for Activity Structures Across Six Experts.**

| Activity structure | Median (in min) | Range (in min) | N |
|---|---|---|---|
| Presentation and review | 7 | 1–22 | 37 |
| Shared presentation | 11 | 3–38 | 46 |
| Drill | 4 | 1–30 | 21 |
| Game drill | 11.5 | 6–40 | 6 |
| Homework | 2 | 1–15 | 11 |
| Guided practice | 10 | 2–52 | 43 |
| Monitored practice | 20 | 4–53 | 50 |
| Tutoring | 7 | 2–41 | 19 |
| Test | 12 | 1–22 | 5 |
| Transition | 2 | 1–14 | 62 |

*Note:* Medial total length of classes was 41 min.

categories are displayed in Table 11.1, which shows that the most frequently occurring categories were presentation, shared presentation, guided practice, monitored practice, and transition. Of the instructional segments (those other than transition), the bulk of the lessons consisted of first presenting or reviewing material, then moving into a dialogue with students in which new material was reviewed, and then practicing the new material in increasingly independent ways.

Figure 6 shows a set of parallel box plots for novices and experts for the four major categories. Box plots are rectangular schematic diagrams that identify the median, quartiles or hinges, and range points. The range points are the end points of lines called *whiskers;* the hinges are shown by the outer edge of the rectangle; and the median is shown by the inner vertical line. The most

---

material while students listen. In *shared presentation,* the teacher presented material, usually through questioning or with the help of one or more students orally or at the board.

*Guided practice* is a form of seatwork in which students work on presented problems at desks or at the board with guidance from the teacher. Students work on five or fewer problems at a time. The teacher keeps up a fairly continuous explanation of the problem and usually gives immediate feedback to the group on the answers to problems. *Monitored practice* is the more traditional seatwork where the teacher moves about the room checking and tutoring while students work.

*Homework* refers to checking and collecting homework or seatwork. Most teachers took care of homework either at the beginning or the end of the day or by a pass-in/check/file system.

*Drill* is timed rehearsal of facts by students, either orally, in writing, or at the board, and is usually paced by the teacher. *Game drill* is timed by virtue of a race between groups or individuals. It involves the rehearsal of facts by students in a loud, usually public atmosphere.

*Tutorials* are extended presentations to a few students (2–5) while other students are working either at the board or at their seats.

*Transition* refers to a change from one activity to another. The teacher usually lists several actions and the students execute them.

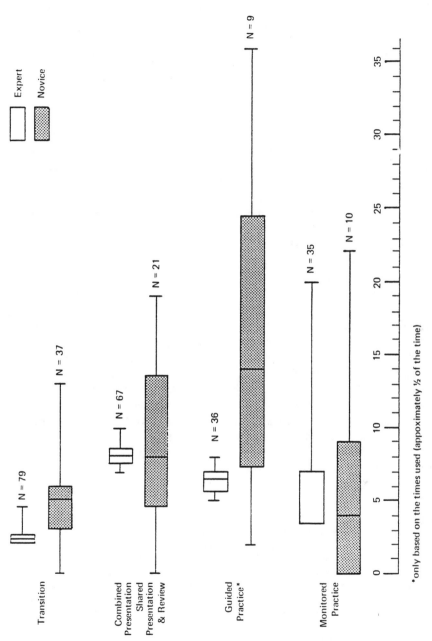

Figure 11.6. Box plots of activity structures for experts ($N = 4$) and novices ($N = 2$).

*only based on the times used (appoximately ½ of the time)

249

striking feature of Figure 11.6 is the difference in spread. The experts' behavior was more consistent over time than the novices'. This was true not only in terms of time, but also in terms of the content of these action segments. Although both the within and between variance were considerable, teachers were consistent in the key activities of presentation, shared presentation, and monitored and guided practice.

*Analyses of Specific Teaching Episodes.* We now describe several protocols of teaching episodes, with interpretations based on the hypotheses about knowledge structures that we presented in the first section of the chapter[3]. The episodes come from a lesson on mixed numbers taught by an expert, Ms. Longbranch, a lesson on equivalent fractions taught by another expert, Ms. Wall, and a lesson on multiplication taught by a novice, Ms. Twain. Longbranch's lesson is presented in considerable detail, and the complete protocol is discussed. The complete protocol for Wall's lesson also is presented, but we discuss it more briefly. Excerpts from two of Twain's lessons are discussed in order to highlight contrasts between expert and novice performance.

Longbranch's lesson began with homework correction; then there was a brief review of terms followed by a shared presentation of how to change a mixed number to a fraction. The shared presentation was continued using a public practice format for a considerable part of the class, with several groups of children called to the board and returning to their seats. Guided practice was started with some children at their desks while others worked at the board. The class ended with enrichment worksheets being done. Twain's lesson started with correction of homework and a brief review of the algorithm to be used. The rest of the lesson was devoted to a game drill of "concentration" in which each child had at least two chances to practice using the algorithm to determine whether the pairs of fractions they uncovered were equivalent.

---

[3]Our interpretations of these episodes organize the teacher's actions into activity structures. We hypothesize goals and subgoals associated with the activity structures and their component activities. Because we assume that performance is often controlled by a simple agenda, the goals of many action sequences are completion of the actions involved. Goals to obtain information may be achieved as incidental effects of the performance of activities; the action sequences include the recording of such information when it is obtained. In our analysis of each activity structure, we traced the action chains and then hypothesized the basic objectives, goals, and subgoals that drove the activities. for each subgoal, the actions used to accomplish it were identified and the functions and/or outcomes were reported. A function is the result of an action; it is not identical to the goal or subgoal but may be relevant to satisfying a constraint or another overriding goal. The basic goals for the lesson do not stand alone, but both receive and produce products from other activity structures. An outcome or product is listed only if the consequence of an action produces something that must be carried forward into another goal or subgoal.

*Homework Check.* The first clear objective in Longbranch's lesson was to get the homework corrected and handed in. Within this goal there were three subgoals: to establish who did or did not do their work (those who did not recorded their names on the board); to have the work corrected; and to assess the general success rate.

Figure 11.7 shows the actions related to achieving the first goal. The actions are listed chronologically down the chart. The teacher gave the cue, "OK, set 43." Attendance was rapidly called; each child answered yes or wrote their name on the blackboard; time to complete was approximately 30 sec. The routine was well rehearsed and universally known. The action provided information and exerted a monitoring and public control function. An outcome was that the teacher knew who had not done the work.

The second subgoal was to correct the homework. The students took

Constraints: Reinforce doing homework
Keep pace moving
Keep attention
Watch for Bryan and Cammy

Expert

Goal 1  Homework check

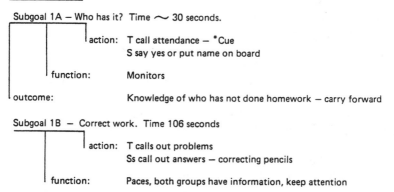

Subgoal 1A — Who has it?  Time ∼ 30 seconds.

action:  T call attendance — *Cue
S say yes or put name on board

function:        Monitors

outcome:         Knowledge of who has not done homework — carry forward

Subgoal 1B — Correct work. Time 106 seconds

action:  T calls out problems
Ss call out answers — correcting pencils

function:        Paces, both groups have information, keep attention

Interruption — "How many reduced it to 1/6?"

Subgoal 1C — How many got it correct? Time 22 seconds

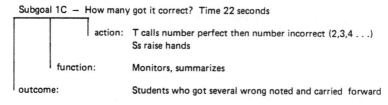

action:  T calls number perfect then number incorrect (2,3,4 . . .)
Ss raise hands

function:        Monitors, summarizes

outcome:         Students who got several wrong noted and carried forward

Conclusion Cue: *Pass to the front, put your books in your desk.

Figure 11.7. Expert homework.

colored pencils but and responded chorally with the correct answer, a fraction in lowest terms. As the teacher called the problem, "1/12 + 1/12," they responded, "2/12 or 1/6." Time to complete was 106 sec. The teacher's calling out of the problem served the function of pacing the class through and reinforcing the pairing of problem and answer. A second function was that it let the teacher note if any of the items produced problems for the group as a whole, as, for example, when multiple answers were shouted. Thus, at one point in the lesson through the use of two of the three homework checking routines, the teacher knew which children she did not know about (namely, the ones who didn't do their homework) and which problems, if any, created difficulties.

The last subgoals was to discover which of the children had difficulty in general with the assignment. This was accomplished in 30 sec by calling out the number of problems missed and having children raise their hands. The homework (or class work) activity structure accomplished a lot in a little time and produced information that could be easily carried forward into the rest of the lesson. The routines used were attendance response, choral response, and hand raising. The teacher thus reduced the amount of potential processing and kept a simple component of the lesson simple.

Another expert lesson, given by Wall, was on equivalent fractions. This lesson also started with the correction of homework and a brief review of an algorithm. The rest of the class was devoted to game drill of "concentration" in which each child had at least two chances to practice using the algorithm to determine if the fractions uncovered were equivalent. As in the first expert's lesson, the first goal of this lesson was to get the homework corrected. The subgoals were also similar: determining completion and the success rate.

The actions in this lesson were slightly different from those of Longbranch. Wall began by telling the students to get out their homework. She then gave a misinterpreted cue of "Ted?" and got the response "Here," obviously calling up the routine for attendance. Wall corrected the routine by immediately saying, "Do you have it?" She got the correct response and continued calling attendance. She marked the responses in a book she was holding. This segment of the homework check was completed in 55 sec.

The second action was, as in the first lesson, to correct the homework. The teacher called out an individual child's name and the problem. The child responded with the answer. During the 165 sec it took to check the problems, Wall asked, "Checking work?" She paced the work by calling out the problem and monitored the class's responses by her reminder to "check work." The calling of individual children's names allowed her to reach her informational subgoal of determining which children had difficulty with the work through a sampling strategy. Although this action did not provide as complete a sampling as Longbranch's, it is interesting to note that it was the three children Wall had described on a separate occasion several months earlier as "daydreamers" who missed the homework problems.

The last action was to assess the success rate of the class. Wall did this by asking, "All right?" and made a quick scan of the room to determine whose hands were raised. This took 5 sec and, in conjunction with the information obtained during the homework correction, gave the teacher information she felt she would need later.

Although the goal and subgoals of correcting homework remained constant over many settings (out of a total of 18 observations on homework check), the actions and routines varied considerably. Sometimes homework was corrected by having individuals go to the board, each one working out a problem while the rest of the group monitored. At other times, papers were traded and corrected; and at still other times, work was simply passed in. Variety itself was valued and often drove a change in approach, but time and depth of knowledge required also constrained the options.

In contrast, a novice teacher doing the homework check activity behaved differently. Figure 11.8 shows the homework check activity for one novice. It was an extended activity (6 min) in which the goal was reached somewhat indirectly and without the type of teacher control present in the previous examples. The homework activity included two subgoals: first, identifying who did the homework and, second, orally correcting the problems. For the first subgoal, the novice, Twain, stood up at the front of the room and asked, "Who doesn't have their homework?" The students did one of the following: stayed seated and held up completed work; stood up, walked to the teacher, and said either they had it or did not have it; or called out from their seats that they did not have it. The novice teacher responded that homework is important and there were no acceptable excuses, and marked on a posted sheet whether work was completed or not. She included no summary action; thus, she did not have accurate information about the homework status of everyone (that is, the check sheet was not systematically reviewed). The informational effects of the action system were not available as they were for the experts. The novice used a less effective question, did not have a routine to obtain the information, and did not maintain control of the flow of information. The students, in an attempt to comply with the somewhat unclear request, responded in a variety of confusing ways. Not only was her attempt at accomplishing the first subgoal time-consuming (it took 85 sec), but Twain was also unable to retain the information in memory to carry it forward and her information was incomplete, as will be seen later. She apparently terminated the action because of time constraints and the press of the next subgoal rather than because the goal was met.

The second goal was to correct the problems. This could have been done

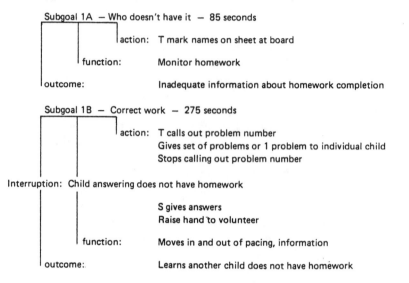

Constraints:  Reinforce doing homework
              Call on student
              Who rarely volunteers

Novice

Goal 1 Homework Check

Subgoal 1A  — Who doesn't have it  —  85 seconds

    action:    T mark names on sheet at board

    function:        Monitor homework

outcome:              Inadequate information about homework completion

Subgoal 1B  —  Correct work  —  275 seconds

    action:    T calls out problem number
            Gives set of problems or 1 problem to individual child
            Stops calling out problem number

Interruption:  Child answering does not have homework

            S gives answers
            Raise hand to volunteer

    function:        Moves in and out of pacing, information

outcome:              Learns another child does not have homework

Conclusion Cue:  *Clear desks

Figure 11.8. Novice homework.

as the experts did it or by the teacher's collecting the work, correcting it, and returning it. Twain chose to call on students to give the correct answers (an action experts do use). She called out a set of problem numbers (1–10) and assigned a child to call out the answers as she called the problem number. The student slowly called out the answers in order. (The first child chosen was the lowest in the class, did not have her work done, and was doing the problems in her head.) Thus, for the first 10 problem answers, the teacher lost control of pace *and* correctness of answers; however, it was only when the child failed on the sixth problem that Twain realized the student had not done her homework. (To get to the seventh problem took 105 sec.) Twain then called on four separate children, each of whom gave the answer to one problem. The rest of the class was checking the work at their desks. Twain then picked her main "troublemaker" to do the next block of 10. The rationale that she gave later for choosing that child was that it was the first time the child had volunteered for anything. He missed one problem, but then continued, going through 10 problems in 70 sec. The last child chosen went through the sequence quickly, but the sound of the child saying the problem number and answer next to each other was confusing (e.g., 24, 27; 25, 64). The novice teacher clearly had the beginning of a strategy for getting homework checked. First, she did it. Second, she realized that she should have some structure and that time was a constraint. During each cycle, she started by having the child pace it, and then she took over the pacing.

In the homework check segment of a lesson, a general goal was to get the homework corrected. Both experts activated similar schemata: attendance, oral-correction, and oral-summary. Longbranch and Wall differed slightly in the *actions* they used for oral-correction—one used choral responses, the other used individual responses. Both experts operated within similar constraints— to move quickly, to get all items corrected, and to know the approximate status of all students. The novice, on the other hand, did not have an attendance schema. Therefore, when the goal of assessing the homework status of students was recognized, she had to construct a set of actions that would satisfy it. The action of calling out "Who doesn't have their homework?" did not carry as a postrequisite that the status of all students was checked. Therefore, the novice ended the action prior to satisfying that condition. This, in turn, did not produce the effect of her knowing about the students, knowledge that the experts were able to secure. The failure to have the postrequisite also influenced the "effect" of the second schema used, oral-correction. For the experts, oral-correction had the effect of informing them about problematic items unambiguously. For the novice, the information that an item was failed could be attributed to the responding student's inability to do the item mentally or to its general difficulty. The novice also showed no schema such as oral-summary and no goal surrounding homework difficulty, whereas both experts used such a schema. In terms of Figure 11.1, experts gave evidence of meeting all of the top-level goals described and showed considerable consistency in their use of action schemata. The novice showed no use of constraints in terms of meeting lower level goals in order to accomplish the basic objective. Thus, attendance was incomplete and there was no assessment of difficulty.

*Presentation.* Returning to Longbranch's lesson, the second goal was to present the topic of the lesson. For this class, the presentation and shared presentation activity structures were always used. Lesson presentation of the new material and mixed numbers is outlined in Figure 11.9. There were three subgoals: The first was to review the labels (vocabulary) needed; the second was to present the rules for the algorithm; and the third was to demonstrate the algorithm. Overlaid on these three subgoals were several systems of constraints that themselves helped to construct the solution: Keep the lesson moving,[4] get through the task,[5] call on different children,[6] watch for the stragglers and help them,[7] keep interest and action up,[8] and do not embarrass children.

To review the labels, the teacher asked for a definition. She selected one of the weakest children, Cammy, to answer. This was both to encourage Cammy and to do a bottom-level check—if a weak student could get it, the lesson could move rapidly. Cammy did not get the definition, and her failure produced another subgoal (2A1 in Figure 11.9), which was to check on her for the rest of the lesson. The teacher then moved to one of her strongest students for the definition—she also failed. Longbranch tried again with a middle-level student—he failed. She then called on a top child, who was correct; she repeated the definition after the student; and she had the class rehearse it chorally.

In the time constraint system, Longbranch was behind; and in terms of Figure 11.2, a teacher would now suppress the goal of keeping interest and move to that of keeping the lesson moving. For the second subgoal of the presentation, the definition of how to change mixed numbers to fractions, Longbranch felt she must move ahead, so she increased the pace but still tried to maintain involvement. She did this by having a choral reading of the rule from the rule cards at the front of the board. So, within 1 1/2 min, she had

---

[4]Ms. Longbranch's concern about keeping the lesson moving is exemplified in the following excerpts. Interviewer: "What are the advantages of using choral check that you did for homework and for this?" Longbranch: "It's quick. It's very quick" (12/14/81, lines 401-403). "It seems the way I have math scheduled I only have that 40 minutes so I really have to know what I'm doing. I have to have my 40 minutes organized" (11/19/81, lines 201-205). "My math is 40 minutes . . .I can never drag math out for a couple of extra minutes (1/06/82, lines 244-245).

[5]Ms. Longbranch's underlying constraint of getting through the task is expressed in this quote (12/03/81, lines 342-347): "I don't have this written down anywhere, but in my mind, I have it. I'm going to be finished with fractions before Christmas. I have to be, you know, to get on. So I'll just pace myself now so that I will get finished."

[6]Ms. Longbranch tried to call on different children: "Everyone doesn't get to the board everyday. But most of them do" (1/06/82, lines 291-292). "I think I was trying to get all the children to the board that I thought would have any difficulty at all" (12/14/81, lines 151-153).

[7]One important concern of Ms. Longbranch was to watch for stragglers and to give them additional help: "I can tell (the ones that have trouble), they're always the last ones to stand up. So I know they need special attention" (11/24/81, lines 38-41). "But usually the ones who have trouble will get to the board that day. The better ones will get turns, you know, every day, or three" (12/11/81, lines 447-451). "Then when you see the same person is always the last one getting up, well you know he or she is really having a tough time of it" (12/14/81, lines 358-361).

[8]Ms Longbranch is operating within the constraint of keeping the children interested and action moving: "There's no specific reason why I have them stand—just to keep them moving" (1/06/82, lines 462-464). "I feel like if I don't have them keep moving constantly, or doing something constantly, their attention span, I don't care how good they are, it just floats away" (1/06/82, lines 464-466).

Constraints: Keep lesson moving
Complete task
Call on different children
Watch for stragglers
Keep up interest
Do not embarrass child

Expert

Goal 2 <u>Presentation</u> — Time 4½ minutes

Subgoal 2A: Define a mixed number

action: T asks for a definition
Weak child is selected — fails

function: Involves students,
Check on first child

outcome: Goal 2A1 — Check on Cammy

action: T calls on Tara
Child fails — confused

action: T calls on Chuck
Child fails — confused

action: Trish called on — gets it . . .
T repeats definition, writes 2½ on board
Ss choral repeat

function: Get definition across
Don't waste time

Outcome: Time is lost — make it up
Goal 2A2

Subgoal 2B: Define operation of changing a fraction to a mixed number

action: Teacher leads choral reading of rule

function: Clearly state algorithm, sacrifice student involvement for time

outcome: Time is caught up — goal 2A2 is met

Subgoal 2C: <u>Demonstrate rules</u>: Select student, select problem — 1st iteration

Problem 1 — 2½

action: T puts 2½ on board, says rule — part 1 — calls on strong student, Tom
Ss misspeaks but says it correctly
T executes

function: T controls fit between rule and action and involves students

action: T says rule — part 2 — calls same student
Ss adds numerator, states answer
T executes

function: Same

action: T says rule — part 3 — and pauses
Ss chorally respond, in part incorrectly

Interruption: Teacher calls to order and reprimands

function: Keep students obedient

Subgoal 2C: <u>Demonstrate rules</u>: 2nd iteration

Problem 2 — 3 2/5

action: T puts problem on board 3 2/5
Calls on middle child (Emmett)
Ss says rules and executes
T writes, pacing through each step

function: 2nd clean demonstration, mid level check, more independence

outcome: Success means can try on a lower student

Subgoal 2C: <u>Demonstrate rules</u>: 3rd iteration

Problem 3 — 2 3/4

action: T puts problem on board
Calls on Cammy
T calls for rule (step by step)
Cammy executes
T writes reinforces last step

function: Check weakest child, check for success of rule presentation

outcome: Success — move on

Figure 11.9. Expert presentation.

reviewed the definitions, introduced an algorithm, and rehearsed it. (It should be noted that the prior lesson involved extensive "conceptual" work drawing representations of mixed numbers and talking about 1 1/2 of a sandwich and 3/2 of a sandwich, etc.) Longbranch was then ready to use a routine of public practice in which a problem would be put on the board and a child would be called on to guide the teacher orally through the operation. Longbranch shared control slightly by permitting volunteers but called on one child at a time to do each of the three steps of the algorithm.

The first problem (Subgoal 2C in Figure 11.9) was 2 1/2, a relatively easy problem. A child (middle level) was called on to perform a part of the algorithm (multiply the whole number by the denominator), and then the teacher followed the rule for the second step while the student dictated to her (add the numerator). These actions were carefully watched by the students; it was the first real demonstration of the algorithm, and interest may have been raised by watching a student tell the teacher what to do. At the third part of the algorithm, Longbranch asked for the answer to "keep the same denominator" and both 2 and 4 were shouted out by the entire class. This was an interesting failure in routine. Longbranch usually gave a problem, then called a name. When a name was not called, a choral answer was usually expected. In this case, Longbranch meant to continue with the same child, but the time lapse had been too long. She instead got a choral answer, which she interpreted as shouting out. She pulled the children together by telling them to sit up, put their pencils down, and not call out. The mutual misunderstanding was not recognized by the teacher (either when it occurred or later, when she viewed the tape), who simply saw the event as one in which she was trying to keep the children in control. ("And I like, as you have seen so far, I like order in my room. I can't stand that when they start all hollering out.") The second problem given to the students was 3 2/5, which was assigned to a top-level child. He went through all the steps smoothly, thus publicly rehearsing the algorithm. To check how the lesson had been understood, she called on the weakest child (from Goal 2A1) and rehearsed the steps for changing 2 3/4 to an improper fraction. As the child gave the answers, Longbranch wrote the answers on the board. The actions produced a third example on the board, rehearsal of the algorithm, and a check of the weakest child, who was by then caught up. The teacher was then ready to begin public practice on the blackboard with groups of students. Longbranch completed the demonstration portion of the lesson and went into the next segment, *public practice*. The students then rehearsed the algorithm for changing mixed numbers to fractions.

Goal 3 is summarized in Figure 11.10. The objective was to have public practice at the blackboard. The action helped to meet the larger goal of going through a lesson and getting material learned. This is similar to the goals and actions in Figure 11.4. The activity structure was still part of a shared

Expert

Goal 3  Public practice:  Time 4½ minutes
        Rehearse algorithm — 2 cycles  Select Problem
                                       Select Students
                                       Orchestrate

Subgoal 3A:  Set up board

        action:   T selects six students by name
                  T assigns to boards
                  T selects problem — 3 1/3
                  T asks for definition of type of number
                  Ss choral response
                  Ss at board do problem
                  T respond:  walks through problem with child at the board

        function:    Fun, public rehearsal

Subgoal 3B:  Monitor seated students (cycles) in parallel

            action:   T watch students to see if paying attention

Interruption — catches a student commenting to one at the board — assigns him to the board, too

        function:    Keep seated attending, punish inappropriate behavior

    action:           T select 2nd problem — 5 2/6
                      T calls on punished child to perform
                      S makes minor error
                      T does problem publically and corrects
                      *erase be seated
                      Call wave two

        function:    Public rehearsal and public chastisement

Subgoal 3C, 2A and 2B:  Move to second cycle, rehearse

            action:   T *"Erase be seated", calls names to go to board
                      Group 1 sits
                      Group 2 goes to board — Keeps Bryan
                      T calls 4 1/2

            (2A):     T — to 2A1 — "What kind of number?" to Cammy, seated
                      S gives answer — slowly with prompts

            (3C & 2B):  T to another — (Tom at board) How do we change
                      S gives algorithm, and answer
                      T repeats answer
                      Ss do at board — Teacher corrects

        function:    Keep pace moving, keep action going, rehearse lesson topic

    outcomes:        Changed groups, algorithm is firm, can change to practice

action:              T says — 6 3/5
                     Calls on seated to define steps
                     Continues oral problem solution
                     Ss at board do problem

Alright, erase, be seated

Figure 11.10. Expert public practice.

259

presentation because the particular event involved only teacher-generated problems, not dittos or books. The routines were assigning to the board, student monitoring of board performance, and explanation of answers. The first action was to call students to the board by calling names of children. Before the children reached the board, the problem 3 1/3 was called out. At that moment, Longbranch had to shift attention from the six children she had assigned to boardwork to those that were seated. She continuously looked for signs of restlessness, confusion, or inattentiveness—those at the board were under public control and needed less attention than the others. The students at the board wrote their solutions to the problem, and one child was called on to solve the problem orally, thus rehearsing the algorithm. While Longbranch watched the seated group and tutored, she saw Emmett make a comment to one child at the board. Longbranch assumed it was a negative comment and sent Emmett to the board as a reprimand. After the 3 1/3 problem was finished, the teacher asked, "Everybody else correct? Erase? Put 5 2/6. Emmett, you tell us this time. What are you going to do?" Emmett forgot to add the numerator, and his failure produced a "seeee" from the teacher. Longbranch had thus constructed a win/win situation. If Emmett did not get it, she could point out his error; if he did, she could rehearse the correct answer.

To move to the second cycle, Longbranch called for the students to erase and be seated; identified the second group, retaining Bryan, a weak student; called out the new problem, 4 1/2, and checked with Cammy to define the type of problems (as mixed number; Goal 2A1). In one breath, she had shifted almost half of the class around, checked on a goal carried forward, given special attention to a child who needed it, and made progress toward completing her goal. With the second group of students, she reviewed the rules and got an answer from a seated child to retain attention. The activity was completed by saying, "Erase, be seated."

The second expert, Wall, used her presentation slot for a partial review of material introduced in the previous lessons—reducing fractions. She reviewed the algorithm of finding factors to help reduce the fraction. Wall used a shared presentation for the review. To pace the lesson, she wrote six fractions on the board (3/6, 6/16, 10/15, 2/16, 4/12, 12/15). She called on a top-level student to read the fraction. She gave them a cue from a previous lesson: "Ask the first question." The children gave her a choral response, "Is 3 a factor of 6?" She then asked Kali, a middle-level child, to identify the next step; and when Kali failed, Wall immediately called on a consistently top-level child, Aaron, who gave the right answer. The class then solved the problem chorally. She called for an individual response on the second fraction, got a choral response, and promptly regained her control by loudly repeating the child's name. The class went through the remaining five fractions using a mixture of individual and choral responses. Each problem was stated, "the question" was asked, and it was answered; if the numerator was not a factor of the denominator, the factors were listed and the largest common one was chosen, tested, and then used. The teacher checked on the three children who missed homework problems and all of them were able to answer correctly.

Wall ended her lesson with a game drill activity in which the children practiced using the algorithm by deciding if the fractions on two cards they turned over were equivalent. She described the game, set the rules, and then practiced by turning over two cards for the class to determine chorally if they were equivalent. Four teams were set up. The game proceeded with each child turning over two cards, writing the fractions on the board, and then orally going through the steps.

The novice's presentation shown in Figure 11.11 was chosen from a lesson different from that of the homework check in order to have an example of a cohesive presentation. This presentation did not proceed with the same fluidity as either of the experts'. The novice, Twain, introduced the concept of multiplication although the students already knew their multiplication tables through at least the fours. She started with the subgoal of arousing interest. Her actions were to (a) tell the students that this was so important that, if they missed it, they would be lost for the rest of the year; (b) cue students to chorally read the word *multiplication*—only a few participated; and (c) describe at length some word problems the students wrote out several days earlier, one of which required repeated addition. These actions did not achieve the subgoal of arousing interest very well. The students responded to the three verbal actions, each one of which ended with a type of rhetorical question, with decreased volume and participation. Finally, in response to the failed oral routine, Twain said, "Am I talking to myself?" A second subgoal was to introduce chips as a way of demonstrating multiplication, but she had failed to complete the presentation portion that included defining terms. She may have recognized this after mentioning the chips; she said, "Not now. Oh no, no, no, no, no!" The students chorally responded, "Aw, aw." Twain was in some trouble at this point but proceeded.

She pointed to the board and said," Here is your typical multi—pli—ca—tion pro—blem," and then referred to parts of addition problems and parts of multiplication problems— "The two numbers are called what?" A modest choral response stated "factors," which was written on the board, but when she asked for "product," she lost the students and reprimanded them for not paying attention. Twain then responded to a child who called out. She then directed the students to open their books to page 98. This led into a 10 1/2-min discussion and semipublic practice of problems in the book.

In our theoretical discussion of content presentation (see Figures 11.2–11.5), we conceptualized four basic goal states that would govern the actions: definition or terms defined, algorithms presented, algorithms learned,

Novice

Transition is first followed by explanation of video equipment

Goal 1 <u>Presentation</u> — Time 3½ minutes

Subgoal 1A — Introduce multiplication by arousing interest, giving terms

action:   T directs attention to board
Calls for choral response

S few respond

function:   Involve students (fail)

action:   T reminds them of word problems several days earlier
Calls for choral affirmation

S no response

T "Am I talking to myself?"

function:   Remind students of other lesson,
Reintroduce problem, motivate students

action:   T prepare to hand out chips
Changes mind

outcome:   Do not change to another subgoal

Subgoal 1B — Define terms in multiplication

action:   T directs attention to board
Calls for choral response

S several students respond

Interruption:   T catches students looking around — "Get your eyes up here".

function:   Keep attention

Subgoal 1C — Demonstrate importance

action:   T shows them speed they need when doing times tables

S complains she will forget tables

T refuses to accept complaint that they will forget

function:   Encourage students to learn tables (partial success)

Present level of competency beyond students

outcome:   Distracting argument
Time lost
Thread lost

Figure 11.11. Novice presentation.

and algorithm understood (through learning and explanation). The presentation of new information is a central part of most math lessons. Presentational objectives consist of a complex system of goals and actions and represent a potential quagmire for the novice. Our two experts started their lesson with an introduction or review of terms. Both experts started with volunteers who were considered weaker and produced failures and moved on to students who were more competent. Subgoal 2A in Figure 11.4 corresponds to the first goal in Figure 11.2. The novice did not introduce terms until well into the lesson (Subgoal 1B in Figure 11.11) and instead used a rather lengthy action string involving conversation routines that seemed to be aimed at arousing interest. In fact, after defining terms midway through the lesson, she omitted most of the presentation and went into the beginning of a guided practice. Thus, she seemed to lack both major goals for presentation as well as automaticity of action.

The second goal that we hypothesized was to present an algorithm (see Figure 11.3). Both experts did this. Longbranch presented the algorithm by reading with the class a verbal list of steps and then linking each action in the list to an action with numerals. Wall, who presented the second lesson on reducing fractions, prompted a verbal chain and asked for individual and choral responses in going through the steps of the first problem. Both experts used actions of verbally stating and demonstrating; both selected the numeral and verbal representations (as opposed to pictures, number lines, etc.); neither differentiated very much between new and old material although both had done some of that during the prior conceptual lesson. It is interesting that the novice tried to identify the familiar elements but not in the process of presenting the procedure, and thus the identification was not clear.

The third goal of getting the procedure learned (see Figure 11.4) was recognized by both experts and to some extent by the novice. The experts called on all the action systems available—board work, choral rehearsal, individual responses, and, in Longbranch's case, statement by the teacher. For both experts, learning is the goal for presenting, and frequent tests of various students are built in to assure that it is achieved. The novice's action of student oral review of problems seems to have been governed more by the goal of getting through the problem than by the goal of learning the material.

Presentation encompasses a large number of routines, actions, and goals. Our description has of necessity been sequential, giving a chronological flavor to the segments. However, actions often occur in more complex patterns, partially satisfying a segment of one goal system or another. Thus, learning actions occur simultaneously or intertwined with presentational ones. The important point is that when presentation is completed, several different goal states have been achieved and the teacher can move to another segment.

*Guided Practice.* The next major lesson segment was guided practice, which serves as a bridge from the lesson to the students' independent work. The transition from presentation to guided practice was accomplished using four separate subgoals: Children at the board were seated, books were taken out, paper was distributed, and the second group was sent to the board. This was a particularly interesting 1-min segment because it demonstrated the effective call-up of four routines, none involving interactive responses and all of which were simply executed. The teacher's closing statement from the previous activity, "Erase and be seated," initiated the transition. As six children moved back to their seats, the teacher simultaneously said, "Take out your books. Turn to page 169," and passed the paper out to each child in the first row. The books emerged and were opened and paper was passed over heads, one by one, to the last row. There was a brief pause and the teacher said, "Michael's row to the board—first three to the front, second three to the back."

In the first portion of guided practice some children were at the board while others were seated—all were working out problems from the book. There were six cycles of problems. The first subgoal was to work through a problem while keeping both the seated children and the children at the board engaged. The teacher did this by identifying the problem number and having a seated student read it aloud while the students at the board solved it. A second seated child stated the answer and a third explained. This system kept the pace going, involved the whole class, and rehearsed the work.

In the second portion of this segment all of the children were seated while Longbranch called out problem numbers to be done. She went through four sets. The first involved three problems, and each child stood when he or she had completed it. Longbranch gave the answers, then gave five more problems, and went to the desks of the children who were last to stand. She helped them do several problems and then repeated the procedure several more times.

Two experts teaching two lessons on different topics differed, but both used familiar grouping of verbal and physical behaviors to facilitate the smooth running of the class. There was little confusion in cues. What did get confused was quickly cleared up. Without feeling rushed, both experts completed their lessons and provided between 40 and 50 opportunities for rehearsal of the newly learned material.

The differences between novices and experts with respect to lesson structure centered not solely around activity structures, but around routines as well. The novice spent a little more time than the experts in presenting, but not much, and spent considerably more time than the experts in guided practice and less time in monitored practice. However, the novice showed a constantly changing pattern in how she went about these activities. One day, there was a lengthy lecture; the next day, lengthy filling in of a chart of number facts on the blackboard; and the next day, two quizzes sandwiching a presentation. The failure of routines existed in part because there was little or no repetition of them and in part because the novice had not worked them out.

## 6. IMPLICATIONS AND IMPORTANCE

Expert teachers constructed their mathematics lessons around a core of activities. This core moved from total teacher control to independent student work. The teachers started with presentations or reviews of information that frequently involved students in some form of focused discussion and moved to public, shared working out of problems; then to very interactive seatwork; and occasionally to independent seatwork. In our observations, teachers used review, drill, tutoring, and testing irregularly but frequently enough that students behaved predictably during them. Occasionally, teachers used an entire lesson to present an especially complex piece of material. They did this by alternating presentations with guided practice.

The presentations and shared presentations of expert teachers were usually quite short. Expert teachers used efficient routines to make effective use of the time spent in guided or monitored practice. For example, Longbranch regularly started by assigning two problems and having the students stand when they finished. This provided her with an easily interpreted perceptual cue as to how students were doing and provided the students with an "action" to engage in upon completion. The teacher used the standing to identify the slowest children and then gave one of those children tutoring during the next round of problems. This routine provided pacing and gave rapid feedback on performance to all of the children. The experts regularly assigned homework but did so only after there had been at least two rehearsals in class, such as guided and monitored practice or textbook plus workbook. With novice teachers, the class was rarely involved in guided practice; instead, the novice often jumped from presentation to practice. Further, the novice teachers often used homework to finish an incomplete lesson. This had two consequences: It made the homework more difficult to do and hence more punishing, and it decreased the chance that it would get done.

The expert teachers had, with the class, a large repertoire of routines, usually with several forms of each one. In some cases, we observed teachers apparently teaching new routines to their classes. The main features of these mutually known routines were that (a) they were very flexible, (b) order could be shifted and pieces taken from one segment and applied to another, (c) little or no monitoring of execution was required, and (d) little or no explanation was required for carrying them out. These routines had simple, transparent objectives: to increase the amount of time that the students were directly engaged in learning or practicing mathematics and receiving feedback, to reduce the cognitive load for the teacher, and to establish a frame that permitted easy transmission of information in mutually known and recognized settings.

In contrast, novices did not work in a routine or habitual way, so each portion of a lesson was different from the next and each day was different. Students, therefore, had to be instructed in their roles and the teachers had to take time and energy to explain each action. Novices spent a little less time than experts presenting material, but the difference was small. Novices spent considerably more time than experts in guided practice and less time in monitored practice. The main difference, though, was that novices displayed a constantly changing pattern in how they performed these activities. A novice might give a lengthy lecture one day, endlessly fill in a chart of number facts on the blackboard the next day, and give two quizzes sandwiching a presentation the third day. A major difference between expert and novice teachers was in the experts' use of well-practiced routines. The absence of routines in the performance of novices was due mainly to their lack of experience, but this was exacerbated by the lack of repetition in the activity structures that the novices used.

The expert's lesson can be characterized as an action agenda consisting of a list of action segments. Each segment has a substantive and unique content, a goal structure, and a consistent knowledge base that is accessed for its completion. Each segment needs certain unique information in order to function. The routines within the segment either produce the information (Who has homework?) or use information recorded from the outcomes of actions occurring in prior segments (Is there a particular type of problem generating difficulty in the homework?). The information schema that retains and makes available information throughout the course of the lesson seems to be arranged very efficiently. The schema lists information with critical properties appended so that information can be assembled in redundant lists for use as needed throughout the lesson and for modification, if necessary, of more stable knowledge, especially about children. Throughout the lesson, the teacher is seeking and using information about the progress of students and the progress of subject matter coverage.

When we consider the massive amount of information that teachers and students must deal with in the course of a single math class, it becomes clear that some techniques must be used to structure the information and limit its complexity. This structuring occurs in part by dividing the 40-min class time into action segments in which the overt behaviors are routinized. The new material can then be plugged into these segments.(This routinization means teachers do not need to take time from instruction to explain how to do boardwork, for example.) A part of the new material is preplanned, whereas another part is a response to the teacher's on-the-spot reading of the way the preplanned segments are going. The use of routines means the teacher has freed herself or himself to focus on the important and/or dynamic features of the material to be transmitted and the information from the students about how the lesson is progressing. Each teacher has three or four variants on each of the approximately 15 routines that are used. The expert teachers retain clearly defined information and are in control of the agenda. New teachers are less able both to obtain and to retain information as well as to maintain control of the agenda. New teachers can benefit from information about different routines, methods of teaching them to students, and ways of using them effectively to maintain student interest. The use of routines reduces the cognitive processing for teachers and provides them with the intellectual and temporal room needed to handle the dynamic portions of the lesson, but we have also seen that experts assemble these actions to achieve goals that, in some cases (presentation, for example), the novice does not seem to recognize as desirable or necessary.

Students also benefit from the presence of goals, action segments, and routines. They can follow instructions and catch up because the sequence of behavior is familiar. They have more time to concentrate on the content of the lesson, or if they prefer, to let their minds wander. The student is relieved of both an interpretation and decision-making element (What am I supposed to do with these six sheets of paper? Which book?).

This type of analysis of routines and activity segments is a useful way of starting to understand how teachers and students deal with a dynamic, ill -structured task setting. Routines and activity segments constrain some of the task elements by making them more or less static and transform some of the tasks into highly standard elements that call up entire repertoires of mutually understood behaviors.

## REFERENCES

Berliner, D.C., King, M., Rubin, J., & Fisher, C.W. (1981). *Describing classroom activities*. Unpublished manuscript, Far West Laboratory for Educational Research and Development, San Francisco, CA.

Bossert, S.T. (1981). Understanding sex differences in children's classroom experiences. *Elementary School Journal, 81,* 255-266.

Brown, J.S., & Burton, R.R. (1978). Diagnostic models for procedural bugs in basic mathematical skills. *Cognitive Science, 2,* 155-192.

Chaiklin, S. (1984). On the nature of verbal rules and their role in problem solving. *Journal of Cognitive Science, 8,* 131-155.

Chase, W.G., & Simon, H. A. (1973). Perception in chess. *Cognitive Psychology, 4,* 55-81.

Good, T.A., Grouws, D.A., & Ebmeier, H. (1983). *Active mathematics teaching*. New York: Longman.

Greeno, J.G., Magone, M., & Chaiklin, S. (1979). Theory of constructions and set in problem solving. *Memory and Cognition, 7*(6), 445-461.

Greeno, J.G., Riley, M.S., & Gelman, R. (1984). Young children's counting and understanding of principles. *Cognitive Psychology, 16,* 94-143.

Hayes-Roth, B., & Hayes-Roth, H. (1978). *Cognitive processes in planning* (Report R-2366-ONR). Santa Monica, CA: Rand Corporation.

Johnson, P.E., Duran, A.S., Hassebrock, F., Moller, J., Prietula, M., Feltovich, P.J., & Swanson, D.B. (1981). Expertise and error in diagnostic reasoning. *Cognitive Science*, 5,

235-283.

Leinhardt, G. (1983, April). *Routines in expert math teachers' thoughts and actions.* Paper presented at the annual meeting of the American Educational Research Association, Montreal, Canada.

Leinhardt, G. (1987). The development of an expert explanation: An analysis of a sequence of subtraction lessons. *Cognition and Instruction,4* (4), 225-282.

Leinhardt, G. (1989). Math lessons: A contrast of novice and expert competence. *Journal for Research in Mathematics Education,20* (1), 52-75.

Leinhardt, G. (in press). On teaching. In R. Glaser (Ed.), *Advances in instructional psychology, Vol.IV.* Hillsdale, NJ: Erlbaum.

Leinhardt, G., & Smith, D. (1985). Expertise in mathematics instruction: Subject matter knowledge. *Journal of Educational Psychology, 77*(3), 247-271.

Leinhardt, G., Weidman, C., & Hammond, K.M. (1987). Introduction and integration of classroom routines by expert teachers. *Curriculum Inquiry, 17,* 135-176.

Lesgold, A.M., Glaser, R., Feltovich, P., and Wang, Y. (1981, April). *Radiological expertise.* Paper presented at the meeting of the American Educational Research Association, Los Angeles, CA.

Newell, A., & Simon, H.A. (1972). *Human problem solving.* Englewood Cliffs, NJ: Prentice-Hall.

Polson, P.G. (1972). A quantitative analysis of the conceptual processes in the Hull paradigm. *Journal of Mathematical Psychology, 9,* 141-167.

Polson, P.G., Atwood, M.E., Jeffries, R., & Turner, A. (1981). The processes involved in designing software. In J.R. Anderson (Ed.), *Cognitive skills and their acquisition* (pp. 255-283). Hillsdale, NJ: Erlbaum.

Pople, H.E. (1982). Heuristic methods for imposing structure on ill-structured problems: The structuring of medical diagnostics. In P. Szolovits (Ed.), *Artificial intelligence in medicine* (pp. 119-185). Boulder, CO: Westview Press.

Sacerdoti, E.D. (1977). *A structure for plans and behavior.* New York: Elsevier-North-Holland.

Smith, D.A., Greeno, J.G., & Vitolo, T.M. (1989). A model of competence for counting. *Cognitive Science, 13*(2), 183-211.

Soloway, E., Ehrlich, K., Bonar, J., & Greenspan, J. (1982). What do novices know about programming? In B. Schneidermann & A. Badre (Eds.), *Directions in human-computer interactions* (pp. 853-860). Norwood, NJ: Ablex.

Stefik, M. (1981). Planning with constraints (MOLGEN: Part 1). *Artificial Intelligence, 16,* 111-140.

Stodolsky, S.S. (1983). *Classroom activity structures in the fifth grade* (Final report, NIE Contract 400-77-0094). Chicago: University of Chicago.

Wilkins, D. (1980). Patterns and plans in chess. *Artificial Intelligence, 14,* 165-203.

# 12

## REPRESENTATIONS OF TEACHERS' KNOWLEDGE

JAMES CALDERHEAD

### 1. INTRODUCTION

Teachers possess a wide variety of knowledge which can potentially inform their classroom work. This might include knowledge of children, curriculum, teaching methods, classroom organization, educational goals, and subject matter. In the everyday tasks of planning, in the organization of the class, in instruction, in the diagnosis of children's difficulties, and in the moment-to-moment reactions to classroom situations, teachers' actions might well be guided by a very extensive knowledge base.

The nature of teachers' knowledge, how it is developed, and the processes by which it informs classroom action are questions of interest to teacher educators and curriculum developers who are keen to facilitate the improvement of practice. This area of enquiry has also become of interest to designers of AI tutors (Ohlsson, 1985) who argue that the knowledge and principles underlying pedagogical action may have potential for the structuring of ITSs. This chapter aims to draw upon recent research on teaching to examine the teacher's task, to consider the possible nature and structure of the knowledge that informs teaching, and to speculate on the relationship of current theoretical frameworks in research on teaching to some objectives in ITS design.

### 2. THE TASK OF TEACHING

Recent research on teaching has highlighted the complex nature of the teacher's task. Doyle (1986) well describes this complexity in terms of six general characteristics of classroom teaching. Teachers' work, he claims, is *multidimensional.* They face numerous demands and often have to make decisions which are compromises among various costs and benefits. It is *simultaneous,* teachers having to deal with several tasks at once. Teachers' work is also *immediate* in that they have little time for reflection and are faced with situations which frequently demand an instant response. The *unpredictability* of teachers' work is apparent in the difficulty of knowing how any particular lesson will be received by children or what they will learn from it. The *publicness* of the classroom situation enables children to note how their teachers respond to classroom events, and their interpretations of teachers' actions and expectations can influence future interactions: an inept analogy, for instance, which is spontaneously produced in response to one child's difficulty, but overheard by, or passed on to, other children may have wide-ranging and cumulative effects in leading the children's thinking astray. In addition, each teacher and class develops its own *history:* as a teacher and class become accustomed to interacting with one another, a set of norms, ways of interpreting each other's actions, and ways of behaving and coping with classroom work become established.

Some of these characteristics of teaching are attributable to the organizational context in which teachers work, having sole responsibility for 30 or so children in a classroom for 6 hours a day with limited curriculum resources. Some are attributable to the nature of children's learning. Considerable evidence from research on learning suggests that children approach the school curriculum with various understandings that predispose them to learn in particular, sometimes quite idiosyncratic, ways (e.g., Resnick, 1987; Driver, 1983). In a class, children will have had different past experiences, will have acquired different understandings, and may approach a given task in a variety of ways. Consequently, teachers, in order to instruct effectively, need to be aware of these differences and take account of them where possible.

Recent research on teaching has been particularly concerned with how teachers come to make sense of their complex environment. How do teachers think about children, teaching, and the context in which they work? What knowledge do they acquire and use in their teaching? What is the knowledge base of teaching? How is this knowledge base developed and used?

## 3. CHARACTERISTICS OF TEACHERS' KNOWLEDGE

Some approaches to exploring teaching have attempted to map out the knowledge base of teachers (particularly of teachers judged to be expert) using interviews and stimulated recall (e.g., Leinhardt & Smith, 1985). This research has frequently depicted teachers' knowledge in terms of semantic networks, diagrammatically represented as node–link chains. Various distinctions have been made about the types of knowledge teachers possess—the concepts of procedural and declarative knowledge noted by Anderson (1983) have been particularly influential in this respect. The knowledge that guides action has been viewed as oriented towards problem solving and qualitatively different from the knowledge of facts and subject matter that informs the content of teaching. This is an analytical distinction, however, and procedural knowledge and subject matter knowledge may well not exist as such discrete knowledge bases in the mind of the teacher. The knowledge teachers possess on the teaching of fractions or the teaching of reading or of a particular science topic may not be readily segmented into subject matter and procedural categories. Learning to teach a new topic or subject area, for instance, may involve more than simply mapping new subject matter knowledge onto existing procedural routines.

Research which has attempted to map out the knowledge of both beginning and experienced teachers in a systematic manner suggests a number of interesting characteristics.

Firstly, the knowledge base of teachers appears to be vast. Even focusing on one particular segment of a lesson, and dealing only with subject matter and procedural knowledge categories, Leinhardt and Smith (1985) describe large interconnected bodies of knowledge.

Secondly, when learning to teach, student teachers approach the task from different starting points, with different subject matter knowledge, different background experiences, various beliefs about the nature of teaching, and different ideas about themselves as teachers (e.g., Lanier & Little, 1986) which appear to influence how they analyze and construct their own practice (Calderhead & Robson, 1988).

Thirdly, student teachers take various routes through their teacher training course, extracting different knowledge, developing different attitudes or approaches to learning, perceiving classroom processes in a variety of ways, and acquiring their own particular behavioral skills (Korthagen, 1988; Russell, 1988).

Fourthly, student teachers who at the end of their course are regarded as competent teachers by their tutors display quite a diverse range of knowledge, skills, and ways of thinking about teaching. There appears to be no prototypical model of the good teacher, or of one way of learning to teach (Robinson, 1988). Though there are inevitably some general broad areas of agreement, teacher educators themselves often disagree over specific criteria for good teaching (Stones & Morris, 1972).

## 4. STRUCTURE OF TEACHERS' KNOWLEDGE

Several attempts have been made to explore the nature and structure of teachers' knowledge, considering the content of the knowledge that teachers draw upon and how it is held and used. Two research approaches in particular have attempted to address these questions. One is expert–novice research, which has compared the thought processes of beginning and experienced teachers in specific contexts, using methods such as stimulated recall and simulation tasks (e.g., Berliner, 1987; Carter, Sabez, Cushing, Pinnegar, & Berliner, 1987). The other is research which has followed student teachers through their period of training and into full-time work as a teacher, attempting to monitor the acquisition, use, and structuring of knowledge, employing mostly interview techniques, diaries or journals, and field observation (e.g., Borko, Livingston, McCaleb, & Mauro, 1988).

One of the features of this research is that it has drawn attention to the importance of a body of typificatory knowledge or case knowledge that teachers possess about children and teaching situations which they appear to use to highlight various possibilities for action. *Case knowledge* refers to a memorized repertoire of events or people which are highly significant for the kinds of tasks teachers face.

In one study, for instance, a group of student teachers and experienced teachers were presented with a series of classroom critical incidents, one at a time, and asked to say what more they needed to know in order to make up their minds about how to deal with the incident and what they would do (Calderhead, 1981,1984).

A common response was for experienced teachers to recall a series of typical incidents rather like the one presented to them and to suggest how they might cope. Student teachers, on the other hand, usually gave much simpler responses. For example, one of the incidents was, "The class is working quietly when a group of children start talking among themselves." Experienced teachers frequently recounted six or more typical incidents of this kind—the class clown playing up, a child having a difficulty and asking around for help rather than approaching the teacher, a child not having listened to instructions and having to ask others what to do, a distraction like a wasp flying in through the window, or another teacher coming into the room, etc. In contrast, one student teacher responded to the same critical incident, saying, "I'd wait until the noise reached an intolerable level, then I'd tell them to shut up." The experienced teachers had more elaborate perceptions of the critical incidents and perceived the incidents in terms of an example of a possible range of typical incidents, this range being readily brought to mind.

Interestingly, some situations didn't elicit such marked differences between experienced and student teachers, and some elicited no difference at all. In addition, the experienced teachers didn't provide such an extensive list of ready action solutions: they could perceive various problem situations, but the number of solutions offered was usually considerably less. One interpretation of this is that teachers' knowledge is not held in the form of action recipes for typical situations. There no doubt are occasions when teachers need action-recipes. They have to respond quickly to classroom incidents, and they acquire an established routine on which they can draw. But depending on the situation, teachers may at times be able to take a more reflective stance, monitoring their own behavior, and adopting a more problem-solving approach to classroom incidents. The readily recalled mental repertoire of incidents may provide a set of initial problem formulations for thinking about particular events, in what amounts to an ill-defined problem-solving context. Their response to a particular situation, however, may in part be determined by the peculiarities of the child, situation, or context involved. For example, if a teacher engages the class in discussion, the topic being discussed may develop along various routes, depending on the type and level of participation of the pupils, the interests they express, and the ideas the teacher has in mind for the lesson. Similarly, if the teacher presents a class with a mathematical problem, children's responses might reveal an array of misconceptions that teachers might choose to respond to. This process of interactively tailoring knowledge and action to a particular situation has been described by researchers in several ways. Yinger (1987) suggests teaching be conceptualized as an improvizational activity in which teachers engage in successive cycles of problem setting and problem solving. This views teachers' cognitive activity as akin to Schon's (1983) 'reflection-in-action,' a constant monitoring of the situation and one's own interaction with it.

An alternative conceptualization is of different levels of routine, some routines being analogous to simple if–then responses, others amounting to a complex network of conditions and responses resulting from the practice of fine discriminations in a complex environment. Leinhardt and Greeno (this volume) suggest that teachers might handle this complexity through a mental agenda of concerns and actions for the situation at hand. The agenda is largely informed by teachers' rich memory of children, curriculum, classroom situations, and teaching strategies, but is regularly updated in response to ongoing classroom activity.

## 5. THE DEVELOPMENT OF TEACHERS' KNOWLEDGE

Some researchers have suggested that the differences between expert and novice teachers are not unidimensional: The process of learning to teach is not characterized simply by the accumulation of knowledge as a result of classroom experience. Experience has to be analyzed and knowledge processed before it becomes relatable to classroom action, and knowledge growth may be characterized more by a process of various alternating advances and regressions, cycles of understanding and confusion, rather than unidimensional progress (Stoddart, 1988; Roehler & Duffy, 1988).

The processes of knowledge growth are well illustrated by Wilson,

Shulman, and Richert (1987; see also Shulman, 1986), who, in investigating the use of subject matter knowledge by student secondary teachers, suggest that, in learning to teach, new forms of knowledge and understanding are created. In thinking about the teaching of particular subject matter and in reflections on one's own classroom action, a form of knowledge termed *pedagogical content knowledge* is created, which consists of the metaphors, analogies, illustrative examples, demonstrations, etc. that are used in order to teach specific topics or specific areas of subject matter. In order to teach a particular topic, teachers need to know ways of presenting the material, key examples to use, what common misconceptions children develop, etc. Furthermore, since children approach classroom tasks with different preconceptions, encountering a range of various difficulties, teachers, in order to instruct, need to develop a "representational repertoire." They need to have at their disposal numerous ways of communicating content and understanding. Wilson et al. describe a process of pedagogical reasoning in which teachers, faced with the task of teaching new material, draw upon their own understanding of the material together with their understanding of children, teaching strategies, and the curriculum to generate teaching plans. The teaching of the material, and the later reflection and analysis of how satisfactorily the plans worked out in action, lead both to a fuller understanding of the subject matter and to the accumulation of a representational repertoire for the teaching of this subject. Shulman (1986) suggests that pedagogical content knowledge is part of the case knowledge of teachers, indicating typical ways of explaining, communicating, and representing particular topics or subject material.

## 6. CASE KNOWLEDGE, IMAGERY, AND PROBLEM SOLVING

Experienced teachers faced with a particular task or situation seem to be able to call to mind a body of significant case knowledge. This knowledge may be related to routine responses but also enables other levels of reflection and subsequent action. Case knowledge may provide the initial problem formulation from which other knowledge or current observations can be used to modify the perception of the problem teachers face and the strategy to be adopted in its solution. Precisely what form case knowledge takes is a topic demanding much further research. However, several researchers have adopted the term *image* to describe case knowledge. Although the term has been used in various ways to describe knowledge at different levels of abstraction, it is generally argued that images of practice are economical ways of storing the vast amounts of knowledge that teachers appear to draw upon, and that they represent appropriate means of encoding complex classroom situations, enabling a ready association between a complex knowledge base and ill-defined classroom situations. Images also seem to represent well the ways in which teachers talk about their own knowledge—often in terms of mental pictures, capable of manipulation.

Connelly and Clandinin (1985) describe a category of teachers' knowledge as personal practical knowledge which they suggest takes the form of images, defined as powerful metaphors with affective and moral associations. An image, in this sense, is a way of conceptualizing what teaching ought to be and presents a way of generally 'framing' teaching situations. They describe, for example, a teacher of infants with an image of 'classroom as home.' This image influences how she perceives her work, and in consequence how she organizes and manages her class, how she relates to the children, and how she arranges the classroom environment.

At a lower level of abstraction are the images that student teachers have sometimes been found to have of models of teaching. These are rather more partial and specific, but have been found to influence how student teachers interpret their own and others' practice (Knowles, 1987; Calderhead & Robson, 1988). One student teacher, for example, was found to hold a model in mind of a teacher who managed the class through her relationships with the individual children. The model was derived from the memory of a teacher whom the student had encountered as a pupil at school. The teacher had a warm, concerned, sympathetic relationship with children, which permeated the whole classroom environment. It had become so important to the children to get on well with the teacher that the teacher's threat of 'falling out' was itself sufficient to maintain control. The student viewed this model as an ideal to be achieved; it influenced her evaluations of her own practice in the classroom and also how she perceived other teachers at work. In commenting on videotapes of classroom teaching, for example, she would be very much more discriminating than other students about the quality of teacher–pupil relationships as indicated by such features as their tone of voice, manner of address, physical proximity, and the teacher's response to the moods and personalities of the children.

At a still lower level of abstraction are the lesson images noted by Morine-Dershimer (1979). Teachers have been found to have images or 'mental pictures' of what an arithmetic, spelling, or practical science lesson typically involves. Experienced teachers can readily 'picture' what a particular lesson will be like.

The concept of image has also been used to refer to the many visual memories, or snapshots of perception, of individual children and situations that enter teachers' minds in the course of everyday teaching (Eraut, 1985). Stimulated recall protocols frequently suggest that teachers evoke images of particular children or incidents in the course of their interactions in the classroom.

The term image is clearly still in need of much tighter definition, though it can serve to conceptualize, in a loose sense, part of the case knowledge format of teachers' practical knowledge. The concept of image highlights the perceptual/experiential nature of teachers' practical knowledge and, in some cases, the affective associations that teachers' knowledge sometimes appears to possess. Images or models of practice appear to be an economical way of storing knowledge about teaching which is readily related to the practical situations that teachers face. Images may also cut across such divisions as procedural and declarative knowledge, in that images can refer to action within particular contexts and with reference to specific subject matter.

There are parallels between this account of teachers' knowledge and those of other human 'experts' whose knowledge bases psychologists have studied. Chess players and medical diagnosticians, for example, have similarly been found to have rich, particularistic, episodic knowledge bases that are readily retrieved in an action context (Chi, Glaser, & Rees, 1982). Though part of this knowledge might take the form of rules capable of verbalization, some theorists have argued that there is, inherent in problem solving, a form of knowledge which lies in imagery and which cannot be reduced to linguistic propositions (Kosslyn, 1985).

## 7. TEACHERS' KNOWLEDGE AND THE DESIGN OF ITSs

Such a description of teachers' knowledge raises a number of interesting questions concerning teachers' own development. What kinds of images do student teachers bring to the teacher training context? How are they influenced by the experiences they are offered in college and school? What influences the evolution of particular images? How are images at different levels of abstraction interrelated? What are the cognitive and metacognitive processes involved in the creation and use of images? We know little about these processes.

Such a conceptualization of teaching also raises questions about the direction of research and development concerning intelligent tutoring systems. ITSs may well function in different contexts from those of the school teacher, or in a subset of those contexts in which teachers work. ITSs are more likely, for instance, to be engaged in individual or small group instruction as opposed to class teaching. The question remains, however, whether the study of teachers in individual or small group teaching situations can yield appropriate theoretical frameworks for the design of ITSs. If we were to generalize from the literature discussed above, it suggests that the characteristic features of an ITS would be an extensive knowledge base of typical situations, representing a repertoire of ways of initially framing teaching/learning problems, and a set of heuristics for using these to match particular instructional strategies to particular learning difficulties, together with a means of monitoring how teaching and learning are interacting. This is an interesting framework to pursue, but how the case knowledge or images of the teacher are to be represented in an ITS is problematic. How this case knowledge is to be developed and employed, what form the manipulating heuristics might take, and how the effects of using the case knowledge can be monitored are also challenging questions.

The task of mapping out teachers' pedagogical knowledge, systematizing it, and incorporating it into an ITS is fraught with difficulty. The development of ITS technology may depend as much on investigating the differences between human and artificial tutors, the contexts of their work, and their differing representations of knowledge, as attempting to promote their similarities. The outcome of research in both fields, and the exchange of models from these fields, may, however, provide the basis for developing improved theoretical frameworks with which to enquire further into the complex processes of instruction, and to develop the instructional potential of both teacher and computer.

## REFERENCES

Anderson, J.R. (1983). *The architecture of cognition*. Cambridge, MA: Harvard University Press.

Berliner, D.C. (1987). Ways of thinking about students and classrooms by more and less experienced teachers. In J. Calderhead (Ed.), *Exploring teachers' thinking*. London: Cassell.

Borko, H., Livingston, C., McCaleb, J., & Mauro, L. (1988). Student teachers' planning and post-lesson reflections: Patterns and implications for teacher preparation. In J. Calderhead (Ed.), *Teachers' professional learning*. London: Falmer Press.

Calderhead, J. (1981). A psychological approach to research on teachers' classroom decision-making. *British Educational Research Journal, 7*, 51-7.

Calderhead, J. (1984). *Teachers' classroom decision-making*. London: Cassell.

Calderhead, J., & Robson, M. (1988, September). *Images of teaching and learning: Student teachers' early conceptions of practice*. Paper presented at the British Educational Research Association annual conference, Norwich.

Carter, K., Sabers, D., Cushing, K., Pinnegar, S., & Berliner, D.C. (1987). Processing and using information about students: A study of expert, novice and postulant teachers. *Teaching and Teacher Education, 3*, 147-57.

Chi, M.T.H., Glaser, R., & Rees, E. (1982). Expertise in problem solving. In R. Sternberg (Ed.), *Advances in the psychology of human intelligence* (Vol.1). Hillsdale, NJ: Erlbaum.

Connolly, F.M., & Clandinin, D.J. (1985). Personal practical knowledge and the modes of knowing: relevance for teaching and learning. In E. Eisner (Ed.), *Learning and teaching the ways of knowing* (84th Yearbook of the National Society for the Study of Education). Chicago, IL: University of Chicago Press.

Doyle, W. (1986). Classroom organisation and management. In M.C. Wittrock (Ed.), *Handbook of research on teaching* (3rd ed.). New York: Macmillan.

Driver, R. (1983). *Pupil as scientist?* London: Open University Press.

Eraut, M. (1985). Knowledge creation and knowledge use in professional contexts. *Studies in Higher Education, 10*, 117-33.

Knowles, J.G. (1987, November). *What student teachers' biographies tell us: implications for preservice teacher education.* Paper presented at the joint conference of the Australian and New Zealand Associations for Research in Education, University of Canterbury, Christchurch, New Zealand.

Korthagen, F.A.J. (1988). The influence of learning orientations on the development of reflective teaching. In J. Calderhead (Ed.), *Teachers' professional learning.* London: Falmer Press.

Kosslyn, S.M. (1985). Mental imagery ability. In R.J. Sternberg (Ed.), *Human abilities: An information-processing approach.* New York: W.H. Freeman & Co.

Lanier, J.E., & Little, J.W. (1986). Research on teacher education. In M.C. Wittrock (Ed.), *Handbook of research on teaching* (3rd ed.). New York: Macmillan.

Leinhardt, G., & Smith, D.A. (1985). Expertise in mathematics instruction: Subject matter knowledge. *Journal of Educational Psychology, 77,* 247-271.

Morine-Dershimer, G. (1979). *Teacher plan and classroom reality: The S. Bay study, part 4* (Research monograph). Ann Arbor, MI: Institute for Research on Teaching, University of Michigan.

Ohlsson, S. (1985) Some principles for intelligent tutoring. *Instructional Science, 14,* 293-326.

Resnick, L.B. (1987). Learning in school and out. *Educational Researcher, 16* (9), 13-20.

Robinson, P. (1988, June). *The quality of novitiate primary teachers, with special reference to the teaching of writing and science.* Paper presented at the ESRC Teacher Education Workshop, Edinburgh.

Roehler, L.R., & Duffy, G.G. (1988, April). *Unexpected patterns in the development of teachers' knowledge structures.* Paper presented at the American Educational Research Association annual meeting, New Orleans.

Russell, T. (1988). From preservice teacher education to first year of teaching: a study of theory and practice. In J. Calderhead (Ed.), *Teachers' professional learning.* London: Falmer Press.

Schon, D.A. (1983). *The reflective practitioner.* London: Temple Smith.

Stoddart, T. (1988, April). *Non-linear patterns of development: Implications for research.* Paper presented at the American Educational Research Association annual meeting, New Orleans.

Shulman, L.S. (1986). Those who understand: Knowledge growth in teaching. *Educational Researcher, 15,* 4-14.

Stones, E., & Morris, S. (1972) *Teaching practice: Problems and perspectives.* London: Methuen.

Wilson, S.M. Shulman, L.S., & Richert, A.E. (1987). '150 different ways' of knowing: representations of knowledge in teaching. In J. Calderhead (Ed.), *Exploring teachers' thinking.* London: Cassell.

Yinger, R.J. (1987, April). *Teaching by the seat of your pants: Improvisation in an algebra classroom.* Paper presented at the American Educational Research Association annual meeting, Washington, DC.

# 13

# TEACHING AND TUTORING SYSTEMS: EXPLANATORY DIALOGUES IN CONTEXT

MICHAEL BEVERIDGE
RACHEL RIMMERSHAW

Psychological theories of learning have in general seemed unsatisfactory to those people who are engaged in the teaching process. Taxonomies of learning (Bloom, 1956), and learning hierarchies (Gagne, 1970), have been found helpful in curriculum planning but have not been successful in explaining success and failure in classroom teaching. Similarly, developmental approaches (Piaget, 1959; Sternberg, 1984) have given us a limited understanding of why some concepts are difficult to teach but have not explained how they are learned (Wood, 1988).

However, more recently an approach to the analysis of learning has emerged which is having more direct impact on learning and teaching. This approach takes the events of classroom life as its starting point. It looks at the way that teachers and students interact during lessons. Classroom activities are analyzed in order to see how the students' knowledge is constructed. Conceptual development is identified as a social process with its roots in the practices of the classroom. The reasons why children succeed or fail are investigated by looking at the lengthy and complex interchanges through which ideas are built up. This *constructivist* approach is useful to teachers because they can recognize these processes from their own experiences. They recognize the ways students' conceptions and misconceptions are changed through the ways that language weaves experience into knowledge.

Constructivist approaches to understanding student learning have been applied to a number of domains of knowledge, most notably science (Driver

& Oldham, 1986) and economics (Thomas, 1985). As well as offering a useful account of the process of teachers and learners jointly constructing knowledge in the course of classroom dialogue, we shall argue that this approach suggests implications for the interactive models which are designed into ITS. In particular, insight can be gained into the way that explanations contribute to the success of teaching. This insight is not only useful for understanding how classroom explanations work, but also offers some guidance to the tutoring systems designer. In this chapter we will look at some examples of explanatory dialogues in the classroom and suggest some ways that AI-based tutoring might be enhanced by modeling some features of these processes. In order to motivate this discussion, we first give a brief overview of the way explanations have been treated in the research literature.

## 1. ANALYSES OF EXPLANATION

A common basis for discussing explanation has been to use a taxonomic approach and distinguish between different kinds of explanation. This approach is evident in several different literatures. It is to be seen for example in the philosophy of science, from Aristotle's "four causes" to the classic treatment of Nagel (1961), who classified scientific explanations into four types: deductive, probabilistic, teleological (functional), and genetic (developmental). More recently in the philosophy of science Van Fraassen (1980) has drawn attention to the contexts in which explanations are given; and the influence of people's orientation, interests, and the way they have come to the problem on what they pick out as salient features to be cited in an explanation. In addition he points out that requests for explanation have an implicit 'in contrast to . . .' clause, or set of alternatives in relation to which a phenomenon needs explaining. In his view typologies such as Aristotle's reflect (but probably oversimplify) the variety of interests determining relevant factors for explanatory requests.

Some educational writers have taken such classifications wholesale as the basis for discussing explanation in education. Green (1971), for example, uses Nagel's taxonomy, and argues that making such distinctions should be helpful in teaching, as it would be "a mistake to answer one kind of 'why' with an explanation appropriate only to another kind" (p. 147). Other philosophers of education (Ennis, 1969; Swift, 1961) have used other taxonomies. Ennis distinguished between descriptive, interpretative, and reason-giving explanations, and also between those which are analytical, empirical, causal, reason-for-acting, or associated with value or obligation. More simply, Swift only distinguished between relational, nonrelational, and scientific explanations. However, while such taxonomies can usefully distinguish the kinds of explanations which are tendered, they offer no assistance in determining what Van Fraassen (1980) calls the relation of explanatory relevance; that is, what kind of explanation is required by any request to explain.

Recent work in the expert systems area has similar limitations. Hughes (1986), for example, has suggested that Lenhnert's (1981) classification of questions for a question-answering program (QUALM) could be exploited fruitfully. However, QUALM was used in story-understanding programs, where prior knowledge in the form of generalized scripts was used as the basis for determining what kind of explanation was required. Such an assumption of common expectations is likely to be violated frequently in teaching and learning contexts. So, for example, irrespective of whether the 'Photon' explanation (referred to at the beginning of the next section of this chapter) is classified as *descriptive* (Ennis), *nonrelational* (Swift), or *feature specification* (Lehnert), these labels provide no basis for judging the circumstances in which such an explanation would be apt.

In other respects there are differences in emphasis or perspective in the literature on explanation. On the whole the educational literature has concentrated on explanation as exposition or even lecturing (Brown, 1978; Gage, 1971; Swift; 1961). This reflects a concern with classroom processes and whole-class or large-group teaching. Some educational writers however (e.g., Thyne, 1966) have taken the individual learner's perspective. This is also apparent in recent work (Bennett, Desforges, Cockburn, & Wilkinson, 1984; Edwards & Mercer, 1987). In the expert systems literature this individual focus has been oriented particularly towards problem-generated explanations, either as responses to learners' requests (Rymaszewski, 1987; Weiner; 1980), spontaneously offered (Draper, 1987) or both (Beveridge, 1989). Such treatments have tended to deal with explanation as something tutors do (Hughes, 1986; Rymaszewski, 1987; Swartout, 1983; Weiner, 1980). However, learners' explanations have been addressed. Much of Swift's (1961) paper, for example, is concerned with discussing the adequacy of students' explanations demanded by way of assessment. Miyake (1986) takes a different perspective on learners' explanations and is concerned with explanations generated for each other by students working collaboratively in a problem domain.

Cutting across these perspectives is another set of constraints on the content of explanation as domain dependent (Swift, 1961; Weiner, 1980; Collins, 1987), purpose dependent (Rymaszewski, 1987; Draper, 1987), and audience dependent (Beveridge, 1989). Swartout (1983) describes an attempt to refine and improve the usefulness of the explanations generated by expert consulting programs. The proposed basis for this improvement is the explicit representation of domain heuristics and procedural principles as well as, but separately from, the declarative domain knowledge of causal relationships and classification hierarchies. On this basis the program is able to offer an account, not only of what rules it used in making a diagnosis, but also why it was reasonable to use these rules.

We shall argue, however, that while the system-user foci in discussions of explanation in the expert systems literature have their value, emphasis on the domain at the expense of context (purpose, audience, history) is a serious flaw.

## 2. ANALYSIS OF EXPLANATIONS IN CONTEXT

"Photons are about this long," explained the physics teacher, stretching out her hands to about a meter apart. "They vibrate along their length and come into existence at one end and disappear at the other."

This teacher was clearly not giving *the* explanation of the physics of light; she was responding to a student's question, "What is a photon?" Her response was set in the context of a lesson on how modern physics has integrated corpuscular and wavelength theories of light. Without this context her response appears bizarre and lacks explanatory power.

The teaching and learning of science makes extensive use of explanatory acts which, like the one above, are brief and only have power because of their place in the history of student and teacher exchanges. Each explanation is given its scientific meaning by the action and dialogue which have led the students to their current understanding. Knowledge is constructed in these encounters. Explanations are successful when their form and content and timing is appropriate. Put more simply, explanations are more likely to work when they take account of the processes of learning that students have already experienced. And, furthermore, delivering appropriate explanations requires that teachers have both monitored and remembered the routes to understanding which their students have taken.

Single explanations rarely have full power to make issues and concepts immediately clear to students. They are most typically part of a patchwork created by the teacher. The teacher attempts to repair holes in the students' knowledge while also making their knowledge structures more open to new possibilities. This increased assimilative power will , it is hoped, make new information more intelligible to the student. Teachers use explanations in this way to build up knowledge over long periods of time. There is rarely *one* explanation but different interrelated acts of explaining which are effective through their cumulative power.

The following outline of a typical lesson in secondary school physics [1]

---

[1] This lesson is summarized, with permission, from the following report:

Wightman, T.(1986). *The construction of meaning and conceptual change in classroom settings: Case studies on the particulate nature of matter*. Leeds England: Children's Learning in Science Project. CSSME, University of leeds.

shows how an explanatory patchwork can be constructed. What follows is a schematized summary of a lesson on the topic of Brownian motion. (The words which appear below indicate the meaning the participants were expressing and are not those actually used. This change is necessary because of available space. The actual lesson contained considerably more dialogue.)

T: We've been thinking of materials as made up from particles. Now we're going to get as near as we can to seeing a single atom. You'll have realised from what you've done so far that atoms are very tiny, so they'll be difficult to see.
We're going to use what we can see through a microscope, and a model, and a computer simulation to try to get the idea.
Here's the apparatus (container, bulb, glass rod 'lens', plastic tube). I'm going to put smoke into the plastic tube.. Is it empty at the moment?

P: No! Air's in it.

T: Here we go. (Puts smoke in.) What can you see?

P: Little white bits.

T: Are they doing anything?

P: Moving.

T: How?

P: Jumping.

P: Sharp.

T: Yes, fast movement.

P: Little bits, white circles.

P: Flashing on and off.

T: Do you mean they disappear sometimes?

P: Stardust, I think they're gold.

P: Dodging, bumping, shooting away from each other.

P: Like two magnets going for each other, but when they get near to each other they shoot away to the sides.

P: Is it?

T: Or is there a simpler explanation?

P: Are they just not attracted?

P: Is it cohesion being reversed, pushing each other away?

T: Let's piece together all these observations. First the colours—white, gold. What is it you're seeing?

P: Particles.

T: Of?

P: Smoke.

T: What is smoke?

P: Gas.

T: Alright, but it's tiny debris. This microscope isn't powerful enough for you to see the individual flakes. What is it you're seeing?

P: Heat—energy—oxygen burning.

T: What does energy do?

P: Makes things move.

T:  So maybe it's involved in the movement. What about what you can see. When sunlight reflects off the car windscreen or a house window in the distance you don't know anything about the shape or size of the pane of glass. You're seeing particles of dust reflecting light in the same way.

T:  Now what about the movement. You used the word 'dodgy'. Look at this computer simulation of just one speck, slowed down. The motion you're seeing is called Brownian motion. Could you predict which way that speck was going to move.?

P:  No.

T:  So how is it moving?

P:  Irregular.

P:  Random.

T:  Notice it's still there under the microscope as vigorous as ever. So it's also rapid and continuous. This is what the track of single particle could be like (computer demonstration). Some of you noticed the speck of light disappear. Remember, the microscope is focussed on one level, but the movement is vertical as well as horizontal. So if the speck moves up or down it goes out of focus and you can no longer see it.

T:  What causes the movement? What else is in the tube?

P:  Air.

T:  Air is also made of particles. Too tiny to reflect the light, but not to do something to the dust particles. A crowd in the corridor can't follow a straight path.

P:  They zig zag, bumping and bouncing of each other.

T:  So what might the air particles be doing to the smoke particles?

P:  Deflection.

P:  They're both moving, and bouncing off.

T:  Yes, that's what we think is happening. A chap called Brown first discovered it by seeing floating pollen grains shimmering. Particles of water were moving at random and colliding with the pollen grains.

T:  Here's a model to help you understand. Ball-bearings represent particles. I'll set the motor to give only a small amount of energy. The ball bearings are moving, but just vibrating up and down, closely packed together. That's how we think they might be in a solid. I'll give it more energy. What happens when it's heated?

P:  Expands.

T:  Becomes a liquid.

T:  Look the particles are moving more freely. What about the spaces?

P:  Further apart.

T:  Right, so what about the forces between them?

P:  They'll be weaker.

T:  Yes and what's the next stage?

P:  Gas.

T:  Now here's a piece of paper representing a smoke particle. I'll put it in. Watch how it moves, what sort of path does it follow?

P:  Zig zag.

T:      Right, like the computer model showed. The ball bearings are bom-
        barding it, pushing it sometimes one way sometimes another, giving a
        random motion.
        So that's Brownian motion. It's close to seeing individual particles. It's
        evidence of the existence of particles, because how else would you explain
        what you're seeing under the microscope?

In terms of its aims this whole lesson is an explanation of the concept of
Brownian motion. During the lesson the teacher elicits ideas from the
students. Sometimes he leaves their suggestions on one side and picks them
up later. On other occasions he builds on them immediately. Sometimes
pupils' ideas are ignored, usually by the teacher giving another idea himself.

All the time he is leading the children to understanding that the movement
of the smoke particles is caused by other invisible particles bumping into them.
And that the movement is seen by the reflection of light off the smoke particles.

The nature of the movement is crucial to the understanding of this
concept. The children must perceive its apparently random quality and that
it is not associated with forces between the smoke particles. The explanation
required is more than mere description.

In the lesson the teacher spends almost all the time establishing that the
phenomenon to be explained is correctly perceived by the children. It is
clearly not enough to show it to them. The phenomenon itself needs
explaining as random movement revealed by reflected light.

Once the phenomenon is correctly seen, the teacher uses the 'crowd'
analogy to explain the movement. The relevant features of this analogy are
themselves elicited from the children. These are then related to the motion of
the smoke particles. The relationship between the movement in the smoke
tube apparatus and the originally noted Brownian motion of pollen grains on
water is established.

This lesson is typical of the way many teachers explain concepts in science.
The lesson is not simply problem specification followed by a solution or
explanation at the end. The whole lesson is a patchwork of pupils and teacher
constructing an interpretation of the events which occur under the microscope—events which, once correctly perceived, can be explained by the
concept of Brownian motion.

Embedded within this constructivist process, various subordinate explanations are given both by the students, for example, energy, attraction, cohesion,
air as cause; and by the teacher, such as, reflection and vertical movement.
These embedded explanations are woven together in a way that reveals the
scientific world as a place in which explanations of one phenomenon have to
be consistent with those of others. In this way students participate in the
process of scientific understanding as a coherent and logical process. They are
experiencing, not merely an explanation, but also the way scientists evaluate

alternatives. They are learning how to think about this problem as scientists. The dialogue of the classroom reveals the practices of a scientific community and the inner thoughts of the scientist. The children are being taught to use discourse to think in a particular way. The implicit rationale for this kind of teaching is that merely demonstrating phenomena and presenting accounts, without offering a model of the dialogical processes which relate them, does not teach children how to think scientifically.

To the extent that the aims of science education are similar both in the traditional classroom context and through interaction with a tutoring system, the important message for ITS design is that they must be able to handle interactive procedures which reflect these processes of thought. We are not suggesting, however, that all features of classroom explanation should be modelled by tutoring systems. There are some features of classroom explanation which the designers of ITS would do well to avoid. Hull (1985) provides a vivid example of how the exigencies of a syllabus or the teacher's preconception of a lesson serve to keep the teacher's purposes uppermost at the expense of the explanations demanded by the students. The transcript below is an extract from a top set fourth year (10th grade) physics lesson.

T:   Who knows anything about the structure of the atom? (No reply)

T:   No? (Pause) Well, an atom is made up of a nucleus with a positive charge, and around it it has a field of negative charge . . . the nucleus is very small . . . you could compare it with the size of a pea on the center spot of Wembley Stadium . . . So an atom is mostly . . .? (Pause) What's in between?

P7:   Air

T:   Air is made up of atoms . . . What's in [indistinct]?

P5:   How do you split them?

T:   We're interested in . . .

P5:   How did they find out about the nucleus and [indistinct]?

T:   It would take too long to tell . . . it would take half a term in the sixth form. (Noise) All right, then . . . there was this chap called Rutherford . . . he produced a sheet of atoms of [indistinct].

P5:   How?

T:   . . . and bombarded it with particles.

P5   *Where* did he [bombard them?]

T:   Well, it would take a long time.

PP:   Half a term in the sixth form! (Small chorus)

P2:   How did he get the atoms off it?

T:   He knocked them . . .

P2:   (Interrupting) *HOW*?!! How did he get them . . .

T:   Well . . .

P2:   I want to KNOW!
      (Voice rising in exasperation.)

T:   Jane!

After this small explosion his exposition went on for a short while uninterrupted by questions, or anything else.

T:  They thought an atom was just solid, but because . . . [indistinct] they found that 99 per cent went straight through, 0.9 per cent got deflected, but 0.1 per cent got bounced straight back.
PP: Cor!
T:  They couldn't explain it . . . they thought the only reason could be . . . the mass was concentrated at one particular point . . . if all the rest went through [indistinct] . . . RIGHT, so we have . . .
P8: (Interrupting) is that splitting the atom?
T:  No, we'll get on to that later.

The teacher then rather abruptly started hid dictation of notes. The note-taking was completed two minutes or so later with the words: 'surrounding this are electrons in constant motion'. Immediately, a pupil spoke.

P9: Do they go round?
T:  Yes, but it's not as simple as that, because they behave both as particles and as waves—it's a very complex part of chemistry.
PP: Half a term in the sixth form? (Small chorus)
P5: University.

(Hull, 1985, pp. 122-123)

In this short extract the teacher has received seven requests for explanations from four different students, only one of which is grudgingly gratified ("All right, then . . ."). What the students receive by way of explanation from the teacher, apart from the account of the discovery of the nucleus they asked for, are either explanations offered by the teacher when the students don't demonstrate their own knowledge, as in the teacher's opening moves, or indications that there are explanations which the students are not going to be offered. The teacher explains, in the sense of 'gives reasons for,' his own refusal to answer the students' questions.

The exchange at the end of the extract is particularly interesting, as pupil 9's question "Do they go round?" does not have the surface features of an explanation request like "How . . .?" and "Why . . .?" questions do. Yet the teacher recognizes by his reply that this question, signaling that the student is checking out his or her mental model of atomic structure, requires an explanation that will confirm, qualify, or develop it.

Despite not volunteering any knowledge of the structure of the atom in response to the teacher's opening request, the students' questions, as Hull points out, indicate that they are at least familiar with talk of atoms ("How do you split them?" "Is that splitting them?" "Do they [electrons] go round?"). Now they see an opportunity to "fix" this language, or harden up or revise the mental models they have developed so far, but their starting points are not for the most part allowed on the agenda. So, while this transcript is untypical of classroom dialogues presented in the educational literature in having a high level of students' (rather than teachers') questions, the teacher's need to maintain control, or stick to the lesson, or cover the syllabus ("We're interested in . . .") prevents a genuine negotiation of what is to be explained.

Thus the students' initiatives can be seen as lost opportunities. While classroom teachers analyzing such a lesson transcript may draw useful conclusions of their own practice, the analysis we have offered also has an important lesson for the design of tutoring systems. It concerns the relative usefulness of student models as opposed to features which allow the students to have some control over what is explained.

Recognition of the interactive nature of explanation implies that knowing the constraints of the person to whom an explanation is directed ought to help in formulating successful explanations. But how can student models containing such information be developed? In practice students often have a rich repertoire of "minitheories" about whatever they are learning (Driver, 1983). Research into how children learn science has shown that they use their own theories to interpret the explanations which they are offered by teachers (Solomon, 1983; Bell, 1985). But the unpredictability and variation of the learners provides an "open system" (Wilden, 1972) model of learning which would be very difficult to model computationally. Learners are active theory builders, but not always to their advantage, at least in the short term. For example, Beveridge (1985) showed that giving young children lessons on one concept (absorption) led children to give a false explanation of another (evaporation). They developed the theory that metal was porous and that water could disappear through it. This can be seen either as an "incorrect" explanation or an appropriate adjustment of a mental model based on new information or a new question. A series of such adjustments can be seen in Miyake's (1986) study of the recursive construction of explanations at different levels by two learners in coming to understand a mechanical system. Here two learners worked together to develop an understanding of how a sewing machine works. As each explanation or model was constructed it became clear to the learners that a new explanation at a different level of description was needed.

Beveridge's 'absorption' example shows how students tend to assume that the last concept learned explains the next problem presented. Edwards and Mercer (1987) have shown how this skill can be to children's advantage in learning the "ground rules" of classroom life. The extent to which children can work out these rules is illustrated by the child who was asked by a priest, "Do you know what is grey, furry, and hides nuts" to which the child thoughtfully responded, "I know the answer must be Jesus but it sounds like a squirrel to me." The central point is that explanations have a history and a heuristic function based on their place in the learner's experience. Successful explanation often means getting inside the head of the learner, which as Edwards and Mercer have shown, means knowing a lot about their learning history.

While some aspects of a student's learning history are shared in a learning community and can be drawn on to construct successful explanations, as the example of the lesson on Brownian motion demonstrates, others may often be particular to an individual, as with the snippets of knowledge about atomic structure revealed in the second transcript. Since both common and individual knowledge histories are bound to extend beyond the interaction with a particular program or teacher, even the most elaborate of student models based on a student's interaction with a tutoring system may have a limited capacity to predict what explanations are needed, or what will satisfy a particular learner.

Equally, whether a particular learner would be satisfied by a given explanation cannot be judged by analyzing either the "correctness" of its content or type (Ennis, 1969; Green, 1971) or the "adequacy" of its structure (Weiner, 1980). So a more useful approach may be to consider the rhetorical status of explanations. The expository or "lecturing" explanations discussed in the educational literature of the 1960s and 1970s, and exemplified in the lesson transcripts offered here, will have a different function to those generated in a problem-solving dialogue. But as O'Malley, Draper, and Riley (1984) have shown, even in that sort of context, explanations are typically grounded in the knowledge of the explainer and may meet resistance if that mental model is not shared by the explainee. Observation and analysis of explanatory dialogue may reveal both how a repertoire of explanatory devices (examples, analogies, generalizations and so on) is used by successful explainers, and also how learners use their discourse repertoire to negotiate what is to be explained, what kind of explanation will suffice, and what explanatory devices are helpful. Such studies have been begun (Rymaszewski, 1987). If either of these repertoires turn out to be manageably small, as we suspect they might, then implementing the appropriate discourse machinery could be a more efficient way forward for intelligent tutoring systems than the use of elaborate student models.

## 3. WHAT CAN TEACHER AND ITS DESIGNER LEARN FROM EACH OTHER?

Since the existing explanation facilities of expert systems, including intelligent tutoring systems, are widely criticized, an urgent task for the designers of tutoring systems is to select from the perspectives discussed above those whose exploration is most likely to bear exploitable fruit. This is an important strategic issue for ITS development. One can take the attitude of "never mind the ball, let's get on with the game,'' but tackling theoretical issues should enable better progress on the practical front. One of the strengths of A I is its resistance to the philosophy of essentialism, which attempts to define answers to empirical questions in advance of their being tested.

The limitations of the taxonomic approach have already been noted. The designer of an intelligent tutoring system with only a classification schema to hand is left with all the decisions about how to implement explanations. Taxonomies do not tell the designer in what circumstances to offer explanations (Draper, 1987), how to judge what kind of explanation will satisfy a particular user on a particular occasion, or even what the user is puzzled about (Rymaszewski, 1987).

What the ITS designer needs is an account, not of kinds of explanation, but of the explanation process. This includes the functions explanations serve in the sociocognitive contexts of learning. For example, the explanation of a photon given earlier is unlikely to stand alone as a generally applicable response to a request. Rather it would most typically represent a local and context-dependent decision on the part of the teacher. He or she would use this explanation after deciding on how it can be fitted into a chain of EXPLANATION – RESPONSE – EXPLANATION – RESPONSE – EXPLA- NATION moves. Within such a sequence an explanation is offered according to a continually updated model of the learner, or in response to a new expression of puzzlement.

So far we have been arguing that the intelligent use of explanations in tutoring systems must take account of both the learner's needs and purposes and of the dialogic and learning context in which the explanations are to be framed. Such an approach to studying explanation is not easy to find in the literature on education, with its emphasis on the traditional classroom context. So the perspectives on explanation argued for as useful here may not only help apply our understanding of human explanation in designing improved tutoring systems. They may also prove a useful impetus to classroom research which is directed towards more effective teaching and better quality student learning experiences in the classroom. Recent class- room research, such as that of Bennett et al. (1984), Hull (1985), or Edwards and Mercer (1987) has begun to reveal the dynamics of explanation in relation to the tensions between teachers' and learners' goals. The individual and problem-based perspectives on explanation currently being explored in the expert systems context (Beveridge, 1989), might also with profit be more widely applied in educational research.

We are suggesting that studying the dialogue of teaching can reveal procedural models of the process of understanding. And, furthermore, that teacher and student jointly construct the pathways to understanding. Com- puter modelling of human interaction is as yet inadequate to the task of providing the full range of subtle responses available to teachers (Goodyear,

1987; Beveridge, 1989). But there are some interactive procedures which can be identified from teacher–pupil dialogues and which may be within the compass of the systems designer.

Firstly, could systems be designed to allow students to discover the limits of plausibility of their own explanations? For example, they could hold student explanations in memory for reintroduction at points where their plausibility may be reduced or increased. The Brownian motion example shows how the teacher leads the children to a different perspective on the problem such that their original explanations of 'attraction,' 'repulsion,' and so on, are no longer as plausible. The teacher is formulating the lesson plan to increase the plausibility of the Brownian motion explanation. He also, and to some degree independently, uses strategies to decrease the plausibility of the children's initial attempts to account for the visible movement of the smoke particles. Secondly, tutoring systems can hold a repertoire of analogies and microenvironments, like those of the ballbearing model referred to in the transcript, which can be examined in the light of the explanations offered by students. Thirdly, students can be asked to examine their own explanations and to assign probabilities, implications and advantages to them. These approaches do not treat students' responses as mistakes but as theories to be explored. ITSs operating in this way will help the learners with 'how to think' as well as with 'what to know.'

It has often been noted that the world of scientific objects is not the same as that of experience (Bruner, 1986). Teachers attempt wherever possible to bridge this divide; but as diSessa (1987) argues

> One of the essential gaps in public education is its failure to convey the sense of incredible complexity, interrelatedness and depth of scientific knowledge as compared to commonsense reasoning. (p. 71)

Because scientific understanding is so powerful and multileveled, it requires complex explanatory procedures. These are themselves little understood at present, but, in our view, tutoring system design constraints do allow for inclusion of some of their features. And, by attempting to achieve this goal, we should both understand more about the explanatory process and avoid reproducing the 'gap' referred to above by diSessa.

In this chapter we hope we have shown that the successful use of explanation in a tutoring system is likely to require more than the domain models and problem-solving heuristics currently assumed (Swartout, 1983; Weiner, 1980). However, modeling the students' understanding, including inferring what follows from the students' own theories, is itself a far from trivial task. We argue for a system design which is in accord with the procedures of reasoning needed to develop adequate explanations. This implies increased attention on the repertoires of explanatory devices available to the system and of the dialogic moves available to both system and user.

# REFERENCES

Bell, B. (1985). 'Students' ideas about plant nutrition—what are they? *Journal of Biological Education, 19(3),* 213-218

Bennett, N., Desforges, C., Cockburn A., & Wilkinson, B. (1984). *The quality of pupil learning experiences.* London: Erlbaum.

Beveridge, M. (1985). The development of young children's understanding of the process of evaporation. *British Journal of Educational Psychology, 55,* 84-90

Beveridge, M. (1989). The educational implications of intelligent systems. In L. Murray & J. Richardson (Eds.), *Intelligent systems in a human context.* Oxford, England: Oxford University Press.

Bloom, B. S. (1956). *Taxonomy of educational objectives. The cognitive domain.* New York: Longman

Brown, G. (1978). *Lecturing and explaining.* London: Methuen.

Bruner, J.S. (1986). *Actual minds: Possible worlds.* Cambridge, MA: Harvard University Press.

Collins, H. M. (1987). Expert systems and the science of knowledge. In W. Bijker, T. Hughes, & T. Pinch (Eds.), *New developments in the social study of technology.* Cambridge, MA: M.I.T.

Disessa, A.A. (1987). Artificial worlds and real experience. In R. W. Lawler & M. Yasdani (Eds.), *Artificial intelligence and education* (Vol. 1, pp. 55-77). Norwood, NJ: Ablex Publishing.

Draper, S.W. (1987). The occasions for explanation. *Proceedings of the Third Workshop.* Guildford, England: Alvey Knowledge Based Systems Club Explanation Special Interest Group, University of Surrey.

Driver, R. (1983). Pupils' alternative frameworks in science. *European Journal of Science Education, 3(1),* 93-101.

Driver, R., & Oldham, V. (1986). A constructivist approach to curriculum development in science. *Studies in Science Education, 13,* 105-122.

Edwards, D., & Mercer, N. (1987). *Common knowledge: The development of understanding in the classroom.* London: Methuen

Ennis, R. H. (1969). *Logic in teaching.* Englewood Cliffs, NJ: Prentice-Hall.

Gage, N.L. (1971). The microcriterion of effectiveness in explaining. In I Westbury & A. A. Bellack (Eds.), *Research into classroom processes.* New York: Teachers' College Press.

Gagne, R.M. (1970). *The conditions of learning.* New York: Holt.

Goodyear, P. (1987). *Approaches to the empirical derivation of teaching knowledge for intelligent tutoring systems.* Tubingen, Germany: European Seminar on Intelligent Tutoring Systems.

Green, T. F. (1971). *The activities of teaching.* New York: McGraw-Hill.

Hughes, S. (1986, March). *How and why: how far will they take us and why should we need any more?* Paper presented at the First Alvey Explanations Workshop, University of Surrey, Guildford.

Hull, R. (1985). *The language gap: How classroom dialogue fails.* London: Methuen.

Lehnert, W. (1981). A computational theory of human question answering. In A. K. Joshi, B. Webber, & I. Sag (Eds.), *Elements of discourse understanding.* Cambridge, England: C.U.P.

Miyake, N. (1986). Constructive interaction and the iterative process of understanding. *Cognitive Science, 10,* 151-177.

Nagel, E. (1961) *The structure of science: Problems in the logic of scientific explanation.* London: Routledge.

O'Malley, C.E., Draper, S.W., & Riley, M.S. (1984). Constructive interaction: A method for studying computer-user interaction. In B. Shackel (Ed.), *Interact '84 First Conference on Human-Computer Interaction.* Amsterdam: North-Holland.

Piaget, J. (1959). *The language and thought of the child.* London: Routledge.

Rymaszewski, R.H. (1987). *Negotiating cooperative and effective explanations* (CERCLE Technical Report No 39). Lancaster, England: University of Lancaster, Centre for Research on Computers and Learning.

Solomon, J. (1983). Learning about energy: how pupils think in two domains. *European Journal of Science Education, 5(1),* 49-59.

Sternberg, R. (Ed.). (1984). *Mechanisms of cognitive development*. New York: Freeman.

Swartout, W.R. (1983). XPLAIN, a system for creating and explaining expert consulting programs. *Artificial Intelligence, 21,* 285-325.

Swift, L.F. (1961). Explanation. In R. H. Ennis & B.O. Smith (Eds.), *Language and concepts in education*. Chicago, IL: Rand McNally.

Thomas, L. (1985). The core of economics—A psychological viewpoint. In G.B.J. Atkinson (Ed), *Teaching economics*. London: Heinemann Educational.

Thyne, J.M. (1966). *The psychology of learning and techniques of teaching*. London: University of London Press.

Van Fraassen, B.C. (1980). *The scientific image*. Oxford, England: Clarendon Press.

Weiner, J. (1980). BLAH, a system which explains its reasoning. *Artificial Intelligence, 15,* 19-48.

Wilden, A. (1972). *System and structure: Essays in communication and exchange*. London: Tavistock Press.

Wood, D.J. (1988). *How children think and learn*. Oxford, England: Blackwell.

# SECTION IV

## KNOWLEDGE-BASED SYSTEMS AND TEACHING TASKS

# 14

# A MODEL OF CLASSROOM PROCESSES: TOWARDS THE FORMALIZATION OF EXPERIENCED TEACHERS' PROFESSIONAL KNOWLEDGE*

SHARON WOOD

## 1. INTRODUCTION

Teaching expertise is passed on by word and example to trainee teachers throughout their teaching practice by their more experienced colleagues. The knowledge of the experienced teacher may therefore be regarded as something amenable to an expert systems approach, that is, to formalizing that knowledge computationally. This chapter describes a project embodying this assumption, an attempt to develop a *trainee teacher support system* (TTSS). (Further details of the project can be found in Wood, 1987a, b.)

Underlying the approach taken in this project is a regard for the professional status of teaching expertise. The skills of the experienced teacher are not considered solely to be an extension of general social skills acquired by all members of society to a greater or lesser degree. Rather they are seen as a reflection of the professional knowledge of teachers regarding their knowledge and understanding of classrooms and how to teach in the classroom setting, which are acquired through study and practice. The project has been concerned with identifying the teacher's professional knowledge in use in the

*Development of the TTSS was funded by the Renaissance Trust. This project has a steering group whose members include Ben du Boulay, Trevor Pateman, Mike Scaife, and Aaron Sloman, to whom much is owed for the successful progress of this research.

classroom and rendering this implicit knowledge explicit, so that it may be passed on directly to trainees in order to complement the knowledge they acquire through teaching practice.

## 2. TEACHING KNOWLEDGE AS PROFESSIONAL KNOWLEDGE

The view that some subset of teachers' knowledge is professional knowledge upon which they base their teaching decisions carries with it certain implications. Most important, from the point of view of the intelligent teaching systems research community, is the view that teaching is not synonomous with presenting subject matter, however appropriately structured and manageable the chunks' of knowledge to be imparted. There are other important factors to be taken into consideration. For example, experienced teachers have ways of making learning tasks more interesting and enjoyable, such as through the use of games in mathematics. This is because enjoyment is an important component of the learning process (this of course will be no revelation to teacher!). They also need to be adept at striking a balance between the help they give to a child and that child's sense of autonomy and personal responsibility for success in learning.

Discovering the basis upon which teachers come to make important decisions of this kind can only enhance our understanding of the learning process and our ability to construct useful teaching systems. But this is not the only purpose of such research. Owing to the very nature of the experienced teacher's knowledge acquired through practice, it is not readily available in any form other than through the process of direct experience. The motivation behind the work on the TTSS is to enhance its accessibility. Viewing the knowledge of the teacher as professionally acquired knowledge suggests we might be able to make this accessible.

A helpful experienced colleague will happily advise the trainee on the problems they encounter in the classroom. It is the basis upon which that experienced teacher is able to advise that we are interested in. What enables experienced teachers to comment wisely upon situations they have not even seen and about which they can have only a rough approximation of a subset of what really took place? It would appear that the experienced teacher has some generalized model of classroom situations, representing what is common to all classroom contexts, rather than the individual classroom setting experienced on any particular occasion. This model enables the teacher to interpret the nature of the problem described by the trainee and to advise accordingly. It is this which constitutes an important part of their professional knowledge. Owing to its implicit, experientially embodied nature, however, the 'surface appearance' of the advice given to trainees may bear little resemblance to the model from which it is derived, manifesting itself instead as intuitions regarding how to respond to various problem scenarios.


## 3. FORMALIZING TEACHERS' PROFESSIONAL KNOWLEDGE

In attempting to 'capture' and formalize the experienced teacher's knowledge in computational form, we are not attempting to simulate in all its fine detail the complexity of the classroom in which the teacher practices. Indeed, even the experienced teacher is not in a position to notice everything which takes place within his or her lessons. Rather, we attempt to identify those aspects of the classroom setting which play a crucial role in teachers' decision making—those things which the teacher notices and which determine what he or she does next. We are therefore identifying the components of teachers' decision making skills, not simulating classroom settings. The model of classroom processes discussed here is not, therefore, a model of 'how a classroom works' but of the teacher's understanding of how key aspects of a classroom situation (e.g., the extent to which every pupil is encouraged to participate) interact with general classroom processes (e.g., the motivation of the whole class as an entity) to bring about desired or undesired situations.

To a large extent teachers are unaware of any so-called 'model' upon which they are drawing in giving advice. It is probably true to say that they do not have any such coherent model of the kind we are proposing here, but a collection of things they know about classrooms—ways of interpreting particular nuggets of information and 'intuitions' about how to deal with different kinds of situations—which effectively form their knowledge about classrooms.

The current trend in 'knowledge engineering' (the process of obtaining knowledge from an expert and representing this in a computational form) has been to move away from the concept of 'knowledge mining' (Welbank, 1983), where the head of the expert is viewed as a storehouse of information to be 'mined' by the knowledge engineer with his or her metaphorical pickaxe. It has, to some extent, been replaced by the view of knowledge engineering as a collaborative enterprise of knowledge construction (Young, 1988), where the knowledge engineer and expert together infer the knowledge the expert is using. It is often the case, during the knowledge engineering process, that the expert feels he or she has discovered things he or she did not (or thought he or she did not) know beforehand. Rather than modelling something that already exists in the head of the expert, therefore, it is probably more accurate to say that we are attempting to construct some external coherent representation of what an expert knows, which does not necessarily exist prior to this construction process.

It is not surprising, therefore, that teachers cannot freely and easily elaborate the basis upon which they impart advice to trainees (although they may offer coherent justifications of their reasoning). Obtaining our model therefore requires us to go beyond simply asking experienced teachers what they know in order to render this implicit knowledge explicit in some structured form. The approach of this project has been to adopt expert systems techniques in order to identify and formalize this expertise.

## 4. IDENTIFYING EXPERIENCED TEACHERS' PROFESSIONAL KNOWLEDGE

Trainee teachers usually receive advice about their lesson practice in the context of discussing some particular classroom experience—an event, perhaps, which troubles them. The teacher tutor will usually seek further information about the context of the situation, then provide advice on how to deal with or avoid it, and explain why the problem may have arisen. For instance, in the excerpt below a trainee is having problems with a class's lack of incentive for a lesson. Although it is wise for trainees to be clear about what they are hoping to achieve, the need to convey this to the pupils is emphasized, expressing the pupils' need to know why they are doing things and for them to have an interest in the work.

> **Trainee:** "...I had problems starting the lesson...they want to know why they should do it..."
>
> **Teacher-Tutor:** "...it's a good idea to start by recapping on previous lessons. Outline the course and tell them the aims of the course. Also breaking down the lesson gives you confidence; knowing why you're doing what you're doing helps if you're worried about getting started. It can help in starting lessons if you can give them a reason why you're doing it; they may rather be doing something else, so you must explain aims and where the course is going. Pupils have high expectations in humanities for the lesson to be interesting." (Wood, 1984, p. 5)

In order to advise trainees appropriately, the teacher tutor often needs to go beyond the superficial characteristics of a particular situation in order to analyze what led to the situation arising in the first place. For instance, an uncontrolled class might either be bored with the activity or simply not aware of what the teacher wants it to do. Information about the circumstances under which the situation arose might indicate that the pupils had been working well until there was a change in what they were expected to do. Or one might discover that the class had been occupied with the same activity for the past half hour and were becoming progressively less interested. In the one case, appropriate advice might be to give better explanations to the pupils about what they are meant to be doing, and to be sure that they are aware when the lesson is meant to be moving on, by giving clear instructions at the appropriate juncture. In the other case the advice might be to make lessons more interesting by providing the pupils with more challenge.

Identifying the causal antecedents to a situation often requires knowledge about processes such as 'motivating' and 'communicating' which underly events in the classroom and their outcomes. For instance, in the example below, the teacher tutor focusses on the process of 'comprehending.' when discussing a problem brought about by a decline in the pupils' ability to understand the work—due to which they are no longer participating in the lesson.

**Trainee:** "...the first lesson went very well, but I had a struggle to keep them quiet and teach in the second lesson..."

**Teacher-Tutor:** "...when kids start to play up in lessons when previously they have been good, this can be because the work starts to get a bit beyond them, and their whole pattern of behaviour can change." (Wood, 1984, p. 6)

Occasionally, the teacher tutor will refer directly to the underlying processes which are implicated in this way. In the example below, the teacher tutor advises the trainee about motivating a class by constantly relating the work to their experiences.

**Trainee:** "...as I was talking, the class started to split off into small groups which were talking amongst themselves..."

**Teacher-Tutor:** "...the attention span of the 4th year CSE group is not long enough for a whole lesson based around a talk; if the standard is low, you must go quicker to keep attention, and relate the content to the kids more." (Wood, 1984, p. 3)

The implicit nature of teachers' knowledge makes elicitation hard. We therefore had to develop techniques for facilitating teachers' recourse to their deeper understanding of these classroom processes, in order to explain the reasons underlying their decision making. We found (Wood, 1985) that, by showing videos of trainee teachers taking lessons to groups of experienced teachers, the experienced teachers were able to identify ways in which their teaching would have differed from that of the trainee. By asking them to articulate when, what, and why they would have taught differently, we were able to identify a range of commonalities in their interpretation of the classroom situation.

Teachers referred to a range of processes which we labeled *control, motivation, communication, comprehension, relating, recalling,* and *learning*— although we were able to discover more about some than others.

**controlling:** the process governing the extent to which a class is engaged in task appropriate behavior;

**motivating:** the process governing the class's predisposition to participate in the lesson, to pay attention, listen, understand, and generally to make the effort to learn;

**comprehending:** the process by which pupils come to understand the material presented to them through its structure and relationship to previous knowledge, and its pacing relative to the pupils' rate of comprehension;

**communicating:** the process by which pupils remain aware of what they should be doing and why they should be doing it (in contrast to imparting the subject matter itself);

**learning:** the combination of all the aforegoing processes—going beyond mere rote memorizing of the material presented, and involves its apprehension and retention as the basis for subsequent learning and application to new situations;

**recalling:** the process of accessing from memory things that have been learned in earlier lessons or over the duration of a course.

**relating:** describes the process underlying the relationship developing between class and teacher.

These descriptions characterize the informal theory/theories of classroom processes (implicitly and explicitly) existing in the minds of teacher-trainers/experienced teachers. We have also been able to identify some components of the model, described informally at this stage, which characterize the experienced teacher's understanding of some of the causal antecedents to changes brought about through these processes.

Control, for instance, may be gained through ensuring the class is engaged in an activity. It is also influenced by the relationship existing between pupils and teacher, while the motivation of the class and effective communication also play a part in establishing control.

Motivation may be gained through involving the pupils in whatever activities are taking place, allowing them to play an active role where possible. Also the experience of a sense of progress, challenge, and achievement in their work is instrumental in maintaining the level of class motivation. The teacher's own enthusiasm for the subject matter may also influence the motivation of the class, as do appropriate levels of communication and comprehension by the class.

Comprehension, or pupil understanding of the subject matter, is affected by the structured presentation of the subject matter. It is also influenced by such factors as its level of difficulty for the class concerned and whether or not its presentation is paced to their rate of comprehension. What may be understood in a lesson may also depend on what is previously learned and how well the class remembers this.

Effective communication with pupils requires that they be kept informed of what they should be doing and why. This depends not only upon their being told, but upon ensuring that they actually receive the information—especially when there are other demands upon their attention.

Counteracting the process of forgetting requires that pupils have adequate recourse to prior knowledge. Ensuring that pupils have this knowledge to begin with, reminding them of previous work where appropriate, and including revision where necessary, helps to counteract this process.

The relationship which exists between class and teacher appears highly dependent on the degree of respect the pupils have for the teacher. It is easily lost if the teacher demonstrates an insincere or 'couldn't care less' attitude, or seems ineffective in disciplining the class.

For pupils to learn, some combination of control, motivation, communication, comprehension, remembering, and a good relationship are required. The other antecedents of learning still remain unclear in this model of classroom processes, which does not seek to model the learning of individual pupils themselves, but is concerned with the *collective learning of a class as a whole*. Although this is a feature of the way in which teachers tend to think about classroom teaching, as a way of characterizing the classroom teaching experience (as there is clearly no such entity as the 'collective student'), it appears to exist as a useful mental construct in the heads of teachers (Bromme, 1987).

## 5. MODELING CLASSROOM PROCESSES AS A BASIS FOR CONSULTATION

The processes described informally above, which correspond to the teacher-trainer's/experienced teacher's conceptualization of the classroom in which they teach, have been represented within a process model which describes different situations as states and the changes from one situation to another as transitions. A description of a class's behavior may be viewed as lying somewhere along a continuum. For instance, if looking at the degree of control a teacher has over a class, the class may be described as either doing completely what the teacher desires for the activity they are engaged in, or at the other extreme, doing nothing like what the teacher desires. There are many shades of greater or lesser compliance in between. We have identified points along this continuum which distinguish between qualitatively different states of control over the class. What would be considered an appropriate response by the teacher to a situation characterized as being to the one side of this point would be different from what would be considered appropriate in a qualitatively different situation characterize as being to the other side of this point. So, for instance, a reasonably well-controlled class may be kept in that state by beings kept occupied with some work. A less well-controlled class, however, may require some threat to be administered, in order to gain better control of it, before successfully being given some work. Otherwise it may simply ignore the teacher. Once the desired state has been achieved, maintaining it depends very much upon what the teacher does next. If the class is kept occupied, control will be maintained; if not, then the class will again slip into a state of disarray.

The changes which may be brought about, and the situations which result, depend partly on the initial situation the teacher finds himself or herself in, and partly on how he or she responds to this. In addition, processes interact, so that, for instance, one might anticipate a highly motivated class to be more likely to keep on task than one which is bored with the work. Similarly, pupils having difficulty understanding the work will find it difficult to participate in the lesson, perhaps becoming demotivated and less likely to do what the teacher would like. In this way processes act causally upon each other.

The process model captures some of what experienced teachers know about events and their outcomes in the classroom. The model provides us with a basis for reasoning about the causal antecedents to a particular outcome, in the same way that a teacher might reason about a trainee's difficulties and what gave rise to them. By identifying which state within the model corresponds to the situation the trainee describes, and which state within the model corresponds to the earlier classroom context, one is able to identify the type of transition brought about during the lesson. The knowledge associated with various transitions within the model provides a means of focusing on those actions which are implicated in giving rise to the problem situation, so that their contribution to the problem situation may be investigated further.

The potential exists for the process model to support advice on how to *improve* situations. Given a situation and a desired outcome, it may indicate how the desired outcome might be achieved, by referring to the range of factors critical in teachers' decision making that are causally associated with the transition to be made. The model may also support commentary upon the potential of achieving a desired state from a given situation or using an intended plan of action.

We have implemented a prototype TTSS which pursues an analysis of a trainee teacher's difficulties using this approach. It presents a series of menu-based questions aimed at identifying which states in the model most aptly correspond to those the trainee experienced, and what actions on the part of the trainee were responsible for bringing about that situation. Preliminary trials with the system indicate a reasonable analysis can be achieved using this approach; albeit the analysis currently supported by the process model is somewhat abstract in terms of the way situations are accounted for.

In developing this model, we must not forget about the context of advice giving. It takes place in the context of particular problems which trainees encounter—problems which motivate them to better their understanding in order to find appropriate solutions and to which they must then designate an appropriate response next time they encounter that class. No one can offer a 'prescription' for a successful lesson; the trainee must try to understand the situation well enough to decide upon the appropriate course of action as and when the lesson proceeds. Essentially, then, it is imparting the knowledge inherent in the underlying model which is of most value to the trainee who is developing this understanding, rather than imparting the 'advice' itself.

## 6. THE MODEL

The TTSS currently models the seven processes described above. The transition of processes into qualitatively different states may be marked by a set of conditions. These relate to the existing state of the process, events in the classroom which may act causally in engendering a new state and the indirect effect of events through engendering states in other processes which then influence the process concerned. For instance, a very demotivated class may be unlikely to excel in what it learns, even though conditions are otherwise ideal in enabling the class to understand the subject matter.

The criteria for making a distinction between states are where one can characterize two (or more) situations to which the effects of one's response vary (rather than that the response carries a greater or lesser weight or effect). For instance, interactions between processes depend on the state a process has been allowed to get into—so comprehension may be motivating, and inability to understand subject matter may reduce motivation; but in a state of very low motivation (perhaps brought about by inability to understand) improving understanding will not alter motivation. Something purely motivational has to be done to regain attention (alter the *state* of the process) before one can get back to a situation where the influence of comprehension again applies. This differential response of motivation to the affects of comprehension characterises at least two distinct states of motivation.

Similarly, when low motivation leads to loss of control, one doesn't get around a rowdy class through motivation (bribery or pleading, say) once control has been lost but purely through control measures. These would be legitimate grounds for distinguishing between two states of a process. Other grounds might be internal restrictions on a transition. One might want to characterize a state of motivation (of a highly participant class, say) where it was inconceivable except under some extreme conditions that a class could make a direct transition into the state of motivation where it would only respond to purely motivational measures. Thus the initial state of a process may lead it to suffer the effects of causes and other processes in characteristically different ways. Hence the variable effects of one's response to a situation, depending on the internal state of the process.

The model of classroom processes is represented as an augmented transition network: a network of state connected by pathways corresponding to the transitions from one state to another. Transitions between states are recursive and represent the passing of processes into either the same or different states over a period of time. Three different sets of conditions have been identified in marking transitions between one state and another: the internal state of the process, primary context of events, and secondary context of other processes.

*Internal state conditions.* These specify which states a process may move into given the existing state of that process. For instance, if a process has three possible states, it may be valid for state A to pass into state B, and for state B to pass into state C, but not for state A to pass directly into state C.

*Primary context.* Certain conditions appear causal in the way they affect a particular process; their existence, alone or in combination with other events, may also enable the transition of a process. However, they may be choosy in which transitions they mark. For instance, a condition may be significant in enabling a transition from state A to state B, but perhaps not vice versa; or, say, from state A to state B but not state B to state C, as in the variable appropriateness of control measures, discussed above.

*Secondary context.* The state of the other processes sometimes has a bearing on the kinds of state transitions that can be made. The causes acting on the other processes may not have a bearing themselves on the state of a process; but should they engender a transition in those other processes—that resultant state(s) can. Thus the causal influences on one process may have an indirect bearing on another, as when participation in work during an activity requiring the active involvement of pupils (e.g., class discussion) enhances control through maintaining the motivation of the class.

These conditions implicitly embody constraints on possible combinations of process states.

The process model functions in two ways: firstly, it represents a range of states and transitions between them; by mapping the state description provided onto this model, the system is able to identify the range of states that are in some way related to the described state. Even where the number of states is potentially large, the amount of search required can be kept to a minimum; the system is restricted to obtaining further information about just those states which are known to have some relationship to the described state. Similarly, searching for the cause of the described state is focused on transitions between those identified states.

Secondly, the knowledge embodied in the process model describes the relationship between particular causal conditions and process states (it is the representational structure of this model as a transition network which assists the search capability of the system). The insight provided by the model into this causal relationship makes it possible to identify the contextual relationship between what the trainee teacher did and the outcome which was described. This then provides the basis for providing accurate and appropriate advice on a particular user's problems.

Diagnosis may be achieved through reference to the process model by identifying (according to their observed characteristics) the problem state of the class and state(s) prior to that. Read as a grammar, transition rules can describe possible pathways from one (perhaps desirable) state to another (perhaps less desirable) state, under alternative contextual conditions. This representation may then be used to identify possible pathways from an earlier state to the problem state, including the potential causal agents operating on such a transition. Interpreting the underlying route of a problem might involve evaluating these causal properties in order to identify causes; these causes might operate directly through events, via other process states (indirectly through events), or through the state the process has been allowed to get into itself, making it less responsive to measures for preventing problems and therefore requiring quite different remedies.

By focussing on the context in which a problem state has arisen, this representation presents the means for addressing novel problems. Hence this model is capable of supporting the kind of reasoning usually associated with recourse to 'first principles.' One cannot possibly anticipate all the things which might go wrong for a teacher in any classroom, that is, use a 'checklist' approach. Nevertheless, part of the task of uncovering the root of a problem lies in being able to pose the right questions.

For instance, some initial diagnosing might suggest a problem communicating with a class; the task is then to pinpoint how this has come about. Knowing the contexts in which lack of communication arises enables sensible questioning strategies to be formulated. If one can discount the class having not actually been told what to do, then one might focus on the *means* of communication. Verbal instructions are known for their failings: you need the *complete* attention of *all* the class—failings of memory apart. So in a situation where instruction must be referred to over a period of time, or where their importance to some operation is paramount, for example, a biology practical, they are best written down somewhere: in a book, on a worksheet, or on the board, for instance. This situation, however, is satisfied in this example, as the instructions are constantly accessible in this way. Therefore, one might begin to suspect a *problem* with the medium of communication. This might be poor photocopying or printing which is too faint to read. With a blackboard the problem might be one of many: dark chalk on dark board, shortsightedness of class members, distance of the class from the board, size and legibility of handwriting, or the board being too shiny.

One does not need a checklist of such failings. What pinpoints the problem is knowing that questioning the medium of communication is sensible and appropriate. It works just as well if the medium involved is a book, for one may discover, for instance, that a child has reading difficulties. We as intelligent users can be quite creative in pinpointing a problem, once we know the type of problem and where we should be looking.

The potential also exists for this model to be used opportunistically. Given a current state and a desired state, one may advise upon how to achieve the desired learning state by reference to the conditions associated with a transition, or comment upon the potential of achieving a desired state from a given situation or intended plan of action.

## 7. THE EXPERT SYSTEMS METHODOLOGY

The TTSS has a conventional expert system architecture. It has a knowledge base of rules, corresponding to the knowledge elicited from the teacher tutor. It accumulates a database of facts, and has a goal-directed rule implementation program (inference engine) for evaluating the antecedents to rules from the knowledge base, on the basis of accumulated data from the user, and its own internal reasoning using the rules in its knowledge base.

The approach described here has many similarities with traditional expert systems developed in the field of medical diagnosis. The evaluation of symptoms, diagnosis of disease, and recommendation of an appropriate course of therapy are activities which have parallels in the functioning of the TTSS. In fact, an interesting classroom simulation program which mimics a class's 'vital signs' in response to teacher inputs was itself based on an early medical expert system (Dunn, 1979).

The rationale underlying the typical expert systems architecture is that knowledge can be represented modularly—as independent rules—and can be incremented gradually to increase the specificity, accuracy, and variety of instances the system can respond to. However, in practice, we find that knowledge is highly structured and that knowing one thing affects how we evaluate another. Making an inference that takes us nearer to a solution is partly based on knowing it is a sensible inference to pursue.

For example, a doctor may see two patients who present very similar symptoms, indicating a range of possible causes. However, he or she obtains the additional information that one of his or her patients has just returned from a trip abroad. He or she is more likely then, in evaluating the symptoms of this patient, to take into consideration diagnoses which are linked to diseases endemic to the part of the world just visited. Whereas for his other patient, the range of diagnoses the doctor considers will be limited to those diseases he or she believes the patient could possibly have come into contact with in his or her locality.

The information an experienced practitioner uses when undertaking a task such as solving a problem can have two roles: it can provide information about the problem, enabling the expert to deal with the task in hand; or it can indicate how the investigation should proceed—what information should be selected next, for instance, or whether a particular aim should be pursued. In this example, the doctor has decided that a particular range of inferences is not appropriate or sensible, because of the additional information he or she has obtained.

Similar observations pertain to teaching. Typically this knowledge would be represented as rules, for example:

*Antecedent:* class is not behaving as teacher wishes; loss of control occurred
   during transition between activities
*Consequent:* problem is possibly one of communication
and:
*Antecedent:* class is not behaving as teacher wishes; loss of control occurred
   during course of activity.
*Consequent:* problem is possibly one of comprehension or motivation

This affects the diagnosis subsequently pursued. On the one hand, a sudden change in the teacher's control over the class indicates the class no longer knows what it should be doing: a communication problem. On the other, a gradual loss of control indicates the class's lessening participation in the lesson, indicating its inability to follow the work or its loss of interest: comprehension or motivation problems, respectively. There is a branch in the line of reasoning or decision making, and the system takes one path over another.

The TTSS uses metarules which control when an inference may be appropriately made or when it is sensible to pursue another scenario. Our rules look more like this:

*Antecedent:* class is not behaving as teacher wishes
*Consequent:* problem is possibly one of communication
and:
*Antecedent:* class is not behaving as teacher wishes
*Consequent:* problem is possibly one of comprehension or motivation

While our metarules would look like this:

*Antecedent:* loss of control occurred during transition between activities
*Consequent:* consider communication
and:
*Antecedent:* lost of control occurred during course of activity
*Consequent:* consider comprehension and motivation

The metarules are used to constrain the set of ordinary rules applied in making the diagnosis. That is, they embody a judgment, based on the evidence currently available to the system, about the set of rules that are relevant to meeting a 'sensible' diagnostic goal. At all times, however, it is as valid to infer that the problem is one of communication as that it is one of comprehension or motivation. The metarules simply specify the differing circumstances under which the teacher may prefer to pursue one hypothesis over another. This strategy does not determine the final conclusion of the system—further evidence may prove one conclusion totally invalid—it simply constrains or controls the search for a solution in the same way as a teacher constrains his or her own reasoning.

The current phase of development of the TTSS knowledge base focuses upon the way in which the teacher tutor modifies the analysis being made in finding out certain key items of information from the trainee. There are some situations which leave a trainee open to particular types of problems. For instance, a real problem for trainee teacher is getting a lesson started. It is one of the major obstacles to be overcome by the trainee, very often lying at the heart of a conviction that they can't control classes. If we look very closely at the problem of starting lessons, we find what appears to be a distinct scenario for within-lesson teaching. At the heart of this observation lies a recognition of the fact that the behavior of the class is not solely the responsibility of the teacher. The class may have just come from a boring or unsuccessful lesson, or returned from a lunch break. In such circumstances, the range of actions available to the teacher, faced with difficulty in gaining control of the class, is different from that which would be acceptable in mid-lesson.

Under closer analysis, therefore, it appears that the relevance of a process to the interpretation of a situation varies in relation to other processes according to a wider contextual appraisal of events. Much of the reasoning appropriate to understanding a trainee's problem within a lesson just does not apply to the beginning of a lesson. If the problem occurred in the middle of a lesson, the tutor may be concerned with the material presented to the class and how it was presented, or curious about class motivation. In contrast, at the beginning of the lesson there is much more focus on how effectively the trainee is communicating with the class; little else is relevant.

From this it might appear that the notion of a generic process model is misplaced, accounting for only a small range of situations occurring during the middle of lessons, while at the beginning of lessons a different set of states, and a different range of causal antecedents bringing about those states, applies. However, communication fails at the beginning of lesson for exactly the same reasons as at other points in the lesson. What is significant about starts of lessons is that communication problems are *more likely* to be the reason that the lesson grinds to a halt or simply fails to take off. Experienced teacher tutors know this. On learning that a problem occurred at the beginning of a lesson, they will focus on communication problems first. The information about the start of the lesson is used *strategically* to guide the tutor's diagnosis. This strategic information is therefore represented within the metarules of the TTSS, specifying the conditions under which particular goals are most aptly pursued. So, for instance, the TTSS might incorporate a metarule like this:

*Antecedent:* it is the beginning of the lesson
*Consequent:* investigate communication

Consultation with our domain expert has enabled us to develop the knowledge base of the system in other ways. For instance, failing to gain the attention of the class is currently interpreted within the process model as a special kind of failure to make an appropriate transition between two states of communication. However, we have discovered that gaining the attention of the class can itself be described quite naturally in some detail in terms of states and transitions. Although not having the attention of a class can be a reason for a failure in communication, inattentiveness is itself a state on the continuum of preparedness on the part of a class to begin a lesson or pay attention to what the teacher tells them to do next. This state of preparedness might be influenced either positively or negatively by what the teacher says or does, or by external factors, such as distractions from outside the classroom. Attentiveness therefore appears to be an additional process which we can represent in the same way as other processes within our model. Our model now represents the fact that failing to have the attention of the class while communicating is sometimes a cause of a particular state of communication. In pursuing a diagnosis, we are now in a position to investigate what caused a state of inattentiveness in the same way that we explored the causes acting on transitions brought about through other processes.

We propose to continue this theoretical development of the classroom process model through its extension at a more detailed level of analysis, in order to capture the experienced teacher's understanding of classroom dynamics on a finer timescale. Through the continued formalization of the experienced teacher's knowledge regarding classroom practice, we hope to support a wider differentiation in advising trainees, as well as increasing our understanding of classroom practice. We are currently working with our domain expert on developing our understanding of pupils' comprehension of subject matter.

We have been able to identify some of the knowledge experienced teachers have about classrooms and have represented this explicitly within an expert system architecture in order to verify the model of classroom processes. We achieve this through testing the performance of the system in terms of the dialogue it pursues—the appropriateness of various questions at different points during the consultation—and the analysis and explanation brought to bear on a typical problem. Where this doesn't fit or seems inappropriate, we supplement the information contained in the knowledge base in order to modify the behavior. We attempt to do this in a principled way—thinking through the reasons for the errors and omissions and how these affect our overall conceptualization of the domain knowledge. Very often a simple detail results in a substantial revision of the knowledge base. This may not be apparent in the performance of the system—the changes may appear very few or insignificant—but may have important repercussions for the way in which the model is developed.

## 8. SUMMARY

I have presented here some thoughts about the constituents of experienced teachers' professional knowledge—the understanding of classroom processes upon which they base their teaching decisions and advice. This knowledge is not merely an extension of social interaction skills. Through the nature of its acquisition in practice, it is largely implicit. This poses the problem of how to render it explicit so that it may be articulated, rather than passed on through direct personal experience.

We anticipate that a system of this kind will have a useful role to play in teacher education. The levels of explanation provided by the TTSS are necessarily rudimentary at present—we are applying new techniques in a novel way to a difficult area—but we propose to continue developing the knowledge base, using the framework the current model provides and in time have plans to pilot the TTSS within the Sussex teacher education programe in order to evaluate its role as a pedagogical tool.

Apart from the development of a specific pedagogical tool, however, the AI approach to formalizing what we know about classroom processes appears to have interesting implications for the development of educational theory into the area of classroom practice. Independent of the successful, or otherwise, development of a TTSS, we can, perhaps, still gain insight into what we should be attempting to achieve in the classroom and how we may help trainee teachers achieve it.

## REFERENCES

Bromme, R. (1987). Teachers' recall of students' difficulties and progress in understanding in the classroom. In C. Clark, J. Lowyck, & R. Halkes (Eds.), *Teacher thinking and professional action*. Swets & Zeitlinger, Lisse, Holland.

Dunn, W.R. (1979). *Computer assisted learning programme on classroom management in the primary school* (Project Proposal). Glasgow, Scotland: University of Glasgow, Department of Education.

Welbank, M. (1983). *A review of knowledge acquisition techniques for expert systems* (British Telecom Reseach Report No. 283). Ipswich, England: BT Research Labs.

Wood, S. (1984). *Observation of school tutoring groups* (Progress Report). Brighton, England: University of Sussex, Cognitive Studies Programme.

Wood, S. (1985, October). *Eliciting teaching expertise using videos of trainee teachers*. Paper presented at the 3rd ISATT Conference on Teacher Thinking and Professional Action, Leuven, Belgium.

Wood, S. (1987a, April). *The Trainee Teacher Support System: An expert system for advising trainee teachers on their classroom practice*. Paper presented at the Third International Conference on Artificial Intelligence and Education, University of Pittsburgh, Pittsburgh, PA.

Wood. S. (1987b, June). *Expert systems and understanding teacher education and practice*. Paper presented at the BERA Conference, Lancaster University, Lancaster.

Young, R. (1988). Role of intermediate representations in knowledge elicitation. In D.S. Moralee (Ed.), *Research and development in expert systems IV*. Cambridge, England: Cambridge University Press.

# 15

## PROJECT DOCENT: DESIGN FOR A TEACHER'S CONSULTANT*

### PHILIP H. WINNE

### 1. WHAT IS A DOCENT?

Webster's Ninth New Collegiate Dictionary gives this definition for the word, docent:

**Docent 1:** a college or university teacher or lecturer
**2:** a person who conducts groups through a museum or art gallery

A university lecturer commands deep and broad knowledge about a discipline plus methodological procedures for investigating, verifying, and modifying disciplinary knowledge to add to and refine it. Thus, a teaching docent would command two forms of disciplinary knowledge: research-based principles derived from fundamental investigations in instructional psychology and research on teaching, and expert teachers' first-hand experience. Methodological expertise about teaching corresponds to methods for gathering data, organizing it, characterizing its patterns, and deriving valid implications from it about how instruction can be adapted to a classroom's local situation.

*This work was supported by grants from the Social Sciences and Humanities Research Council of Canada (#411-09-0085), Simon Fraser University, and Sun Microsystems of Canada, Ltd.

As a guide in a gallery, a docent introduces novices to the gallery's displays of interesting information, addressing visitors' questions and giving them knowledge to "take home." A teaching docent would introduce novice teachers to interesting and verified information about teaching effectiveness. In a gallery of instructional knowledge, a docent would respond to a teacher's questions with information selected to fit into the large, complex, and personal puzzle of how to teach effectively, and it would explain its answers. To give teachers information to "take to teaching," a docent could help them script plans for teaching. As well, informing teachers about means for gathering data on instructional processes and products in their classroom would help them create information to carry forward in their work.

## 1.1. What DOCENT Is

DOCENT is being designed to be a unique docent—a very large, artificially intelligent computing system with many of the qualifications and qualities of a human docent in the realm of teaching. DOCENT will be used in two contexts. In the first, a sector of DOCENT called TUTOR will provide students with a state-of-the-art instructional environment for individualized learning. As an intelligent tutoring system (ITS), TUTOR has two main functions: (a) to instruct students by supplementing teachers'lessons; and (b) to gather information about students' learning processes and their achievements that can supplement data which their teacher gathers by other means such as questions asked in class.

DOCENT's second context is serving as an expert planning system for teachers. In this role, DOCENT also has two main functions: (a) to collaborate with a teacher, especially student and novice teachers, in developing plans for teaching that take maximum advantage of principles of instruction previously validated by research and by expert teachers' experience; and (b) to work with the teacher to analyze data on teaching processes and students' learning from teaching.

## 1.2. What DOCENT Will Do

Before the start of a student teaching practicum or the academic year, the teacher will work with DOCENT to describe for the system global parameters of instruction. For instance, the teacher would specify preferred routines (Leinhardt & Greeno, this volume), frame overarching objectives for the instructional period, and describe the period's curriculum in broad but thorough terms. Initial data about students also would be cataloged, some solicited from the teacher and some from school records. (As DOCENT is used over years, its accumulated portfolio about students would be accessed directly.) Other critical information about students will be gathered early in the instructional period when students and TUTOR work through diagnostic sessions.

Throughout the instructional period, the teacher will use DOCENT to create plans for units and component lessons, and to develop scripts for teaching (Clark, Gage, Marx, Peterson, Stayrook, & Winne, 1979; Good & Grouws, 1979). The flow of information in planning sessions will be two-way. First, when information encoded in DOCENT bears on elements of the teacher's proposed plan for teaching, DOCENT will suggest optional methods for instructing and for managing lessons. These will help the teacher shape each lesson for maximum effectiveness. These suggestions will be based on extensive knowledge from research and from expert teachers which resides in DOCENT and which the system consults, analyzes, and matches jointly to the historical context of the class and the immediate objectives in the lesson being planned. Second, when DOCENT recognizes that data about instructional events are needed to help match its encoded knowledge to a teacher's classroom, or to extend its knowledge of that teacher's instructional setting, it will request the teacher to gather such data during an upcoming lesson. Based on its catalog of knowledge, DOCENT also will be able to suggest means for gathering this data.

After teaching, the teacher will return to DOCENT to enter these specific data as well as other information about the lesson's instructional processes and products. As the practicum or school year unfolds, the data accumulated about past lessons will provide grounds for customizing plans and tailoring them to the teacher's specific and changing instructional environment.

Interleaving with the teacher's lessons, students will use TUTOR to participate in individualized, computer-based tutorials. Tutorials will supplement instruction that students receive in their teacher's lessons by individualizing practice and assignments, and by diagnosing and remediating difficulties. TUTOR's plan for a tutorial will be guided by general knowledge encoded in DOCENT and by specialized information about tutoring that resides in TUTOR. The student's accumulating portfolio of data—gathered by the teacher and through the student's previous tutoring sessions—will form an extensive backdrop for adapting a tutorial to each student's achievement and motivation.

Within a tutoring session, moment-to-moment interaction between TUTOR and the student will be adjusted dynamically to optimize the fit between instruction and a student's participation in the tutorial. Information about the student's performance in tutorials will be added to the student's portfolio, thereby extending the teacher's capacity to stay abreast of each student's progress. This also broadens the scope of information available to the teacher and DOCENT for formatively evaluating lessons and tutorials for improvement.

### 1.3. What This Chapter Reports

Designing, prototyping, and field testing the enormous DOCENT system is a 10 to 15-year enterprise. A more detailed report is provided in Winne (1988a). In the next section, four cornerstones are laid to build an argument that an artificially intelligent planning and tutoring system, such as DOCENT, could make a substantial contribution to improving the quality of education in today's schools. In particular, I suggest that student teachers and beginning teachers need much more ready access to knowledge about how to teach. Such knowledge can be found in published research and in practicing teachers' expertise. One objective of Project DOCENT is to cull this knowledge, make it available to novice teachers, and especially, to give novice teachers guidance about how to incorporate such knowledge into lessons.

Following this argument, the overall architecture of DOCENT is described. This section maps DOCENT's internal territories, describing what goes on in each sector of the large system and the kinds of informational commerce between sectors. The design attempts to reflect conceptually sensible and computationally feasible partitions of the organic activities that comprise teaching.

The penultimate section sketches accomplishments of the project. A major product is a scheme for representing knowledge about teaching. Also, brief mention is made of software systems developed to implement this scheme and to use when translating information from in journal articles into this representational scheme. These systems allow us to take the first steps toward creating a knowledge base about teaching for DOCENT.

## 2. IS THERE A NEED FOR DOCENT?

There are four cornerstones in an argument that DOCENT can make a substantial contribution to improving teaching and boosting teaching effectiveness:

1. Novice teachers' lesson plans are incomplete and features of them correlate with suboptimal teaching. These conditions probably depress teaching effectiveness.

2. Students' cognitive participation in instruction is a prime determinant of their achievement. Teachers' attempts to optimize their students' cognitive participation may fail, however, because of inadequate training and because the practicalities of lessons interfere with obtaining valid information that teachers need to improve students' cognitive participation in instruction.
3. DOCENT can mitigate the first problem and TUTOR can help solve the second. Moreover, these advantages may be unreachable by means other than DOCENT.
4. Project DOCENT can contribute substantially to basic research on instruction and to research on applying artificial intelligence to education.

## 2.1. Teachers' Planning, Teaching, and Instructional Effectiveness

Clark and Peterson (1986) recently reviewed research on teachers' planning and cognition during lessons. They concluded that a teacher's plan significantly influences "[students] opportunity to learn, content coverage, grouping for instruction, and the general focus of classroom processes" (p. 267). Clark and Peterson also note that studies of planning during the first weeks of a school year indicate that the ". . . 'problem space' (Newell & Simon, 1972) within which [the] teacher and students operate is defined early, changes little during the course of the school year, and exerts a powerful, if subtle, influence on thought and behavior [in lessons]" (p. 260). In short:

- Plans establish the context for students' participation in instruction, and plans strongly influence a teacher's day-to-day instructional processes.

Clark and Peterson's review also reveals an important correspondence between the decisions teachers make while planning and decisions they face during teaching. In planning, about 40%–50% of teachers' decisions address objectives and the content they will teach. During teaching, however, only 15%–20% of teachers' decisions address content. Approximately 20%–30% of planning decisions concern instructional processes, and these are described in global terms (e.g., "*discuss* parliamentary procedure"or "*review* erosion"). The same frequency, 20%–30%, of decisions during instruction concern instructional processes. Only 5%–10% of planning decisions are about students and their cognitive mediation of instructional events. Notably, though, 40%–50% of the teacher's decisions during teaching are about learners, especially their cognitive and motivational states. These figures display a strong inverse correlation between topics considered during planning and those needing teachers' attention during lessons.

• Topics that a teacher considers in planning for lessons do not consume the teacher's attention during teaching. Topics that a teacher underemphasizes during planning require frequent decision making during teaching.

The nature of planning to enact instructional processes (as opposed to considerations about managing classes) and its link to instruction merits elaboration. Expert teachers have rich, interconnected schemata that articulate information about students' cognition and motivation with instructional processes (Carter, Sabers, Cushing, Pinnegar, & Berliner, 1987; Peterson & Comeaux, 1987). Research shows that expert teachers translate these schemata into integrated, efficient routines during instruction (Leinhardt & Greeno, this volume; Leinhardt, Weidman, & Hammond, 1987) which coordinate multiple, detailed instructional actions. In turn, these actions can be mapped readily onto independent variables studied in basic research on teaching and in instructional psychology (Winne & Marx, 1988).

Leinhardt and colleagues' research also shows that expert teachers weave together routines to form an agenda which structures a lesson. This eases the teacher's need for decision making during instruction, leaving cognitive "room" to handle perturbations and unpredictable dynamics. Students whose teachers organize routines in an agenda also benefit because, when students are familiar with their teachers' routines and agendas, they are relieved of the constant need to interpret cues about cognitively mediating instruction (Leinhardt & Greeno, this volume; Winne, 1985).

In contrast, novice teachers "have less well developed knowledge structures than experts" (Borko, Lalik, & Tomchin, 1987, p. 87). This shallow and unelaborated knowledge accounts for their sparse attention during planning to instructional routines and their detailed components, precisely those aspects of teaching that learners seek out in cognitively mediating instruction. Thus, it is not surprising that novice teachers' lesson plans "are generally crude and lacking in detail" (Calderhead, 1984, p. 118); that, during instruction, they face many decisions about instructional processes and learners' cognitive mediation of them; and that their lessons generally are less effective. In sum:

• Novice teachers' weaker lessons can be traced, in part, to shallow unelaborated knowledge of (a) routines and (b) detailed instructional processes that comprise routines; and to (c) vague or imprecise agendas which give order to routines.

A series of final observations concludes this line of argument. Nowhere in the published literature on teachers' planning is there evidence that teachers

(a) identify criteria to use for monitoring students' progress during a lesson, (b) specify tolerances for deviations from plans, or (c) posit alternatives to planned actions when a lesson strays too far off track. As reported previously, however, 60%–80% of teachers' decisions during lessons address how instructional processes unfold and how students cognitively mediate these instructional events. This absence becomes disturbing when juxtaposed with three further findings.

First, at decision points during lessons where instructional processes stray outside tolerances that may be implicit in plans, less-than-expert teachers rarely adjust instructional processes (Clark & Peterson, 1986).

Second, Marland (1986) found that, although teachers report knowing about general principles governing classroom teaching, they apply principles in teaching opportunistically rather than deliberately. In his words: "Teachers generally did not foresee that classroom conditions might possibly lend themselves to use of a particular principle. Most instances of principle application were thus reactive rather than proactive—teachers reacted to lesson events rather than shaped them" (p. 218). Indeed, in Marland's data, only 2 in 500 segments of interviews with teachers after lessons reflected a teacher's planned application of principles! This suggests that, whenever teachers do adjust instructional processes to situations where a lesson strays beyond tolerances implicit in a plan, they do not do so in a deliberate principled way.

Third, no experiments have investigated the relation between training teachers' interactive decision making and students' achievement. A correlational study (Peterson & Clark, 1978), however, reports two critically relevant findings. In situations where experienced teachers judged that lessons were outside tolerances, failure to substitute or reshape instructional processes correlated -.50 and -.64 with two measures of students' achievements. In other words, not changing a lesson in the face of perturbations seems to depress students' achievement. In situations where these experienced teachers did make adjustments to planned teaching "on the fly" (since alternatives had not been planned), correlations with students' achievement were not statistically distinguishable from zero. To sum up these facts:

- When nonexpert teachers plans do not include (a) tolerances for how lessons should unfold, and (b) alternatives to follow when lessons are perturbed: Adaptations are not made during lessons and this depresses teaching effectiveness; or adaptations are made opportunistically, but these have no benefit.

Shortly, it will be argued that DOCENT could substantially redress these deficiencies in teachers' plans for lessons.

## 2.2. Students' Cognitive Mediation of Instruction and Achievement

Paralleling the newer perspective of teaching as expertise based on complex cognitive skills, the student's role in learning from teaching recently has been similarly reconceptualized (Winne & Marx, 1977; Wittrock, 1986). Modern research no longer views teachers or instructional processes as direct causes of student achievement. Rather, students' cognitive and motivational processing of information in the instructional environment, that is, their cognitive mediations of instruction, account for their achievements and attitudes (Winne, 1982, 1985; Winne & Marx, 1982).

- Teaching effectiveness pivots on students' cognitive processing during lessons.

Winne and Marx (1982; see also Wittrock's, 1986, review) explored this topic. They videotaped lessons and replayed them twice. First, the teacher identified spots where she intended to cue students' about particular paths of cognitive processing to pursue in learning from teaching. Second, students were interviewed about their cognitive participation in the lesson. Teachers frequently reported that they attempted to cue students' about cognitive processes to use. Students, however, had varied success in making use of cues. Logically, four kinds of mismatches can exist between an instructional cue and how a student cognitively participates in learning when a cue is presented (Winne, 1982). Specifically, when a cue is provided, students may not (a) register that it was delivered, (b) correctly perceive which cognitions the cue signals to be used, (c) be able to carry out cognitive processing, or (d) be motivated to perform cognitive processing that is perceived. Students evidenced all four types of mismatches in Winne and Marx's study. Thus:

- Teachers' attempts to guide students' cognitive processing during lessons by providing cues aren't consistently effective.

Peterson and her colleagues (Peterson, Swing, Braverman, & Buss, 1982; Peterson & Swing, 1982, 1985) investigated relations among students' aptitudes, their cognitive mediations of events in lessons, and achievement. Students whose cognition matched their teacher's cues had higher achievement, and this relation remained statistically reliable even after statistically controlling for students' aptitude. The researchers noted that "students' reported thought processes may be better predictors of student achievement than observations of student behavior" and urged teachers to "acquire important information about student's learning through questioning students about their thought processes" (Peterson & Swing, 1982, p. 489).

Such information seems essential because teachers may be misled in judging students' cognitive participation since "apparent student attention (observed time-on-task) does not reliably measure anything" (Wittrock, 1986, p. 301). These findings lead to two conclusions:

- When students make appropriate use of cues, achievement is enhanced.
- Teachers need information about students' cognitive mediations of instruction to design instruction that optimizes students' cognitive participation in learning from teaching.

How might teachers acquire such data? In a typical class of 25–30 students, it is infeasible for the teacher to interrupt lessons every few seconds to ask each student about cognitions. Fortunately, Marx, Winne, and Walsh's (1985) review of methods for obtaining data about students' cognitive processing identified a better method, one called *traces* (Winne, 1982; Winne & Marx, 1983).

Traces are observable responses that teachers design for students to make in the presence of cues. A complete trace reflects (a) which cognitions a student applies to (b) which item(s) of content that are to be processed. For instance, suppose that, while listening to a lecture, students also work with a worksheet handed out at the lecture's beginning. They underline specific terms, among many listed in the left column of the worksheet, and write an example for each underlined term in space provided in the right column. This exercise creates a trace of whether, during the lecture, students attend to and elaboratively rehearse (two specific cognitive operations central in learning; see Winne, 1987a) new vocabulary terms and their meaning (the content). Winne (1987b) showed how instant-to-instant data about cues and traces establish superior grounds for generating psychological interpretations of students' cognitive participation in instruction. Data from traces can be especially revealing of how students adapt cognitive mediations of instruction and how they develop metacognitive strategies for learning. In short:

- Traces can provide teachers with information that is critical to understanding how students cognitively mediate instruction.

Traces are a kind of performance assessment, "observation and rating of student behavior and products in contexts where students actually demonstrate proficiency" (Stiggins & Bridgeford, 1985, p. 273). Performance assessments are prominent features of teaching in general (Stiggins & Bridgeford, 1985), although no data are available specifically about teachers' use of traces. However, teachers also "rely heavily on mental recordkeeping to store and retrieve information on student performance" (Stiggins & Bridge ford, 1985, p. 281). In light of known problems of remembering information and using it validly in making judgments and decisions (Nisbett & Ross, 1980), this might explain why Allal (1988) concluded that "teachers need explicit training in . . . how to avoid or reduce biases (errors of estimation and judgement) that commonly occur in informal, intuitive assessment procedures" (p. 50) such as performance assessments. Moreover, the nature and tempo of teaching in group-based lessons make it difficult for teachers to design traces, develop materials students can use in tracing, obtain and score traces, and integrate this information with data about lessons from other sources (Allal, 1988). To sum up:

• Practical matters attending regular classroom teaching impede and may even prohibit teachers from obtaining and using data from traces to map students' cognitive participation in lessons.

## 3. HOW DOCENT HELPS AND WHY IT MAY BE A BETTER FORM OF HELP

The preceding review suggests that two cases need to be developed as grounds for reasoning that DOCENT may be a useful system. The first is that DOCENT can supply means for redressing deficiencies that appear to be characteristic of nonexpert teachers' plans for lessons. The second is that DOCENT may be able to boost a teacher's ability to enhance students' cognitive participation in learning from teaching.

### 3.1. The Case that DOCENT Can Help Teachers Plan Better Lessons

Rhetoric about school's role in building foundations for children's futures must be backed by concrete steps that assure teaching is as effective as it can be. Research can help, as one recent report on the state of American education noted:

> [Teacher] preparation programs must rest on a research base of knowledge about classrooms and instruction, and knowledge about education, otherwise new teachers will have no professional knowledge to practice. (American Educational Studies Association, 1984, p. 37)

Despite this and other calls for teacher education to insure that teachers-in-preparation are informed by knowledge from research, Gage (1985), concluded that:

generations of teacher education students have been given inadequate grounding in how to teach. They have not been taught how to organize a course, how to plan a lesson, how to manage a class, how to give an explanation, how to arouse interest and motivation, how to ask the right kinds of questions, how to react to students' responses, how to give helpful corrections and feedback, how to avoid unfair biases in interacting with students—in short, how to teach. (pp. 27–28)

Do beginning teachers acquire research-based expertise during practica by observing practicing teachers? In one critical domain, problem solving, it seems not. Teachers with an average of 11 years of experience had "limited . . . knowledge about how to teach problem solving. Few of the teachers described problem solving activities that went beyond having students practice word problems [and]...pedagogical concerns were not paramount" (Burns & lash, 1988, p. 375). Without role models, novice teachers' outlook on research may begin to reflect the general professions' "scornful [view] of research and the possibility of its being used in practice" (Richardson-Koehler, 1988, p.74).

Because experts are rare in a population, there necessarily are fewer experts to observe than student teachers, and few student teachers will be able to profit from apprenticeship to an expert during teacher training. Can gaps can be closed during novice teachers' first years of teaching? The U.S. Department of Education (1986) notes:

> *Research Finding:* Teachers welcome professional suggestions about improving their work, but they rarely receive them.
> *Comment:* When supervisors comment constructively on teachers' specific skills, they help teachers become more effective and improve teachers' morale. Yet, typically, a supervisor visits a teacher's classroom only once a year and makes only general comments about the teacher's performance. (p. 52)

Perhaps this explains why most beginning teachers "believe that they were virtually abandoned during the year of induction" (Joyce & Clift, 1984, p. 5).

This "combination of inadequate training and chaotic conditions in the workplace make it difficult to bring about curricular changes or for teachers to expand their repertoire of effective teaching strategies" (Joyce & Clift, 1984, p. 6). Unfortunately, this situation is not ameliorated through inservice education (Joyce, Hersh, & McKibbin, 1983). If it were possible to provide supervision, what kind of supervision might introduce teachers to research and interest them in making use of it? Clark (1988) suggests a model of consultation that begins in a program of teacher education and extends into schools. He characterizes a good consultant for teachers as one who has experience and a perspective different from that of the client, and engages this expertise in the service of the client's own ends. A consultant seldom solves major problems, but often contributes important pieces to the client's own solutions ...who leave[s] something interesting and provocative to think about as the clients continue to wrestle with the complexities of the local problematic situation. (p. 6)

*3.1.1. Summary of the Case.* An expert teacher plans for instruction, makes rapid decisions in an ill-structured, dynamic classroom environment, and modifies instruction to improve it. To perform these tasks, an expert teacher calls on rich schemata that extend well beyond knowledge gained and skills achieved in preservice and inservice programs of teacher education (Berliner, 1986). Support for developing these schemata, however, is meager. Thus, to develop expertise, novice teachers need consultation that supplements resources available to them in university courses, student teaching practica, and on-the-job experience.

DOCENT will be a consultant that can serve these needs. The system's knowledge will be grounded solidly in extensive research and extended by expert teachers, thus supplementing human resources in a program of teacher education and a school. Because DOCENT can be introduced when teachers-to-be elect to apprentice themselves, the choice to seek and apply research-based options is the teacher's rather than another's. DOCENT's suggestions naturally fit locally relevant conditions, because options are grounded initially in the teacher's own objectives and subsequently constrained as the teacher continuously updates DOCENT with data about teaching and learning *in situ.*

As an archive of past instruction, DOCENT stores data that a teacher needs to investigate, evaluate, and improve teaching. Across time, DOCENT will allow the teacher to focus more on instruction and less on curriculum development because lesson plans can be retrieved and easily edited rather than needing to be created anew. By following a student teacher into the first job, DOCENT offers continuity between campus-based teacher education, practicum experiences, and the first years of work in the schools. DOCENT will be available for consultation at the flick of a switch, has no calendar other than the teacher's, and can't intrude.

Beyond these advantages, DOCENT offers three unique opportunities. First, should teachers network their systems, DOCENT provides a medium for communication which otherwise is blocked by classroom walls, individual schedules, and meager budgets for inservice education. Collegiality can replace the isolation that teachers, especially beginning teachers, now suffer. Second DOCENT creates means by which teachers can establish ties with research and undertake their own professional development. Third, DOCENT will significantly boost the amount and the relevance of research on teaching. Fifty teachers using DOCENT daily over a school year would provide as much data and more pertinent data about instruction than has otherwise accumulated to date. DOCENT's tools can assist teachers and researchers alike to organize this mass of data, thus contributing to advancing knowledge and enhancing mutual understandings about teaching.

### 3.2. The Case that TUTOR Can Boost Students' Cognitive Participation In Instruction

The central role now accorded students' cognitive processing in learning from teaching revives an old dilemma. Recent empirical evidence leads to the same conclusion that the Chinese scholar Yuezheng reached in the 4th century B.C.: "The success of education depends on adapting teaching to individual differences among learners" (cited in Corno & Snow, 1986, p. 605). Corno and Snow (1986) continue: "Unfortunately, systematic procedures for accomplishing instructional adaptations of the sort envisioned through all these years have never been clearly established and validated" (p. 605). They may be overly pessimistic.

Corno and Snow describe a continuum of adaptation. Macroadaptations aggregate over students (e.g., collecting students into reading groups) or generalize over time (e.g., routines such as review). Microadaptations accommodate one student at one point in time (e.g., asking a special question of Sally to reinstate particular information in her working memory during a review). In tutorials, adaptations *always* can be micro.

An ITS can implement systematic microadaptation much more readily than teachers in classrooms (Corno & Snow, 1986, p. 614). Two reasons account for the ITS's advantage. First, a teacher can not gather traces of each student's cognitive mediation of every cue in lessons and analyze these data "on the fly." These data, however, are precisely what an ITS uses to sculpt its model of a student, its theory of *learning in process* (Corno & Snow, 1986). Second, even if a teacher could obtain such data, microadaptations would differ among students at one point in a lesson. Working with individuals, however, an ITS can pose a series of exercises that are dynamically tailored, first to diagnose a student's cognitive participation in instruction, and, then, optimize it.

Although this scenario might appear to argue that students not be taught in group-based lessons where evaluative sensitivity and instructional adaptability have practical limits, completely individualized education is not likely in the foreseeable future. However, if tutorials given by an ITS such as TUTOR are coordinated with a teacher's lessons through a system such as DOCENT, four hypotheses predict substantial gains nonetheless.

First, adaptations are necessary to accommodate heterogeneity among students. Grouping in classes (Slavin, 1987) reduces heterogeneity only minimally, as expected in less than a true tutoring environment. This begs for a more individualized intervention such as TUTOR.

Second, TUTOR is an instructional system which research, although limited, suggests will be very effective (Lawler & Yazdani, 1987). Since knowledge is one of the strongest factors underlying heterogeneity among students, when TUTOR's tutorials focus on prerequisite knowledge before a teacher's lesson, students should be less heterogeneous.

Third, macro-and microadaptations should be shaped jointly by principles and by context. Any teacher, especially a novice, will have trouble keeping track of hundreds of research-based principles, identifying subtly different contexts, and matching principles to a particular context. TUTOR collects and stores extensive data about each student's achievements and also promises a superior environment for learning more about how students learn from instruction (Winne, 1989). Thus, DOCENT's already extensive store of knowledge about microadaptations that teachers could apply in group-based lessons is expanded significantly and contextualized. With these resources, a teacher's ability to customize class-based lessons may increase substantially, because DOCENT, as an AI system, is especially suited to analyzing and coordinating myriad facts upon which to identify microadaptations and suggest how to incorporate them coherently in group-based lessons. This, too, should help to reduce heterogeneity.

Fourth, any single instructional system has limitations. An exciting hypothesis is that the strengths of class-based lessons, planned collaboratively with DOCENT and given by a teacher, and the strengths of tutorials, provided by TUTOR, might compensate for the weaknesses of one another. Research into coordinating these two instructional environments to maximize students' achievements will add to general understandings of instructional effectiveness.

*3.2.1. Summary of the Case.* Students' cognitive mediation of instruction determine their achievements. In group-based lessons, teachers cannot track students' cognitive mediations punctually and sensitively. Consequently, heterogeneity always makes teaching in groups suboptimal for some students. An ITS, however, thrives on these kinds of data, gathering and using them to develop and revise instruction dynamically. Thus, it should be able to diagnose and repair gaps among students' achievements that group-based lessons inevitably create which, in turn, will reduce heterogeneity in group-based lessons. Cumulatively, TUTOR should have a direct positive effect on making those lessons more effective.

TUTOR, through DOCENT, also can share data with a teacher about students' achievements and learning processes. This provides a broader and more valid set of data that the teacher and DOCENT can use to tailor lessons to meet students' needs. By this path, TUTOR contributes in an indirect way to improving the teacher's plans for class-based lessons at both macroadaptive and microadaptive levels.

## 4. DOCENT'S SYSTEM ARCHITECTURE

DOCENT's modules and their interrelationships are rooted in research on teaching, instructional design, expert systems, ITS, and artificial intelligence in general. Two especially innovative objectives unique to Project DOCENT are coordinating instruction across two instructional environments, a teacher's class-based lessons and students' computer-assisted tutorials; and taking advantage of each instructional system's strengths to compensate for weaknesses of the other.

DOCENT's architecture (see Figures 15.1 and 15.2) is divided into four sectors, each of which corresponds to one major task relating to instruction: developing principles of pedagogy, designing a syllabus for teaching, planning the forms of interaction that comprise instruction, and tutoring students. All sectors share four features:

1. *Knowledge Base.* This bank of information stores facts that figure directly in the instructional task assigned to a sector. Each knowledge base represents knowledge by a scheme that is uniquely matched to tasks performed in its sector.

2. *Archivist.* This program has three functions. It (a) receives information from a teacher or a student using the system or from another sector, (b) formats this data for a sector's knowledge base (s), and (c) fetches information in response to specific requests by people or by another program in DOCENT.

3. *Reasoning Engine.* To approach a goal set by a person or which a reasoning engine may develop itself, this program requests selected facts from its own sector's knowledge base and/or specific data from a user or another sector. Using these facts, the reasoning engine creates principles and, if asked, can explain how it produced them. Because of the centrality of this program, each sector is named after its reasoning engine.

4. *Interface.* The information that a person exchanges with DOCENT is unique to each sector and, occasionally, unique to one aspect of the overall job that a sector does. Interface programs supply special formats that ease communications and guide exchanges of information between DOCENT, teachers, and students.

### 4.1. Sector PEDAGOGUE

This sector answer simple queries using information stocked in a knowledge base about teaching, and creates principles of instruction that it predicts will

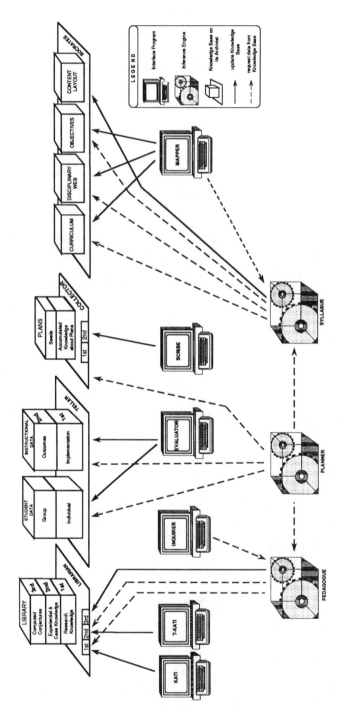

Figure 15.1. Architecture of the DOCENT system.

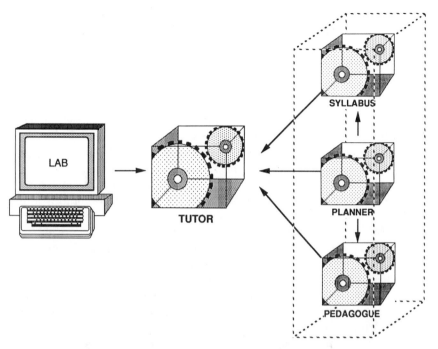

Figure 15.2. Architecture of the TUTOR sector within the DOCENT system.

be effective under specified conditions. These tasks can be set either by a teacher or by the sector called PLANNER (described later).

The knowledge base supporting these functions is the LIBRARY; its archivist program is the LIBRARIAN. The LIBRARY has three "floors." The first floor shelves empirically validated knowledge about instruction that has been translated from published educational research. Project staff use a smart interface program, the Knowledge Acquisition Tool for Instruction (KATI), to make these translations. The LIBRARY's second floor shelves expert teachers' experiential and case knowledge about teaching. Teachers will use an extension of KATI, T-KATI, to translate their knowledge into the LIBRARY. The third floor of the LIBRARY stocks conjectures about principles of instruction. Given constraints that specify a particular situations, the reasoning engine PEDAGOGUE computes conjectures using information stocked on the first and second floors plus a growing set of computed conjectures stored on the third floor. Thus, computed conjectures are principles of effective instruction that are grounded on empirical knowledge but are not yet empirically validated.

The interface INQUIRER links a teacher to the LIBRARIAN and to PEDAGOGUE. Using INQUIRER, teachers can ask straightforward questions of the LIBRARIAN, such as, "What information is there about motivating students to do homework?" Teachers also can address problems for which PEDAGOGUE develops principles, for instance, "How can I motivate my top students to do the enrichment exercises?"

## 4.2. Sector SYLLABUS

This sector represents the subject matter to be taught and coordinates it with instructional objectives specifying tasks in which students apply knowledge and demonstrate competence with it. SYLLABUS also helps the teacher design a coherent series of lessons and tutorials.

The archivist program in this sector, SOCRATES, works in and among four knowledge bases. CURRICULUM contains translations of information from two sources: scope and sequence information commonly provided with school textbooks, and descriptions of a jurisdiction's (e.g., a province or district) required content. The DISCIPLINARY WEB stores facts about how knowledge of a topic is structured on grounds of the subject's discipline. This knowledge includes, for example, the flow of cognitive activities in a strategy for monitoring reading comprehension (e.g, Paris, 1987) or the semantic network of concepts for correct knowledge and misconceptions about physics (e.g., Champagne, Klopfer, & Gunstone, 1982). Thirdly, the OBJECTIVES WEB records information about the tasks in which the subject matter is used (Marx, Winne, & Walsh, 1985).

The reasoning engine SYLLABUS selects, integrates, and fuses information in these three knowledge bases and, occasionally, queries the LIBRARIAN. With this diverse knowledge, SYLLABUS creates a fourth knowledge base called CONTENT LAYOUT. CONTENT LAYOUT is used to navigate within the subject matter. It maps knowledge and skills in terms of prerequisites and corequisites, core and enriching concepts, examples, elaborations, and links among topics within lessons and across units of lessons.

The interface program in this sector is MAPPER. Using MAPPER, teachers and curriculum developers can create or edit a knowledge base, weight material's importance according to their own preferences, and adjust the CONTENT LAYOUT on the basis of experience with lessons and tutorials.

## 4.3. Sector PLANNER

The main job of the PLANNER sector is consulting interactively with a teacher to design the instructional events of lessons to maximize teaching effectiveness. PLANNER also helps the teacher evaluate agendas for lessons and routines that comprise agendas. Teachers interact with PLANNER using the interface program SCRIBE.

PLANNER draws on three knowledge bases within its sector. PLANNER also requests information from sector PEDAGOGUE so that plans are solidly grounded in empirical knowledge about effective instruction. As well, PLANNER relies on SYLLABUS's sector to insure that lessons and tutorials involve appropriate content and organize it well.

Two of PLANNER's knowledge bases accumulate evaluative data about the teacher's (and TUTOR's) instruction for continuous formative evaluation of instructional processes. This allows PLANNER to identify past deviations from plans and to forecast future deviations of actual instruction from planned instruction. One of these knowledge bases is STUDENT DATA. It has two partitions served by the archivist TELLER. The first records data about each student's intralesson and postlesson achievements, motivations, styles of learning, and behavior. Data for the this partition are provided to DOCENT by the teacher, using the interface program EVALAUTOR, and by TUTOR. The second partition of STUDENT DATA reflects similar information about groups of students, such as the degree of cooperation in a small group or the performance of a group which the teacher uses as a basis for gauging the class's overall mastery of content (a steering group; Dalloff, 1971). Data for the second partition are recorded by the teacher. Both partitions share an archivist, TELLER.

The second knowledge base in PLANNER that contains evaluative data is INSTRUCTIONAL DATA. It also has two partitions. The first records data about the match between aspects of a lesson or tutorial as planned and instruction as actually implemented and adapted. The second partition of records are measures of outcomes achieved relative to goals set for a lesson or its parts. These data might include the amount of academic learning time (Fisher et al., 1978) or the ratio of correct to incorrect student answers in a socratic questioning strategy (Collins & Stevens, 1982). All these data are gathered during or after instruction and entered in INSTRUCTIONAL DATA by the teacher, using EVALUATOR, or by TUTOR.

The third knowledge base in PLANNER's' sector is PLANS. Before a teacher begins to work with DOCENT, PLANS will be seeded with instructional tactics (Winne, 1985), routines and agendas (Leinhardt & Greeno, this volume), and models of teaching (e.g., Joyce & Weil, 1986). Seeds can supply initial structure when teachers work with DOCENT to develop experimental formats for teaching or for trial agendas which TUTOR may follow in a tutorial.

As the teacher works with DOCENT over the course of an instructional period, seeds will be adapted and extended. First, any relatively constant parameters which might affect lessons or tutorials, such as excessive traffic noise around 10 a.m. or the absence of a calculator at center #2, will be stored. Subsequently, the teacher will develop, illustrate, annotate, and store for future use the instructional agendas and routines that have demonstrated value for reaching particular objectives in lessons and tutorials. Two other important items will be included in these records: tolerances for deviations of actual instruction from planned events, and connections between instructional events and students' mediation of them. In short, PLANS becomes a growing repository of what works in a teacher's particular situation, a record that teachers can revisit as they develop and adapt their own repertoires for te⸗ ing. PLANS uses an archivist called COLLECTOR. SCRIBE provides tʰᵉ interface.

## 4.4. Sector TUTOR

This sector provides students with tutorials that address small, focused parts of content that is covered or introduced in a teacher's lesson(s). Its reasoning engine TUTOR consists of rules and heuristics that are unique to managing tutorials and to collecting data about a student's participation in instruction in tutorials.

The knowledge the TUTOR needs relates to all the functions carried out in DOCENT's other three sectors. Because searching and processing very large knowledge bases overwhelms current technology, it is impractical for these other sectors to be "up, running, and fully involved" during a tutorial. However, the architecture of DOCENT lends itself to selecting from other sectors' knowledge bases small, well-defined subsets of information that apply to a single 20–30-minute tutorial. Consequently, these knowledge bases and reasoning engines can be pared and imported to TUTOR just prior to tutorials (e.g., the morning before), lowering computational demands to levels that are feasible. This notion parallels virtual processing—what is really external to TUTOR can be used as if it were an integral, internal feature. With data from a student's responses to tutoring, TUTOR will be able to develop, evaluate, and adapt a tutorial script interactively.

The LAB interface provides a student with a window into TUTOR. LAB contains several modules. PostOffice will give students and their teacher access to electronic mail delivered over a local area network. Logbook, Notebook, and Quizzer will be modifications of the teacher's SCRIBE and MAPPER programs. In their LAB version, these programs will be tutoring tools that are "soft" in that direct instructional intervention by TUTOR is minimal unless a student asks for help. Logbook will post assignments from the teacher or TUTOR and chart a student's developing mastery. Here, based on research into metacognitive skills in self-regulated learning (Corno, 1986), TUTOR will softly guide students to develop macrolevel self-regulation. Students will use Notebook to rework new information and to organize it as a cumulative hypertext of notes. TUTOR also "softly" helps students develop microlevel metacognitive skills for studying (Weinstein, Goetz, & Alexander, 1988) and strategies for spatially representing information (Holley

& Dansereau, 1984). Quizzer will give students a facility to develop and take self-tests while, in the background, TUTOR helps students review content. TEACHER2 is the interface for direct tutorial instruction provided by TUTOR. It uses hypertext and graphic facilities to communicate with students about content and to reflect their cognitive interactions with instructional events (Winne, 1989).

## 5. STOCKING THE LIBRARY

As noted earlier, the LIBRARY will contain information about instruction that is gleaned from three sources: studies published in journals reporting basic research about instruction, experienced teachers' expertise, and conjectures which are computed by the reasoning engine PEDAGOGUE based on information extant in the LIBRARY. To stock the LIBRARY, a scheme has been developed which represents information about teaching in computable from (see Winne & Kramer, 1989). As well, software tools have been designed and implemented that assist staff with the tasks involved in representing information about instruction.

### 5.1. The Expression Language for Instruction

Teaching is a field rich with information. This feature makes knowledge representation especially challenging. Lessons vary widely in format, teachers individualize goals, and instructional researchers make their living, in part, by devising new instructional methods. Despite this heterogeneity, some aspects of instruction must be fundamental or none of students, teachers, and researchers would be able to converse meaningfully about teaching. These fundamental elements of knowledge about instruction are reflected as low-level frames in a subsystem of the Expression Language for Instruction (ELI) called the Basal Language for Encoding Educational Processes (BLEEP).

Each frame in BLEEP represents a basal feature of instruction. Examples of frames are AFFECT, CLIMATE, DEMOGRAPHICS, INFORMATION, and SETTING. A frame is elaborated by slots which identify facets of the primitive concept to which a frame refers. Each slot is further differentiated into values. For example, the frame INFORMATION includes slots and values for slots that can represent aspects of information such as (a) whether it is part of a taught curriculum (yes, no), (b) its origin (given to a student as part of instruction, in the student's mind as prior knowledge, or in the student's mind at a point in instruction), and (c) its mode of representation (semantic, figural, quantitative). By selecting values for these and other slots on the INFORMATION frame that pertain to a given instance of information, say a sentence describing directions for a task, the frame is instantiated to describe a specific instance of information. Many frames in BLEEP have a cascading structure of slots and subslots that permit quite detailed instantiations. Also, BLEEP includes modifiers so that instantiations of frames can be qualified. These qualities are necessary for BLEEP to capture some of the richness of information about teaching.

Individual frames typically are constructs, primitive concepts that rarely correspond to objects, events, or "things" that teachers and students actually experience. Consequently, BLEEP also includes operators so that instantiated frames can be joined or clustered to create composites. For instance, directions for a task often include two sorts of information—a rule students follow about when the directions should be applied (a classification rule, one of the values for the slot labeled *structure* of the INFORMATION frame) plus comparative information that characterizes what adequate performance on the task consists of (another value for the slot labeled *structure*). An operator within BLEEP called a joint permits these two frames, each instantiated individually to identify each type of information, to be joined into one unit. This unit then can be related, using a relationship operator, to another instantiated INFORMATION frame that describes the task which the directions are about, thereby creating what is called a *structured object* in BLEEP.

This simple hypothetical example demonstrates BLEEP's abstractness, an attribute which gives rise to its capacity to represent very detailed information about teaching. Detail at this level is both what research in instructional psychology frequently observes to make a difference in students' motivation and achievement and what is absent in teachers' plans for lessons. To serve PEDAGOGUE well, the LIBRARY must stock such details, but this makes the job of using BLEEP to represent knowledge a very complex one.

ELI is a scheme that evolved to address the difficulties of using BLEEP to represent knowledge about teaching. ELI consists of *terms*, which are collections of BLEEP's units more akin to the experiences, objects, and events of teaching, plus *templates* that relate terms to one another. For example, the term DIRECTIONS is defined such that many slots on several component frames are set at default values and the frames are set in particular relations to one another. These default values and relations reflect the generally shared meaning of what directions typically are about, when they are given, who provides directions, what role directions play in subsequent events, and so forth. Specializations of the generic notion of directions are created by entering values on only a few slots or modifying defaults, if necessary. Thus, relative to BLEEP's frames and structured objects, terms have substantially more internal structure and are constrained by direct relations to other terms.

ELI's virtues as a scheme for representing knowledge about teaching are three. First, the set of terms comprising the scheme is readily extended. This accommodates the heterogeneity so common in the field of research and experience. Second, ELI's terms are easily used without intrinsically degrading the detail of an uncommon occurrence of the term. Third, because terms can be reconfigured as to their BLEEP units and the templates in which they are embedded, the scheme can be altered to reflect different perspectives about instruction. In short, ELI's structure is plastic enough to bend with growth in knowledge about teaching.

## 5.2. Software

Having designed ELI, the scheme needed to be implemented in computational form, and software had to be developed which staff could use to translate instances of information about teaching into a form for the LIBRARIAN to store. An editor which creates units in BLEEP was created early in the project (Xie, Dumaresq, & Winne, 1988). Subsequently, it has been extended to create and edit terms for ELI.

An early system also was developed in instantiate units of BLEEP, thus creating representations of information about instruction appearing in research articles. This system is now being massively restructured and extended to create KATI (see above).

## 6. CONCLUSION

Delivering on DOCENT's promises poses significant challenges for both educators and computer scientists. For example, our scheme for representing knowledge about instruction in published research articles illuminates many ambiguities in both theoretical and operational descriptions of instruction. Suggestions about principles for teaching that derive from ambiguous and incomplete evidence call for deep reflection by educators about what we believe to be our current "state of the art." DOCENT also breaks a new path for knowledge engineering. DOCENT's experts, rather than one or a very few people, are many and diverse journal articles and teachers. Because their topics, methods for reasoning, and conclusions follow many different lines, substantial work is called for on issues such as conflict resolution and generalization. Juxtapostions of just these two examples invites questions ranging from metaprinciples for developing theories to efficiency of search and inferencing mechanisms. in short, DOCENT provides fertile ground for addressing and attempting to integrate diverse perspectives that are central to each of the fields on which the project draws.

Beyond stimulating research, DOCENT is planned to evolve into a working and useful tool for teachers, students, and researchers. As parts of the overall system are developed, field tests of prototypes in schools will play a prominent role in feeding back information about how advanced technology can fit into and contribute to improvements in classroom teaching. This feature is too infrequently a part of applying artificial intelligence technology in education. Our firm commitment to the interplay between developing DOCENT and tracking its use promises to advance the project and spur new research.

## REFERENCES

Allal, L.K. (1988). Quantitative and qualitative components of teachers' evaluation strategies. *Teaching and Teacher Education, 4,* 41-51.

American Educational Studies Association. (1984). *Pride and promise: Schools of excellence for all the people.* Washington, DC: Author.

Berliner, D.C. (1986). In search of the expert pedagogue. *Educational Researcher, 15*(7), 5-13.

Borko, H., Lalik, R., & Tomchin, E. (1987). Student teachers' understanding of successful and unsuccessful teaching. *Teaching and Teacher Education, 3,* 77-90.

Burns, R.B., & Lash, A.A. (1988). Nine seventh-grade teachers' knowledge and planning of problem-solving instruction. *Elementary School Journal, 88,* 369-386.

Calderhead, J. (1984). *Teachers' classroom decision making.* London: Holt, Rinehart & Winston.

Carter, K., Sabers, D., Cushing, K., Pinnegar, S., & Berliner, D.C. (1987). Processing and using information about students: A study of expert, novice, and postulant teachers. *Teaching and Teacher Education, 3,* 147-157.

Champagne, A.B., Klopfer, L.E., & Gunstone, R.F. (1982). Cognitive research and the design of instruction. *Educational Psychologist, 17,* 31-53.

Clark, C.M. (1988). Asking the right questions about teacher preparation: Contributions of research on teacher thinking. *Educational Researcher, 17*(2), 5-12.

Clark, C.M., Gage, N.L., Marx, R.W., Peterson, P.L., Stayrook, N., & Winne, P.H. (1979). A factorial experiment on teacher structuring, soliciting, and reaction. *Journal of Educational Psychology, 71,* 534-553.

Clark, C.M., & Peterson, P.L. (1986). Teachers' thought processes. In M. Wittrock (Ed.), *Handbook of research on teaching* (3rd ed., pp. 255-296). New York: Macmillan.

Collins, A., & Stevens, A.L. (1982). Goals and strategies of inquiry teachers. In R. Glaser (Ed.), *Advances in instructional psychology* (Vol. 2, pp. 65-119). Hillsdale, NJ: Erlbaum.

Corno, L. (1986). The metacognitive control components of self-regulated learning. *Contemporary Educational Psychology, 11,* 333-346.

Corno, L., & Snow, R.E. (1986). Adapting teaching to individual differences among learners. In M. Wittrock (Ed.), *Handbook of research on teaching* (3rd ed., pp. 605-629). New York: Macmillan.

Dalloff, U.S. (1971). *Ability grouping, content validity, and classroom process analysis.* New York: Teachers College Press.

Fisher, C., Filby, N., Marliave, R., Cahen, L., Dishaw, M., Moore, J., & Berliner, D. (1978). *Teaching behaviors, academic learning time and student achievement: Final report of Phase III-B. Beginning Teacher Evaluation Study.* San Francisco, CA: Far West Laboratory.

Gage, N.L. (1985). *Hard gains in the soft sciences—the case of pedagogy.* New York: Teachers' College Press.

Good, T.L., & Grouws, D.A. (1979). The Missouri mathematics effectiveness project. *Journal of Educational Psychology, 71,* 355-362.

Holley C.D., & Dansereau, D.F. (Eds.). (1984). *Spatial learning strategies: Techniques applications and related issues*. Orlando, FL: Academic Press.

Joyce, B., & Clift, R. (1984). The Phoenix agenda: Essential reform in teacher education. *Educational Researcher, 13*(4), 5-18.

Joyce, B., & Weil, M. (1986). *Models of teaching* (3rd ed.). Englewood Clifts, NJ: Prentice-Hall.

Joyce, B., Hersh, R.H., & McKibbin, M. (1983). *The structure of school improvement*. New York: Longman.

Lawler, R.W., & Yazdani, M. (Eds.). (1987). *Artificial intelligence and education* (Vol.1). Norwood, NJ: Ablex, Publishing Corp.

Leinhardt, G., & Greeno, J.G. (1986). The cognitive skill of teaching. *Journal of Educational Psychology, 78*, 75-95.

Leinhardt, G., Weidman, C., & Hammond, K.M. (1987). Introduction and integration of classroom routines by expert teachers. *Curriculum Inquiry, 17*, 135-176.

Marland, P. (1986). Models of teachers' interactive thinking. *Elementary School Journal, 87*, 209-226.

Marx, R.W., Winne, P.H., & Walsh, J. (1985). Studying student cognition during classroom learning. In M. Pressley & C. Brainerd (Eds.), *Cognitive learning and memory in children*. New York: Springer-Verlag.

Newell, A., & Simon, H.A. (1972). *Human problem solving*. Englewood Cliffs, NJ: Prentice-Hall.

Nisbett, R., & Ross, L. (1980). *Human inference: Strategies and shortcomings of social judgment*. Englewood Cliffs, NJ: Prentice-Hall.

Paris, S. G. (1987). *Reading and thinking strategies*. Lexington, MA: D.C. Heath.

Peterson, P.L., & Clark, C.M. (1978). Teachers' reports of their cognitive processes during teaching. *American Educational Research Journal, 15*, 555-565.

Peterson, P.L., & Comeaux, M.A. (1987). Teachers' schemata for classroom events: The mental scaffolding of teachers' thinking during classroom instruction. *Teaching and Teacher Education, 3*, 319-331.

Peterson, P.L., & Swing, S.R. (1982). Beyond time on task: Students' reports of their thought processes during classroom instruction. *Elementary School Journal, 82*, 481-492.

Peterson, P.L., & Swing, S.R. (1985). Students' cognitions as mediators of the effectiveness of small-group learning. *Journal of Educational Psychology, 77*, 299-312.

Peterson, P.L., Swing, S.R., Braverman, M.T., & Buss, R. (1982). Students' aptitudes and their reports of cognitive processes during learning. *Journal of Educational Psychology, 74*, 535-547.

Richardson-Koehler, V. (1988). "What works" and what doesn't. *Journal of Curriculum Studies, 20*(1), 71-79.

Slavin, R.E. (1987). Ability grouping and student achievement in elementary schools: A best-evidence synthesis. *Review of Educational Research, 57*, 293-336.

Stiggins, R.J., & Bridgeford, N.J. (1985). The ecology of classroom assessment. *Journal of Educational Measurement, 22*, 271-286.

U.S. Department of Education. (1986). *WHAT WORKS: Research about teaching and learning*. Washington, DC: Author.

Weinstein, C.E., Goetz, E.T., & Alexander, P.A. (Eds.). (1988). *Learning and study strategies: issues in assessment, instruction, and evaluation*. San Diego, CA: Academic Press.

Winne, P.H. (1982). Minimizing the black box problem to enhance the validity of theories about instructional effects. *Instructional Science, 11*, 13-28.

Winne, P. H. (1985). Steps toward promoting cognitive achievements. *Elementary School Journal, 85*, 673-693.

Winne, P.H. (1987a). Students' cognitive processing. In M. Dunkin (Ed.), *The international encyclopedia of teaching and teacher education* (pp. 496-509). Oxford, England: Pergamon.

Winne, P.H. (1987b). Why process-product research cannot explain process-product findings and a proposed remedy: The cognitive mediational paradigm. *Teaching and Teacher Education, 3*, 333-356.

Winne, P.H. (1988a). *Project DOCENT: Interim Summary Report on Phase I.* Burnaby, BC: Instructional Psychology Research Group, Simon Fraser University.

Winne, P.H. (1989). Theories of intelligence and of instruction for artificially intelligent tutoring systems. *Educational Psychologist, 24,* 229-259.

Winne, P.H., & Kramer, L.L. (1990). Representing knowledge about teaching: DOCENT—An artificially intelligent planning system for teachers. In C. Frasson & G. Gauthier (Eds.), *Intelligent tutoring system. At the crossroads of artificial intelligence and education* (pp. 162-187). Norwood, NJ: Ablex Publishing Corp.

Winne, P.H., & Marx, R.W. (1977). Reconceptualizing research on teaching. *Journal of Educational Psychology, 69,* 668-678.

Winne, P.H., & Marx, R.W. (1982). Students' and teachers' views of thinking processes for classroom learning. *Elementary School Journal, 82,* 493-518.

Winne, P.H., & Marx, R.W. (1983). *Students' cognitive processes while learning from teaching* (NIE Final Report, NIE-G-79-0098). Burnaby, BC: Instructional Psychology Research Group, Simon Fraser University.

Winne, P.H., & Marx, R.W. (1988). The best tool teachers have—Their students' thinking. In D. Berliner & B Rosenshine (Eds.), *Talks to teachers* (pp. 267-304). New York: Random House.

Wittrock, M.C. (1986). Students' thought processes. In M. Wittrock (Ed.), *Handbook of research on teaching* (3rd ed., pp. 297-314). New York: Macmillan.

Xie, S-E., Dumaresq, D.F., & Winne, P.H. (1988). PRED: An interface development tool for editing primitives in knowledge representation languages. In *Proceedings:Knowledge Acquisition for Knowledge-Based Systems.* Banff, Canada: American Association for Artificial intelligence.

# 16

# COMPUTER SIMULATION IN TEACHER EDUCATION: ENHANCING TEACHER DECISION MAKING*

ANNE SHELLY AND ERNEST SIBERT

Simulations in teacher training are receiving renewed attention as computing and audiovisual equipment have become more accessible and as the research base on effective teaching has been expanded. Interest in teacher-training simulations has been traced back to the mid-1960s with the work of Dwight Allen at Stanford University and Bert Kersh at Western Oregon State College (Doak & Keith, 1986). These projects, and the ones that followed, such as Smith's *protocols* and Cruickshank's *reflective teaching*, were excellent prototype work that were much hampered by the lack of accessible technology and of an explicit research base as a foundation for simulation development.

With advances in both areas, educational researchers such as Berliner (1985) suggest that simulations are potentially useful as one method of supporting teacher-education students who need guided practice in decision-making skills and interactive behaviors before they apply such skills in the classroom environment. Simulation on Teacher Decision Making (STDM), the project reported here, enables prospective teachers (a) to practice teacher-planning decisions as they make a variety of instructional decisions for

---

*The project reported here is a collaborative research effort by Greta Morine-Dershimer and Berj Harootunian of the School of Education, and Ernest Sibert and Anne Shelly of the School of Computer and Information Science, all at Syracuse University. The project was supported in part by a grant from the Comprehensive Program Fund for the Improvement of Postsecondary Education (FIPSE), 1985-1987.

a simulated classroom, (b) to receive research-based feedback on the probable effects of these decisions on pupil learning, and (c) to respond to this feedback through changes in their instructional decisions (Morine-Dershimer, Harootunian, Shelly & Sibert, 1985).

We divide the following discussion into three sections: (a) an overview of the system, (b) a description of the technology on which the system is based, and (c) a preliminary analysis of student use of the system.


## 1. OVERVIEW OF THE SYSTEM


Specific simulation tasks in this project include: (a) decisions on grouping for reading instruction, (b) scheduling lesson time, and (c) adapting instructional materials. The simulation setting is a fifth-grade classroom; the data set is information on 14 pupils over 5 years, i.e., grades K through 4. The information was collected initially from school records; then composite portraits of 14 pupils were developed from the data to protect the identities of the original pupils. Types of information in the data bank include health and attendance records, IQ tests and creativity measures, parent-teacher conferences, report card grades, sociograms, teacher-reported special interests of pupils, standardized achievement test scores, and teacher comments.

Engaging in the simulation, the student-teacher uses this information and practices a variety of instructional decisions (e.g., grouping for reading instruction, allotting time for math instruction). The computer has two functions during the simulation: (a) it guides the student-teacher through an interactive sequence to record the products of the simulation (e.g., reading groups, weekly instructional schedules) and the rationale for the products (e.g., memos), and (b) it builds a knowledge base representing this record of the student's decisions and rationale statements. Many such student-teacher knowledge bases are combined for analysis by teacher-educators. In addition to the knowledge-base information representing the record of student-teacher decisions, the teacher-educator can expand the knowledge base by adding information characterizing the student teachers individually (e.g., major in undergraduate program, concepts discussed in course papers) or as a group (e.g., course in which simulation was conducted, course instructor(s), time period in which simulation was conducted). Such additions allow the teacher-educator to explore the connections between student-teachers' background and experience and their rationales for using (or for not using) particular sets of information when making specific instructional decisions.

Figure 16.1 summarizes the structure developed for the task of grouping for reading instruction (i.e., the first task of three in this simulation set).

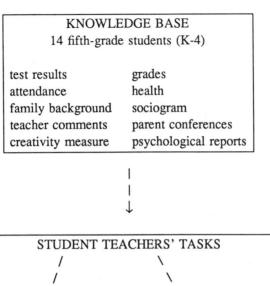

KNOWLEDGE BASE
14 fifth-grade students (K-4)

test results          grades
attendance            health
family background     sociogram
teacher comments      parent conferences
creativity measure    psychological reports

↓

STUDENT TEACHERS' TASKS
/                           \

choose information                choose information
make grouping decisions           make grouping decisions
given information                 choose/add information
make grouping decisions           make grouping decisions
receive research-based feedback   create queries
                                  analyze queries/decisions

↓

STUDENT-TEACHERS' KNOWLEDGE BASES

↓

TEACHER EDUCATORS' TASKS
/                           \

analyze responses          add student-teacher information
                           analyze responses

Figure 16.1. Simulation on Teacher Decision Making (STDM)
Morine-Dershimer, G., Harootunian, B., Shelly, A. & Sibert, E. *Enhancing teacher Decision Making Through Computer Simulations*. Project Funded by the Fund for the Improvement of Postsecondary Education (1986-1987).

## 1.1. Building a Knowledge Base: Sample Task - Grouping for Reading Instruction

The following pages provide a sample of the grouping task with responses by a student in the teacher-preparation program at Syracuse University. The task began with an introductory statement printed by the program (see Table 16.1). After the introductory message, the student was presented with a menu of the pupil information and with a request for her selections (see Table 16.2).

After the student made her choices, which were report-card grades and teacher-comment data, the program proceeded to print the information requested. Table 16.3 shows a sample of the report-card data; Table 16.4 shows a sample of the teacher-comment data.

**Table 16.1.  Grouping exercise, session 1.**

---

Simulation on Teacher Decision Making

TASK I: Grouping for Instruction in Reading

---

Introduction

Some of the most important decisions that teachers make are made before they ever meet their students, or during the first few days of instruction. Decisions about grouping for instruction are one example of this type of decision.

Prospective teachers rarely have the opportunity to practice grouping pupils for instruction before they face their own first class of pupils. This simulation provdes you with an opportunity to practice grouping a "class" of fifth-grade pupils for instruction in reading. You will receive feedback at the end of this exercise, so that you can learn from this experience.

Your fifth-grade class for this simulation includes ony 14 pupils. A real class will have about twice as many students, and some classes may have 30 or more. As you form groups, remember that a group of 4 or 5 students in this simulated class would turn out to be a group of 8 to 10 students in a regular class.

The 14 students in this class are each a composite, based on real information from real school records of real pupils in urban schools. The information available to you is the kind of information collected by most schools, and kept in student record files.

There is quite a bit of information available on each student in this computer "data bank." But a teacher is very busy in the early days of a school year, and would rarely have or take the time to look at all the available information. Your first decision will be to determine what type of information will be most useful, since you will only have time to study a limited amount of data.

You should begin by studying the attached photographs of your students, and sheets of information on their family background. You will then be given a list of the other types of information available. You will have an opportunity to select two more sets of information for study before making your initial decision about how to group these pupils for instruction in reading.

Press RETURN when you are ready to proceed.

---

**Table 16.2.  Grouping exercise, session 1 (continued).**

The following is a list of information available for these students:
— Health and Attendance Records (health—grades 3 and 4, attendance—all)
— IQ Tests and Creativity Measures (all records on file)
— Parent Conferences (all conferences on file)
— Report Card Grades (for grades 3 and 4)
— Sociogram Information (children's choices of neighbors in grade 4)
— Special Interests (comments about students' special interests)
— Standardized Achievement Tests (all tests on file)
— Teacher Comments (for grades 3 and 4)

What is your information choice? Report Card Grades
What is your second information choice? Teacher Comments

---

**Table 16.3.  Grouping exercise, session 1 (continued).**

| Report Card Grades—Grades 3 and 4 | | |
|---|---|---|
| Bob W 83–84   Grade 3 | | |
| Eng C | Math C | Writing B |
| Read B | Music C | Sci C |
| Spell C | Art B | Soc St C |
| Bob W 84–85   Grade 4 | | |
| Eng D | Math D | Writing B |
| Read D | Music B | Soc St C |
| Spell D | Art C | Sci C |
| Carmen V 83–84   Grade 3 | | |
| Eng C | Math C | Writing B |
| Read C | Music C | Sci C |
| Spell D | Art C | Soc St C |
| CarmenV 84–85   Grade 4 | | |
| Eng D | Math C | Writing C |
| Read C | Music C | Sci C |
| Spell D | Art C | Soc St C |
| Esther T 83–84   Grade 3 | | |
| Eng A | Math A | Writing B |
| Read A | Music A | Sci A |
| Spell B | Art A | Soc St B |
| Esther T 84–85   Grade 4 | | |
| Eng A | Math A | Writing B |
| Read A | Music A | Soc St A |
| Spell A | Art A | Sci A |

The instructions shown in Table 16.5 end the first session of the grouping task.

A log of the first session, including the requested pupil data, was automatically printed at the end of this session. The student studied the pupil data, made her grouping decisions, and wrote a rationale statement in preparation for the second session at the computer, which occurred approx-

**Table 16.4.  Grouping exercise, session 1 (continued).**

| THIRD.083 614 643 (Bob W) 83 |
| --- |

| 0614 | Teacher's Comments |
| --- | --- |

0614                                          Teacher's Comments
0615
0616
0617 Name: Bob W.
0618
0619 Year: 83–84                              Grade: 3
0620
0621 Teacher: Miss L.S.
0622
0623 Academic Achievement:
0624
0625    Bob has been at "loose ends" academically and socially much of this
0626 school year. Part of this has been caused by emotional problems,
0627 one of which was the death of his father this spring. His work is
0628 always spotty: at times he does well, and at other times he does
0629 nothing. He has achieved very little in math. In reading he has
0630 progressed very nicely, so well that he jumped ahead one year
0631 in reading.
0632
0633
0634 Social Development:
0635
0636    Bob has been a behavior problem in class. He frequently
0637 gets out of his seat and gets into fights. He is quite
0638 un-self-disciplined: if not watched carefully, he is likely
0639 to be roaming around the room, lying on his desk, or
0640 even taking a walk out into the hall!
0641 Parent-Teacher Relationship:
0642
0643 Additional Comments:

**Table 16.5.  Grouping exercise, session 1 (conclusion)**

When you come back, you will be asked to enter your decision about student groups and a memo discussing your reasons for the groupings.

imately 1 week after the first session. Table 16.6 shows the beginning of the second session, during which the student entered her groups, correcting a few mistakes after the initial entry.

At this point, the student responded with the memo reproduced in Table 16.7.

When the student exited from the word-processing program, she was given another set of information about the elementary pupils. This additional information was preselected for students on the basis of their first two choices. The explanatory statement for the information given to this student

Table 16.6. Grouping exercise, session 2.

Simulation on Teacher Decision Making

Session 2

Press RETURN when you are ready to proceed

Besides the class list and family background information, you have examined

Report Card Grades

Teacher Comments

You have grouped the students using the information provided.

Enter your student groups. For each group, type the (first) names of the students in the group. Press RETURN after each name. Type the word 'end' when you are finished with a group. Don't worry if you make a mistake, you'll get a chance to correct it later. If you can't remember who's left, type the word 'who'.

[The student entered her groups, corrected a few errors, then the computer printed the groups for confirmation.]

Students in group 1:

| Esther T | Jeff M | June M | Neil L |
|---|---|---|---|

Students in group 2:

| Jane A | Joe K | Robin E | Ruth B |
|---|---|---|---|

Students in group 3:

| Bob W | Jim G | John M |
|---|---|---|

Students in group 4:

| Carmen V | Ira M | Jose D |
|---|---|---|

Are these correct? (y or n)y

is shown in Table 16.8. A sample of the pupil data (standardized achievement tests) is found in Table 16.9.

The instructions which conclude the second session are shown in Table 16.10.

The exercise illustrated by Tables 16.11 through 16.15 is the third session in the grouping task. The student's responses are included. The session begins with the instructions in Table 16.11. As shown in Table 16.12, the student entered her revised reading groups. She then typed the memo explaining her revision (shown in Table 16.13).

The session continued with a request for information from the student about the simulation exercises (shown in Table 16.14). The student responded with the memo in Table 16.15.

As the last part of the grouping task, the student received research-based feedback that could be reread as many times as she wished. She was asked to respond to the feedback when she finished reading it.

All session logs, memos, and grouping decisions were recorded by the programs. These files were available to the teacher-educator for analysis.

Table 16.7.  Grouping exercise, session 2 (continued).

---

Memo on First Grouping Decision

---

Upon reviewing the students's third and fourth-grade report cards and teacher comments, I devised a reading grouping for these 14 fifth-grade students.

My method of proceeding for grouping these students involved looking at each individual's third- and fourth-grade report card grades in reading, spelling, and English. These grades enabled me to see how the students did overall academically in these three areas. But this was insufficient information to enable me to place them into groups. Therefore, I resorted to a second set of information—the teacher comments.

As I read through the teacher comments for each individual student, I made note of specific improvements and/or deterioration in their reading work. I also took note of specific individual differences. For example, Bob cannot function in a group situation and thus he needs individual help. Also, Jim has family problems and he also needs remedial help; along with John. Furthermore, we have Jose who should be placed in a special class—perhaps a mentally handicapped class. These are just a few of the cases which I had to take into consideration when devising the reading groups. This information given by the teachers made it easier for me to devise the reading groups; rather than relying solely on the report card grades.

I have divided the class into four groups (I, II, III, IV). My goal was to attempt to choose the most suitable place for each student in order that they may benefit the most academically and socially.

Groups I and II consist of the above average (A) and the students who are on the borderline (B− B+), students whom teachers feel are capable of obtaining A grades. I have purposely intermixed these students, so that there will be an incentive to place a little extra effort in their work. The only precaution that I had to deal with in Group I and II is that I wanted to split Neil and Joe apart so Joe wouldn't feel intimidated by the gifted child Neil.

Groups III and IV consist of the average to below average students. Most of these students need to go to remedial reading classes outside of the classroom. I have placed Carmen and Jose in the same group for the very fact that Carmen is the "class mother" figure and she can be of assistance to Jose. Perhaps these students will benefit from this grouping academically and socially. Furthermore, I have separated Bob and Carmen because Bob cannot function in a group situation, and I feel Carmen's personality would upset him. I feel this is the best grouping for Group III and IV.

---

## 2. LOGIC PROGRAMMING AS A BASIS FOR SIMULATION

The system grew out of our interest in symbolic computation and mechanized deduction and in the analysis processes teachers use as they make instructional decisions. Their analyses involve observational and inductive processes as well as deductive processes. A complex effort is involved in the careful observation and interpretation of many sources of richly detailed information about students. Our interest is in applying computers to these activities, doing so in a manner consonant with the processes teachers use.

We approached the development of this system using methods of computing which have evolved within the broad perspective of artificial intelli-

Table 16.8.   Grouping exercise, session 2 (continued).

You will now be given the information about
Standardized Achievement Tests (all test on file)

Press RETURN when you are ready to proceed

Standardized Achievement Test Results—
Here are the standardized achievement test results for your students. The achievement test
results are given in "grade level equivalent" scores. The scores are related to national norms,
or average achievement of large numbers of pupils. A score of 3.0 means the child has scored
as the average child entering third grade would score on that particular subtest. The 3 stands
for the grade level, and the 0 for the months completed in that grade. A score of 4.9 means
that the child has scored as the average child completing the fourth grade would score on
that subtest. (Test makers consider that there are nine months in the school year.) If a test
was administered in early February of the third grade year, and the child taking the test was
exactly average, according to national norms, then the score on the test would be 3.5, for the
child would have completed five months of the third grade.
   A child tested in March of the third grade and scoring 5.4 (fifth grade, fourth month) is
exhibiting above average achievement. A child tested at the same time, and scoring 2.3 is
exhibiting below average achievement. Extreme scores, such as 1.2 and 8.6 for a third grade
child, do not mean that the child is really reading or doing mathematics as a first grader or an
eighth grader would be. Such extreme scores simply mean that the child is well below (or
above) average in achievement in a particular subject area, relative to other childen at the
third grade level.
   As you interpret these scores, you should note the grade and month in which the test was
administered to the child. Also note the child's age. Most children are eight years old in the
third grade. Children who are much older may have repeated an earlier grade.

gence research. The first of these emphasizes symbolic, as opposed to
numeric, computation, and is best exemplified by LISP (McCarthy, 1960;
McCarthy, Abrahams, Edwards, Hart, & Levin, 1965), one of the oldest and
best known languages for symbolic computation. The symbolic approach
offers the advantage that the user can express information using freely chosen
symbols and creating expressions freely constructed from those symbols. The
second computing methodology we have borrowed is that of mechanized
deduction (Robinson, 1965), which makes it possible for the computer to
deduce logical consequences of information provided by the user. In
particular, we have used logic programming methods (Kowalski, 1974,
1979), which offer the advantage of very efficient implementation at the price
of a slight restriction in expressive power. Using logic, users can enter
information as assertions, which may be either particular statements of fact or
general statements expressing rules. Such a collection of assertions is usually
called a *knowledge base*. The implicit content of the knowledge base can be
deduced in response to queries, which request the system to establish the
existence of objects (actually, expressions denoting objects) satisfying some
combination of logical conditions. Such an approach yields enormous
flexibility, both for recording information and for querying this information

Table 16.9. Grouping exercise, session 2 (continued).

Bob W

Grade 3 Age 8 yrs. 7 mos.
Stanford-W administered 7 Feb 84
Results:

| | |
|---|---|
| word meaning 1.8 | language 3.1 |
| paragraph meaning 2.2 | arithmetic computation 1.5 |
| spelling 1.9 | arithmetic concepts 2.3 |
| word study skills 1.5 | science-social studies 1.6 |

Grade 4 Age NL
Stanford-W administered NL
Results:

| | |
|---|---|
| word meaning 3.3 | language 1.4 |
| paragraph meaning 3.2 | arithmetic computation 3.6 |
| spelling 3.3 | arithmetic concepts 3.2 |
| word study skills 2.6 | science-social studies 2.9 |

Carmen V

Grade 3 Age 9 yrs. 10 mos.
Stanford-W administered 7 Feb 84
Results:

| | |
|---|---|
| word meaning 1.7 | language 1.9 |
| paragraph meaning 2.0 | arithmetic computation 2.7 |
| spelling 1.7 | arithmetic concepts 1.6 |
| word study skills 2.2 | science-social studies 3.6 |

Grade 4 Age 10 yrs. 10 mos.
Stanford-W administered ? Feb 85
Results:

| | |
|---|---|
| word meaning 2.3 | language 1.4 |
| paragraph meaning 2.1 | arithmetic computation 3.2 |
| spelling 2.6 | arithmetic concepts 2.8 |
| word study skills 3.1 | science-social studies 3.4 |

Table 16.10. Grouping exercise, session 2 (conclusion).

For your next session you should consider your groupings using this new information about the students, and prepare to write another memo explaining your reasons for changing or maintaining your original groups.

in ways that were not anticipated by the user at the time the information was entered.

The best known implementations of logic programming are the various forms of PROLOG (e.g., Roussel, 1975; Pereira, Pereira, & Warren, 1978). For these investigations, however, we have chosen a programming system, LOGLISP (Robinson & Sibert, 1982, 1984), which integrates logic with LISP and retains the benefits of both. In LOGLISP, information is represented and stored as *facts* (i.e., unconditional, specific statements asserted to

Table 16.11. Grouping exercise, session 3.

---

Simulation on Teacher Decision Making

Session 3

---

In this session, you should accomplish four tasks:

1. Enter your "new" groupings, which could be the same as before, or could be entirely different. You will be using a program just like the one you used in the second session.
2. Type a memo explaining your reasons for these groupings, and how they relate to the previous ones. You will use EDT, just as before.
3. Type another memo discussing questions you have about the information you were given.
4. Read the research-based feedback about this simulation exercise. Write a memo (on paper) giving your reactions to the feedback.

You will be given further instructions as you proceed.

Press RETURN when you are ready to proceed

---

Table 16.12. Grouping exercise, session 3 (continued).

---

Now that you have also examined
    Standardized Achievement Tests
you have had an opportunity to reconsider your initial groups.

Enter your student groups. For each group, type the (first) names of the students in the group. Press RETURN after each name. Type the word 'end' when you are finished with a group. Don't worry if you make a mistake, you'll get a chance to correct it later. If you can't remember who's left, type the word 'who'.

[The student entered her groups, corrected a few errors, then the computer printed the groups for confirmation.]

Students in group 1:

| Esther T | Jeff M | June M | Neil L |
|---|---|---|---|

Students in group 2:

| Joe K | Robin E | Ruth B | |
|---|---|---|---|

Students in group 3:

| Bob W | Jane A | Jim G | John M |
|---|---|---|---|

Students in group 4:

| Carmen V | Ira M | Jose D | |
|---|---|---|---|

Are these correct? (y or n)y

---

be true) and as *rules* (i.e., possibly conditional, generalized statements asserted to be true). Users can develop *relations* (i.e., sets of assertions) by using words and symbols in forms they establish, thus creating representations of concepts they wish to express.

## 2.1. Building a Knowledge Base

We emphasize the use of relations as a vehicle for representing simulation data (i.e., pupil information) and for recording the thinking processes that

**Table 16.13.  Grouping exercise, session 3 (continued).**

Memo on Second Grouping Decision

Upon reviewing the third set of data, (The Standardized Achievement Tests), I have decided to switch only one student from the four groupings.

I have basically maintained the same groupings except for Jane—the bilingual student, whom I feel needs a little extra help. I have placed her in Group III instead of Group II.

I feel that Jane would feel too pressured by being in an above average group. I feel this would lead to a loss of confidence in her work, and she would not benefit academically and emotionally.

Basically, this new data is not a shock to me. This data reinforces my reasons for choosing the first groupings. The Standardized Achievement Test Scores are very consistent with the students' third and fourth grade report card grades, and their teacher comments.

Finally, after reviewing my groupings I again feel that only one additional change will provide the most suitable place for each student. Each student will benefit the most academically, socially, and emotionally.

Note: All students in Group III except for Jane go for
      individual help on different days of the week.
      Jose attends a special class—English as a Second
      Language.

*** If any student shows signs of improvement and/or
    deterioration in their work, each student will have to
    be evaluated and placed in the appropriate group.

**Table 16.14.  Grouping exercise, session 3 (continued).**

Simulation on Teacher Decision Making

Session 3—Discussion of Student Information

In this part of the exercise, you are to type a memo discussing your views concerning the information you received about the students. We are interested in the questions you may have about interpreting any of the information. Your responses in this memo will be useful as we consider revisions to these programs.

  1)  What student information did you receive?
  2)  Did you have any questions about how to interpret the information?
Refer to "Introduction to Fullscreen EDT" if you need help typing the memo. When you finish this task, you must exit from EDT; then the program will start you on the next task.

characterize each student-teacher's use of the pupil information. For example, the simulation knowledge base includes the following relations:

Attendance, Classmember, Creativity, DataBank, Grades,
Health, Parent, Parent-Conference, SeatChoice, Sibling,
Sociogram, Stanford-W, Student-Interests, Teacher-Comment

Our choice of names for these relations is not constrained by the programming system; they are labels of our choosing, each representing a specific grouping of pupil information.

**Table 16.15. Grouping exercise, session 3 (conclusion).**

Memo on Interpreting Student Information

All of the information that I was given: Report Card Grades, Teacher Comments, and Standardized Achievement Tests seemed to be consistent and reliable. This information enabled me to select the most appropriate reading grouping for each individual student.

It seems to me that the only information given to me was from the viewpoint of the teacher or information that evaluted each student's academic performance. I was not able to find out about each student's feelings concerning reading, school and their feelings towards their peers. Furthermore, I was not able to find out about any special interests they had.

If I were given the additional information mentioned above, would this have any effect on my grouping selection? Would different combinations of information change my grouping choice?

I only have some specific questions concerning the last set of information: the Standardized Test Scores. What is the difference between the Standard- W, x, and L exams? Are these exams administered nationally or state-wide? Furthermore, what does NL mean?

---

These relations differ not only in substance, but in structure as well. We have used three devices for formulating our relations. The most common form records specific information for each student within logic assertions. To illustrate, the Attendance relation has the form:

Attendance $student $year $grade-level $present $absent $tardy

We use the convention that logic variables begin with a dollar sign. Attendance is defined by assertions such as:

Attendance (Ira M) (81 82) 1 160 20 0
Attendance (Ira M) (82 83) 2 165 15 0
Attendance (Ira M) (83 84) 3 163 17 0
Attendance (Carmen V) (79 80) K 158 22 0
Attendance (Carmen V) (80 81) 1 160 20 0
Attendance (Carmen V) (81 82) 1 164 16 0
Attendance (Carmen V) (82 83) 2 173 7 0

A second structuring device involves the use of text files. Lengthy, prose-text information for each student is contained within text files, and access information for the text relevant to each student is contained within a set of logic assertions; for example, the Parent-Conference relation has the form:

Parent-Conference $text-file $file-lines $student $group $fn

where:

$text-file and $file-lines denote text-file access information
$student denotes the student of reference
$group denotes the grade level for each instance of text
$fn denotes the academic year for each instance of text

and is defined by the assertion:

assert relation:
   Parent-Conference $file $lines $student $group Sfn
if:
   Ftype $file ParConference
   Code $file $lineŝ   $student
   Fgroup $file $group
   Fnumber $file $fn

In this system, we decided to organize parent-conference notes in files labeled
*ParConference*. These files are grouped by grade level and are numbered by
academic year. The portion of each file containing the conference notes for a
particular student is identified by a *Code* assertion.

We also use a third structuring device for relations in which information for
all students is accessed through a combination of LISP functions and logic
assertions, and in which information among relations is represented by a
higher-order relation. For example, we can define the notion of having a
"good" attendance record for a particular year by:

assert relation:
   Good-attendance $student $year
if:
   Attendance $student $year $prs $abs $trd
   < $abs (* 0.05 (+ $prs $abs))

We define *good* to mean absent fewer than 5% of the total number of school
days. The arithmetic is written in LISP style, with expressions of the form
(operator argument argument).

## 2.2. Documenting Simulations of Teacher Decision Making

Applied to this system, then, student-teachers and teacher-educators proceed, and the system documents the analytic processes in a variety of ways:

1. The knowledge base of information about grade-school pupils is stored
   as groups of logic assertions, such as relations. These relations express

specific constructs as well as connections among constructs using symbols (i.e., words and phrases) familiar in the education context.

2. The system generates a knowledge base which records the student-teacher's decisions as relations. Automated queries based on predetermined areas of focus are used to provide the student-teacher with additional information.

3. Queries record the teacher-educator's examination of student-teacher's knowledge bases to gather data or to test decisions around particular foci.

4. Memoranda record: (a) the student-teachers' rationales underlying their decisions, and (b) teacher-educators' thoughts and conclusions during knowledge-base analysis.

5. Chronological information automatically recorded in assertions and memoranda provides traces of the evolution of both students' and educator/researcher's thinking.

## 2.3. Examining Student-Teachers' Knowledge Bases

As student-teachers proceed with the simulation exercises, the system organizes and stores a knowledge base of information about their use of the elementary-pupil data as they make instructional decisions. For example, the system builds a relation, *Chosen*, which indicates the pupil-data choice made by the student-teacher. The assertions below record the facts that a student chose Report Card Grades (RC) and Teacher Comments (TC) in the first (1) session.

```
(DEFINE-PROCEDURE Chosen ()
    ((Chosen) <-)
    ((Chosen RC 1) <-)
    ((Chosen TC 1) <-))
```

This relation, describing one student's choices, can be combined with the same relation for all students participating in the simulation. To illustrate, one teacher-educator chose to represent the combination of all student knowledge-base relations, *Chosen*, as a relation she called *Grouping-Choice-One*. Thus, the *Grouping-Choice-One* relation has the form:

Grouping-Choice-One $student $first-choice $second-choice

where:

$student is student name
$first-choice and $second-choice are types of pupil data chosen

and is defined by logic assertions such as:

Grouping-Choice-One (Stacy S) (teacher comments) (parent conferences)
Grouping-Choice-One (Scott G) teacher comments) (standardized achievement tests)
Grouping-Choice-One (Kathleen K) (report card grades) (teacher comments)
Grouping-Choice-One (Michelle H) (report and grades) (teacher comments)
Grouping-Choice-One (Sarah B) (standardized achievement tests) (teacher comments)
Grouping-Choice-One (Melissa S) (special interests) (standardized achievement tests)
Grouping-Choice-One (Jill G) (report card grades) (teacher comments)
Grouping-Choice-One (Vickie A) (report card grades) (teacher comments)
Grouping-Choice-One (Cindy L) (standardized achievement tests) (special interests)
Grouping-Choice-One (Tara P) (special interests) (standardized achievement tests)
Grouping-Choice-One (Elisa H) (IQ tests and creativity measures) (special interests)
Grouping-Choice-One (Brooke K) (report card grades) (special interests)
Grouping-Choice-One (Robert A) (special interests) (teacher comments)

In a different relation, *Groups* indicates the grouping decisions made by the student-teachers. The assertions below record the facts that a student-teacher decided to group a particular pupil (e.g., Esther) in a particular group (e.g., 1) during session two or three (e.g., 2) of the grouping task.

(DEFINE-PROCEDURE Groups ( )
   ((Groups) < -)
   ((Groups (Esther T) 1 2) < -)
   ((Groups (Jeff M) 1 2) < -)
   ((Groups (June M) 1 2) < -)
   ((Groups (Robin E) 2 2) < -)
   ((Groups (Ruth B) 2 2) < -)
   ((Groups (Jane A) 2 2) < -)
   ((Groups (Bob W) 3 2) < -)
   ((Groups (Jim G) 3 2) < -)
   ((Groups (John M) 3 2) < -)
   ((Groups (Carmen V) 4 2) < -)
   ((Groups (Jose D) 4 2) < -)
   ((Groups (Ira M) 4 2)
   ((Groups (Neil L) 1 2) < -)
   ((Groups (Joe K) 2 2) < -)
   ((Groups (Esther T) 1 3) < -)
   ((Groups (Jeff M) 1 3 < -)
   ((Groups (June M) 1 3 < -)
      ....

The teacher-educator uses mechanized deduction with these knowledge bases to analyze the student-teachers' decisions. The following query by the teacher-educator asked the programs to find the first memo of all student-teachers, dividing them into two groups: (a) those requesting teacher comments as one of their choices for pupil data, and (b) those not requesting teacher comments. The program responded with 13 confirming instances, such as memo information for those students who chose teacher-comment data, and 12 disconfirming instances, such as memo information for those students who did not choose teacher-comment data.

```
hytest
answer template:
    $st $ch1 $ch2 $file $lines
if conditions:
    Grouping-Choice-One $st $ch1 $ch2
    = = $file SPRING86.GM1
    Code $file $lines   $st
then conditions:
    Member (teacher comments) ($ch1 $ch2)
```

13 confirming instances:

1: (Beverly D) (teacher comments) (standardized achievement tests) SPRING86.GM1 (1277 1306)

2: Cheryl G) (IQ tests and creativity measures) (teacher comments) SPRING86.GM1(665 796)

3: (Chris O) (report card grades) (teacher comments) SPRING86.GM1 (1308 1364)

4: (Jill G) (report card grades) (teacher comments) SPRING86.GM1 (266 304)

5: (Kathleen K) (report card grades) (teacher comments) SPRING86.GM1 (75 96)

6: (Michelle H) (report and grades) (teacher comments) SPRING86.GM1 (98 148)

7: (Robert A) (special interests) (teacher comments) SPRING86.GM1 (552 580)

8: (Sarah B) (standardized achievement tests) (teacher comments) SPRING86.GM1 (150 221)

9: (Scott G) (teacher comments) (standardized achievement tests) SPRING86.GM1 (51 73)

10: (Sheri A) (report card grades) (teacher comments) SPRING86.GM1 (634 663)

11: (Stacy S) (teacher comments) (parent conferences) SPRING86.GM1 (1 49)

12: (Theresa S) (teacher comments) (special interests) SPRING86.GM1
(1019 1220)
13: (Vickie A) (report card grades) (teacher comments)
SPRING86.GM1 (306 400)

12 disconfirming instances:

14: (Aimee B) (sociogram information) (special interests)
SPRING86.GM1 (797 879)
15: (Amy A) (IQ tests and creativity measures) (standardized achievement tests) SPRING86.GM1 (938 1017)
16: (Brooke K) (report card grades) (special interests) SPRING86.GM1
(520 550)
17: (Cheryl M) (parent conferences) (special interests) SPRING86.GM1
(881 936)
18: (Cindy L) (standardized achievement tests) (special interests)
SPRING86.GM1 (402 443)
19: (Elisa H) (IQ tests and creativity measures) (special interests)
SPRING86.GM1 (494 518)
20: (Ellen M) (IQ tests and creativity measures) (special interests)
SPRING86.GM1 (1268 1275)
21: (Lisa V) (IQ tests and creativity measures) (report card grades)
SPRING86.GM1 (621 632)
22: (Lori L) (special interests) (standardized achievement tests)
SPRING86.GM1 (582 619)
23: (Mark T) (standardized achievement tests) (health and attendance
records) SPRING86.GM1 (1222 1266)
24: (Melissa S) (special interests) (standardized achievement tests)
SPRING86.GM1 (224 264)
25: (Tara P) (special interests) (standardized achievement tests)
SPRING86.GM1 (445 492)

On the basis of these answers, the teacher-educator called for the memos of
students who requested teacher comments and report card grades. A sample
of those memos follows.

SPRING86.GM1 1308 1364 (Chris O) (report card grades) (teacher comments)
SPRING86.GM1 (1308 1364)
1308 Chris O.
1309 Memo on First Grouping Decision
1310
1311 They were grouped this way because of their grades and
1312 behavior. Superior students, ones with all A's, good
1313 students, ones with a few A's and B's, average students,

1314 ones with a few B's and C's and the fourth group was
1315 the retention students, ones with C's, D's, F's, or
1316 they were recommended for retention.
1317
1318 The four primary grades I selected when looking
1319 over all the students grades were writing, English,
1320 reading and spelling. Behavior, or teacher comments,
1321 also influenced my decision. What past teachers said
1322 about the student, and how the student acted in the
1323 classroom.
1324
1325 Another way I was going to group the students, was
1326 by which student had which teacher. I found that a
1327 number of the students were in the same class(es)
1328 together. But I did not use this in the groupings
1329 because I found it would be difficult. I did find that
1330 Neil and Joe were friends; however, they had not been
1331 in the same classes for a long period of time. Since
1332 they are in my class, I did not group them together,
1333 because they may be disruptive.
1334
1335 The superior students, I found, were not potential
1336 behavior problems, but if some of them were, I
1337 neglected it because of their good grades and
1338 enthusiasm. I also found that these students liked to
1339 read and create books. This would probably benefit both
1340 the class and the group. The only people I would move
1341 based on my findings are: Esther, June, and Neil. The
1342 reason I would move them is because of their behavior
1343 problems.
1344
1345 In the good category, I found that these students
1346 were a bit above average. Their grades and teacher
1347 comments showed that they will do well, or benefit from
1348 this group. The person I would change in this group
1349 is: Ruth. The group I would put her in is the
1350 superior group, but there are too many people in the
1351 group now.
1352
1353 The average group is a small group. These seem to
1354 be the average students in the class. The person I
1355 would move in this group is Jim. The reason for this
1356 is because of his behavior, I would move him to the
1357 retention group.
1358
1359 In the retention group, I found the real behavior
1360 problems. These students have at one time been

1361 recommended for retention. Also their grades are very
1362 bad, and they don't do well in any subject. The person
1363 I would move in this group is John, and I would move
1364 him to the average group because he has potential.

SPRING86.GM1 881 936 (Cheryl M) (parent conferences) (special interests)
SPRING86.GM1 (881 936)
0881 Cheryl M.
0882 Memo on First Grouping Decision
0883
0884
0885 There are two low reading groups in this class.
0886 These two groups are at the same level but since it is
0887 a low reading group I thought that it would be helpful
0888 to have the groups as small as is possible. The low
0889 reading groups include group 1-Bob W., Carmen V., Jane
0890 A., and Jim G. and group 2-Joe K., John M., and Ruth
0891 B. Bob W. has been placed in a low reading group
0892 because in reading about his parent conferences it said
0893 that the teacher agreed to give extra help in reading.
0894 Carmen V. was placed in this same group because in
0895 reading about his parent conferences I read that his
0896 mother agreed to help her at home with her reading even
0897 though she does not have time to spend with her
0898 daughters. Jane A. has been placed in this group
0899 because I read that in her parent conference it was
0900 agreed that she was a slow reader. It also mentioned
0901 that Jane is getting special help with her reading. Jim
0902 G. is in this low level reading group because he has a
0903 hard time staying attentive in school. He also has an
0904 extremely difficult family background and is being
0905 given extra help at home. Joe K. is in this group
0906 because I saw the words-"extra personal help with
0907 reading is needed." John M. is in this group because
0908 he works below grade level in reading and is getting
0909 remedial help in reading. Ruth B. is placed in this
0910 group simply because I have no information that can
0911 prove helpful in placing her in a reading group. Since
0912 it is easier to move a child up than it is down, she
0913 will start in this group. She will be watched
0914 carefully and moved appropriately if needed.
0915
0916 Ira M. is in the middle reading group because he
0917 is known to do well in spelling, sees himself as a
0918 schoolboy and even though he does have problems, they
0919 are being taken care of. Jose D. is being placed in
0920 this group because there is Spanish spoken at home and

0921 there is a new stepmother in the family. I have no
0922 information that she needs to be in a low group but she
0923 shall be watched because there is not much information
0924 on her. June M. is in the middle reading group
0925 because she is reading at her appropriate grade level.
0926 Neil L. is in this group because he has great reading
0927 ability but he sometimes plugs away at books that are
0928 too hard for him and this is of a concern to his
0929 parents. Robin E. has been placed in a middle group
0930 because she does grade level work.
0931
0932 Esther T. is in the high reading group because
0933 she is a gifted and high powered student who has an
0934 interest in writing. Jeff M. is the only other
0935 student that has been placed in the high group. He is
0936 there because he is very intelligent.

## 3. USES OF STUDENT DATA IN INITIAL SYSTEM DEVELOPMENT

Students in a second-year teacher-preparation course at Syracuse University participated in the first task, Grouping for Reading Instruction. In the 1986 spring semester, 20 students completed the simulation using the computer; in the 1987 spring semester, 32 students completed the simulation.

### 3.1. Student Data as Feedback for Simulation Development

Analysis of the 1986 data led to refinements of the grouping simulation in two general areas: (a) computer use, and (b) pupil-data use.

*Computer Use.* Fewer than 10 of the 1986 participants had any previous experience with computers prior to the simulation exercises, and none of the students has any previous experience with the campus mainframe computers. Even with explicit written directions for getting on and off the system, student ability to begin and end sessions without instructor help ranged from fair to hopeless. Session logs and memo source files provided additional evidence that students required extensive guidance in system use. Two students reported their anxiety about computer use in their written memoranda; approximately six students reported their anxiety orally to the simulation instructor.

Less than six of the 1987 participants had any previous experience with computers, and only two had any previous experience with the campus mainframe systems. As a result of the 1986 data and based on the perceived needs of the 1987 participants, the simulation instructor provided additional documentation, guided practice at the terminal prior to the simulation exercises, and visible presence, if not assistance, during all three simulation sessions. Of the 1987 participants reporting anxiety during the first session, more than half expressed relief in "just having the instructor be there." Three of the 1987 participants reported great anxiety about computer use but, with instructor assistance, completed the simulation. In their written memoranda, two other students reported difficulty using the computer, one indicated that the difficulty was overcome by carefully following the documentation and the instructor's advice.

It is clear that students need extensive support in acclimating themselves to computer use. Even students with some word-processing experience need guidance in a different work environment, such as a different set of software and procedures for using it. As a result of these data, we caution that there needs to be a considerable time investment in the initial phase of these simulations. Students must be given substantial support in feeling comfortable about the computing environment in which they are working. The benefit of such support is manifested by increased enjoyment. Approximately one half of all simulation participants reported that the simulations were fun, "once you got the hang of it."

*Pupil-Data Use.* Nine of the 1986 participants reported difficulty understanding the pupil data they received as part of the simulation. Seven of the participants reported difficulty understanding the standardized achievement test data and two reported difficulty understanding the form and content of the IQ and creativity measure data. The following comment from one participant's memo is typical of the 1986 data:

> The problem I had with the achievement tests was that I did not have any idea of what was an average score. I compared the children's scores to each other, but there was a very large range. Some children were getting ones while others were scoring twelves.

Before the second use of the simulation, the research team added explanations of terms such as *sociogram* and of pupil data such as *standardized achievement test scores*. Presuming that the explanations helped clarify student understanding of the test scores, it is interesting to note that there was a shift in the 1987 participant questions about pupil data. Of the six students reporting difficulty understanding the standardized achievement test scores, only two could be characterized as similar to the difficulty reported by the 1986 students. The other four were questions about the context of the tests themselves; for example, how the versions were different, what was actually tested on the subtests. Five students reported that the explanations made the test data clear for them, or that the data seemed straightforward and "easy to interpret." Six students requested information on *interpreting* the test data, such as, how the scores related to other pupil data. The following comment from one participant's memo is typical:

> In looking at the standardized test scores I noticed that some students with good course grades had scored lower than I might expect on the test. Ira and Jane are both students that I would have expected higher scores from. Also I noticed that some students scored highly in one area on the first test taken and went down in that same area on the second test taken.

As the research team seeks to use the student data for evaluation and research purposes, it seems clear that: (a) students' abilities to understand the pupil data precede their abilities to interpret and to use the data, and (b) students need guidance in both areas and in that sequence.

### 3.2. Student Data as Indicators of Potential Research Issues

The student-teacher data show patterns which have potential for contributing useful information to the area of expert vs. novice teacher thinking.

*Interpreting pupil data.* In their memos, simulation participants generally contributed to one or more of the following patterns:

1. Former teachers' perceptions about pupils are more accurate than objective test scores.
2. Pupil social development is more important than academic achievement, even in the context of instruction in basic skills such as reading.
3. Individual types of pupil data are more reliable sources of information than an integration of several types of pupil data.

Berliner and Carter (1986) have identified all of these patterns as characteristics that differentiate expert and novice teachers. It appears that, in the context of these simulations, such as, use of pupil data to make instructional decisions, students do raise issues related to reliability and integration of pupil data. Thus, the grouping simulation has potential for providing data on novice teachers' perceptions on these issues.

*Thinking like a teacher.* Of the 1986 participants, 11 stated that their decision-making processes differed from the research-based feedback process, seven reported that their processes were the same, and two did not commit themselves. Most participants perceived their choices of pupil data as the operational definition of the decision-making process. Thus, their perceptions of employing the same processes rested almost solely on whether or not they chose the data reported as important in the feedback.

One other pattern of interest appeared in the 1986 data. More than half of the participants indicated a change in their thinking as result of reading the feedback. In addition, these participants reported that the feedback provided them with new ways of thinking about the uses of pupil data. If given the opportunity, they would have reconsidered their groupings a third time. The group who said they did not change their decisions voiced strong opposition to the use of objective pupil data such as test scores. These participants tended to be the ones who also had social development as the primary objective of their instructional groupings.

These patterns, related to the process of thinking like a teacher, provide a basis for structuring in-depth analyses of these and future data. One working hypothesis currently under investigation is that novice teachers progress through stages of learning to think like a teacher. The process begins with an early stage of understanding pupil data, moves to a stage of exploring how one type of data relates to any other type, and progresses to a stage of applying inferences about pupil data to instructional activities.

Morine-Dershimer (1986) suggests that there is much work to be done to explicate the process of moving from novice-teacher to expert-teacher thinking. These simulations appear to offer a context in which novices, reacting to research-based feedback, provide information that characterizes their current patterns of thought and that describes conditions which cause them to think differently. Although the research team is focused currently on applying student data as a feedback device for simulation development, our long-term research goal is to contribute information about the characteristics and development of novice-teacher thinking.

## REFERENCES

Berliner, D.C. (1985). Laboratory settings and the study of teacher education. *Journal of Teacher Education*, 36, 2-8.

Berliner, D.C., & Carter, K.J. (1986). *Differences in processing classroom information by expert and novice teachers.* Paper presented at the meeting of the International Study Association on Teacher Thinking, Leuve, Belgium.

Doak, E.D.,& Keith, M. (1986). Simulation in teacher education: The knowledge base and the process. *Tennessee Education*, 16(2),14-17.

Kowalski, R.A. (1974). Predicate logic as programming language. In *Proceedings IFIP 74* (pp. 569-574). Amsterdam, Netherlands: North-Holland.

Kowalski, R.A. (1979). *Logic for problem solving.* Amsterdam, Netherlands: North-Holland.

McCarthy, J. (1960). Recursive functions of symbolic expressions and their computation by machine, part I. *Communications of the Association for Computing Machinery, 3,* 184-195.

McCarthy, J., Abrahams, P.W., Edwards, D.J., Hart, T.P., & Levin, M.I. (1965). *LISP 1.5 programmer's manual* (2nd ed.). Cambridge, MA: M.I.T Press.

Morine-Dershimer, G. (1986). *Creating a "recycling center" for teacher thinking.* Paper presented at the Invitational Symposium on Simulation in Teacher Education, Knoxville, TN.

Morine-Dershimer,G., Harootunian, B., Shelly, A., & Sibert, E. (1985). *Simulation on teacher decision making* [Computer program]. Syracuse, NY: Syracuse University, School of Education and School of Computer and Information Science.

Pereira, L.M., Pereira, F., & Warren, D.H.D. (1978). *User's guide to DEC-system10 PROLOG* (D.A.I. Research Paper No.154). Edinburgh, Scotland: Department of Artificial Intelligence, University of Edinburgh.

Robinson, J.A. (1965). A machine-oriented logic based on the resolution principle. *Journal of the Association for Computing Machinery, 12,* 23-41.

Robinson, J.A., & Sibert, E.E. (1982). LOGLISP: Motivation, design and implementation. In K.L. Clark & S.-A. Tarnlund (Eds.), *Logic programming* (pp. 299-313). New York: Academic Press.

Robinson, J.A., & Sibert, E.E. (1984). *The LOGLISP programming system* (LPRC Tech. Rep.). Syracuse, NY: Syracuse University, Logic Programming Research Center.

Roussel, P. (1975). *PROLOG: manuel de référence et d'utilisation.* Marseille France: Groupe d'Intelligence Artificielle, U.E.R. de Luminy, Université d'Aix-Marseille II.

# 17

## COMPUTER SIMULATION AS A TOOL IN STUDYING TEACHERS' COGNITIVE ACTIVITIES DURING ERROR DIAGNOSIS IN ARITHMETIC

ERIK DE CORTE, LIEVEN VERSCHAFFEL, AND HILDE
SCHROOTEN

## 1. INTRODUCTION

Research on teaching undertaken over the past decades has mainly focused on subject-matter independent teaching behaviors and skills, such as management of classrooms, the cognitive level of questions, allocation of time, and so on. This is certainly true for the vast amount of process-product studies (see, e.g., Brophy & Good, 1986; Gage, 1985; Rosenshine & Furst, 1973), but it also holds for the more recent strand of research on teacher thinking (see Clark & Peterson, 1986; Shavelson & Stern, 1981). In this respect Shulman (1986b) has rightly remarked that questions about the *content* of teaching are lacking in the available research. Commenting more specifically on the work on teacher thinking the same author (Shulman, 1986a) writes:

> Where the teacher cognition program has clearly fallen short is the elucidation of teachers' cognitive understanding of subject matter content and the relationship between such understanding and the instruction teachers provide for students. (p. 25)

The obvious lack of attention in the study of teaching for the content of what is taught is the more remarkable, because in research on children's learning and problem solving the focus has already (since the late 1970s) shifted towards subject-matter areas and the role of domain-specific knowledge in performance and in the acquisition of cognitive skills (see, e.g., Resnick, 1983). In between, several researchers (e.g., Berliner, 1986; Leinhardt & Smith, 1985; Putnam, 1987; Shulman, 1986b) have started work aiming at an analysis of teachers' actions and cognitions in relation to the content being taught. For example, using extensive protocols, Leinhardt and Smith (1985) explored the content and organization of expert teachers' knowledge of fractions. Putnam (1987) studied how teachers structured subject-matter content while tutoring individual students in adding whole numbers. The present study is related to Putnam's investigation and aims at analyzing teachers' cognitive activities while diagnosing systematic errors in the algorithms of addition and subtraction in a simulated environment.

Research has obviously shown that children's errors on arithmetic problems are mostly the result of very systematic but wrong procedures (see, e.g., Brown & Burton, 1978; De Corte & Verschaffel, 1985; Resnick, 1982). At the same time it has frequently been argued that effective instruction and remediation in mathematics requires that teachers have substantial knowledge and understanding of those incorrect procedures. Being able to diagnose them seems therefore a very important teaching skill. However, in spite of the attention for those incorrect arithmetic procedures in recent research, and the frequent claims for the importance of skill in diagnosing them, the way in which teachers determine what students know and how they operate internally has not yet been systematically explored. Consequently, we are also ignorant of how teachers use such knowledge to adjust the content of their instruction to the needs of children. Finally, we know very little about how to teach effectively the skill of diagnosing errors.

## 2. THEORETICAL BACKGROUND

The present state of the art of cognitive instructional psychology and of educational computing research provide us with the necessary tools for developing computer programs that simulate systematic errors on arithmetic tasks. The starting point of the present study was our assumption that administering such an error-simulating program offers an interesting environment for studying student-teachers' cognitive processes during diagnosis. Moreover, we hypothesized that such a simulation program can be useful and efficient for training student-teachers in the skill of diagnosing errors in the algorithms of addition and subtraction.

The basis of the computer simulation program used in this study is twofold. First, there is the work of Brown, Burton, and VanLehn on procedural bugs in basic arithmetic skills (Brown & Burton, 1978; Brown & VanLehn, 1980, 1982; Burton, 1982). The term *bugs* refers to erroneous but systematic procedures that are often a variant of a correct one. An example of a common subtraction bug is called *smaller-from-larger*: Instead of borrowing in a column where it is necessary, the pupil subtracts the top digit, which is smaller, from the bottom one, which is larger. Using computer simulation Brown, Burton, and VanLehn have constructed an extensive catalogue of bugs; furthermore, they have developed a generative theory of those procedural bugs, called the *repair theory*. Starting from the catalogue of bugs of those investigators, computer programs can be written in which a sample of errors is represented for diagnostic purposes, that is, the user of such a program has to discover the simulated bugs.

Second, a rather global process model of competent diagnosing of errors was used as a frame of reference in developing the computer program. The model involves two main phases, namely, a hypothesis-generating and a hypothesis-testing phase. In the first stage the user of the program tries to generate a plausible assumption concerning the erroneous procedure underlying a given error. In the second phase the hypothesis is verified by predicting the wrong responses that would be obtained on a series of problems if the buggy procedure was applied.

## 3. DESCRIPTION OF THE COMPUTER PROGRAM

The computer program used in the present study is based on VanLehn's "Buggy Game." It is written in Basic, runs on an Apple IIe or IIc computer, and simulates 15 frequently occurring, incorrect procedures in addition and subtraction. A description of the program in the form of a flow chart is given in Figure 17.1.

## 4. METHOD

The computer program has been administered individually to 10 student-teachers during the last semester of their training. Each student worked about 2 hours on the computer. To allow a detailed qualitative analysis of their diagnostic processes, all the students' reactions typed on the screen were registered by a videorecorder connected directly to the monitor.

One day after all 10 students had finished the computer simulation program, a collective paper-and-pencil test was administered to this experimental as well as to a control group; the experimental and the control groups were matched on the basis of a rating of their overall capacity by the teacher who was mainly responsible for their training. The test was especially designed to assess student-teachers' diagnostic skill of arithmetic bugs, and consisted of nine items representing nine bugs: two of these errors were also represented in the computer program (no transfer), four related to addition

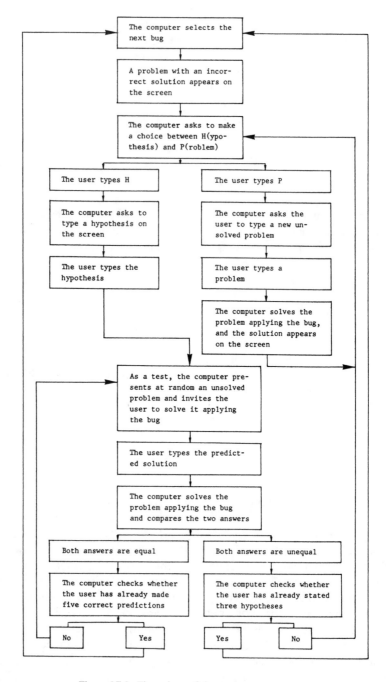

The computer selects the next bug

A problem with an incorrect solution appears on the screen

The computer asks to make a choice between H(ypothesis) and P(roblem)

The user types H

The computer asks to type a hypothesis on the screen

The user types the hypothesis

The user types P

The computer asks the user to type a new unsolved problem

The user types a problem

The computer solves the problem applying the bug, and the solution appears on the screen

As a test, the computer presents at random an unsolved problem and invites the user to solve it applying the bug

The user types the predicted solution

The computer solves the problem applying the bug and compares the two answers

Both answers are equal

The computer checks whether the user has already made five correct predictions

No        Yes

Both answers are unequal

The computer checks whether the user has already stated three hypotheses

Yes        No

Figure 17.1. Flow chart of the computer program.

and subtraction bugs not trained in the program (near transfer), and three others were multiplication and division errors (far transfer). Each item presented the subjects with five incorrectly solved problems, and they were asked first to define their hypothesis concerning the underlying bug, and then to predict the answers on three unsolved problems that would be obtained as a result of applying this bug.

The following procedure was used to score the test. The statements of the hypotheses and the predictions of the answers on the unsolved problems were treated separately. The hypotheses were scored as correct (2 points), incomplete (1), or incorrect (0). The intersubjective agreement between two independent judges who scored all the statements of hypotheses ($n = 150$) was $r = .94$. For the predictions of the answers on the unsolved problems a severe criterion was applied: 1 point was given if the three predictions were correct: the score was 0 in all other cases.

In line with the general hypothesis stated before, we expected that the average score on the posttest for the statements of hypotheses, as well as for the predictions of the answers on unsolved problems, would be significantly better in the experimental group than in the control group.

## 5. PROCESS RESULTS

We collected all the reactions of the student-teachers (their typed input) using a videorecorder connected to the monitor. An analysis of these qualitative data revealed several aspects of the cognitive activities of the subjects during diagnosis. We will briefly report some results relating to the following aspects: (a) hypothesis-generating in the beginning of the diagnostic process, (b) the quality of the hypotheses and their relationship with the results on the prediction tests, and (c) reactions after a hypothesis was rejected.

In view of the presentation of the findings it is useful to mention that no one subject reached the end of the computer program, which contained 15 bugs in all. Most student-teachers did not go beyond the tenth bug, and only two reached the eleventh. Furthermore, the student-teachers were given, at the maximum, three opportunities to state a hypothesis with respect to each bug (see Figure 17.1). In all, 137 hypotheses were formulated: They were distributed as follows over the three consecutive opportunities: 95, 31, and 11.

After a hypothesis was stated, a prediction test was given: The computer presented at random a series of five problem, (maximum), asking the user to predict the answers applying the assumed bug. The hypotheses statements were scored in the same way as on the posttest. For the prediction tests the procedure was also similar: 1 point if the five predictions were correct; 0 in all other cases.

## 5.1. Hypothesis-generating in the Beginning of the Diagnostic Process

The flow chart of the computer program shows that with respect to each bug, the subjects were first given a problem with an incorrect solution, followed by the question to either state a hypothesis (H), or to type a new problem (P). A careful hypothesis-testing phase would be characterized by typing some additional problems and trying to collect more information concerning the bug before stating a hypothesis. The results show that the choice between H and P was student- as well as bug-dependent.

First, there was an obvious trend towards more careful hypothesis-testing as one progressed through the program. However, this effect is difficult to interpret because of the confounding of the difficulty level of the bugs with a possible learning effect. Indeed, the sequence of the bugs was based on their difficulty level starting with the easy ones.

Second, as shown in Table 17.1, the student-teachers consistently seemed to use one of two approaches, namely, either typing a hypothesis immediately after the presentation of the incorrectly solved problem (six out of ten subjects), or typing one or more additional problems to collect more detailed information on the underlying error (four subjects).

The finding that the choice between H and P in the beginning of the diagnostic process was student- as well as bug-dependent also explains why there was not a strong relationship—as one might expect—between the P-choice, indicating that a subject looks for more detailed information on the bug, on the one hand, and the quality of the subsequent hypotheses statements and scores on the prediction tests, on the other. Indeed, the average performance on those two measures following an H-choice was only slightly but not significantly lower.

Table 17.1. Reactions of the Subjects after Presentation of the Problem with an Incorrect Solution.

| Reactions | Subjects | | | | | | | | | |
|---|---|---|---|---|---|---|---|---|---|---|
| | 1 | 2 | 3 | 4 | 5 | 6 | 7 | 8 | 9 | 10 |
| H | 8 | 2 | 10 | 0 | 9 | 5 | 1 | 7 | 3 | 10 |
| P | 2 | 8 | 1 | 10 | 0 | 2 | 9 | 2 | 8 | 0 |

## 5.2. Quality of the Hypotheses and Results on the Prediction Tests

The results concerning the quality of the hypotheses statements and on the prediction tests are summarized in Table 17.2, in which the relationship between both measures is also shown.

**Table 17.2.    Relationship between the Quality of the Hypotheses Statements and the Results on the Prediction Tests.**

| Scores on the prediction tests | Scores for the hypotheses statements | | | Total |
|---|---|---|---|---|
| | 2 | 1 | 0 | |
| 1 | 38 | 24 | 18 | 86 |
| 0 | 4 | 5 | 48 | 57 |
| Total | 42 | 29 | 66 | 137 |

Table 17.2 reveals that only 30% of the hypotheses statements were scored as correct, while almost 50% were definitely incorrect. On the other hand more than 60% of the prediction tests were solved entirely correctly. This shows that, in a number of cases, the subjects made five correct predictions with respect to a bug, although their hypothesis statement concerning the underlying error was wrong, or, at least, incomplete. The point-biserial correlation between both measures was $r_{pbi} = .57$. Assuming that the two measures tap subjects' understanding of the corresponding bug, one would expect a higher correlation. However, several factors had a depressing impact on that correlation.

1. The student-teacher understood the bug, but the hypothesis was stated wrongly or too specifically. This happened frequently when a subject formulated a hypothesis based only on the initial problem with an incorrect solution.
2. The student-teacher stated a correct hypothesis, but made a typing or counting error in the prediction test, which was not discovered afterwards.
3. The student-teacher had initially typed an incorrect hypothesis, but adapted it mentally during the prediction test.
4. The student-teacher succeeded by chance in the prediction test.

## 5.3. Reactions after a Hypothesis was Rejected

When a subject did not succeed in the first prediction test with respect to a bug, the corresponding hypothesis was rejected, and the subject could make a second attempt (31 out of 95 cases), and possibly a third (11 out of 31 cases). The subjects' reactions, following the rejection of a hypothesis, were of two kinds: rigid perseverance and flexible revision.

In the case of rigid perseverance the student-teacher stuck to his first hypothesis, ignoring counter evidence. Consequently, the subject generated new problems—mostly only one—that confirmed the initial hypothesis, and ended with typing it in again. This led to a new failure on the prediction test. Flexible revision, on the other hand, started with accepting that the hypothesis was wrong, and continued with an attempt to change, adapt, refine, or generalize it.

## 6. POSTTEST RESULTS

Table 17.3 shows that the experimental group obtained a better average result on both posttest scores. A $t$-test revealed that, in each case, the difference was significant: $t(18) = 2.12, p < .05$ for the statement of hypotheses, and $t(18) = 2.43, p < .05$ for the predictions of answers. These findings confirm the hypothesis concerning the favorable effect of the computer program on student-teachers' diagnostic skills. However, this effect seemed to be rather specific. Indeed, a further analysis of the data showed that the experimental group outperformed the control group significantly only on the items relating to bugs trained in the computer program. On the near and the far transfer items, the results were in the expected direction, but were not significant.

The specificity of the learning effect can probably be accounted for by the short duration of the training, in which, moreover, only a restricted set of bugs was presented to the subjects.

Table 17.3. Posttest Results of the Experimental and the Control Groups with Respect to the Statements of Hypotheses and the Predictions of Answers.

| Group | Statements of hypotheses (max. score = 18) | | Predictions (max. score = 9) | |
|---|---|---|---|---|
| | M | SD | M | SD |
| Experimental | 11.6 | 2.5 | 6.2 | .9 |
| Control | 9.4 | 1.8 | 5.1 | 1.0 |

## 7. DISCUSSION

A first goal of the present study was to explore the usefulness of the adapted version of the "Buggy Game" as a simulation tool for studying teachers' thinking and decision-making processes while trying to understand children's errors in arithmetic. The investigation has yielded positive results in this respect. By providing a task environment involving some important features of a natural setting, but at the same time permitting careful control and automated recording of the subjects' reactions, the "Buggy Game" constitutes a valuable context for research.

However, the diagnostic computer environment alone does not provide us with full insight into the cognitive structures and thinking processes underlying (student-) teachers' performance. The program informs us about the kinds of problems administered to the child by the (student-) teacher, his or her hypothesis concerning the child's underlying bug, his or her predictions about the child's answer on a series of unsolved problems, etc. But the data collected do not allow us to answer questions such as: Why did the (student-) teacher choose these problems during the hypothesis-generating stage? Why did it take so long before he or she was able to state a hypotheses concerning the bug? Why was there a discrepancy between his or her hypotheses and predictions on the test problems?

To answer this kind of question, we need to increase the richness of the data by making some extensions and alterations to the present program. For example, the (student-) teacher could be given an opportunity to restate his (or her) hypothesis about the underlying bug after the prediction test and before moving toward another bug. A better generator of the test problems can be developed, etc. But undoubtedly the most straightforward way of improving the richness of the empirical data lies in the collection of think-aloud or retrospective protocols of subjects working through the program.

In summary, it seems to us that the combined application of self-reporting techniques, and the registration of teachers' reactions while using the computer program, can lead to a more comprehensive picture of the cognitive processes underlying diagnostic activities.

A second purpose of this investigation was to explore the program's usefulness as a device for teacher training. Two kinds of data represent positive indications in this respect: The program's face validity as evidenced by the enthusiastic reactions of teacher trainers during previous presentations of the "Buggy Game," and the positive empirical evidence found in the present study. However, there remain some critical remarks relating to the value of the program for training the skill of diagnosing errors in algorithms. Two major criticisms are, respectively, based on Putnam's (1987) study of teacher thoughts and actions in live and simulated tutoring of the addition algorithms, and Resnick's (1982) distinction between the syntax and the semantics of arithmetic operations.

Recently, Putnam (1987) explored the thoughts and actions of experienced elementary teachers and nonteachers (mathematics students and prospective elementary teachers) as they tutored individual children in whole number addition, both in a live and a simulated situation. The major goal of the study was to discover the goals and strategies teachers use to infer the state of student knowledge and to adjust their instruction on this basis. More specifically, Putnam (1987) wanted to test the popular idea, in educational and research circles, that a detailed model of a student's knowledge, including his or her misconceptions and faulty procedures, is a prerequisite to successful remediation. This viewpoint underlies also the diagnostic computer environment used in our investigation (see also Sleeman et al., this volume).

Putnam (1987) showed that there is little empirical evidence for this so-called diagnostic-remedial model. Indeed, one of his major findings is that the experienced teachers did not try to construct highly detailed models of the child's wrong procedures before attempting remedial instruction. In other words, they rarely had the subgoal of determining the exact nature of a student's errors. Indeed, only 7% of children's errors and deficient responses were followed by presenting more problems and allowing the pupils to continue working incorrectly in order to reveal more about their wrong procedures or knowledge. On the other hand, in most cases the teachers appeared to move through a predetermined set of skills and concepts that they expected the child to know. This predetermined set of skills and concepts, along with problems, activities, and strategies for teaching the material, is called the *curriculum script* and constitutes a teacher's pedagogical knowledge about addition.

To summarize, Putnam's (1987) study suggests that the diagnostic-remedial model underlying the "Buggy Game" does not correspond to an expert elementary arithmetic teacher's approach to errors and their remediation. However, one first could criticize the way in which teaching expertise was operationalized in this investigation—having at least 10 years of teaching experience at the elementary level was the only criterion. Second, even when a descriptive study with "real" expert teachers would reveal that they operate according to the curriculum-script rather than the diagnostic-remedial model, this would not immediately justify the conclusion that teaching diagnostic skills is inappropriate at any stage during inservice or preservice teacher training. For example, the diagnostic computer environment can probably be very useful in making (student)-teachers aware of the systematicity in a lot of the learners' errors. Moreover, the question can be raised whether remedial teaching would not be more effective if based on the diagnostic-remedial model instead of the curriculum-script approach.

The second major criticism of the "Buggy Game" relates to the restricted scope of its diagnostic process. In this respect Resnick's (1982) distinction between the syntax and the semantics of arithmetic operations is relevant.

According to Resnick, written addition and subtraction "can be analyzed as an algorithm defined by a set of *syntactic* rules that prescribe how problems should be written, an order in which certain operations should be performed, and which kinds of symbols belong in which positions" (Resnick, 1982, p. 137). On the other hand, there is the conceptual or *semantic* basis on which these rules and procedures are based, such as the ten base system and positional notation.

In line with the preceding distinction, instructional interventions can focus either at the syntactic (or algorithmic) or at the semantic (or conceptual) level (Resnick, 1982; see also Putnam, 1987). An algorithmic intervention is an attempt to describe or demonstrate the procedures of addition and subtraction without explaining explicitly the reasons for the various steps, or without linking these procedures to the underlying conceptual knowledge. A conceptual intervention, on the other hand, aims at helping children to understand the arithmetic procedures by linking them to mathematical concepts, for example, through the use of concrete materials.

In terms of this distinction, the "Buggy Game" can be described as a simulation program that is almost exclusively focused on the algorithmic aspects of the arithmetic procedure. Indeed, there is little or no attempt to deal with the concepts on which they are based: the insight in the nature of the child's errors necessary to predict his or her answers on the test problems, is restricted to the superficial, syntactic level of operating. However, recent research on elementary mathematics learning and teaching has shown convincingly that appropriate instructional interventions involve providing appropriate links between the semantics and the syntax of the written algorithms (Resnick, 1982).

The preceding remarks do not imply that using the "Buggy Game" in teacher training is useless or even harmful. Nevertheless they show that the present diagnostic computer environment represents a restricted approach to the remediation of errors. Therefore it should be complemented by the development of diagnostic and remedial teaching skills focusing on the concepts underlying the algorithmic procedures, and at the multiple links between the syntactic and the semantic knowledge base.

## REFERENCES

Berliner, D.C. (1986). In pursuit of the expert pedagogue. *Educational Researcher, 15* (7), 5-13.
Brophy, J., & Good, Th. L. (1986). Teacher behavior and student achievement. In M.C. Wittrock (Ed.), *Handbook of research on teaching* (3rd ed., pp 328-375). New York: Macmillan.
Brown, J.S., & Burton, R. B. (1978). Diagnostic models for procedural bugs in basic mathematical skills. *Cognitive Science, 2,* 155-192.
Brown, J.S., & Vanlehn, K. (1980). Repair theory: A generative theory of bugs in procedural skills. *Cognitive Science, 4,* 379-426.
Brown, J.S., & Vanlehn, K. (1982). Towards a generative theory of "bugs." In T.P. Carpenter, J.M. Moser, & T. Romberg (Eds.), *Addition and subtraction: A cognitive perspective* (pp. 117-135). Hillsdale, NJ: Erlbaum.
Burton, R.B. (1982). Diagnosing bugs in a simple procedural skill. In D. Sleeman & J.S. Brown (Eds.), *Intelligent tutoring systems* (pp. 157-183). London: Academic Press.
Clark, C.M., & Peterson, P.L. (1986). Teachers' thought processes. In M.C. Wittrock (Ed.), *Handbook of research on teaching* (3rd ed., pp. 255-296). New York: Macmillan.
De Corte, E., & Verschaffel, L. (1985). Beginning first graders, initial representation of arithmetic word problems. *Journal of Mathematical Behavior, 4,* 3-21.

Gage, N.L. (1985). *Hard graines in the soft sciences. The case of pedagogy*. Bloomington, IN: Phi Delta Kappa

Leinhardt, G., & Smith, D.A. (1985). Expertise in mathematics instruction: Subject matter knowledge. *Journal of Educational Psychology, 77,* 247-291.

Putnam, R. T. (1987). Structuring and adjusting content for students: A study of live and simulated tutoring of addition.*American Educational Research Journal, 24,* 13-48.

Resnick, L.B. (1982). Syntax and semantics in learning to subtract. In T.P. Carpenter, J.M. Moser, & T.A. Romberg (Eds.), *Addition and subtraction: A cognitive perspective* (pp. 136-155). Hillsdale, NJ: Erlbaum.

Resnick, L. B. (1983). Toward a cognitive theory of instruction. In S.G. Paris, G.M. Olson, & H.W. Stevenson (Eds.), *Learning and motivation in the classroom* (pp. 5-38). Hillsdale, NJ: Erlbaum.

Rosenshine, B., & Furst, N. (1973). The use of direct observation to study teaching. In R.M.W. Travers (Ed.), *Second handbook of research on teaching* (pp. 122-183). Chicago, IL: Rand McNally.

Shavelson, R.J., & Stern, P. (1981). Research on teachers, pedagogical thoughts, judgements, decisions, and behavior. *Review of Educational Research, 51,* 455-498.

Shulman, L.S. (1986a). Paradigms and research programs in the study of teaching. A contemporary perspective. In M.C. Wittrock (Ed.), *Handbook of research on teaching* (3rd ed., pp. 3-36). New York: Macmillan.

Shulman, L.S. (1986b). Those who understand: Knowledge growth in teaching. *Educational Researcher, 15* (2), 4-14.

# 18

## INTELLIGENT ENVIRONMENTS FOR CURRICULUM AND COURSE DEVELOPMENT*

MARLENE JONES AND KEVIN WIPOND

## 1. INTRODUCTION

### 1.1. Motivation for the Project

Recent years have seen a growing concern regarding the effectiveness and efficiency of the education system. One consequence has been the advocacy of individually paced instruction in conjunction with detailed monitoring of student's progress. This has lead to an incresed emphasis on *competency-based* education or *mastery learning*, in which a student's progress through the curricula is monitored in terms of the specified objectives. Because competency-based education advocates self-paced learning, there has been a corresponding increased appeal for *sophisticated* computer-managed learning systems and computer-based curricula including explicitly stated expected performance outcomes by which a student's achievements can be measured.

Any curriculum, regardless of the delivery medium (classroom or computer) should be pedagogically sound. Certain knowledge and skills are expected of a course developer, yet it is not uncommon for instructors to be

---

*The authors would like to acknowledge the contributions of team members Julia Driver, Doug Konkin, Chris Stang, Rick Steele, Alec Stephen, and Dave Stephen, without whom the project described herein would not be taking place. We would also like to thank Julia Driver and Linda Graham for comments on an earlier draft of this chapter.

reponsible for much of the curriculum development. Unfortunately, instructors may have litttle background in the areas of curriculum development and instructional design.

The "Expert" computer-managed learning (CML) project was launched in 1987 by Computer-Based Training Systems Ltd., in conjunction with the Alberta Research Council, with the goal of addressing some of the aforementioned needs of the education community. The system's purposes include assisting developers in producing online curricula and courses, and monitoring individual student's progress according to the learning objectives specified within the curricula. The four main system components, termed *phases*, are as follows:

phase 1 - an environment for curriculum development

phase 2 - an environment for course development from curricula

phase 3 - a component that guides, monitors, and evaluates students as they progress through the courses.

phase 4 - a component which assists the developer with the evaluation of both courses and curricula based on student performance.

It is the first two components, phase 1 and 2, with which we are concerned here. Within the environment for curriculum development (phase 1) users can build up representations that include all curriculum content from the broad goals of a program of study through to the specifics of particular lessons or modules. Within the environment for course development (phase 2), a user can adapt a curriculum representation to meet particular requirements, specifying such things as the preferred order of the material, dates for exams, mastery requirements, and so on. Within both of these components, the user can also develop assessment blueprints (e.g., for exams or assignments). Furthermore, we have captured expert knowledge about the processes of curriculum and course development, and within both components this "expertise" is used to guide and advise the user during the process of development. The system has been designed to be suitable for use by experienced curriculum developers or instructional designers, as well as by instructors with little or no background in these areas, including student teachers.

In the context of the "Expert" CML system, phases 1 and 2 allow the users to build up a rich online representation of one or more courses. In phase 3, students are enrolled in the courses and are guided online by the system through the course material. In phase 4, the tracking of student performance allows the system to suggest how the curricula and courses might be enhanced or changed to facilitate the learning process.

## 1.2. Related Work

Two related projects worthy of note are IDE (Instructional Design Environment) under development at Xerox PARC (Russel, Moran, & Jordan 1988) and ISD (Instructional System Design) Expert (Merrill, 1987a; Merrill & Li, 1988). IDE is an interactive system in which instructional designers can record course content decisions. ISD Expert is an expert system which provides expertise regarding instructional design decisions. Although all three projects share some common goals, the resulting systems are quite diverse and are aimed at slightly different target audiences.

IDE is intended for use by knowledgeable instructional designers, as the system currently does little in the way of automatic structure checking. On the other hand, Merrill's ISD Expert is intended for use by instructional designers with minimal training. Similarly, "Expert" CML can be employed by instructors who have little expertise in the areas of curriculum development and instructional design.

The output of the three systems also differs. IDE is a framework within which the user can record and rationalize decisions regarding the developing curriculum. Similarly, the output of ISD Expert is a set of specifications upon which implementation can then be based. Our system, although similar to Merrill's in terms of target audience and general goals, differs significantly in this regard. "Expert" CML provides assistance in the actual development of online curricula and courses. The user, as part of the curriculum development process (phase 1), specifies curricular content including learning activities and evaluation items; the learner later interacts directly with the system to dertermine which activities or assessments he or she should undertake. It should be noted, however, that Merrill is developing a simple authoring tool that takes the specifications produced by ISD Expert and develops a corresponding lesson (Merrill, 1988). As yet, the domain of operation is extremely limited; the system can generate only one type of lesson, with corresponding restrictions on screen layout and menus.

A final distinction that should be noted concerns the expertise incorporated into ISD Expert and "Expert" CML. The former is based on Merrill's component display theory (Merrill, 1983) an approach to instructional design which requires substantial knowledge of the content material. One criticism of the initial prototype, as described by Merrill (1987a), is the extent of the proposed dialogues by which the expert system would elicit the necessary knowledge from the developer. It is important to note, however, that both component display theory and ISD Expert are still evolving (Merrill, 1987b, 1988) in an attempt to address this and other concerns. Unlike ISD Expert, which adheres to one particular theory, "Expert" CML is based upon knowledge elicited from several domain experts and practitioners. This is discussed further in the next section.

## 1.3. An Expert Systems Approach

"Expert" CML can accurately be classified as an *expert* or *knowledge-based* system, as it captures a variety of expertise concerning curriculum and course development. Both the development of the system and its structure are representative of traditional expert system development. However, by expert system standards, it is a large and complex project. Standard artificial intelligence (AI) representation techniques, such as *rules* and *frames*, are employed to capture the expertise and provide a rich representation framework for curricula and courses. As is typical of expert systems, the expertise or *domain knowledge* is separate from the tools, interface and other parts of the system. System development can be broadly broken into the following stages: knowledge acquisition, conceptual design, prototype development, and implementation.

The knowledge acquisition stage concentrated on the elicitation of principles of "good" curriculum and course development. This task was complicated by several factors. The domain of curriculum development is large and the area abounds with pseudo-experts. Furthermore, many different models of curriculum development have been proposed over the years, yet in practice none is adhered to.

Several educational institutions are participating in the project. They have provided input into desired functionality and expertise in the areas of curriculum development and instructional design. The experts from these sites are all practitioners with many years of experience. In addition, experts were drawn from nonparticipating sites; these experts were all university-based researchers/practitioners. In selecting the participating experts, several factors were considered: the expert's area of expertise and extent of knowledge, communication skills, and enthusiasm for the project.

Although the experts espoused particular philosophies, none adhered to a single theoretical model when developing curricula. So, rather than selecting one particular theory, we tried to determine common principles of "good" curriculum development and instructional design, such as, the common thread among the different philosophies recommended by our various experts. Although the experts did not agree with each other on all points, the amount of agreement was surprisingly high. When apparently conflicting information was elicited, follow-up sessions concentrated on determining the precise situations in which the suggested technique or guideline was to be applied. If this failed to resolve the conflict, the experts were asked to critique the alternative approach. This was typically supplemented by an examination of the research literature, as well as an assessment of the experts' relative expertise regarding the specifics concerned

Because our experts included several well-established practitioners, we were able to elicit information regarding the practicality of various approaches. There is little point in recommending a particular approach or philosophy if it is not going to be used by instructors due to lack of knowledge, unavailability of requested information, or the lack of time to provide the system with the requested information. We also had to take computational restrictions into account; the implementation and performance of the system were important considerations.

During this stage of the project, certain knowledge acquisition techniques were found to be more effective than others. Although structured interviews proved to be an effective technique for eliciting a variety of knowledge, the approach was most efficient for establishing an overall perspective and broad categories of expertise. When developing a more refined picture of the expertise, structured interviews were supplemented with actual sample cases, that is, working though a portion of the developmental process with actual curricula. Occasionally, protocol analysis was also employed but was found to be an inefficient use of time. Cross-checking with research literature proved invaluable and hence was used extensively.

This knowledge acquisition process was carried out in several steps and was interwoven with both the design and prototyping operations. After establishing the initial specifications, a corresponding design was developed. As preliminary prototyping got underway based upon the initial design, the knowledge regarding curriculum development was refined further, including an in-depth examination of expertise and corresponding knowledge structures. The design was then refined accordingly. The interweaving of the knowledge acquisition, the conceptual design, and the prototyping processes proved to be a wise decision. The consequence has been an efficient process of iterative refinement in the development of the system.

The development of the prototype system was carried out with the aid of ART (automated reasoning tool), a high-powered Lisp-based expert system development tool running on a Lisp workstation. This approach facilitated rapid development of a prototype system. After testing of the completed prototype and some redesign, a delivery version of the system was begun. It is written in C and targeted for the VAX family of computers.

## 1.4. Curriculum Development, Course, and Assessment Design

In the remainder of this chapter we describe the curriculum development component (phase 1), the course design component (phase 2), and the assessment design component (accessible from both phases 1 and 2). Before detailing these components, a description is provided of the development monitor, an integral part of each of these components. The structure of the remaining discussion mirrors the order under which the various tools are typically encountered. We begin with a discussion of the specification of curricula, followed by a section on the design of courses based upon the specified curricula. Finally, we address the specification of assessments based upon the material in the courses. The emphasis is on typical use of the system with justifications for the various design decisions provided along the way.

It is important to note that, although the description in this chapter follows the development process of a single user, the system does allow simultaneous development of curricula and courses by several users.

## 2. A MONITOR FOR CURRICULUM AND COURSE DEVELOPMENT

The monitor mechanism oversees the user's curriculum and course development activities, providing advice which guides, and expertise which embodies principles of "good" design. An introduction to the structure and function of the monitor will facilitate a better understanding of the later discussion of its specific interactions in the various stages of the development process. In the following, we briefly discuss design considerations, the difference between *advice* and *expertise*, the priority of violations, and the monitor interface.

The intent of the monitor is to guide the user through the process of curriculum and course development, providing advice and interjecting with criticism when necessary. The effect is that of having an expert looking over the user's shoulder, providing step-by-step assistance throughout the development process. The system was designed to be efficient and easy to use by a wide group of users. It provides a sufficient amount of advice for a novice developer, but does not hinder an expert curriculum or course developer. The monitor serves in an advisory capacity rather than controlling the user's interaction with the system. Furthermore, we strived to achieve a balance between unobtrusiveness and bringing the user's attention to development violations.

The rules in the monitor are naturally divided into two categories: advice and expertise. Advice rules serve to guide the user through the various development tasks by suggesting, in an unobtrusive manner, the next task to be carried out. Two lines at the bottom of the screen always display the "current" advice. This is generally a suggestion to specify a particular piece of information at this time or to refine the curriculum to the next level. In contrast, expertise rules capture the principles of "good" curriculum and course development as identified during knowledge acquisition. Expertise rules interrupt the development process, and it is not unusual to have several expertise rule violations outstanding at any one time.

When several outstanding violations exist, the system employs a ranking scheme to determine which single rule should fire. The priority of any one rule violation is a weighted combination of an assigned initial priority, the number of times it has already fired, and the distance between the user's current location in the curriculum and the detected violation. The display of the current expertise or advice varies both with the type of violation and with whether or not the user has already been warned about it. The display may interrupt the development process, by overlaying a window, or unobtrusively appear at the bottom of the screen, as in the case of advice.

The user may choose to "ignore" a particular instance of a rule violation or "turnoff" the rule altogether. Ignoring the violation instance causes the monitor to disregard that particular violation in the future. Turning off the actual rule causes all previous and subsequent violations of that rule to be ignored. The user may also choose (at his or her peril) to turn off the expertise mechanism altogether. This will leave the advice mechanism still functioning but will suppress the display of expertise messages. We also allow the user to browse the list of all current violations. For further details regarding the monitor mechanism, the reader should consult (Wipond & Jones, 1988b).

## 3. PHASE 1—CURRICULUM DEVELOPMENT

The term *curriculum* is defined as all curricular content from the broad goals of a program of study through to the specifics of particular lessons or *modules*, including learning activities and methods of assessment. Phase 1 of the system provides a rich curriculum represenation along with a set of tools to facilitate this process of curriculum development.

The curriculum representation includes each of the entities that make up a curriculum, such as departments, programs, courses, topics, subtopics, modules, learning objectives, resources, evaluation items, learning activities, and taxonomies. Each of these entities has many attributes. For instance, among other things, courses have names, descriptions, goals, prerequisites, and taxonomies (by which learning objectives are categorized).

The approach to curriculum development that the system encourages is one of *top-down refinement* where the curriculum is refined successively from broad goals down to objectives, learning activities, and evaluation items, Though encouraged, it is not mandatory that the developer take this approach. Typically, the process of curriculum development begins with the specification of departments, and programs within those departments. The user then indicates a particular course within one of the programs. Prior to representing the curricular content of the course, the user can select a curriculum *structure* or *framework*. The user would then specify the topics and subtopics of that course. Next comes that refinement of the course material into modules which are further refined into learning objectives. Objectives can be refined to submodules and submodule objectives. Finally, learning activities, resources and evalutation items can be tied to any objective. Each of these stages is described in detail within this section.

The curriculum representation also includes a mechanism for representing prerequisite and corequisite relationships. One or more objects at any level from topic to module can be prerequisite or corequisite for another. As well, the mechanism allows for the specification of one object out of a set of objects as a prerequisite.

In phase 3 the system routes students through the course material based upon the student's performance. In addition to guiding a student through the various modules specified within the course map (discussed in section 4.3), the system may route a student to remedial or enrichment materials. This routing necessitates that the curriculum representation of phase 1 contains the appropriate information. Routing information can incorporated into the curriculum representation at three levels: module, objective, and evaluation item.

In the following subsections we specify, in more detail, each stage of the curriculum development process.

### 3.1. Department/Program Level

In these top levels, the user creates departments and programs within those departments. The information specified includes the names of the departments and programs, and a description of each. The function of this level is primarily the organization of the various course curricula.

### 3.2. Curriculum Framework Specification

The basic objects that make up a curriculum are linked together in a default framework capturing the relationships that exist between them (see Figure 18.1). For instance, courses have topics, modules have objectives, and evaluation items have instruction statements. When the user initiates the creation of a new course curriculum, he or she is given the option of using the default curriculum framework or modifying it to more aptly suit the needs of the particular course. If the latter is chosen, modifications to the default framework are allowed in certain restricted ways. The user is able to add, delete, rename, and examine the details of particular levels in the curriculum structure. Throughout the remainder of this chpater we assume the use of the default curriculum framework.

The expertise implicit in this process of framework specification includes the allowed variations on the curriculum structure. For instance, the developer cannot create a curriculum framework without the notion of modules, although they may be renamed.

### 3.3. Upper-Course Levels

After specifying a curriculum framework, the user is ready to begin the specification of the course content. This includes the general course infor-

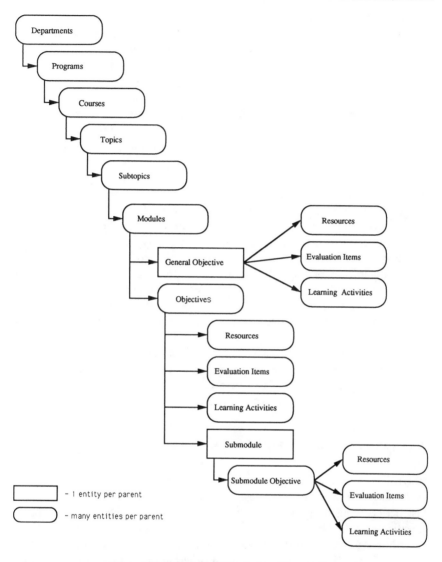

Figure 18.1. The Default Curriculum Framework.

mation as well as the refinement of the course into topics, subtopics, and so on. The user specifies names and descriptions for the course, each topic and subtopic, the broad goals of the course, the goals of each topic and subtopic, time-estimates for each, and prerequisite relationships that hold between the topics and subtopics (some of which may lie outside of the current curriculum)

The user also specifies, at the course level, a variety of taxonomies that will be used to classify the various pieces of the course curriculum. When developing curricula, the instructor may need to categorize given objects according to certain characteristics, for example, indicating that a learning activity is interactive in nature. Taxonomies are used to categorize learning objectives, learning activities, evaluation items, and resources, and are useful in the determination of module completeness and the ordering of the components of the curriculum. A variety of common taxonomies, such as Bloom's Cognitive Taxonomy (Bloom, 1956), are represented in the system. In addition, the user can create his/her own taxonomies or copy and edit existing ones.

Expertise within these levels encourages the user to define the goals for each level of the curriculum before that level is refined further. The expertise reminds the developer that suitable taxonomies should be defined at the course level to cover the material within the course. The expertise warns when topics become too unwieldy; the system employs both the user-supplied time estimates and the system-calculated estimates (recursively employing information specified at the next level of refinement) to determine when topics should be redefined. Under certain conditions, the monitor may suggest the introduction of an additional level of refinement. For example, if the user has introduced a large number of subtopics and feels that the topic itself should not be split, the system suggests introducing an additional level of refinement between the two. The additional level serves as an organizational tool for both the instructor and the learner. The system does not attempt to advise regarding the best criteria for restructuring; this would depend on the developer's own philosophy.

### 3.4. Modules, General Objectives, and Objectives

Regardless of how the user chooses to structure the curriculum, topics must eventually be refined to modules. A module is considered the basic unit of instruction, consisting of a single general learning objective and a number of specific module objectives. In addition, a module is characterized by a description, difficulty and criticality ratings, a user-defined time estimate, a system-calculated time estimate, and an ordering of the objectives within the module.

Learning objectives are one of the fundamental objects in the system. These objectives are the means by which an instructor specifies what the learner will be able to do upon completion of this curricular material. In order to allow the system to reason with/about them, the objectives are specified according to a relatively rigid structure. Each objective consists of a set of conditions under which the objective is to be demonstrated, a description of the performance to be demonstrated, and a list of criteria that are to be satisfied during that performance. Objectives can be classified according to various taxonomies, including a cognitive taxonomy and one or more affective and psychomotor taxonomies. Other information that can be defined for particular objectives includes user-defined and system-defined time estimates, links to resources, learning activities, and pertinent evaluation items.

The expertise at the module level is extensive. It is designed to encourage the proper and complete representation of modules and objectives, which are key components in the curriculum specification. The system employs the wording of the objective, particularly the main verb, for several purposes. First, it automatically classifies the objective according to the chosen cognitive taxonomy. It may recommend classfication of the objective according to the chosen affective taxonomy, or it may suggest rewording of the objective in order to avoid certain ambiguous phrases. The system also ensures that: the general objective is present and defined before any of the objectives are fully specified; all of the necessary information is specified for each objective; the general objective and the objectives are consistent and the module is complete. In checking module completeness, the system examines the taxonomic information associated with each objective. For example, a couple of simple system rules are as follows:

- If the general objective concerns the affective domain, and yet none of the objectives within the module does, the module is incomplete.
- If the general objective is at a higher cognitive level than all of the objectives within the module (as specified by the cognitive taxonomy chosen for this course curriculum), at least one objective is missing.

As well, the size of module, in terms of structure and time, is checked, and help with the sequencing of objectives is provided.

## 3.5. Submodules and Submodule Objectives

Particular objectives may be refined further into submodules and subsequently into submodule objectives. The representation and expertise employed for a submodule are similar to that of a module.

## 3.6. Learning Activities and Learning Resources

Learning activities are associated with given objectives (general objectives, module objectives, and/or submodule objectives) and are intended to aid the student in the mastery of the objective. Possible learning activities include reading a passage of text, a lab experiment, watching a film, etc. Learning resources are sources of further applicable information for the mastery of the objective.

## 3.7. Evaluation Items

Because one of the goals of the system is to accommodate competency-based learning, a major requirement of the project is assessment. The system must be able to determine whether a student has mastered the assigned objectives and route the student through the curricular material accordingly. Therefore, one focus of the overall project is on/offline testing, and for this reason an extensive framework for the representation of evaluation items is provided.

For evaluation items, the developer has control over what is displayed to the student, what answers should be considered correct or partially correct, and what feedback should be given to the student, and so on. The developer is able to specify feedback for any correct or partially correct answer, feedback for all wrong answers, and feedback for particular erroneous answers. This feedback can include references to the student's answer, the correct calculated answer, and any other calculated result. There are eight different question types: true-false, multiple-choice, numeric answer, text answer, matching, instructor-evaluated, multipart, and case-studies. Instructor-evaluated questions include the ability to represent a marking scheme with automatic feedback. For a more extensive discussion of evaluation items, the reader should consult Wipond and Jones (1988a).

## 4. PHASE 2 - COURSE DESIGN

In phase 2 of the system, the user develops courses based on the curricula built in phase 1. It is important not to confuse the term *course* as it is used within phase 2 with *course* as it is used in phase 1. In phase 2, the term *course* means the delivery of selected pieces of one or more curricula to group of students during a particular period of time along with evaluation of those students. Typically, a phase 2 course is offered during a given semester to one or more classes of students. The system provides a set of tools and guidance for building an online representation of a course.

The stages of course development are: the selection of pieces of phase 1 curricula to be included in the course, the specification of ordering information, viewing the course map, specifying the schedule, specifying the marking scheme, specifying module study guides, and specifying other course-related information. By ordering information, we mean information about the order in which students can progress through the material, distinct from prerequisite and corequisite relationships. The course map is a graphical representation of the ordering information.

The selection, ordering, and viewing stages of phase 2 are usually interwoven in the course development process. Typically, a user will select pieces of the curriculum to be incorporated, specify some of the ordering information regarding these selected objects, view the resulting course map, select additional objects, add or delete ordering information and view the map again, until the map is deemed a reasonable representation of the material to be included in the course.

### 4.1. Selection of Curricular Material

In the selection stage of phase 2, the developer selects material to be included in the course from the online curricula developed in phase 1. He or she can select topics, subtopics, or modules (or any level in between, as determined by the curriculum framework). The selection of a topic or subtopic does not imply that all modules within that topic must be included in the course. Although this is the default action, the user can specifically exclude particular objects within a selected level of the curriculum. Note that the user is free to include material from any available curriculum.

Expertise at this stage is limited and largely concerned with ensuring that prerequisites and corequisites for selected material are not violated.

### 4.2. Ordering the Selected Material

The selected material is already constrained by the prerequisite and corequisite relationships specified within phase 1. These requisites can be supplemented or removed by the user. The course developer usually has further preferences about the ordering of the material. It is these additional constraints that are specified in the ordering phase. Note that the user can add so many ordering constraints that there is only one manner in which students can progress through the course. More typically, however, students do have some choice regarding the order in which they will undertake the course material. This flexibility is reflected within the course map.

Ordering constraints are of two forms. The user can specify that $a$ must be completed before $b$ can be started, or that one of $a$, $c$, or $d$ must be completed before commencing b. Actual specifications can include combinations of these two basic forms and be quite complex, such as:

$a$ OR $b$ OR $c$ OR $d$ -> $e$ AND $f$ -> $g$ AND $h$ AND $i$.

### 4.3. Viewing the Course Map

The course map is a graphic representation of the topics, subtopics, and modules being taught in the course, the prerequisite relationships among them, and the ordering constraints that the developer has imposed. There are a number of levels to the course map, corresponding to the curricular levels, topic through module. The module level reflects the ordering information pertaining to all the course modules. It is this information that ultimately determines to which module a student may progress. The other map levels are abstractions of the often large amount of information at the module level. Each level map can be viewed in its entirety, or the user can focus on a particular piece of the map.

Each node in a map represents an object in the curriculum, for example, a topic, subtopic, or module. A directed arc from object $a$ to object $b$ implies that $a$ must be completed before $b$. There are two kinds of arcs in the map: AND arcs and OR arcs (with the standard interpretations).

The map does *not* depict the paths that students can take through the course material. Rather, it represents constraints on the way the students can progress through the course material. In phase 3, the system interprets the course map in order to determine candidate routings or paths through the material based upon a student's achievements.

### 4.4. Specifying the Course Schedule

In the course schedule the developer can assign specific start and/or end dates, either suggested or fixed, to the various components of a course such as learning activities, exams, modules, and so on. There are several options for specifying dates, including calendar dates and elapsed days or weeks in the course. Additionally, the developer can indicate which components of the course are optional. The course schedule represents the final set of constraints on the way in which students may progress through the course. The system ensures that there are no conflicts in the information specified or between the schedule and the course map. Note that dates do not have to be affixed to each component of the course. The fewer fixed dates specified, the more flexibility the students have in their progression through the material.

### 4.5. Course Marking Scheme

For each assessment (assignment, test, or exam), the developer can specify a weight factor to be used in the calculation of the overall grade, and which attempt should be counted (if the student is allowed to attempt a task more than once).

### 4.6. Specifying Other Course Information

Another aspect of phase 2 allows the user to specify other general information pertaining to the course. The developer specifies information such as whether students are allowed to challenge ahead, the maximum number of active modules, the maximum number of attempts at a module, whether and when hints should be issued during assessments, and so on.

## 4.7. Module Study Guides

A module study guide consists of information to be presented to the student, to aid the student's progress through the module. The information presented typically includes learning objectives, learning activities, and practice evaluation items. The presentation of the guide can be online, but it is generally given to the student as hard copy.

Module study guides are developed from a template of all possible information that could be included in the guide; the user simply indicates which options are desired. The user can then rearrange the selected objects via an ordering window, if the desired ordering differs from the default.

Expertise concerning module study guide specification again captures some relevant principles, such as the inclusion of pretests as one type of advanced organizer, inclusion of several learning activities, resources, and sample evaluation items.

## 5. ASSESSMENT DESIGN

The Assessment Design component is accessed from both phases 1 and 2, although the norm is for an instructor to access this component through phase 2. The user employs this component to develop a blueprint for each assessment, whether it be an assignment, midterm, or accreditation exam. The blueprint is a specification of constraints and is employed by the system to generate the required assessment. Within the blueprint, the user specifies both the purpose of the assessment and the type of assessment, as well as various constraints or criteria such as which curricular objects (objectives, modules, topics, etc.) are to be covered and the desired characteristics of candidate items (such as type of evaluation item, candidate categories of associated taxonomies), along with recommended percentages of items with such characteristics, allowable lock levels, allocated time for the assessment, total number of marks, and so on. The user can also specify whether testing emphasis should be placed on certain types of objectives such as problem-solving objectives. Ordering information can also be specified; options include random, aggregated according to objective, ordered according to objective, or user-specified. This is not a complete list of possible constraints but rather an indication of the more commonly specified constraints.

The system then employs the blueprint as a basis for generating the assessment. To do so, the system contains knowledge of which constraints typically can be relaxed and which cannot. For example, one assumes that a time constraint cannot be relaxed, although the system treats the specified time as a narrow range rather than a fixed number. Similarly, coverage of material must be handled as a priority constraint which is not to be violated. The specified percentages of items according to type (true-false, multiple choice etc.) can, however, be relaxed if necessary. Similarly, under certain conditions, the requested percentages of items at the various taxonomic levels can be relaxed. The approach to generating the resultant assessment is a heuristic one employing a generic set of rules which take into account the priority of the specified constraints. Because the generation of the assessment need not be undertaken at the time of blueprint specification, it is essential that the system be able to assess the feasibility of generating the requested assessment. The user is informed if the assessment generation is deemed to be infeasible based upon the system's knowledge of constraint priorities and allowable relaxations, in conjunction with the characteristics of the curricular material to be accessed. If desired, a sample assessment can be generated for the user to examine.

The expertise for this component is currently limited, It does, however, ensure that: essential constraints have been specified, the requested amount of assessment (e.g., a 1-hour exam) is reasonable given the purpose of the assessment, and the specifications regarding retesting are sufficiently stringent. For example, the user is discouraged from allowing a student to be retested on only those objectives which he or she failed if his or her original attempt was substantially below the desired mastery level.

## 6. SUMMARY

The "Expert" CML system will provide instructors with an extensive environment within which to develop and evaluate curricula and courses, as well as a means of monitoring students' progress through given courses. In other words, the system will provide a collection of tools to assist with the various tasks involved in developing, implementing, monitoring, and evaluating curricula. A subset of the system, the curriculum development component, the course design component, and the assessment design component, has been described herein.

The system is unique in both its goals and scope. We are developing tools for use by instructors regardless of the curricular content, educational environment, and the instructors' background and expertise. In developing the system, we assessed the needs of instructors at various educational institutions. To address these determined requirements, the following were undertaken: representation schemes were developed based upon an extensive examination of curricula and courses, tools were developed by which instructors could undertake the various tasks involved in curriculum and course design, and we elicited and formalized knowledge regarding curriculum and course development in order to provide assistance with these tasks. We have employed a knowledge-based approach to curriculum and course design, resulting in sophisticated environments for each. Moreover, one of the long-term benefits of "Expert" CML is assistance with the task of evaluating curricula and courses. The information captured by phase 4 of the system will provide developers with feedback regarding difficulties encountered as students progress through the given courses, This will ultimately provide further insight into the effectiveness of the various instructional methodologies being employed under given learning conditions.

At the time of writing, phase 1 has been prototyped, subjected to external review to evaluate both its functionality and ease of use, and then implemented. The results of the external review were positive. Prototyping of phase 2 has been completed. Both phase 2 and the assessment component are currently being implemented; expected completion date is the spring of 1989.Implementation of phases 3 and 4 will also get underway in 1989. Computer-Based Training System, Ltd. plans to continue developing and enhancing the system once the current version is a marketable product.

## REFERENCES

Bloom, B. (Ed.). (1956). *Taxonomy of educational objectives. Handbook I: Cognitive domain.* New York: Longsman, Green and Co.

Merrill, M.D. (1983). Component display thoery. In C.M. Reigeluth (Ed.), *Instructional design theories and models: An overview of their current status* (pp. 279-333). Hillsdale, NJ: Erlbaum.

Merrill, M.D. (1987a). An expert system for instructional design. *IEEE Expert 2*(2), 25-37.

Merrill, M.D. (1987b). The new component display theory: Instructional design for courseware authoring. *Instructional Science, 16,* 19-34.

Merrill M.D. (1988). Micro-level design strategies and expert systems as instructional design tools. In *Symposium on instruction.* Calgary, Canada: Canadian Centre for Learning Systems.

Merrill, M.D., & Li., Z. (1988). An instructional design expert system. In *Symposium on Instruction. Calgary, Canada: Canadian Centre for Learning Systems.*

Russel, D.M., Moran T.P., & Jordan D.S. (1988). The instructional design environment. In J. Psotka, L.D. Massey, & S.A. Mutter (Eds.), *Intelligent tutoring system: Lessons learned.* Hillsdale, NJ: Erlbaum.

Wipond, K., & Jones, M. (1988a). Curriculum and knowledge representation in a knowledge-based system for curriculum development. *Proceedings of ITS'88: International Conference on Intelligent Tutoring Systems.* (pp. 97-102). Montreal.

Wipond K., & Jones, M. (1988b). Monitoring the user within a sophisticated computer-managed learning environment. *Proceedings of IASTED'88: Expert Systems Theory and Their Application* (pp. 14-18). Los Angeles: ACTA Press.

# CONTRIBUTORS

**Michael Beveridge**
Professor of Education
University of Bristol
35 Berkeley Square
Bristol
BS8 1JA
England

Michael Beveridge has researched and published extensively on cognitive difficulties in relation to Education. He has focused in particular on the role of pictures in text processing and the presentation of graphs and diagrams in science. His work on communication problems has been most recently published in two books: *Language Disability in Children* (Open University Press, 1987), and *Language and Communication in the Mentally Handicapped* (Chapman Hall, 1989). He has also recently co-directed the Staged Assessment in Literacy Project for the Joint Matriculation Board.

**Dick Bierman**
Professor
Psychology Faculty
Department of Psychonomics
University of Amsterdam

Weesperplein 8
1018 XA Amsterdam
Netherlands

Dick Bierman is interested in parallel activation models of memory and concept formation; tutoring strategies and courseware presentation modes, both with regard to classical and intelligent CAI; learner characteristics as they relate to these strategies and presentation modes; evaluation of (I)CAI systems; and computerized management and execution of (psychological) experiments and tests.

**James Calderhead**
Lecturer in Educational Research
Department of Educational Research
University of Lancaster
Lancaster
LA1 4YL
England

James Calderhead's research seeks to understand how student teachers learn to teach, and ways of facilitating this learning. He has engaged in several studies of student teachers in training, investigating the nature and growth of their knowledge, how this knowledge relates to their developing practice, and how it is influenced by the training context in which they learn. Publications include the book *Teachers' Classroom Decision-Making* (Cassell) and two collections of papers on teachers' cognitions, *Exploring Teachers' Thinking* (Cassell) and *Teachers' Professional Learning* (Falmer Press). He is soon to take up a Chair in Education at the University of Bath.

**Allan Collins**
Principal Scientist
Bolt Beranek & Newman Inc.
10 Moulton Street
Cambridge MA 02238

Allan Collins has interests in cognitive science, human semantic processing, and the use of computers in education. He was the first chairman of the Cognitive Science Society. His research, with Albert Stevens and others, on the analysis and computational modeling of expert teaching, has been very influential in the ITS field. His SCHOLAR system, produced in collaboration with Jaime Carbonell (1970-1973), is widely cited as the first ITS.

**Erik De Corte**
Professor of Educational Psychology and

Director of the Institute for Language Teaching
Center for Instructional Psychology
University of Leuven
Vesaliusstraat 2
B-3000 Leuven
Belgium

Major research interests relate to the analysis and improvement of mathematics knowledge and problem-solving skills, especially in elementary school children, and to the effects of powerful computer-based learning environments on children's learning and thinking skills. The more general concern underlying this work is with the development of an instructional theory of knowledge and cognitive skill acquisition.

**Geoff Cumming**
Senior Lecturer and Chairperson of Department
Department of Psychology
La Trobe University
Bundoora
Australia 3083

Geoff Cumming's enduring research interest is in educational uses of computers, with emphasis on cognitive and educational aspects. He has studied computer use by young children learning to read, the classroom use of the Prolog Language, and most recently, as part of the Excalibur Project, the use of artificial intelligence in educational systems.

**Sarah A. Douglas**
Assistant Professor
Department of Computer and Information Science
University of Oregon
Eugene, OR 97403

Current research interests concern human–computer interaction, particularly basic research on the relationship between human understanding and the control, form, and content of communication. These interests have been applied to the design of intelligent tutoring systems, online help, and command languages. Current research involves two ITS projects: one a continuation of the second-language tutoring reported in this article; the second, a system that explores presentation of qualitative causal explanation of the cardiovascular system with a simulation construction kit.

**Mark T. Elsom-Cook**
Research Lecturer in Intelligent Computer Aided Instruction

Institute of Educational Technology
Open University
Walton Hall
Milton Keynes
MK7 6AA
England

Research interests: the nature of educational interaction, particularly in dialogue processes. Interested in designing less directive architectures and integrating educational environments with tutors (i.e., guided discoverey tutoring). Recent(ish) work includes development of systems with multiple teaching strategies, AI models of dialogue, and the use of machine learning techniques in student modeling.

**Barbara A. Fox**
Assistant Professor
Institute of Cognitive Science
University of Colorado, Boulder
Boulder, CO 80309

Current research focuses on the symbiosis of interaction and cognition in language, and on the relationships between general principles and local patterns in language use. Her three main research projects explore human tutorial dialogue, written and conversational argumentation, and relative clauses in English conversation. Her book, *Discourse Structure and Anaphora*, describes the social and cognitive functioning of pronouns and full noun phrases in English conversation.

**Peter Goodyear**
Lecturer in Edcuational Computing
Department of Educational Research
University of Lancaster
Lancaster
LA1 4YL
England

Has research interests in a number of areas of artificial intelligence and education, including the cognitive demands and consequences of learning to program and empirical approaches to the derivation of teaching knowledge for ITS design. He is currently engaged on two DELTA projects concerned with the use of knowledge-based techniques to support the production of intelligently adaptive courseware.

**Dr Marlene Jones**
Senior Research Officer
Advanced Technologies
Alberta Research Council
6815 8th St. NE,
Alberta Calgary
T2E 7H7
Canada

Adjunct Professor
Department of Computational Science
University of Saskatchewan

During the last 8 years research has focused on AI applications in education. Recent projects include expert systems for educational diagnosis, student and user modelling, and expert environments for curriculum and course development. Current interests also include instructional planning within intelligent tutoring systems.

**Paul Kamsteeg**
Researcher
Centre for Educational Research (SCO)
University of Amsterdam
Weesperplein 8
1018 XA Amsterdam
Netherlands

Interested in problem solving in formal domains, and in forms of learning this by doing and computerized coaching of same. Need for and use of individual vs. generalized learner characteristics: What must a coaching system know about a learner, how specific/deep/individualized must this knowledge be, representation of this knowledge and usage in diagnosis, and feedback generation. Coursework development.

**A. Eamonn Kelly**
Assistant Professor
School of Education
Rutgers University
State University of New Jersey
New Brunswick, NJ 08903

Trained as a teacher in Dublin, and then did masters degree in educational psychology at Chico State University in California. He completed his Ph.D. degree from Stanford's School of Education in 1988. From 1984–87, Kelly was a Research Assistant on the PIXIE project, first at Stanford and then in Aberdeen.

**Gaea Leinhardt**
Senior Scientist/Professor
Learning Research and Development Center and
School of Education
University of Pittsburgh
Pittsburgh, PA 15260

Gaea Leinhardt conducts applied research in the classrooms of unusually effective mathematics and history teachers. Effectiveness is an attribute of the student knowledge change of the students of these teachers. She seeks to understand the context, structure, and dynamic processes involved in subject matter teaching. She uses tools of both psychology and anthropology to do this research: extended observations, video recordings, interviews, and analyses of student productions. The analyses depend on both psychological and social constructs.

**David Littman**
Graduate Research Assistant
Department of Computer Science
Yale University
New Haven, CT 06520

David Littman is in his final year of the doctoral program in computer science at Yale University. His area of specialization is artificial intelligence and software design. David Littman holds a doctorate in experimental psychology from Cornell University (1976) and has had a varied research career since then. His main interest is learning.

**Rosemary Martinak**
Douglas Aircraft Company
2450 S. Peoria Street
Aurora CO 80014

Was awarded a Ph.D. in educational psychology from the University of Colorado (Boulder) in 1985, and worked as a Research Fellow on the PIXIE project at Stanford and Aberdeen between 1985–1987.

**Joyce Moore**
School of Education
Stanford University
Stanford, CA 94305

Did her undergraduate training at the University of Pittsburgh, and then joined the Education School at Berkeley as a doctoral student in 1985. She spent the session 1986/87 as a programmer on the PIXIE project. She is now a graduate student at the School of Education at Stanford.

**Stellan Ohlsson**
Research Associate
Learning Research and Development Center
University of Pittsburgh
Pittsburgh, PA 15260

Main research interest is the application of computer simulation techniques to the study of learning and performance in elementary mathematics. This includes formulating models of how mathematical knowledge is represented mentally and how it is applied during the learning of arithmetic procedures, as well as working out the implications of such models for the design of intelligent tutoring systems that teach conceptual understanding of mathematics. Minor research interests include modeling of performance on insight problems, and of the role of cognitive conflict in belief revision.

**Rachel Rimmershaw**
Department of Educational Research
University of Lancaster
Lancaster
LA1 4YL
England

Rachel Rimmershaw's research interests are primarily in the field of educational discourse. Her doctoral research was on the use of pragmatic knowledge in text comprehension. Her current interests are in the negotiation of explanations, in collaborative writing, and in reading strategies for handling complex expository texts.

**Hilde Schrooten**
Research Assistant
Center for Instructional Psychology
University of Leuven
Vesaliusstraat 2
B-3000 Leuven
Belgium

Hilde Schrooten is involved in two research projects: one related to the development of a computer program for training teachers in the skill of diagnosing systematic errors in the algorithms of adding and subtracting, the other to the effects of powerful computer-based learning environments on children's learning and thinking skills.

**John Self**
Reader in Computing
Department of Computing
Lancaster University
Lancaster
LA1 4YR

John Self is interested in the application of artificial intelligence to computer-based learning systems and especially in the use of formal AI techniques to define and reconceptualize learner–computer interactions in order to address the problem of learner modeling.

**Anne Shelly**
Senior Research Associate
School of Computer and Information Science
Center for Science and Technology, Fourth Floor
Syracuse University
Syracuse, NY 13244-4100

Anne Shelly's work in logic programming applications is directed toward aiding research in areas such as the social sciences and the humanities where computer-facilitated research has been relatively limited. Developing conceptual frameworks of text-based methodologies leads to the design of programs that document researcher thinking and that facilitate the mechanical tasks associated with text-based methodologies. Dr Shelly's research is intended to contribute to the understanding of the interface between inference-based research methodologies and logic programming and of representations of the knowledge of system users.

**Ernest Sibert**
Professor
School of Computer and Information Science
Center for Science and Technology, Fourth Floor
Syracuse University
Syracuse, NY 13244-4100

Though his investigations have ranged over processor architectures and real-time data acquisition systems, Ernest Sibert has worked primarily in the area of computational logic, especially logic programming and its applications. He is creator, with J.A. Robinson, of LOGLISP, the first system to integrate logic programming with LISP in a way which allows the programmer to combine the two styles at will. Currently he is studying combinations of logic with advanced functional languages implemented on massively parallel computers, as well as a variety of uses of LOGLISP.

**Derek Sleeman**
Professor and Head of Department
of Computing Science
University of Aberdeen
Aberdeen
AB9 2UB
Scotland

Previously, Derek Sleeman had been on the faculty at Stanford University, and at the University of Leeds, where he co-founded the CBL Unit. He has written extensively on ITSs, cognitive science, and, more recently, machine learning, including the book he co-edited with John Seely Brown, *Intelligent Tutoring Systems,* published in 1982 by Academic Press. He is main editor of the Pitman/Morgan-Kaufman Research Notes in Artificial Intelligence series, and was the BCS 1987 Jubilee lecturer.

**Lieven Verschaffel**
Research Associate of the National Fund for
Scientific Research, Belgium
Part-time Associate Professor
Center for Instructional Psychology
University of Leuven
Vesaliusstraat 2
B-3000 Leuven
Belgium

Leiven Verschaffel's main research interests are the analysis and improvement of elementary school children's mathematical knowledge and problem-solving skills, and the study of the effects of computer-based learning environments on children's learning and thinking skills.

**Robert Ward**
Lecturer
Department of Computing Studies
Coventry Polytechnic
Priory Street
Coventry
CV1 5FB

Completed his Ph.D. in educational psychology at Hull in 1987. From September 1986 to December 1988, he was a Research Fellow in the Department of Computing Science at Aberdeen, working with Derek Sleeman on ITSs, and studies to determine the difficulties users have with expert systems shells.

**Philip H Winne**
Faculty of Education
Simon Fraser University
Burnaby
British Columbia
V5A 1S6
Canada

Phil Winne is an instructional psychologist whose research focuses on students' cognition and teaching effectiveness. In addition to investigating these topics through empirical studies and theoretical syntheses, his work on Project DOCENT is a large-scale investigation of applying artificial intelligence to instruction.

**Kevin Wipond**
Expert Systems Researcher
Advanced Technologies Department
Alberta Research Council
6815 8 St. N E
Calgary
Alberta
T2E 7H7
Canada

Kevin Wipond has been involved in the design and development of Expert Systems for several years. Recent projects include an expert system for well log analysis, an expert system for ice classification and the Expert CML project. He is also currently interested in planning and the abstraction of plans for use on new, related, but different tasks.

**Sharon Wood**
Lecturer in Artificial Intelligence
School of Cognitive and Computing Sciences
University of Sussex
Brighton, BN1 9QN

Sharon Wood is currently lecturing in artificial intelligence in the School of Cognitive and Computing Sciences at the University of Sussex. She graduated from Sussex in developmental psychology with cognitive studies and has a

Ph.D. in artificial intelligence on the topic of multiagent planning systems for rapidly changing environments. Her research interests are in this area and in the field of expert systems. She was employed as Research Fellow for three years on the development of an expert system for advising trainee teachers on the subject of classroom teaching practice.

# AUTHOR INDEX

# SUBJECT INDEX

415